ity Conservation

D0420886

Effective marine biodiversity conservation is dependent upon a clear scientific rationale for practical interventions. This book is intended to provide knowledge and tools for marine conservation practitioners and to identify issues and mechanisms for upper-level undergraduate and master's students. It also provides sound guidance for marine biology field coursework and professionals.

The main focus is on benthic species living on or in the seabed and immediately above, rather than on commercial fisheries or highly mobile vertebrates. Such species, including algae and invertebrates, are fundamental to a stable and sustainable marine ecosystem. The book is a practical guide based on a clear exposition of the principles of marine ecology and species biology to demonstrate how marine conservation issues and mechanisms have been tackled worldwide, with special attention given to the criteria, structures and decision trees that practitioners and managers will find useful. Well illustrated with conceptual diagrams and flow charts, the book includes case study examples from both temperate and tropical marine environments.

Keith Hiscock is an Associate Fellow and Senior Consultant in Biodiversity and Conservation Science at the Marine Biological Association, Plymouth, UK.

Earthscan Oceans

Governing Marine Protected Areas
Resilience through Diversity
By Peter J.S. Jones

Marine Policy
An Introduction to Governance and International Law of the Oceans
By Mark Zacharias

The Great Barrier Reef
An Environmental History
By Ben Daley

Marine Biodiversity Conservation
A Practical Approach
By Keith Hiscock

For further details please visit the series page on the Routledge website:
http://www.routledge.com/books/series/ECOCE

Marine Biodiversity Conservation

A practical approach

Keith Hiscock

Routledge
Taylor & Francis Group

LONDON AND NEW YORK

earthscan

from Routledge

First published 2014
by Routledge
2 Park Square, Milton Park, Abingdon, Oxon OX14 4RN

and by Routledge
711 Third Avenue, New York, NY 10017

Routledge is an imprint of the Taylor & Francis Group, an informa business

British Library Cataloguing-in-Publication Data
A catalogue record for this book is available from the British Library

Library of Congress Cataloging in Publication Data
Hiscock, Keith.
Marine biodiversity conservation : a practical approach / Keith Hiscock.
pages cm. -- (Earthscan oceans)
Includes bibliographical references and index.
1. Marine biodiversity conservation. 2. Marine ecology. I. Title.
QH91.8.B6H57 2014
333.95'616--dc23
2014006327

ISBN: 978-0-415-72355-8 (hbk)
ISBN: 978-0-415-72356-5 (pbk)
ISBN: 978-1-315-85764-0 (ebk)

Typeset in Goudy
Servis Filmsetting Ltd, Stockport, Cheshire

Printed and bound in Great Britain by
TJ International Ltd, Padstow, Cornwall

Contents

Preface

This book is a guide to the conservation of marine biodiversity based firmly on scientific knowledge of marine species and ecosystems and the experience that we now have of managing human impacts for the protection of wildlife. It benefits from the natural history expertise of often aging individuals and, hopefully, provides a starting point for a next generation of naturalists to build on that knowledge and to inform conservation in a wise way. This book is predominantly about benthic species as information on fisheries and on large, highly mobile vertebrates is well covered elsewhere. It provides tools for practitioners to use, aiming to make the best use of the science that we have for marine biodiversity conservation. It is 'practical' because we live in a world with incomplete information on what we need to know for conservation and where we need to make best use of what we do know. It is practical because it tries to interpret the rhetoric that often comes from directives, conventions and statutes into scientifically sound actions. It is practical because it tries to separate actions that will make a difference from those that will not. It is practical because it accepts that human activities are bound to have some impact on marine ecosystems. It is not a textbook about marine processes, ecosystem structure and function or the biology of species (although relevant examples are given to inform conservation action): there are many books that provide such information including the volume on marine conservation ecology by Roff and Zacharias (2011). Nor is it a book about how to implement conservation measures (mechanisms and governance): that is addressed by volumes such as Jones (2014).

The definition of biodiversity used in this book is 'the variability among living organisms from all sources including, *inter alia*, terrestrial, marine and other aquatic ecosystems and the ecological complexes of which they are part; this includes diversity within species, between species and of ecosystems' (UN Convention on Biological Diversity, 1992, cited in Glowka *et al.*, 1994, p16). Essentially, biodiversity is the variety of life from genes to ecosystems.

The definition of 'conservation' that readers should touch back to throughout their reading of the book comes from a time before scientists started to use the term biodiversity: 'the regulation of human use of the global ecosystem to sustain its diversity of content indefinitely' (Nature Conservancy Council, 1984, p7). This definition makes it clear that human activities need to be regulated to protect species and habitats and that protection will not just 'happen' by labelling locations as 'protected'. Good stewardship of the whole of the marine environment is essential, whilst marine protected areas are needed for the most threatened habitats and species to preserve valued resources and to provide examples that are as close as possible to natural for study. Whilst human interest in feathered creatures and large, charismatic vertebrates has led moves for their protection for many years, we also need to identify what is threatened on and near the seabed and action there is well under way.

This book gives the reader:

- reasons for 'doing' marine biodiversity conservation;
- a perspective on how to organise the information that we already have to inform biodiversity conservation;
- a background of knowledge on natural change that is essential if we are to separate natural from human-induced change;
- information on how marine ecosystems 'work': essential for understanding the environmental factors that determine what is where, why change happens and whether we can fix things when we break them;
- examples of the changes brought about by human activities to marine ecosystems that provide a warning of how easily we can adversely affect nature;
- an explanation of ways of assessing degree of threat and of sensitivity of species and habitats to human activities as a starting point to prioritising action;
- a guide to ensuring that the most relevant survey and monitoring methods for answering conservation questions are chosen;
- a view on what marine protected areas can and cannot do and a description of their selection, design and management;
- an account of how long recovery might take after protection is put in place or after some disaster and whether we can do anything to help recovery or to replace what has been lost;
- a final account of what writing the book has reminded or taught the author about marine conservation and a summary (as the 'manager's toolbox') of what the new generation of scientists, policy advisors and managers can use to help sustain the diversity of content of our marine ecosystems indefinitely.

The book is split between Chapters 1 to 5 which are about what we already know and Chapters 6 to 11 that are the 'how to do it' chapters. Chapter 12 concludes the volume and provides a checklist of what the marine conservation manager and policy advisor should have in their box of tools. There is a glossary and list of commonly used acronyms to help the reader.

The book addresses one of the greatest problems that we face in marine environmental protection and management: knowing what is where. The text will help practitioners see how to find, to organise and to make best use of the knowledge that we have for marine biodiversity conservation. New surveys are, however, bound to be needed. Whilst description of specific survey techniques is not included in this book, the matching of methods to objectives is covered. The tabulated summaries provide opportunities to consider specific, perhaps local, examples of management questions and to design survey and monitoring programmes that will answer those questions.

The environmental manager or policy advisor needs to be able to separate what are, or are likely to be, natural changes in environmental conditions and biology from those brought about by human activities and that may therefore be manageable. Examples are given of the scale of change from seasonal to longer-term changes including how some natural change occurs on decadal timescales. The likely consequences of global changes in our climate, especially warming, and of ocean acidification are addressed in the context of whether we can do anything on a local scale to alleviate adverse effects.

Human impacts on marine ecosystems are widespread and are summarised to provide a background to understanding why conservation action is needed. Those impacts extend from the shorelines used for centuries to gather food, harbours that have covered over natural habitats and introduced pollutants, nutrient enrichment that has resulted in deoxygenation, introduction of non-native species and associated disease to a region through shipping and mariculture, and trawling of seabeds with mechanical gear, all during the past 150 years – to seamounts hundreds of kilometres offshore and hundreds of metres deep that have, in the past 30 or so years, been targeted by vessels using heavy bottom fishing gear that destroys organisms which are hundreds of years old. Depressing though some of the evidence of human impacts is, some areas of sea and seabed are close to natural – they are distant from localised pollution and are too rugged for damaging mobile fishing gear to be used. Identification of those areas and knowing how to protect them is informed by this volume.

Much of our understanding of the likely impact of human activities on marine biodiversity comes from studies of past events and from experimental manipulation of natural habitats. We also need to know the biology of species to be able to identify which are sensitive species and habitats in order to create information that is at the core of understanding what really matters for biodiversity conservation. This book can provide examples of the knowledge that we have but wise advice will come from practitioners with both knowledge and experience. Only you, the reader, can augment that experience by doing the survey work, making the natural history observations and monitoring change.

Some conservation action can be described as 'duty of care', meaning to prevent or minimise the adverse effects of human activities across the entire environment. It requires knowledge that enables sustainable use; that identifies lethal or damaging chemicals and the levels of them that are 'safe'; that understands which species and habitats are sensitive to different activities and their recovery potential if damaged; and that institutes relevant and enforced regulatory procedures. As our knowledge of 'safe levels' of extraction and deposition and of actual impacts from human activities improves so management can be more soundly based. Examples are given of how sensitivity can be assessed and of the sorts of measures that have been taken to protect natural communities and 'important' species, their success but also sometimes unexpected consequences. Much more problematic to tackle are those impacts of human activities that are being caused, or may be caused, by inputs to the atmosphere affecting marine life and which require massive efforts to reduce harmful emissions. Those impacts and the prognosis for further change are described as of overarching importance, but this volume will concentrate on local and regional seas' impacts and solutions.

The establishment of well-managed marine protected areas (MPAs) is one of the tools that we have to regulate human use of the seas for the benefit of wildlife. MPAs are encouraged or required by a raft of declarations, directives and conventions, meaning that (if their countries are signatories to those agreements) regulators have to create them. Whether those MPAs are effective depends on the sincerity with which they are identified and established and the measures that are taken to identify and manage them. Such areas have proved highly successful in many parts of the world for developing sustainable fisheries and for protecting biodiversity. As more and more well-managed MPAs are established and their effects on biodiversity within and outside them studied, we can get better and better at instituting measures that will benefit species and habitats and begin to quietly leave behind those that have shown no significant benefits. The criteria that are used to identify areas and the considerations that are applied to make them 'work' are identified and explained, but some critical commentary is included to make the process less difficult and to ensure that the most meaningful (for biodiversity conservation) criteria and measures are applied.

When it is clear that sites have been damaged or species abundance and viability reduced by human activities, is there anything that we can do to assist restoration and recovery? Much depends on whether habitats have been irretrievably lost or species reduced in abundance beyond some 'tipping point' where recruitment is lower than mortality. Examples are given of how restoration and recovery programmes may be applied in the sea and a decision tree is offered to help managers decide if a recovery programme is needed and worthwhile. Sometimes habitat loss cannot be avoided and replacement or biodiversity offsetting may be suggested. Examples and warnings are given for such actions.

The amount of understanding that we need of what is where, of ecosystem processes, of species biology, etc. is intimidating – it is too much and we have too little time, money and knowledge to do everything. Challenging meaningless goals, objectives or slogans and prioritising meaningful action using the knowledge that we have must come to the fore. After reading this book, ecologists, policy advisors, policymakers and the interested public will be better placed to work in a meaningful way to protect our seas and the life in them.

The geographical relevance of this book is particularly to the shallow waters of temperate regions although many of the decision aids can be applied universally.

The book is intended to provide knowledge and tools for marine conservation practitioners but also to identify issues and mechanisms for upper-level undergraduate and master's students as well as the interested and concerned public.

Key references are given, as far as possible, to review papers which themselves lead to a much larger number of references if detailed study is needed. The glossary of terms is invaluable for students struggling with new concepts and an often misinterpreted vocabulary.

About the author

I have been researching intertidal and shallow subtidal marine habitats over the past 45 years and have always worked to ensure that science is used effectively to protect seabed marine life. Much of my career has been organising and undertaking survey and monitoring as well as contributing to developing an understanding of how marine ecosystems are structured and how they function. In 1969, I began work that would lead to the island of Lundy, England becoming the first marine nature reserve in Britain. In 1987, I was appointed to lead the Marine Nature Conservation Review of Great Britain which, for the next 11 years, developed relevant survey and classification methods and undertook surveys around England, Scotland and Wales. During much of that time, I was also Head of the Marine Conservation Branch in the UK Joint Nature Conservation Committee. In 1998, I initiated the Marine Life Information Network (MarLIN) at the Marine Biological Association (MBA) in Plymouth, UK. That programme brought together information about marine life in order to identify its sensitivity to human activities and to provide internet-based tools for marine environmental management, protection and education.

Acknowledgements

As well as reviewing international literature on marine conservation, much of the research that has helped produce this volume comes from work commissioned by the UK's statutory nature conservation agencies, by WWF-UK and by other bodies. That work has been undertaken at the Marine Biological Association in Plymouth, UK since about 2000. Colleagues there have contributed much thinking to the development of practical measures for marine biodiversity conservation, and five in particular have done that work and have reviewed and helped with the contents of this volume: Matt Frost, Harvey Tyler-Walters, Emma Jackson, Olivia Langmead and Jack Sewell. The facilities available through the UK National Marine Biological Library at the Marine Biological Association have been invaluable throughout the many projects that have contributed to the volume.

In addition to those colleagues acknowledged above, many others have helped by reading draft sections and providing source material and comments that make the text as authoritative and up to date as possible: Bob Earll, Dan Laffoley, Nova Mieszkowska, Nick Pope, Dan Smale.

Many colleagues have provided images for the figures and plates and I am very grateful to them. I am particularly grateful to the Marine Biological Association for providing a grant to enable the inclusion of colour plates in the volume.

A note on scientific names

The scientific names for species given in this book are, as far as possible, checked for currency in the World Register of Marine Species (www.marinespecies.org) where authorities and dates can be found.

Chapter 1

The need for marine biodiversity conservation

Introduction

This chapter is about why we need to protect marine biodiversity both as moral responsibility for the good stewardship of a world that we can all too easily damage and from the practical perspective of the value of biodiversity to humans. For policymakers, the need to take action is also based on directives and conventions that their governments are a party to: they need to institute measures because they are required to abide by these agreements.

Historical perspectives

Concerns about human impacts on marine life can be traced back, in England, to the fourteenth century when a petition presented to Parliament in the year 1376–7 (quoted in Hore and Jex, 1880, p55) stated: 'the hard and long iron of the said "wondyrchoun" [a modified oyster dredge] . . . . destroys the spawn and brood of the fish beneath the said water, and also destroys the spat of oysters, muscles [sic], and other fish by which large fish are accustomed to live and be supported'. At that time, certain species were protected perhaps to prevent over-collection or perhaps because they were so tasty that they were reserved for consumption by nobility. They were the 'Royal Fish' in Britain and included cetaceans and the sturgeon. Elsewhere in the world, there was often an understanding that over-exploitation could be bad for stocks of edible species. In New Zealand, Hutching and Walrond (2009) describe how the Māori relationship with the sea included *rāhui* (bans), which limited the harvesting of fish species at certain times and may have included size limits. There were also *tapu* (restrictions) relating to certain practices, such as pollution of fishing areas with human waste, and rules preventing damage to fishing grounds with nets and lines. Sacks and baskets were never dragged over shellfish beds.

There were exceptions to the focus on fish stock conservation including the concern that was expressed about the ravages of curiosity-led collection on the English seashore in Victorian times. In 1906, Edward Gosse wrote critically of the very activities encouraged and pursued by his father, the eminent Philip Henry Gosse FRS.

The world's first area that specifically protected marine habitats was probably the Fort Jefferson National Monument in Florida, which covered 18,850ha of sea and 35ha of coastal land. Although that site was designated in 1935, the main impetus for marine biodiversity protection came much later with the World Parks Congress on National Parks in 1962 and a follow-up meeting in 1982 calling for the incorporation of marine, coastal and freshwater sites.

Box 1.1 Historic 'drivers' for marine conservation

Tunnels Beach, Ilfracombe, England – one of the most popular hunting grounds for Victorian naturalists.

Source: Ilfracombe Museum

'The ring of living beauty drawn about our shores was a very thin and fragile one. It had existed all those centuries solely in consequence of the indifference, the blissful ignorance of man … The fairy paradise has been crushed under the rough paw of well-meaning, idle-minded curiosity.'

Edmund Gosse, 1906, 'Father & Son'

SCUBA divers in 1968.

Source: Keith Hiscock

Although overfishing was already a concern in the nineteenth century and showing signs of severe consequences for fish stocks in the 1960s, issues associated with seabed disturbance by mobile fishing gear were not being considered. Oil pollution was seen as endangering birds and other vertebrates but consequences for seabed wildlife seemed of little concern. And disposal of waste into the sea was, well, 'out of sight, out of mind'. It was SCUBA diving that seemed to be driving calls for conservation.

The wreck of the *Torrey Canyon*.

Source: Photograph from the MBA Archive Collection MB8.2.1(42) – RAF St Mawgan. Crown Copyright: reproduced under the terms of the Open Government Licence.

The wreck of the *Torrey Canyon* in 1967 polluted large areas of Brittany, the Channel Isles and south-west England with crude oil. Subsequent use of toxic dispersants did great damage to marine life. The *Torrey Canyon* disaster was a wake-up call with regard to the dangers of transporting large quantities of oil around the world and resulted in international conventions and agreements regarding compensation and responsibilities, but pollution was not a main 'driver' for conservation action in the 1960s.

It was not until the 1960s that the damage being inflicted by humans on marine wildlife in general became starkly obvious. This was a period when the marvellous character of marine life was beginning to be shown on television through programmes by Hans and Lottie Hass and by Jacques Cousteau. The public were 'wowed' by the aesthetic beauty of the underwater world and, even today, can be surprised when they see images of colourful and fragile marine life in what they might have thought was a marine desert. The 1960s were also a time when pictures of Earth from space showed not only that the planet was predominantly blue ocean but just how small and finite it was. One event, in March 1967, brought into sharp focus the damage that could be caused to wildlife by humans: the *Torrey Canyon* oil spill in south-west England. Oil-covered birds got the greatest publicity but fish and invertebrates were also shown washed up on the strandline having been killed by the oil and by the chemicals that were used to disperse it. There were scientific studies not only of the impacts of the spill on marine life (Smith, 1968) but also experimental studies of oil spill impact and dispersant toxicity (for instance, Baker, 1976). Oil became the 'baddie' and there were more major spills as well as studies that demonstrated the impacts of oil refinery effluents on species and habitats. But oil wasn't the only polluter wrecking marine life. Localised effects of sewage sludge disposal, heavy metal contamination and agricultural run-off of nutrients were all having effects. Persistent chemicals, in particular, were identified in the 1970s and 1980s as highly damaging although their impacts were less conspicuous than those of oil – that is, until the effects of Tributyltin (TBT) antifouling paint expressed itself in oysters and dog whelks (for instance, Alzieu, 1991; Bryan *et al.*, 1986). At the start of the marine conservation movement, it was not oil, it was not fishing and it was not persistent chemicals that 'bothered' conservationists, but it was SCUBA diving. Whatever the reasons, the marine conservation movement saw its origins in the 1960s.

The scale of decline and loss

By the mid nineteenth century, two marine species were known to have been made extinct by human activities: Stellar's sea cow and the great auk. There are many more now although numbers are uncertain (see del Monte-Luna *et al.*, 2007). Many commercially exploited species have been brought to the verge of extinction and the viability of their populations may be in doubt. The evidence for depletion of stocks of fish is overwhelming with populations of many target and by-catch species being severely reduced, sometimes by up to 90 per cent since industrialised fishing took off in the 1950s (see, for instance, Baum and Blanchard, 2010; Collette *et al.*, 2011; Worm *et al.*, 2009). Furthermore, local extinctions have occurred, and species have become ecologically extinct – that is, their populations are now so small that they can no longer play a significant ecological role in a particular community (see, for instance, Steneck *et al.*, 2004). The examples of fish stock collapses as a result of exploitation are many and are catalogued in books by Callum Roberts, *The Unnatural History of the Sea* (2007) and *Ocean of Life* (2012). However, restrictions on fishing were directed at stock conservation and any benefits for other wildlife were incidental. The idea that there might be 'win-win' situations where the same measures would benefit fish stocks and unexploited seabed wildlife has been very slow to take off. A broader view of the threats posed by humans to marine life is summarised in Earle (2009).

Other species have been severely depleted, including through habitat loss. Summarising depletion and degradation of estuaries and coastal seas from historical data from 12 locations worldwide, Lotze *et al.* (2006) paint a grim picture in which human impacts have depleted more than 90 per cent of formerly important species, destroyed more than 65 per cent of seagrass and wetland habitats, degraded water quality and accelerated species invasions in those locations. They further observe (p1809):

> The structure and functioning of estuarine and coastal ecosystems has been fundamentally changed by the loss of large predators and herbivores, spawning and nursery habitat, and filtering capacity that sustains water quality. The erosion of diversity and complexity has slowly undermined resilience, giving way to undesirable algal blooms, dead zones, disease outbreaks, and invasions, and elevating the potential for disaster.

The causes of decline and loss

In looking for solutions to the decline in biodiversity, the first thing to do is identify what are the causes. In this introductory chapter, a list of activities (Table 1.1) that may create adverse environmental factors is given as a starting point. The list is for Great Britain and there will be activities to add or retract for other parts of the world. Later (in Chapter 5), description and some ranking of those threats is undertaken.

Not all of the listed activities may be damaging biodiversity (although all will affect 'naturalness'). Building wind farms, dumping redundant structures (vessels, oil rigs, etc.), placing artificial reefs or the historical dumping of munitions may protect areas of seabed from mobile fishing gear, and the structures themselves will often increase the variety of habitats available for colonisation by adding hard substratum to areas that were previously sediment. Creating new enclosed areas by the construction of dykes can lead to highly diverse and productive habitats. However, 'replacement' of damaged habitats is not always desirable and this is discussed further in Chapter 11.

Costello *et al.* (2010) summarise some of the conclusions regarding drivers of change from the Census of Marine Life which was a ten-year programme, from 2000 to 2010. The programme's Regional Implementation Committees reported overfishing, habitat loss and pollution (contamination by xenobiotics and eutrophication) to be the greatest threats to biodiversity in the regions, followed by the presence of alien species and the impacts of warming due to climate change. Other impacts reported less frequently were related to aquaculture and maritime traffic, which were considered especially important in the Mediterranean Sea.

Driving forces for biodiversity conservation

The drivers for biodiversity conservation range from philosophical (our 'duty of care' for an environment that we can all too easily damage and for species that have their right to exist whether or not they are of benefit to us) to immensely practical reasons concerned with the services that the sea provides (from food to waste remediation through natural coastal defences to recreation). We also need to protect what we have while we learn to understand how it works and what happens when our activities damage it. Although our understanding of the role of biodiversity in ecosystem functioning is often empirical, there are experimental studies and data that suggest the importance of diversity in providing resilience in marine communities, and that this resilience might be especially important in relation to climate change impacts. Worm *et al.* (2006), in their review of the impacts of biodiversity loss on ocean ecosystem services, conclude 'marine biodiversity loss is increasingly impairing the

Table 1.1 Activities that may create adverse environmental factors for biodiversity

Energy production
- At sea (wind turbines)
- At sea (wave turbines)
- At sea (tidal turbines)
- On land (power stations, including nuclear)

Extraction – non-living resources
- Quarrying
- Navigational dredging (capital, maintenance)
- Sand and gravel
- Oil and gas
- Water (freshwater catchment; industrial, e.g. power stations)

Extraction – living resources
- Harvesting – seaweed
- Bioprospecting
- Extraction – maerl
- Fishing – benthic trawling
- Fishing – hydraulic dredging
- Fishing – pelagic trawling
- Fishing – traps (creels, pots)
- Fishing – set netting
- Fishing – angling
- Fishing – blast fishing
- Crab tiling/Bait digging
- Fishing – shellfish harvesting

Food production
- Aquaculture – finfish
- Aquaculture – shellfish

Habitat modification/introduction
- Beach replenishment
- Cables and pipelines (installation)
- Cables and pipelines (operation)
- Ports, marinas, leisure facilities

- Coastal defence and land claim
- Artificial reefs
- Oil and gas platforms (including oil spills, disposal of lubricants)
- Wind and wave turbines

Military
- Military activities including sonar

Recreation
- Tourism and recreation including 'rock pooling' and curio collection

Survey and research
- Seismic survey (exploration, construction)
- Scientific sampling including specimen supply

Transport
- Shipping (including oil spills, use of antifoulants)

Waste disposal – gas
- Waste gas emission (including greenhouse gases)

Waste disposal – liquid
- Industrial chemicals
- Agricultural liquid
- Sewerage disposal
- Oily waste

Waste disposal – solid
- Fish waste (land-based processing, processing vessels)
- Munitions (chemical and conventional)
- Navigational dredging (capital, maintenance)
- Quarrying (geological material)
- Litter

Agriculture (land)
- Fertiliser run-off
- Pharmaceutical products

ocean's capacity to provide food, maintain water quality, and recover from perturbations. Yet available data suggest that at this point, these trends are still reversible' (p787).

Apart from the philosophical and practical matters driving the desire for marine biodiversity conservation, there are political measures that demand action and which scientists should inform. Moves towards protecting marine ecosystems and species, whilst already under way in the late 1960s, saw little progress in the 1970s (except perhaps as an afterthought to terrestrial measures) but began to develop in the 1980s. Internationally, biodiversity conservation saw its beginnings in the United Nations Conference on the Human Environment (held in Stockholm in 1972) and the adoption of the World Charter for Nature by the United Nations General Assembly in 1982 (Resolution 37/7). Many of

How and why we have legislation

1. Evidence of problems

2. Campaigns

3. Directives, conventions
   and statutes

4. Actions (measures, action
   plans, policy statements etc.)

Figure 1.1 Getting to legislation.

those developments, especially the establishment of marine parks, were to protect recreational resources (Björklund, 1974) and many were very controversial, involving powerful lobby groups – especially fishermen. In 1987, the World Commission on Environment and Development (WCED, 1987) introduced the concept of sustainable development (*development that meets the needs of the present without compromising the ability of future generations to meet their own needs*) which influenced initiatives concerned with biodiversity conservation including the Convention on Biological Diversity which was signed at the Earth Summit at Rio de Janeiro on 5 June, 1992. Recommendations (which signatories to the Convention are required to follow) specifically for marine and coastal biodiversity conservation were made in the Jakarta Mandate in 1995. In 2002, at the World Summit on Sustainable Development in Johannesburg, recommendations included the 'establishment of marine protected areas consistent with international law and based on scientific information, including representative networks by 2012' (United Nations, 2002, p25). Meanwhile, in the 1980s and 1990s, regional and national measures for biodiversity conservation had been embedded in directives, conventions and statutes. International, regional and national measures required actions by national governments that were parties to those measures: ministers *needed* to take action for the conservation of marine biodiversity (whether they wanted to or not).

Marine conservation was often led by measures to protect threatened species. Internationally, the World Conservation Union (IUCN) *Red List of Threatened Species* (the latest version is IUCN, 2013) provides a world perspective. Although identifying species as 'threatened' and in need of protection is not protecting 'biodiversity' *per se*, protecting a species often requires protecting its habitat; thus biodiversity conservation on land may have benefited in many cases from that focus on species. In the sea, the majority of species listed in conventions, directives and statutes are highly mobile, charismatic megafauna, and so such benefits for other parts of biodiversity are unlikely.

With perhaps an appreciation that 'marine is different', directives and conventions that specifically address marine environmental protection and management began to appear in the 1990s. An early example is the European Union's Habitats Directive of 1992 (Council Directive 92/43/EEC: http://ec.europa.eu/environment/nature/legislation/habitatsdirective/index_en.htm) which included fine-scale and threatened terrestrial habitats and a rather difficult-to-interpret list of broadscale marine habitats.

More and more, the importance of ensuring that there was an ecological dimension to the sustainability agenda and of taking a whole ecosystem approach in managing human activities for the benefit of wildlife was becoming clear. Relevant concepts were developed and, by the late 1990s, measures were being underpinned by the 'ecosystem approach'.

> The ecosystem approach is a strategy for the integrated management of land, water and living resources that promotes conservation and sustainable use in an equitable way. It is based on the application of appropriate scientific methodologies focused on levels of biological organization which encompass the essential processes, functions and interactions among organisms and their environment. It recognizes that humans, with their cultural diversity, are an integral component of ecosystems.
>
> (Convention on Biological Diversity (CBD), 'Ecosystem Approach': www.cbd.int/ecosystem)

The concept evolved and definitions were adapted. For instance:

> The ecosystem approach is the comprehensive integrated management of human activities, based on best available scientific knowledge about the ecosystem and its dynamics, in order to identify and take action on influences which are critical to the health of the marine ecosystems, thereby achieving sustainable use of ecosystem goods and services and maintenance of ecosystem integrity.
>
> EU Marine Strategy Stakeholder Workshop, Denmark, 4–6 December 2002
> (See Laffoley et al., 2004, p7)

Conserving biodiversity has to be at the centre of 'ecosystem integrity' although the role of biodiversity in maintaining that integrity, in supporting resilience of communities and in maintaining ecosystem services is still a very empirical science. Often, the poor understanding of the importance of biodiversity can be used by industry and by politicians to undermine biodiversity conservation measures. Countering those adverse views are societal values that appreciate the importance of nature and that influence political views.

What we should and can do for biodiversity conservation

After centuries of damaging marine ecosystems and several decades of making that damage widespread and, in places, severe, action is being taken. That action may be to improve water quality and regulate development – undertaken on a national or confederation basis (for instance, via European Union Directives or via Conventions that refer to regional seas such as the Barcelona Convention – the Convention for the Protection of the Mediterranean Sea Against Pollution). Some are international, often regulating a particular sector, such as through the International Maritime Organisation which provides a forum for shipping. For instance, in 2008, the International Convention on the Control of Harmful Anti-Fouling Systems on Ships came into force for all countries that ratified the convention.

'What we should do' is the subject of international meetings (for instance of the Contracting Parties to the Convention on Biodiversity) and of the often very wise observations in books that address human impacts on the marine environment (for instance, Earle, 2009; Roberts, 2007, 2012). The objectives that are promoted, by whatever route, need science to interpret them into practical reality but, most importantly, regulation and enforcement to ensure they work. What we, as scientists, must try to do is to answer the questions from policy advisors and regulators that are often along the lines of: Has there been a change in . . .?; What will happen if . . .?; Can we do anything to prevent . . .?; or How will we know if . . .? Scientists provide evidence and facts to policy advisors who translate that information into suggested measures to prevent or at least to minimise adverse effects of human activities on marine ecosystems within the context of continuing to use the marine environment for food, transport, energy and recreation. We can provide better evidence if we use the knowledge and experience gained around the world of what measures are effective and by using available and new tools to give objective and defensible advice. We know enough now to give that advice and we know enough to advise when caution is needed even if we do not have every last piece of evidence that policymakers may demand.

'What we can do' is the subject of this book but, very specifically, it addresses the biodiversity conservation measures that we can adopt now and on a local or regional seas basis. It purposefully steers away from fisheries – the literature is awash with advice – and what should be done to reduce the likelihood of global impacts from climate change – the measures are global.

What can biodiversity 'do' for us?

The question is inevitably asked by those that want proof that something is 'worth' something (usually in financial terms). There are indeed many services that species and habitat diversity provide, from supply of food through waste processing to recreational enjoyment. Demonstrating that there are values to biodiversity in the form of ecosystem services is worth doing to inform and influence politicians who may be out of touch with nature and societal values. There are many publications that catalogue the services that are provided by marine and coastal systems. Liquete *et al.* (2013) have compared four classifications and Table 1.2 summarises the key points for marine and coastal areas. Some of the localised services that the marine ecosystem provides are illustrated in Plates 1–6.

A next stage is to place a financial value on those services, which is reasonably easy for some and difficult for many and is rarely attempted now.

Worm *et al.* (2006) conclude that, overall, rates of resource collapse increased and recovery potential, stability and water quality decreased exponentially with declining diversity. Some examples of the importance of biodiversity in supporting resilience and resistance in marine communities are mentioned in Chapters 3 and 4. However, there is much that we do not understand about which species are the ones that are critical to ecosystem functioning and what is the importance of diversity in making ecosystems resilient. At its crudest, ecologists need fully stocked habitats to understand the complex relationships that exist between species to help understand when a system is broken and how to fix it. At its most influential, humans enjoy diverse and colourful habitats and charismatic species and want to know that marine life is being 'looked after'. At its most philosophical, we have the ability to cause severe damage and disruption and that makes us responsible for ensuring that nature survives and thrives. To reword a famous quotation from John F. Kennedy's inaugural speech in 1961 – ask not what biodiversity can do for you, but ask what you can do for biodiversity.

Table 1.2 List and description of marine and coastal ecosystem services

Marine and coastal ecosystem services	Specific component
Provisioning services	
Food provision	a Fishing activities (including shellfishing) industrial or artisanal (either commercial or subsistence fishing). In general, fisheries are reported as total landings or catch per unit effort and, sometimes, corresponding jobs. b Aquaculture is the farming of aquatic organisms, including fish, crustaceans, molluscs, seaweeds and algae.
Water storage and provision	a Water abstraction in marine and coastal environments is mostly associated with coastal lakes, deltaic aquifers or desalination plants. b Marine water may also be used for industrial cooling processes or coastal aquaculture in ponds and raceways.
Biotic materials and biofuels provision	a This includes medicinal (e.g. drugs, cosmetics), ornamental (e.g. corals, shells) and other commercial or industrial resources (e.g. whale oil, fishmeal, seal leather, algal or plant fertilisers). b Biomass to produce energy can have a solid form (like wood from mangroves), liquid (like fuels extracted from algal lipids or whale oil) or biogas (from decomposing material).
Regulating and maintenance services	
Water purification	Treatment of human wastes (e.g. nitrogen retention); dilution; sedimentation, trapping or sequestration (e.g. of pesticide residues or industrial pollution); bioremediation (e.g. bioaugmentation after marine oil spills); oxygenation of 'dead zones'; filtration and absorption; remineralisation; decomposition.
Air quality regulation	Vegetation (e.g. in mangroves), soil (e.g. in wetlands) and water bodies (e.g. open ocean), due to their physical structure and microbiological composition, absorb air pollutants like particulate matter, ozone or sulphur dioxide.
Coastal protection	Natural defence of the coastal zone against inundation and erosion from waves, storms or rise in sea level. Biogenic and geologic structures that form the coastal habitats can disrupt the water movement and, thus, stabilise sediments or create buffering protective zones.
Climate regulation	The ocean acts as a sink (and only a very marginal source) for greenhouse and climate-active gases. Inorganic carbon is dissolved into the seawater, and organic carbon is formed through primary producers, a percentage of which is stored and a percentage of which is sequestered.
Weather regulation	For example, the influence of coastal vegetation and wetlands on air moisture and, eventually, on the saturation point and the formation of clouds.
Ocean nourishment	Natural cycling processes leading to the availability of nutrients in the seawater for the production of organic matter. Pedogenesis could be observed at the margin of certain wetlands and mangroves, depending on hydrodynamic conditions.
Life cycle maintenance	The maintenance of key habitats that act as nurseries, spawning areas or migratory routes (e.g. seagrasses, coastal wetlands, coral reefs, mangroves). These habitats and the connectivity among them are crucial for the successful life cycle of species. This also includes pollination (e.g. mangrove pollination) and seed and gamete dispersal by organisms.

Table 1.2 (continued)

Marine and coastal ecosystem services	Specific component
	This service guarantees the maintenance of genetic diversity or gene pool protection.
Biological regulation	Control of fish pathogens, especially in aquaculture installations; role of cleaner fishes in coral reefs; biological control of the spread of vector-borne human diseases; control of potentially invasive species.
Cultural services Symbolic and aesthetic values	Coastal communities have always shown strong bonds to the sea due to local identity. Natural and cultural sites linked to traditions and religion are numerous in the coastal zone. Both coastal and inland societies value the existence and beauty of charismatic habitats and species such as coral reefs or marine mammals.
Recreation and tourism	The appeal of marine ecosystems is usually linked to wilderness, sports or iconic landscapes and species. It can be related to coastal activities (e.g. bathing, sunbathing, snorkeling, SCUBA diving) and offshore activities (e.g. sailing, recreational fishing, whale watching).
Cognitive effects	Inspiration for arts and other applications (e.g. architecture designs inspired by marine shells, medical applications replicating marine organic compounds). Material for research and education (e.g. discoveries of new deep-sea species). Information and awareness (e.g. respect for nature through the observation of marine wildlife).

Source: Based on Liquete *et al.* (2013).

Conclusions

1   Whilst human activities and the associated changes made to the environment have affected marine ecosystems for hundreds of years, it is mainly since the 1960s that impacts on ecological processes and on biodiversity have expressed themselves to the extent that action is needed.

2   Maintaining the diversity of habitats and of species in the sea is a 'duty' of the present generation but is also a very practical need: biodiversity provides tangible 'services' for humanity. Both duty and practicality need to be emphasised to users of the sea, to politicians and to others who have lost touch with nature and with societal values.

3   A difficulty that managers often have is translating political imperatives into action using meaningful and available science.

4   Conservation is a key part of the 'ecosystem approach' which guides much of how we manage human activities. Ensuring that conservation plays its role successfully needs knowledge and an understanding of how to use that knowledge.

5   The need for biodiversity conservation is driven by public concern, scientific advice and political action as expressed in directives, conventions and statutes. The information resources that inform application of those conventions may not be particularly relevant to the conservation of marine biodiversity, and marine ecologists need to influence future developments internationally and on regional scales to ensure that all species and habitats are considered – not just the charismatic ones or the ones with quantitative information indicating decline.

6   Managing human activities for the benefit of biodiversity and for sustainable use of our seas, including for societal benefits, is what 'conservation' is all about. That conservation should pervade everything we do in using the seas.

Chapter 2

What is where and how much of it is there? The role of science

Introduction

Knowing what is where, how much of it is there and what is its condition are fundamental starting points for effective conservation including assessment of the likely impact of human activities through to selection of representative MPAs. How to organise existing data and information (taking the science-based approach that is the foundation of this volume) is the subject of this chapter. The text begins with an account of the early sources of information that laid the foundations of what we know today. It continues by explaining that the data we collect needs to be organised within a common vocabulary that identifies similar entities so that we can compare like with like. Examples are given of terminology and classifications that help to do that. Then, we need to see data in context, including where else species and habitats occur and how rich those other locations are, to assess 'quality'. The application for practical conservation of that now-organised data and information as well as the collection of new data is for later chapters.

Natural history – the starting point

At the core of biodiversity conservation is not only an understanding of what is 'out there' but also how much there is and how it 'works'. To have that understanding requires knowledge (that we get from training and literature) and experience (that we get from making field observations and conducting experimental studies).

Studies of marine life started with a desire to document the species that existed in the sea. In the heyday of natural history, during the nineteenth century, many species new to science were catalogued and monographs that described species within the major taxonomic groups were written. Those publications would provide the essential support for resource surveys that underpin our knowledge of biodiversity hotspots, including the locations of rare species, and allow us to give structure to the otherwise impossibly complicated world of the 0.7 to 1 million marine species (of which, to date, 226,000 have been described) that are believed to exist in the world (Appeltans et al., 2012). The structures that we have work well for taxonomy, and the Linnean system of biological nomenclature allows us to give names to distinct entities. Classifying habitats is much less easy and there are continua between distinctly different habitats. Nevertheless, if we are to be able to represent examples of different habitats and to compare like with like when identifying the best examples for conservation, we need a robust classification in the biogeographical area in which conservation measures are being considered. Biogeographical provinces have been identified

Figure 2.1 During the middle part of the nineteenth century, naturalists were beginning to catalogue which species were where and the sort of assemblages that they lived in. The dredge was a key piece of equipment.

Source: Harvey (1857).

on a world scale (see Chapter 9 on selection of representative MPAs) but also on more local scales – unfortunately, the boundaries of those biogeographical areas rarely correspond with political boundaries, and conservation objectives for a particular country or union of countries may not make sense biogeographically.

Structuring what we know about species and habitats

Introduction

Organising data and information requires using a common language. There are well-developed taxonomies for species that are kept up to date on the World Register of Marine Species (www.marinespecies.org) so that we call those species by their proper names. Some countries also have taxonomies for classifying their marine ecosystems, and that is an essential starting point for understanding whether a full range of habitats are being surveyed or are being encompassed within protected areas and for considering their expected condition. Detailed knowledge of what is where is inevitably restricted mainly to the coastal zone, but it is important to be able to describe where rare or fragile species occur, to compare habitats that are like with like, and to identify which are representative (and which are the best) examples of habitats.

Organising the information that we have and planning new surveys to describe the range of biodiversity features in a country or regional sea requires a nested approach. That approach is likely to start with identifying large areas with broadly similar biological, physiographic and oceanographic characteristics throughout (as realms or ecoregions), moving to smaller areas sharing physiographic features within those regions and then to the specific assemblages of plants and animals (as biotopes) that occur in those physiographic features.

Ecoregions

'Ecoregions' are biogeographical provinces that may include distinctive physiographic characteristics. Spalding et al. (2007) have identified a nested system of 12 realms, 62 provinces and 232 ecoregions for coastal and shelf areas of the world (illustrated in Chapter 9). For the open ocean and deep-sea areas, UNESCO (2013) have developed a biogeographic classification. Ecoregions will be replicated, although often with local boundary variants, by the states and other regulatory bodies in the various regional seas of the world. They will also be further subdivided on the basis of more localised physiographic features or, perhaps, local biogeographic boundaries. For instance, Wilkinson et al. (2009) identify 24 Level 1 and 86 Level 2 ecoregions in North America with some finer-scale subregions also identified. Hale (2010), taking advantage of extensive data sets for sediment communities in US Atlantic estuaries, identified seven subregions: two based on salinity (oligohaline, mesohaline) and five based on latitude. Zacharias et al. (1998) produced a marine ecosystem/ecological classification for British Columbia. Such studies will be repeated wherever data sets exist but it is often the knowledge and experience of marine naturalists that enables identification of the distinctive regions within which representative protected areas should be located. In other words, don't wait until you have the detailed data sets.

Physiographic features

Physiographic features often hold distinctive habitats and communities of species and are identified mainly to assist in planning surveys to ensure that the range of marine habitats in an area are censused. Some physiographic features such as estuaries, saline lagoons and tidal sounds have clear boundaries which are convenient for the enclosure of protected representative sites. In any case, the distinctive communities that exist within physiographic features will contribute to the development of a biotopes classification or link to an existing one.

Biotopes

Biotopes 'fit' within physiographic features, being the smallest geographical unit of the biosphere or of a habitat that can be delimited by convenient boundaries, and that are characterised by their biota (Lincoln et al., 1998). Biotopes are defined by their physical and chemical (salinity) 'habitat' along with their biological 'community'. Biotopes are often synonymised with 'habitats'. Having a classification of biotopes allows us to map biodiversity resources and to compare like with like to identify typical or richest examples. Within biogeographical regions and physiographic features, it will be biotopes that are used to identify representative areas for protection. Characterising examples of each biotope by the species present in it may also provide a starting point for estimating the species and their abundance that would be expected in a particular habitat and, therefore, whether or not it is likely to be a typical, a rich or, perhaps, a degraded example.

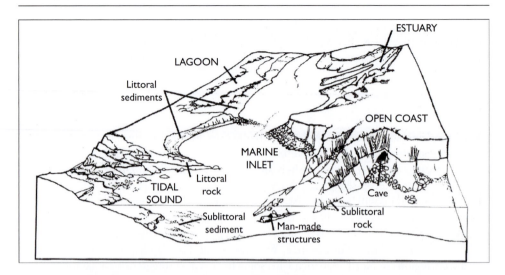

Figure 2.2 Coastal physiographic features identified for separate survey in a region as part of the Marine Nature Conservation Review (MNCR) of Great Britain. Physiographic types are in capital letters and examples of subsidiary habitats include lower-case letters.

Source: Reproduced with permission from Hiscock (1996). © JNCC

Costello (2009) lists various classification schemes for habitats in different parts of the world. Two examples of biotope classification hierarchies are given here. In Europe, classification schemes are led by the European Nature Information System (EUNIS) (Davies *et al.*, 2004; see: http://eunis.eea.europa.eu/habitats.jsp) (Figure 2.4). For that classification, survey data should allow differentiation of habitats to at least Level 4 and preferably Level 5 of the classification. In the USA, the Coastal and Marine Ecological Classification Standard (CMECS) is a catalogue of terms that provides a means for classifying ecological units using a simple, standard format and common terminology (Federal Geographic Data Committee, 2012) (Figure 2.5).

Other well-developed classifications are noted in Costello (2009).

Species distributions and abundances

Having information on the geographical distribution and abundance of species underpins the selection of representative MPAs (see Plate 8), helps to identify biodiversity hotspots and is a starting point for predicting changes in distribution of species as a result of climate change. For non-native species, information on rate of spread will inform any action that may possibly limit that spread. Knowing the distribution of a species also helps to 'test' survey results or newly submitted records for likely accuracy: unusual occurrences will need a much higher level of proof than for species already known to be present in an area. Unusual occurrences can include the presence of rare species which may indicate a special location where biodiversity may be particularly high or unusual conditions exist. Historical data is also important, especially in demonstrating reductions in range or abundance for species that may be threatened by human activities and that may benefit from a species recovery programme.

CR.HCR.XFa.ByErSp.Eun
Eunicella verrucosa and *Pentapora foliacea* on wave-exposed circalittoral rock

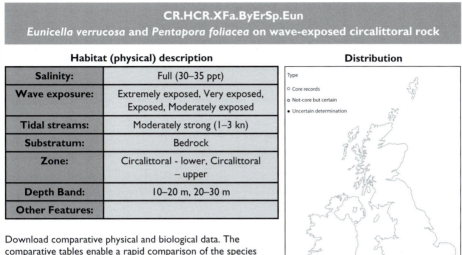

Habitat (physical) description	
Salinity:	Full (30–35 ppt)
Wave exposure:	Extremely exposed, Very exposed, Exposed, Moderately exposed
Tidal streams:	Moderately strong (1–3 kn)
Substratum:	Bedrock
Zone:	Circalittoral - lower, Circalittoral – upper
Depth Band:	10–20 m, 20–30 m
Other Features:	

Distribution

Type
○ Core records
○ Not-core but certain
● Uncertain determination

Download comparative physical and biological data. The comparative tables enable a rapid comparison of the species composition and principal physical characteristics between a given set of biotopes.

Previous code
This biotope occurred in previous versions of the classification as:
CR.MCR.XFa.ErSEun - Version: 97.06

Biotope description

This biotope typically occurs on wave-exposed, steep, circalittoral bedrock, boulder slopes and outcrops, subject to varying tidal streams. This silty variant contains a diverse faunal community, dominated by the seafan *Eunicella verrucosa*, the bryozoan *Pentapora foliacea* and the cup coral *Caryophyllia smithii*. There are frequently numerous *Alcyonium digitatum*, and these may become locally abundant under more tide-swept conditions. *Alcyonium glomeratum* may also be present. A diverse sponge community is usually present, including numerous erect sponges; species present include *Cliona celata*, *Raspailia ramosa*, *Raspailia hispida*, *Axinella dissimilis*, *Stelligera stuposa*, *Dysidea fragilis* and *Polymastia boletiformis*. *Homaxinella subdola* may be present in the south west. A hydroid/bryozoan turf may develop in the understorey of this rich sponge assemblage, with species such as *Nemertesia antennina*, *Nemertesia ramosa*, crisiids, *Alcyonidium diaphanum* and *Bugula plumosa*. The sea cucumber *Holothuria forskali* may be locally abundant, feeding on the silty deposits on the rock surface. Other echinoderms encountered include the starfish *Marthasterias glacialis* and the urchin *Echinus esculentus*. Other fauna includes aggregations of colonial ascidians *Clavelina lepadiformis* and *Stolonica socialis*. Anemones such as *Actinothoe sphyrodeta* and *Parazoanthus axinellae* may be seen dotted across the rock surface. This biotope is present in south west England and Wales.

Situation

This biotope is commonly found on rocky outcrops, surrounded by coarse sediment. This may be in the form of shelly gravel or muddy gravel, supporting *Urticina felina*, *Cerianthus lloydii* and *Neopentadactyla mixta*. Above ByErSp.Eun, dense kelp forest containing *Saccorhiza polyschides* is usually found.

Temporal variation
Not known

Similar biotopes
[A list of four similar biotopes is given]

Characterising Species
[Twenty-five characterising taxa, and their frequency of occurrence, typical abundance and percentage contribution to similarity in examples of the biotope are listed]

Figure 2.3 One of the biotope descriptions from the JNCC Britain and Ireland classification. The code is for version 04.05 and each biotope is compatible with the EUNIS European classification. The biotope is illustrated in Plate 7.

Source: Copied and reformatted with permission from JNCC: http://jncc.defra.gov.uk/page-1584 (accessed 4 November 2013).

A [Level 1]: Marine habitats

    A1 [Level 2]: Littoral rock and other hard substrata

        A1.1 [Level 3]: High energy littoral rock

            A1.11 [Level 4]: Mussel and/or barnacle communities

                A1.111 [Level 5]: *Mytilus edulis* and barnacles on very exposed eulittoral rock

                    A1.112 [Level 5]: *Chthamalus* spp. on exposed upper eulittoral rock

                        A1.1121 [Level 6]: *Chthamalus montagui* and *Lichina pygmaea* on steep exposed upper eulittoral rock

Figure 2.4 A small section of the EUNIS biotopes classification hierarchy

Source: Reformatted from: http://eunis.eea.europa.eu/habitats

Biotope: *Phragmatopoma lapidosa* Reefs on High Energy Sand

    Biogeographic Component:
    Realm: Tropical Atlantic
    Province: Tropical Northwestern Atlantic
    Ecoregion: Floridian

        Aquatic Setting:
        System: Marine
        Subsystem: Nearshore
        Tidal Zone: Intertidal, Subtidal

            Geoform Component:
            Tectonic Setting: Passive Continental Margin
            Physiographic Setting: Continental/Island Shore Complex
            Geoform Origin: Geologic, Biologic
            Level 1 Geoform: Beach
            Level 1 Geoform Type: Wave Dominated Beach
            Level 2 Geoform: Worm Reef
            Level 2 Geoform Type: Linear Worm Reef, Patch Worm Reef

                Substrate Component:
                Substrate Origin: Geologic Substrate
                Substrate Class: Unconsolidated Substrate
                Substrate Subclass: Fine Unconsolidated Substrate
                Substrate Group: Sand, Mud

                    Biotic Component
                    Biotic Setting: Benthic Biota
                    Biotic Class: Reef Biota
                    Biotic Subclass: Worm Reef
                    Biotic Group: Sabellariid Reef
                    Biotic Community: *Phragmatopoma lapidosa* Reef

Figure 2.5 A small section of the Coastal and Marine Ecological Classification Standard (CMECS) hierarchy

Source: Reformatted from Federal Geographic Data Committee (2012).

Surveys range from those driven by curiosity about what is at a location ('pure' natural history), through resource surveys (e.g. measuring fish abundances) that incidentally collect data on invertebrates, to environmental impact assessments or surveys for conservation that seek a knowledge of the biological character of a location (Plates 9–12). Early studies may have resulted in the inclusion of locations of occurrence of species in descriptive text or monographs about a particular group of organisms. Some of the most valuable sources of information are the 'marine fauna lists' that were often published for the area around a seaside laboratory (Figure 2.6) or the checklists of seaweeds from a particular area. Those lists are published in or are copied from paper publications, and it is only since the 1980s, as computerised databases and spreadsheets have become widely used to store information, that data can be brought together to map species distributions and abundances. Furthermore, historical records were often very vague or descriptive about where a species had been recorded. Many recent surveys have been funded by industry and companies may see biological data as 'commercial capital' (it can be sold on to another company undertaking an environmental assessment in the same area), and so it becomes unavailable to science and broadscale conservation assessments. Nevertheless, the disparate sources of data which are available can be brought together with appropriate validation and using imagination about how to georeference locations where data was collected.

One of the largest efforts to gather together data from different sources was the Census of Marine Life (COML) (www.coml.org). COML was an international project that, for ten

---

146

ANNELIDA: POLYCHAETA

Family Serpulidae

SERPULA VERMICULARIS L. [*McIntosh*, 1900–23, IV, 2, p. 353]
> Occasional specimens in the Sound; in small numbers from Mewstone Grounds, Looe-Eddystone, Rame-Eddystone and Eddystone Gourd (E.J.A.): obtained at a number of positions S.S.W. of the Eddystone in depth of 42–49 fm. (Crawshay, 1912, p. 346); large masses were obtained by a diver somewhere in the Hamoaze, and brought to the Laboraty (Allen, 1915, p. 643)
> Breeding: specimens from Eddystone Grounds in Aug. and Sept. were ripe (C.S.): ripe 12.4.20, successfully fertilized (H.O.)

HYDROIDES NORVEGICA (Gunnerus) [*Saint-Joseph*, 1898, p. 440]
> Common on stones and shells from the shore to 30 fm., increasing in abundance in the deeper water (E.J.A): dredged at a number of positions S.S.W. of the Eddystone in depths of 40–49 fm. (Crawshay, 1912, p. 347)
> Breeding: Aug. (C.S.)

POMATOCEROS TRIQUETER (L.) [*McIntosh*, 1900–23, IV, 2, p. 362]
> Common, attached to shells and stones on all grounds from the shore to 30 fm. (E.J.A.): River Tamar, up to Hole's Hole, dredged from main channel, and collected on bank; River Lynher, up to beach 100 yds. above Antony Creek, dredge and hand, June-Oct. 1928 (E.P.): dredged at several positions S.S.W. of Eddystone in depth of 42–51 fm. (Crawshay, 1912, p. 347)
> SALCOMBE. Common in dredge material from Salcombe Harbour and the Kingsbridge Estuary (Allen and Todd, 1900, p. 199)
> Breeding: March–April, successfully fertilized, Rum Bay, Wembury, below Laboratory (J.H.O., H.O.): almost any time of year, successfully fertilized (M.V.L.)

Figure 2.6 Regional marine fauna lists provide valuable information on the distribution and abundance of species and on breeding periods, unusual events, etc. In this example, from the Plymouth Marine Fauna (Marine Biological Association, 1957), 'large masses' of *Serpula vermicularis* were recorded from the Tamar Estuary (the Hamoaze) early in the twentieth century but are not found there today.

Source: Marine Biological Association (1957).

years until 2011, brought together survey data and information that would inform marine science and especially biodiversity conservation. The data sets collated as a part of COML provided a foundation for the Ocean Biodiversity Information System (OBIS) under the auspices of the International Oceanographic Data and Information Exchange (IODE) programme. Much of the work that will inform the 'what is where?' of biodiversity conservation is now being undertaken by the Global Biodiversity Information Facility (GBIF). GBIF envisions '[a] world in which biodiversity information is freely and universally available for

Figure 2.7 For areas that are well surveyed, it is possible to map species distributions as a means of establishing how widespread species are and, in the long term, to track range extensions and contractions. An example from the UK National Biodiversity Network (NBN) Gateway (https://data.nbn.org.uk). The NBN enables participating organisations to share data on species, sites and habitat. This information is collated in a standard format and made freely publicly available via the NBN Gateway and web services. This enables users to explore the data and create products ranging from simple grid maps and site reports to complex predictive models.

Source: Data courtesy of the NBN Gateway with thanks to all the data contributors who can be seen at: https://data.nbn.org.uk/Taxa/NBNSYS0000173675/Grid_Map. The NBN and its data contributors bear no responsibility for the further analysis or interpretation of this material, data and/or information.

science, society, and a sustainable future' (see: www.gbif.org/whatisgbif). GBIF's mission is to be the foremost global resource for biodiversity information and to engender smart solutions for environmental and human well-being. GBIF operates through a network of nodes, coordinating the biodiversity information facilities of participant countries and organisations, and collaborating with each other and the Secretariat to share skills, experiences and technical capacity. The NBN is the UK node of GBIF and a major data contributor. GBIF resources link to other international resources such as the World Register of Marine Species and its publications provide standards that can be applied worldwide (for instance, for the establishment of regional marine species checklists: Nozères *et al.*, 2012).

The World Register of Marine Species identifies the geographical areas in which a species occurs. GBIF provides maps of known distribution of species worldwide. Those facilities and national databases such as the UK National Biodiversity Network (Figure 2.7) may be only a starting point if something rare or unusual is being recorded: checks of correct identification and contact with national or international experts may be needed to verify the observation.

Resources that provide information on the locations and abundances of species will vary greatly from one country or geographical area to the next. Often, the knowledge is in the heads and notebooks of naturalists or in limited circulation reports that may even be confidential. Capturing that information remains a difficult and often costly task. The need for surveys to fill gaps in information is clear. Anyone can contribute to our understanding of the distribution of marine species, from expert amateur naturalists and professional marine biologists to dedicated volunteer 'citizen scientists'. Sharing biodiversity data is becoming easier thanks to the development of new websites and apps for biological recording and species identification, and a growing number of national and international projects which facilitate volunteer participation in studying and recording marine wildlife and habitats. Modelling of the distribution of species using algorithms informed by physical information is being developed and tested (see, for instance, Robinson *et al.*, 2011) but taking account of all of the distributional barriers and habitat preferences will always be difficult and field data is bound to be the most reliable source of information.

How much of it is there? Assessing 'rarity'

Having described the various ways of identifying and displaying information on what is where, we should be in a position to identify what is rare, scarce, uncommon or widespread: key concepts in conservation. Rarity, whether of species or habitats, is important in its own right as a conservation driver and is often used as a surrogate for 'degree of threat'. Quoting measures of rarity may be highly persuasive when seeking action to protect a species or habitat. However, rarity is a difficult concept to define (see Chapter 7). Some species will never be present in large numbers and others are so poorly surveyed that we do not have measures of their abundance. Similarly, some habitats will always be very extensive (sediment plains of various sorts) and some will always be isolated and have a small surface area (for instance, caves, saline lagoons and seamounts). Often, we know that a species was once more abundant than it is today, or a valued habitat more extensive, but the historical records that tell us are usually descriptive and difficult to use as evidence.

Sloppy use of words such as 'rare' and 'scarce' is widespread especially amongst those in the voluntary conservation movement, but finding quantitative measures – let alone the reliable data – with which to apply those terms is challenging. The important thing to do in providing the starting point for assessing rarity is to ensure that information on species distributions is georeferenced and that it is, as far as possible, quantified. Then, the ways of assessing rarity described in Chapter 7 and new approaches that still need to be developed can be applied.

Identifying 'quality' and biodiversity hotspots

'Quality'

Many directives, conventions and statutes desire to maintain 'quality' of marine ecosystems. Where that quality is concerned with the species composition of undisturbed habitats, we face two difficulties. First, we often do not know what would have been the pristine condition of a particular habitat and its assemblage of species (explored in Chapter 11) and, second, we often do not know what would constitute 'normal' or 'expected' species composition or abundance in a habitat. If the way to identify quality or degree of recovery after damage is to compare survey results with the characteristics of undamaged examples of particular habitats, we may be hard put to work out what is representative or 'normal' when local conditions cause so much natural variability in composition. More likely, we will find that the quality of survey data is too 'uneven' to characterise biotopes from different regions in a way that enables reliable comparison (the problem that Hiscock and Breckles, 2007 found when analyzing data to identify biodiversity hotspots).

Biodiversity hotspots

Biodiversity hotspots are often sought out for conservation as the high species richness is often because of the presence of rare species; for a policy advisor working with a 'shopping list' of species or habitats, it is possible to get more 'bang for your buck' at a location which has a high species or biotope richness. Experienced naturalists will all have their favourite biodiversity hotspots – places where they can explore a range of habitats and find a wide range of species, often including rare or scarce species. The concept of biodiversity hotspots is explored by Hiscock and Breckles (2007), who define them as 'areas of high species and habitat richness that include representative, rare and threatened features' (p6). In their study in Great Britain, they only considered areas that had detailed and comparable levels of survey data, trialing six measures of 'richness'. However, despite having data that was considered to provide good accounts of the character of the areas compared and a methodology that adjusted for high levels of survey intensity, there was still a great deal of 'unevenness' in survey data that made the resulting measures equivocal. Measures of taxonomic distinctness (Warwick and Clark, 2001) most closely matched what might have been expected by those with knowledge of the areas concerned, and it was felt that, in the absence of fully comparable data sets, average taxonomic distinctness provided the most robust measure of biodiversity. Langmead and Jackson (2010) explore methods for mapping large-scale patterns of biodiversity in support of prioritising areas for protection. Their methods, described most fully in Jackson et al. (2010), identified hotspots of marine biodiversity in Wales as a way of informing the process of selecting MPAs.

Conclusions

1   Having classification schemes for species and for ecoregions, physiographic features and habitats to provide a practical vocabulary for conservation is important. The Linnean system of classification for species serves us well, and there are global and regional schemes that exist for ecosystems and habitats. Further development is needed, at least on a regional scale, of habitat classifications.

2   Identification of distinctive biogeographical provinces and regions can be achieved using survey data but the knowledge and experience of marine naturalists is invaluable.

3   Bringing together existing data and information about the occurrence of species and habitats (as physical habitats and as biotopes) is the starting point for identifying representative sites for conservation and for tracking changes in distribution and abundance. However, accessing, validating, mapping and presenting that data as information for conservation science is often problematic because of ownership and accuracy issues.

4   Assessing 'rarity' is fraught with problems but pragmatic measures are needed as a contribution to identifying species that need protection.

5   Experienced naturalists 'know' a biodiversity hotspot when they see it, but how can such a concept be translated into the analysis of data sets when data is so uneven and incomplete? Methods have been developed but more work is needed to accommodate the time when the experienced naturalists are no more.

6   Schemes that assess 'biological quality' need reference points in terms of what would be expected of a site or a specific biotope that is unaffected by human activities – is this possible?

Chapter 3

Ecosystem structure, functioning and viability

Introduction

Understanding how marine ecosystems operate is something that we can work towards through observation, recording and experiment. However, the interactions between weather, ocean processes and the organisms that live in the oceans are highly complex and predicting or accounting for change is fraught with uncertainties. This chapter is a summary of some of the things that we know about ecosystem structure, functioning and viability and that are relevant knowledge for anyone who needs to manage or advise on the management of human activities to protect biodiversity.

An 'ecosystem' is the combination of organisms with their physical environment, interacting as an ecological unit (from Lincoln *et al.*, 1998). An ecosystem can be as large as the Baltic Sea or as small as the bacteria and their environment in the gut of a fish. For fisheries conservation, it will most likely be necessary to assess ecosystems at the large (Baltic Sea) scale while for nature conservation and assessing the likely impacts of human activities, consideration is more likely to be at the scale of physiographic (landscape) features such as an estuary or an offshore reef.

Ecosystem 'structure' includes the way in which both biological and non-biological components of the ecosystem are arranged. The physical structure of substratum or the physical and chemical structure of the water column is highly influential in determining the sort of marine life that is likely to be present at a location. Ecosystem 'functioning' depends in part on physical and chemical processes and in part on 'the activities, processes or properties of ecosystems that are influenced by its biota' (Naeem *et al.*, 2004, p3). That influence of organisms on ecosystem functioning is expressed as a result of the functional traits of species (see, for instance, Díez and Cabildo, 2001). 'Viability' is related to the concepts of minimum size of area needed to sustain populations of different species and how large populations need to be to reproduce and repopulate. Viability of an assemblage of species may also depend on the amount of functional redundancy in the assemblage – if one species is lost or declines, are there other species that will take over its role? Understanding, as far as possible, concepts of structure, functioning and viability help to address the desire to 'maintain or restore ecosystem integrity' and other similar policy imperatives.

The importance of maintaining ecosystems

It is important to convey to policy advisors or policymakers and to managers what are the consequences of action that reduce diversity across the board and not just in terms of loss of commercial species or species that provide obvious services (such as the coastal protection provided by salt marshes or mangroves). 'Collapsing ecosystems' are often illustrated by the 'fishing down the food web' diagram (Box 3.1) where parallel declines

Box 3.1 Fishing down the food web

Pauly (2005)* has suggested three phases of the impact of fisheries on marine ecosystems:

- **Pristine** – the first phase. In pristine ocean environments, the biomass of the large predator fish are 10 to 100 times greater than their present biomass. This implies a large supporting biomass of small prey fishes and invertebrates. On the seafloor, the benthos is dominated by deposit feeders which prevent resuspension of sediments and filter feeders which keep the phytoplankton down. Thus the water column tends to be oligotrophic, free of both suspended particles and of the nutrients that leach from them.
- **Exploited** – the second phase. It is characterized by declines in the biomass of large predator fish, declines in the diversity, size and trophic level of captured fish, and declines in the benthos. Bottom trawlers progressively destroy the biogenic structures built over many years on the seafloor by the filter and detritus feeders. As these structures and animals that were filtering the phytoplankton and consuming the detritus (marine snow) disappear, they are replaced with the polyp stages of jellyfish and other small errant benthic animals. Storms resuspend the marine snow, and the water column gradually eutrophies. In the early part of this phase, cascade effects compensate these declines with the emergence of new fisheries for opportunistic feeders, such as squid, shrimp and other invertebrates. But eventually these decline also.

- **Fully degraded** – the third phase. The dead zone is the biological end point of a fully degraded marine ecosystem. The dead zone is a zone with excessive nutrients in the water column, resulting in the depletion of oxygen and the elimination of multicellular organisms. The abundant detritus and marine snow is processed by bacteria rather than by the benthic animals. These dead zones are currently growing throughout the world in places such as the Bohai Sea in China, the northern Adriatic Sea, and the northern Gulf of Mexico. Some estuaries, such as the Chesapeake Bay estuary, also display features associated with a fully degraded marine ecosystem. In Chesapeake Bay, overfishing eliminated the benthic filter feeders, such as oysters, and most predators larger than a striped bass which is the current apex predator. One hundred and fifty years ago, the oysters formed giant reefs and filtered the waters of Chesapeake Bay every three days. Because the oysters are gone, pollution entering the estuary from rivers now produces harmful algal blooms.

*Text is from: http://en.wikipedia.org/wiki/Fishing_down_the_food_web and the wording differs slightly from Pauly (2005).

Source: Illustration copied from: http://en.wikipedia.org/wiki/Fishing_down_the_food_web. © Hans Hillewaert. This file is licensed under the Creative Commons Attribution-ShareAlike 3.0 Unported License.

in finfish stocks and benthos are illustrated. Some of those changes are consequential and some are coincidental, resulting from different sorts of human activities. The progressive declines and changes degrade ecosystem structure, functioning and viability so that ecosystem services are no longer supported. In biodiversity conservation, the aim must be to maintain or restore ecosystems and that means maintaining or restoring viable populations of key functional or structural species as well as (and not only) species that are valued because of their rarity, commercial use or cultural importance. These objectives are different to those pursued in fisheries conservation which usually aims to maintain or restore only the target commercial species of finfish or shellfish and only acts with regard to non-commercial aspects of the ecosystem if those aspects constitute food for the exploited species.

Ecologists and policy advisors should not rely on models from terrestrial or freshwater systems to inform marine conservation. Marine ecosystems are different from terrestrial ecosystems in a number of ways including greater propagule and material exchange and more rapid biological processes (Giller et al., 2004). These processes are due to the fluid nature of marine ecosystems which make them dynamic, often unpredictable and, ultimately, highly complex systems. As a result of this fluidity, the boundaries of marine ecosystems are often difficult to identify. Larvae and propagules, where they are long-lived, are readily dispersed, and movements of planktonic and fish species are generally unimpeded by barriers. Thus, many marine ecosystems are considered more open than terrestrial ecosystems such as grasslands or freshwater ecosystems such as ponds and lakes.

This chapter repeats material in Hiscock et al. (2006) taking account of recent developments.

Structure

Introduction

The term 'structure' is commonly understood to mean: 'the arrangement of and relations between the parts of something complex' (Pearsall, 1999). In ecology, the 'structure' of an ecosystem is usually defined to include amounts and nature of both biological and non-biological components of the ecosystem.

Physical structure

The physical structure of substratum or the physical and chemical structure of the water column is highly influential in determining the sort of marine life that is likely to be present at a location.

Biological structure

'Biological structure' refers both the actual physical structure provided by animals and plants (e.g. biogenic structures) and the structural organisation of the community

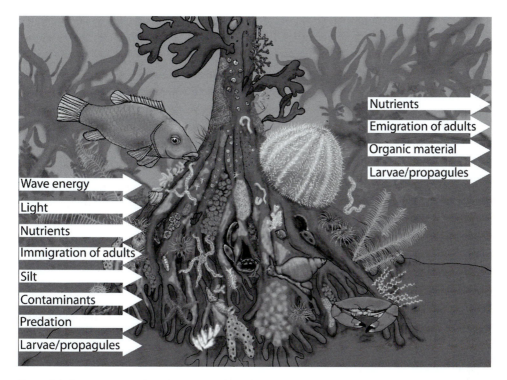

Figure 3.1 A community of species associated with a structural feature: a kelp holdfast. The main inputs and outputs (arrows) in terms of properties and processes are shown. Drawing: Jack Sewell.

Source: Adjusted from Hiscock *et al.* (2006) with permission.

Box 3.2 Categories of structure recorded in Marine Nature Conservation Review surveys

For the seabed, the categories of structure recorded in Marine Nature Conservation Review (MNCR) surveys (Hiscock, 1996) were:

Features – Rock

Surface relief. Overall relief of the habitat from **very even** (unbroken bedrock with uniform inclination) to **very rugged** (highly broken slope with wide range of surfaces, possibly with gullies or rock pools breaking up the overall inclination considerably).

Texture. An indication of the smoothness of the rock type from **very smooth** (a hard and well-worn rock such as granite or well-rounded cobbles) to **highly pitted** (a highly pitted or bored rock such as some forms of limestone, or very fragmentary and jagged rock such as shale).

Stability. An indication of the stability of the rock, and related to wave action, from **very stable** (bedrock; boulders which are never moved by wave action) to **highly mobile** (frequently turned pebbles, cobbles or even boulders, where colonisation is considerably affected because of such movement).

Scour. An indication of scour by sand (not abrasion from mobility of rocks – see above), from **none** (no scour present) to **highly scoured** (very highly scoured by sand – rocks likely to be smooth and without colonisation).

Silt. The amount of silt settled on the rocks, from **none** (very clean rock surfaces) to **highly silted** (thick layer of silt on all surfaces). Where sand deposits on rocks from wave action note under this section.

Fissures. The amount of fissures (over 10mm wide) present, from **none** to **very many** (accounts for high proportion of habitat).

Crevices. The amount of crevices (less than 10mm wide) present, from **none** to **very many** (accounts for high proportion of habitat).

Rock pools. The amount of rock pool present, from **none** to **very many** (accounts for high proportion of habitat).

Boulder, cobble and pebble shapes. From **highly rounded** (very rounded boulders, cobbles or pebbles) to **very angular** (highly angular boulders, cobbles or pebbles, e.g. slates).

In addition to the information required by MNCR surveys, the softness and hardness of rocks is important. For instance, rich algal communities may occur if the rock retains water or is soft enough to allow penetration of holdfasts. Rocks which are soft enough to allow animals to bore into them provide security from predators and, when the inhabitant dies, a habitat for nestling species.

Features – Sediment

Surface relief. Overall relief of the habitat, from **very even** (surface completely uniform) to **highly uneven** (surface perhaps with numerous mounds or drainage channels).

Firmness. An indication of the degree of softness or compactness of the sediment, on the scale (with littoral and sublittoral guides): 1 = **very firm** – no indentation when walked on; difficult to dig with fingers; 2 – can make a slight indentation;

fingers only can go in; 3 – can sink ankle deep; hand can go in; 4 – can sink knee deep; can penetrate up to elbow; 5 = **very soft** – can sink thigh deep; whole arm can go in).

Stability. From **highly stable** (movement of sediment very unlikely) to **highly mobile** (sediment constantly being moved).

Sorting. Particle size distribution – an indication of the uniformity of the particle size, from **very well sorted** (sediment composed of a single grain size) to **very poorly sorted** (sediment with wide range of grain sizes).

Black layer. An indication of the depth of the anoxic layer, on the scale: 1. not visible; 2. >20cm below surface; 3. 5–20cm below surface; 4. 1–5cm below surface; 5. < 1cm below surface.

Figure 3.2 Biogenic reef structures such as those formed by horse mussels *Modiolus modiolus* increase habitat complexity and provide a home for a wide range of species. Drawing: Sue Scott.

itself – the composition and relative proportions of species present at a locality. Plants and animals create physical structures that are, in some cases, essential for maintaining species richness and influencing ecosystem processes. Some of those structures are biogenic reefs that may be an 'oasis' of species richness in often apparently barren or impoverished settings.

Plants and animals may also provide microhabitats for refuge from predation, including grazing, or protection from adverse conditions such as strong tidal currents (Plates 13 and 14). Often, they are nursery areas for juvenile fish or shellfish. Often, they are easily destroyed or damaged by human activities.

Figure 3.3 Some species are capable of boring into soft rock such as chalk and limestone, creating a structure of holes and galleries where they are protected from predators. When they die, those holes become available for cryptic species to use. Section of limestone rock from Firestone Bay, Plymouth, UK. Species illustrated include: 1. *Scrupocellaria* sp.; 2. *Scypha compressa*; 3. *Aiptasia mutabilis*; 4. *Dendrodoa grossularia*; 5. *Flustra foliacea*; 6. *Hiatella arctica*; 7. *Polymastia* sp.; 8. *Ophiothrix fragilis*; 9. *Pisidia longicornis*; 10. *Amphilectus fucorum*; 11. *Phoronis hippocrepia*; 12. *Cliona celata*; 13. *Alcyonidium diaphanum*; 14. *Bugula plumosa*; 15. *Haliclona* sp.; 16. *Verruca stroemia*; and 17. *Dilsea carnosa*. Drawing: Sue Scott.

Source: Adjusted from Hiscock (1998a) with permission.

Species that themselves create structure because of their physical presence or their activities, especially burrowing, are described as 'key structural species' or 'ecosystem engineers'. The sorts of important structures that they create include:

- hard substratum for attachment of sessile species;
- surfaces suitable for laying eggs on/in; and
- burrows that provide a refuge for other species (Figures 3.3 and 3.4).

Structural species may also change aspects of the physical and chemical environment by, for instance, trapping silt or by facilitating oxygenation of sediments (see 'The importance of functional diversity', p40) Key structural species and ecosystem engineers are usually dominant species in an assemblage.

As with processes, structure can operate on many scales. Small-scale structure might include the habitat offered by an empty burrow. At a larger scale, structure might refer to the organisation of the community as a whole, in terms of trophic levels, species richness and functional diversity. These attributes can also be viewed as properties.

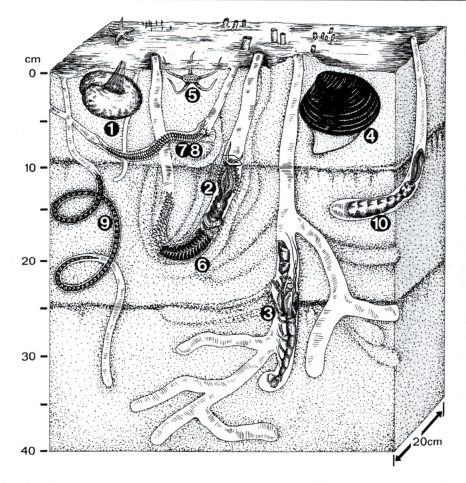

Figure 3.4 Sediments may appear barren on the surface or occupied by a few crawling species but the majority of species are hidden and many create burrows and galleries that structure and restructure the sediment enabling its irrigation. The community present on the Oyster Ground, Belgium. 1. Spatangoids (includes *Echinocardium cordatum*, *Echinocardium flavescens*, *Brissopsis lyrifera*). 2. *Chaetopterus variopedatus*. 3. Callianassids (includes *Callianassa subterranea*, *Upogebia deltaura*). 4. *Arctica islandica*. 5. Ophiuroids (includes *Amphiura filiformis*, *Amphiura chiajei*). 6. *Gattyana cirrosa*. 7. *Glycera rouxi*, *Glycera alba*. 8. *Nereis* (now *Hediste*) and *Nephtys* spp. 9. *Notomastus latericeus*. 10. *Echiurus echiurus*.

Source: de Wilde *et al.* (1984).

Structural integrity – its importance for conservation

Architectural structure, whether of burrows in sediments, biogenic reefs or the shelter afforded by seagrass beds, mangroves or kelp forests, is highly vulnerable to physical disturbance. Maintaining that structure helps to maintain rich communities that rely on the many different microhabitats in the habitat. Some examples of consequences of destroying structural features of habitats are described in Chapter 5.

Figure 3.5 In the Netherlands, the invasive Pacific oyster *Crassostrea gigas* has displaced the previously harvested mussel *Mytilus edulis*. Although the oysters cannot be harvested due to the fact that they are concreted together, they probably fulfil the same role as mussels in terms of ecosystem structure.

Source: Norbert Dankers.

Community structure includes the balance between the relative abundance of different species. For key functional species, a change in the balance can lead to major changes in the dynamics of the community which in turn can affect the functioning of the system (see for example Chapter 4).

Alien species may also threaten structural integrity. For instance, the slipper limpet *Crepidula fornicata* changes the substratum where it is dominant. That change can be from coarse sediments to shell and pseudofaeces-characterised sediments, creating an entirely different biotope that is less rich than the native biotope it replaces. On the other hand, some non-native species may increase structural complexity: for example, although much-valued naturalness is lost, shores on the Atlantic coast of Europe that are now dominated by Pacific oysters, *Crassostrea gigas*, host a wide range of associated species.

Functioning

Introduction

Smith *et al.* (2006, p1153) observe that:

> Biodiversity is an integral part of ecosystem function, affecting ecosystem productivity, decomposition rates, nutrient cycling, stability, and resistance to perturbations. Declines in biodiversity are of great concern as forces such as habitat destruction, global environmental change, pollution, and exotic species cause continued extinctions and declines in species abundances and community biodiversity.

Attributes of coastal and nearshore ecosystems that are important to the functioning of those systems include:

- the oceanographic and coastline setting including currents, upwelling, waves and coastline complexity;
- the fact that those ecosystems are largely 'open' and therefore the import and export of material (detritus, plankton) is facilitated;
- the presence of sharp physical gradients (especially on shores and in estuaries) including variations in depth, tidal elevation, wave action and salinity;
- little primary production consumed at the place of origin;
- fluctuations driven by variability in recruitment;
- strong biological interactions with a few species or functional groups having disproportionate effects.

The elements of ecosystem functioning that are influenced by biota include:

- energy transfer;
- elemental cycling (carbon, silicon, nitrogen, phosphorus, sulphur, calcium);
- productivity;
- food supply/export; and
- modification of physical processes.

Now, 'functional diversity' (see 'Functioning: the importance of knowing biological traits', p37) of the species in biotopes and as a part of food webs is considered as important or more important than taxonomic diversity in ecosystem functioning. And, food webs can be extremely complex with several hundred species in a biotope or associated with a particular habitat interacting as a part of the food web as well as relying on each other for places to live and places to feed (see, for instance, O'Gorman *et al.*, 2008, 2010).

Properties and large-scale processes

The functioning of an ecosystem is affected by its properties and the processes occurring within it, including those influenced by its biota. Properties can affect processes and *vice versa*. For example, the turbidity (a property) within an estuary will affect the level of primary production (a process), with lower turbidity leading to enhanced primary productivity. Conversely, bioturbation (a process) can increase small-scale turbidity at the sediment-water interface in silty areas. This section concentrates on the properties and processes that are the broadscale features of marine ecosystems and which influence large-scale biological properties such as biogeographical distribution. The predominant physical and chemical properties defined at a large scale (beyond that of a particular biotope or biotope complex), are:

- temperature range (air and sea for intertidal areas, seawater for subtidal areas);
- salinity including maxima and minima;
- substratum type;
- light regime;
- turbidity;

- residual current strength and direction;
- strength of wave action;
- strength of tidal streams;
- stratification of the water column;
- nutrient status; and
- contaminant levels.

Biological properties include assemblage (biotope) composition and trophic structure. At a community or biotope level, properties can include resilience and resistance (Giller *et al.*, 2004) which are themselves influenced by the trophic structure and composition of those communities.

'Processes' exert a dynamic influence on the marine environment that 'drives' what is present where, and how it changes. They can be physical, chemical and biological. Figure 3.6 highlights some of the process that control shallow marine communities in temperate ecosystems. Processes can act together to influence the properties and structural elements of marine ecosystems. For example, physical properties such as tidal flow and processes such as sedimentation can greatly influence the sediment characteristics and presence or absence of certain species at a given location. Strong tidal currents favour coarse sediment, such as gravel and pebbles, while slow currents favour muddy sediment.

Other processes which often have physical, chemical and biological elements include:

- dispersal of water quality characteristics brought about by movement of water masses;
- gas exchange;
- nutrient exchange;
- primary and secondary production;
- bioturbation;
- reef-building; and
- propagule dispersal brought about by movement of water masses.

Water movement is important on global, regional and local scales. Oceanic currents distribute warm or cold waters and transport the dispersal phases of some species to distant locations. Regional currents assist dispersal of species with long-lived larvae and distribute water masses with different characteristics (for instance, warm, cold, high salinity, variable salinity, turbid, clear). Local currents (usually wind-driven in tropical locations and tidal currents in temperate or arctic regions) distribute larvae or propagules but also determine, through their strength, the sorts of communities that develop at a location.

Primary production is the basis of almost all living processes. The most visible primary producers are the macroalgae and angiosperms (seagrasses) that live attached to the seabed. But the highest levels of primary production come from minute planktonic organisms. Primary producers assimilate carbon through photosynthesis and take up nutrients (nitrogen, phosphorous and other minerals) to create biomass. In turn, carbon is passed on as plants are consumed by animals, or the carbon is made available in other ways such as by death, fragmentation and decomposition that create the detritus (seston) that suspension feeders may use.

Primary productivity is often restricted by limited nutrient availability. However, where nutrients are enhanced, for instance from agricultural run-off or sewage disposal, green

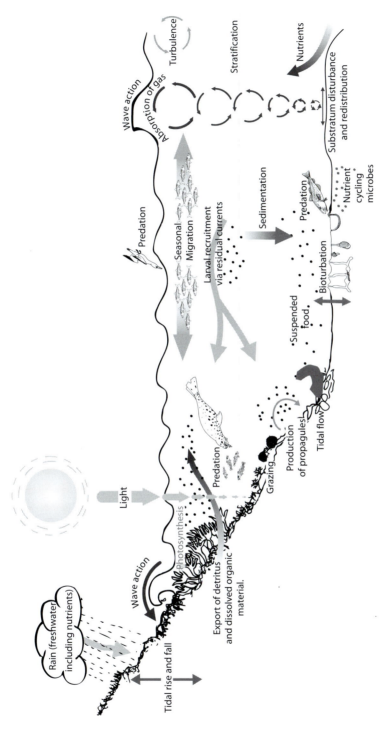

Figure 3.6 Physical, chemical and biological processes that influence shallow marine communities in the NE Atlantic. Drawing: Keith Hiscock and Jack Sewell.

Source: Hiscock et al. (2006) with permission.

Box 3.3 Oceanic currents as a key structural feature: the East Australian Current

The East Australian Current. Lighter shading shows surface currents and darker shading, subsurface currents.

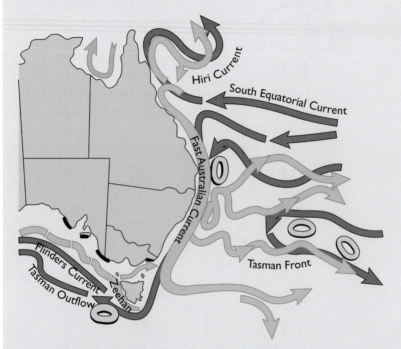

Source: Ridgway and Hill (2009).

Oceanic currents act on a regional scale to transfer water masses and to carry larvae and propagules. The East Australian Current (EAC) carries warm water south along the eastern coast of Australia. It has surface and subsurface elements. The current and its associated eddies contribute to determining the location of fisheries and to vertical mixing which is important for nutrient exchange and plankton abundance. Flow varies seasonally and on decadal timescales, but, in the past 60 years, the southward penetration of the EAC has increased. The east coast of Tasmania has become both warmer and saltier, with mean trends indicating a rise of 2.28°C/century and of 0.34 psu/century over the 1944–2002 period, which corresponds to a poleward advance of the EAC of about 350km. That warmer water is resulting in changes to seabed ecosystems, especially related to the increased southerly extent and abundance of sea urchins (*Centrostephanus rodgersii*) which has resulted in catastrophic overgrazing of productive Tasmanian kelp beds, leading to loss of biodiversity and important rocky reef ecosystem services. The projected strengthening of the EAC and continued warming of the southern part of the Tasman Sea is predicted to have a detrimental effect on cold temperate species in South East Australia and also to impact on commercially important fisheries such as abalone and rock lobster. (Ridgway and Hill, 2009; Ling *et al.*, 2009)

algae may become extensive on the shore and phytoplankton blooms may occur. Nutrient status is often of key importance in influencing the quality and character of marine ecosystems, and it is mentioned frequently in this volume as the cause or part of the cause of regime shifts including the severe effects on marine communities via deoxygenation when eutrophication creates blooms of plankton that die, sink to the bottom and decompose.

Properties and small-scale processes: connectivity

Many processes, including freshwater run-off, warming and localised sedimentation, occur on small scales. Dispersal of species may occur on small to large scales and contributes to a very important biological process that is much misunderstood or misused in marine conservation – connectivity. Adult movement (for mobile species) and larval or propagule dispersal (for sedentary or sessile species) is extremely important to the continued presence of species at a location, including the ability of a species to colonise or recolonise (after damage) habitats. Connectivity between MPAs has been promoted as a core consideration in the design of networks (but see Chapter 9).

Dispersal scales in marine species are extremely wide-ranging – from a distance of millimetres from the adult producing larvae or spores to hundreds of kilometres. Kinlan and Gaines (2003) reviewed the topic of propagule dispersal in marine and terrestrial environments and some of their results are illustrated in Figure 3.7. Not only are dispersal distances of benthic species often very small, the larvae may not behave in a passive way like the sediment particle dispersal algorithms that are often used as a model for larval dispersal.

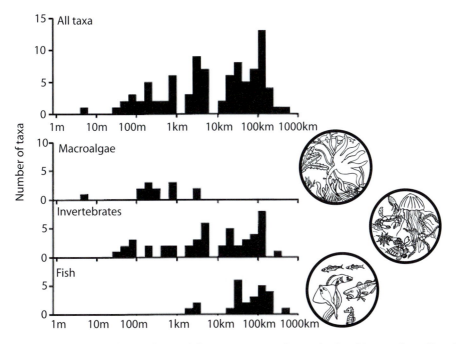

Figure 3.7 Distribution of mean dispersal distance estimates for marine benthic organisms. Drawings of organisms: Jack Sewell.

Source: Based on Kinlan and Gaines (2003).

Todd (1998) reviewed aspects of larval dispersal and addressed the concept of 'realised larval dispersal' by analysing population genetic differentiation in two mollusc species with contrasting larval types. The planktotrophic species showed genetic homogeneity of populations over a 1600km range, displaying large-scale larval dispersal. The pelagic lecithotrophic species revealed population differentiation on a very small scale (< 10km), despite local currents being very strong. If larvae are dispersed passively, then the direction that they go in and the distance they travel will depend on current direction and strength. That direction might be linear or circular, leading to markedly different dispersal distances for species with similar larval dispersal times. Even large, highly mobile fish species may confound ideas of long-distance dispersal. Cowan and Sponaugle (2009) explain the processes that drive larval dispersal and population connectivity:

- spawning output;
- larval dispersal (via currents);
- larval dispersal plus behaviour (e.g. vertical migration, horisontal swimming);
- predator/prey-mediated survival;
- available settlement habitat; and
- post settlement survival.

They observe (p459) that 'although the task at hand may be daunting, the more we can learn about population connectivity, the more nuanced and integrated those [referring to genetic exchange theory] theoretical treatments will become, which will ultimately lead to better design of MPAs.'

The dispersal capability of larvae is often overestimated. Timmers *et al.* (2012), trying to establish the validity of the paradigm that outbreaks of the crown of thorns starfish *Acanthaster planchi* (Plate 15) in one area 'seeded' other areas with large numbers of larvae, concluded (p1) that:

> successive outbreaks within and across regions are assumed to spread via the planktonic larvae released from a primary outbreak. This secondary outbreak hypothesis is predominantly based on the high dispersal potential of A. *planci* and the assertion that outbreak populations (a rogue subset of the larger population) are genetically more similar to each other than they are to low-density non-outbreak populations . . . Substantial regional, archipelagic, and subarchipelagic-scale genetic structuring of A. *planci* populations indicate that larvae rarely realize their dispersal potential and outbreaks in the central Pacific do not spread across the expanses of open ocean.

The concept of 'open' and 'closed' systems is important to bear in mind when considering MPA design, especially with regard to the potential for recruitment from other areas to assist recovery of damaged areas (including whether MPAs will act as donors to other areas) or whether the species and biotopes in a particular physiographic feature or habitat type are self-sustaining and will not benefit from recruitment from outside (see, for instance, Jessopp and McAllen, 2007).

Bearing in mind that many seabed species seem to have short-lived larvae, the curious ecologist or manager may wonder how they get to be in a location distant from the nearest known colonies. There are several possible explanations:

Box 3.4 Currents and connectivity. HMS Association with the Eagle, Rumney and the Firebrand, lost on the rocks of the Isles of Scilly, UK on October 22, 1707

Source: Eighteenth-century engraving accessed from: http://en.wikipedia.org/wiki/HMS_Association_(1697).

Before accurate position fixing at sea was possible, many sailing ships found themselves in a very different position to where they thought they were. Non-permanent currents may often have been to blame. One of the most notorious events in the history of the British Navy was the wreck of the fleet of Sir Cloudesley Shovell. Navigators on the flagship, *HMS Association*, thought the fleet was off Ushant (France) when it appears that in fact they had been swept northwards by a strong current to strike rocks in the Isles of Scilly off south-west England. That current, described in 1793 by James Rennell and now known as Rennell's Current, is relatively strong (1.0 to 1.5 knots) and could take a ship (or the larva of a species) up to about 60km distance in one day. Such currents could account for unexpected occurrences of southern species further north – for example, assisting the migration of species such as triggerfish from warmer waters to British coasts.

- In the case of algae and seagrass, fertile plants detach and float with currents, shedding their spores or seeds some distance from their source.
- Not all larvae produced by adults are short-lived. Some, perhaps ones that are produced by well-fed parents and have large reserves of sustenance, will stay in the water column much longer than normal.

- Larvae that are normally short-lived or are restrained by local currents to a small area are occasionally taken long distances by 'jet-stream' currents (see Box 3.4).

Functioning and small-scale processes: competition and disturbance

Species themselves exert an important influence on the stability and constancy of a community through competition for space and resources whilst disturbance may open up spaces for new recruitment of different species. Such processes are most often studied on settlement panels and through manipulative experiments. Some examples are given in Chapter 4. The importance for biodiversity conservation is to understand that some communities are dynamic in nature and may have 'good years' and 'bad years' for species.

Functioning: the importance of knowing biological traits

Ecosystem functioning is determined by physical and chemical processes and is mediated through the activities of species that make up the biodiversity in an area. For instance, ecosystem functioning may greatly depend on the proportions of producers and consumers and the presence of grazing species. By looking at certain characteristics that govern the lifestyles of species, it may be possible to indicate how those species influence ecosystem structure and functioning. Such features include size, mobility, feeding methods, reproductive strategy and dispersal potential. Such characteristics are often referred to as 'traits'. Biological traits can be assigned to any aspect of the life of the species including reproduction, habitat preferences and general biology (see Box 3.5).

Reproductive traits include fecundity (number of eggs/young) and developmental mechanisms, and it is often possible to make inferences about one from the other. For example, an animal that broods its offspring will most likely produce far fewer offspring than an animal producing planktotrophic (feeding on plankton) larvae.

Traits can be used to make some assumptions about how an organism might respond to disturbances. With regard to the environmental position and mobility traits of a species for example, a permanently attached species growing on the seabed (such as a sea fan) is much more likely to be damaged by beam trawling than a burrowing animal that lives deep down in the sediment. Traits information is essential to assessing species sensitivity to different environmental factors and human activities (Chapter 7) and can be used to predict likely impacts of particular human activities in an environmental impact assessment or to establish or predict likely changes in abundance and distribution as a result of, for instance, seawater warming (see Hiscock *et al.*, 2004). For fishing pressure, there have been several papers describing differences in the occurrence of traits in areas under differing pressure (reviewed in Bremner, 2008). Traits can be scored according to the extent to which the species express them, and these scores can then be weighted by abundance/biomass and summed to provide a measure of the prevalence of each functional trait over an entire assemblage in a way that informs conservation (see Bremner, 2008).

What is now being investigated is 'functional diversity' (what organisms 'do') rather than taxonomic diversity (what they 'are'). Investigating functional diversity of assemblages may not only be more meaningful for understanding threats to their continued presence and their recovery potential if change has occurred, but may also require many less samples to characterise (see, for instance, Törnroos and Bonsdorf, 2012).

Box 3.5 'Biological traits' that distinguish one species or group of species from another

MarLIN (www.marlin.ac.uk) key information reviews for marine species contain the following traits information:

General biology	Body size
	Mobility: e.g. *sessile/swimmer/crawler/burrower*
	Environmental position: e.g. *infaunal/pelagic/epibenthic*
	Feeding method: e.g. *predator/suspension feeder/deposit feeder/parasite*
Range and distribution/ habitat preferences	Resident/migratory: e.g. *resident/diel/seasonal feeding*
	Substratum preferences: e.g. *maerl/cobbles/muddy sand*
	Tidal strength preferences: e.g. *weak (negligible)/strong (3–6 knots)*
Reproduction and longevity	Reproductive type: e.g. *fission/permanent hermaphrodite*
	Fecundity: e.g. *1/1,000–10,000/1,000,000*
	Dispersal potential: e.g. *< 10m/10–100m/> 1,000m*

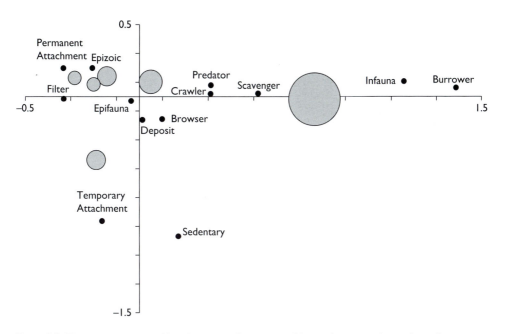

Figure 3.8 Trait composition of benthic invertebrate assemblages along a gradient of trawling intensity in the Long Forties area of the northern North Sea. Ordination scores from fuzzy correspondence analysis of ecological variables (●). Trawling intensity is indicated by area of circles. Sites of high-intensity trawling are characterised by burrowers, infauna and scavengers; low-intensity sites are characterised by filter feeders and attached fauna.

Source: Re-drawn from Tillin *et al.* (2006).

Species with similar traits often have similar habitat preferences and so it is possible to derive information about the functional requirements of groups of animals and algal species. This is important when determining the habitat requirements that underpin essential processes and functions for species and within systems.

The importance of functional diversity

Certain traits will be of critical importance to ecosystem processes. Critical processes include oxygenation, nutrient cycling and gas exchange. For instance, the process of bioturbation has been reported as being essential for nutrient cycling, oxygenation of the sediment and maintaining biodiversity in many sedimentary communities (see later). Suspension feeding species may be important in reducing turbidity and therefore improving light penetration for photosynthetic species (e.g. Cloern, 1982).

Species that provide critical services or greatly influence the type of community that develops at a location and whether or not other species will occur may be described as key functional species. Key functional species include grazers and predators.

Functional diversity occurs in communities with species that fulfil several different functional roles in the community. A community may include many passive suspension feeders, a few grazers and a few predators. Loss of one of those suspension feeders may cause little difference to the overall functioning of the community, including food supply for predators ('functional redundancy'), but loss of one previously abundant predator may make a great difference if there is no other species that can replace it in terms of function. The maintenance of multiple ecosystem functions is explored in Thrush and Dayton (2010).

Recently, there has been growing concern about how loss of biodiversity might affect ecosystem functioning. In sediment communities, it is often key functional species that dominate and bioturbation is especially important. Aside from the structure that can be provided by the burrowing and feeding habits of various infauna, functional influences of bioturbation include increasing oxygen penetration into the sediment, enhancement of nutrient cycling and increased biodiversity. Osinga et al. (1995) looked at the effects of the sea urchin Echinocardium cordatum (a burrowing deposit feeder) (Plate 16) on organic-enriched benthic boxcosms. They found that the activity of the sea urchin led to enhanced transport of oxygen into the sediment, which resulted in a reduction in the accumulation of toxic sulphide compounds in the sediments. Widdicombe et al. (2004) investigated the potential knock-on effects of losing bioturbating species that may be vulnerable to fishing disturbance. The heart urchin Brissopsis lyrifera, sea mouse Aphrodite aculeata and brittlestar Amphiura chiajei are all potentially sensitive to fisheries disturbance; their importance is demonstrated by results from the mesocosm experiments that showed a positive linear relationship between their abundance and species richness. The sea mouse and heart urchin were both said to 'bulldoze' through the sediment in search of food. As a result, their activities may promote diversity through increased oxygenation and sediment mixing which may enhance the cycling of nutrients between the benthos and the overlying water column and also ameliorate the impacts of eutrophication. This cycling of nutrients, termed 'bentho-pelagic coupling' is achieved through the activities of microbes, bioturbators, macrofauna and fish (Weslawski et al., 2004). Another species, Nereis diversicolor, through the irrigation of its burrows, significantly increases the total surface area over which sediment-water exchange can take place (Davey and

Watson, 1995). The authors also reported that *Nereis diversicolor* in the Tamar estuary could account for fluxes to the water column of an order of magnitude more soluble ammonium than is derived from riverine and sewage sources. Costanza *et al.* (1997) calculated that the average global values of nutrient cycling services provided by estuaries and seagrass/algal beds were in the region of US$21,000 and US$19,000 per hectare per year, respectively.

Unfortunately, neither the presence of bioturbating species nor the benefits associated with their activities are conspicuous in the same way that, for example, the loss of a biogenic reef may be. Thus, their sensitivity to disturbance is all too often ignored in terms of fisheries management and biodiversity conservation.

The character of many coastal communities is changing as a result of depletions or extinctions of some species, increased abundance of some other native species able to thrive in their absence, and the arrival of non-native species that are mostly macroplanktivores, deposit feeders and detritivores. The overall effect, according to Byrnes *et al.* (2007), is a situation where food webs change from being capped by a diverse array of predators and consumers to a shorter, squatter configuration dominated by filter feeders and scavengers. Those reorganised ecosystems will continue to function, but valued ecosystem services and species may have been lost and the naturalness that is highly regarded in biodiversity conservation is unlikely to return. 'The unintended consequences of simplifying the sea' are explored in Howarth *et al.* (2013, p1) who conclude that 'the transition from multi-species fisheries to simplified invertebrate fisheries is causing a global decline in biodiversity and is threatening global food security, rather than promoting it'. But, it is not just fisheries that are becoming simplified: seabed communities are also likely to be reduced in species richness with a consequent reduction in resilience (see Stachowicz *et al.*, 2007). Resilient communities can absorb perturbations to return to their previous state (see Chapter 4) because loss or decline in one species will be compensated for by other species that have the same functional role. The maintenance of multiple ecosystem functions is explored in Thrush and Dayton (2010).

Functional diversity in the assemblage of species at a location is just one part of the variety of processes that determine the health, resilience and persistence of that assemblage and the species in it. However, the identification of functional traits is a significant tool that can be used to help understand why change occurs and what that change might be if conditions change.

Viability

Viability refers to the ability of an area to be an effective self-sustaining ecological entity (Salm *et al.*, 2000) or, in the case of the population of a species, the ability to be sustained through:

- being in the 'correct' (for that species or assemblage of species) physical and chemical conditions, including light penetration;
- finding nutrition or being brought nutrition (by currents);
- finding shelter;
- finding mates (for species that recruit locally) or being in the path of larvae coming from elsewhere; and
- being able to avoid predators or tolerate predation.

A species may not be 'viable' when larvae or adults settle or occur outside the range of conditions that it normally lives in. Such species may be rare in a biogeographical region but should not qualify for protection as their occurrence is transitory and they will not reproduce successfully. Examples are given in Plates 17 and 18. It may be that a species was viable in a location but its food source or critical habitat has now been destroyed or reduced and it can no longer survive. Or it may be that a minimum population size (abundance or extent) is needed for purposes of reproduction and that this minimum size has been degraded. Whether or not a population of a species or the continued presence of a community of species is 'viable' is often reflected in its persistence from year to year, decade to decade and even century to century (see Hiscock, 2012). There are many examples of isolated (patch) habitats and populations of species that are present year after year and, in the case of the cup coral population described in Chapter 3, more than a hundred years. Those patches may be small (some less than a metre across or confined to a particular rock pool or cave). Such communities may persist because they reproduce asexually. For instance, a bed of seagrass extends via its rhizome growth; although it produces seeds, they may not be relevant to survival at that location. Many species that reproduce sexually may, nevertheless, produce larvae and propagules that go no distance, and the colony thus becomes self-recruiting with the individuals possibly being clones. Some species may reproduce extremely infrequently but have existing individuals that are very long-lived – a settlement may even have happened hundreds of years ago to establish the population. Such species are unlikely to recover if damaged and lost. For some species, there may be a frequent recruitment of larvae from afar to maintain a viable population; that may be the case especially for persistent species such as mussels. An example of a population that is not viable is one where a chance recruitment has established a population which is not reproducing or, if they are reproducing, larvae are being swept away. The concept of only a large area being viable comes into play when considering mobile species that have a foraging territory. There are many wrasse species that would fit that description and perhaps forage over an area of a few hundred square metres (a moderately large area). Species such as lobsters may forage much further afield although studies of the European lobster *Homarus gammarus* suggest that the great majority showed a strong fidelity to their release sites (hatchery-reared lobsters) and in general moved only a few kilometres within their habitat (summarised in Schmalenbach *et al.*, 2011). 'Viability' is further explored as a criterion in MPA design (Chapter 9).

Using knowledge of ecosystem structure, function and viability in biodiversity conservation

Understanding how marine ecosystems 'work' is a fundamental skill for all policy advisors and managers. But, rather than just satisfying curiosity about nature, that understanding needs to be used to stop systems becoming broken, to inform what it is most important to do in order to mend them, and to target monitoring and reporting on key structural or functional habitats and species including identifying indicators. In managing human activities to maintain marine ecosystems, it may be important to know what environmental and biological factors are essential or important to the maintenance of a particular species or community ('limiting factors') – and what factors are most likely to result in damage to or destruction of that species or community.

Conclusions

1   Ecosystems and the species in them 'function' if the ecological processes that create and support them are maintained. Those processes range from physical and chemical characteristics of habitats (which are rarely changed by human activities outside of harbours) to ensuring that food is available and that the constituents of the community do not become food.

2   Ecological processes in the sea are very different to those on land and so transferring terrestrial management paradigms to the marine environment is unwise.

3   'Connectivity' is a particular difference between terrestrial and marine ecosystems. In the sea, there is natural connectivity (for larvae, propagules and migratory species, but also contaminants) via the water column between locations – and the water column is always there.

4   High biodiversity may lead to improved functioning of ecosystems because the presence of more species increases the likelihood that taxa that perform important roles in the community will be present. Also, if species are lost from a location, it is more likely that there is another species in the community that can take over the functional role of the lost species. Overall, although with exceptions, higher diversity habitats have more resistance to change and better potential for recovery (resilience).

5   If key structural or functional species are lost or if new species (including non-native species) arrive in a location, the interactions within food webs are likely to change. Predicting whether those changes will affect the services provided by those ecosystems – the 'will it matter?' question – is going to be difficult.

6   Whether or not the population of a species is viable in an area depends on it being in the 'right' habitat, on the characteristics of the population (especially minimum population size for reproduction), whether the population has regular recruitment, whether an adequate food supply is available and whether the population is large enough to withstand being preyed upon.

7   Viability, in terms of reproductive/recruitment success, may also be adversely affected by introduction of pollutants, competition with non-native species or long-term changes in climate. The first may be reversible, the second and third may not.

Chapter 4

Understanding change

Introduction

It is important to be able to interpret change – whether small, subtle and scarcely detectable, or massive and obvious even without monitoring – if policy advisors and managers are to respond to those changes in an informed way. Separating what is natural variability (management action is unlikely to be required) from what is change brought about by human activities (management action *may* be possible) is an important part of biodiversity conservation. This chapter describes change that is natural or, in the case of global warming, widespread and which is outside of the control of a site manager.

The chapter starts with a provocative section: 'Change, what change?' Many marine communities and species persist at a location year after year with very little change. Such lack of change is particularly important to understand when considering if losses might have been brought about by human activities or if an 'old' data set can be used to indicate the communities and species likely to be still present today. However, lack of change does not attract research and is unlikely to be of interest to a publisher. The content of this section is therefore, perhaps, more brief than it might have been if more studies describing lack of change were published.

The most substantial part of this chapter is on different types of natural change in the occurrence and abundance of species at a location. Those changes range from seasonal fluctuations, through occasional catastrophic declines (followed by recovery), to large recruitments that might occur on decadal timescales that are often followed by gradual decline until the next recruitment event. Habitats may also change naturally through, for instance, extreme events such as storms that destroy structures and structurally important species. Some communities are inherently unstable and may exhibit multiple or alternative stable points.

Reasons for natural change are many and two are described: warming (as 'events', 'trends' and 'shifts') and disease. But, what might be natural change is often mixed in with change brought about by human activities and examples where multiple stressors have caused change are given – oysters in Chesapeake Bay and seagrasses in the north Atlantic.

Another type of change that is important to be aware of is 'regime shift' where a change in conditions, which may be gradual or sudden, causes the characteristics of an ecosystem to move to a new 'norm' (the section on 'Changing from one state to another'). Such changed ecosystems and associated communities are unlikely to revert to the original state. They can happen as a result of shifts in hydrographical conditions, but most examples are from the impacts of human activities.

'Shifting baselines' mean that our starting point for assessing degree and character of change may be unknown and that monitoring studies are using a reference point that is already a changed population or community from what might have been present before human activities started to influence marine biodiversity. Nevertheless, there are often good indications of what should be present at a location.

To be able to attribute change to natural fluctuations, to human activities or to a mixture of both is an expectation by policy advisors of ecologists but is no simple matter! Case studies are important and so is knowledge of the biology of the species that change. The former gives us historical context and, perhaps, reassurance; and the latter, an idea of whether a species has life history characteristics that would predispose it to change. Only a small number of examples can be given here, but case studies give an experienced scientist clues that may help solve a new puzzle. The chapter concludes with a decision tree to identify the significance of change, including separation of natural changes from change brought about by human activities and therefore, where possible, needing action.

It is important to define the terms used:

Intolerance: The susceptibility of a habitat, community or species to damage, or death, from an external factor.

Persistence: The continued presence of species or communities at a location.

Resistance: The tendency to withstand being perturbed from the equilibrium.

Resilience: The ability of an ecosystem to return to its original state after being disturbed.

Recoverability: The ability of a habitat, community or individual (or individual colony) of species to redress damage sustained as a result of an external factor.

Stability: The ability of an ecosystem to resist change. (Connell and Sousa, 1983 refer to 'adjustment stability' which is the ability of a perturbed population or community to return to the same stable equilibrium point or limit cycle.)

('Resilience' and 'Recoverability' have similar meanings)

(See the Glossary for references and links.)

Change, what change?

A community can be regarded as most 'stable' when the absolute abundance of each species remains constant over time and least stable when even the presence or absence of component species is unpredictable over time (Rahel, 1990). At intermediate levels of stability, the absolute abundances of individual species fluctuate, but the same species are always present and their abundance rankings (measures of quantity within a defined range) remain constant. However, it is usually only the most abundant species in a habitat that can be compared because of sampling limitations (where the great majority of species sampled will be 'rare' and therefore unlikely to be consistently sampled). Bearing that restriction in mind, Gray et al. (1985) found that five common species sampled over two years in Oslofjord, Norway showed stable equilibria, being persistent within bounds of ±10 per cent of the transformed mean. They cite other examples of stability in sediment communities. In another example, Turner et al. (1995) sampled sediment communities in Manukau Harbour, New Zealand from October 1987 to February 1993 to find that, 'despite the physically and biologically dynamic environment, the communities were persistent and exhibited both resistance and resilience to physical disturbance and major recruitment events' (p219).

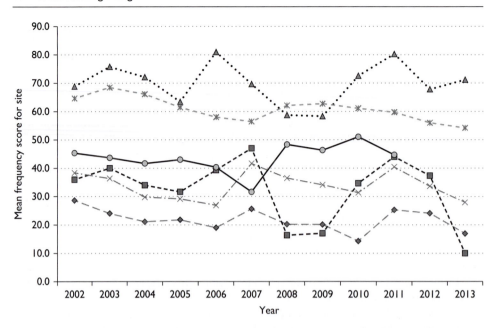

Figure 4.1 Transect frequency counts of the anthozoan *Parazoanthus axinellae* (Plate 19) at six monitoring sites within the Skomer Marine Nature Reserve, West Wales. All of the colonies measured are present every year but abundance as measured by transect frequency is erratic. Overall, the populations may be described as of 'intermediate' levels of stability.

Source: Figure redrawn with permission from Burton *et al.* (2014). The methods used and other monitoring results are described in Burton *et al.* (2014).

Turning to rocky habitats, most habitats and associated species seem to have 'intermediate' levels of stability (see Figure 4.1). Others demonstrate significant change with time but broadly retain the presence of the same communities: for instance, see Lundälv's (1985) study of subtidal rock wall communities in Sweden. Hiscock (2012) reported that his overwhelming impression, based on further surveys at previously studied sites – involving his returning to the same locations that he had surveyed up to 40 years previously as well as his looking back through records from sites that were described up to 160 years ago – was that much the same biology was there on resurvey as on previous occasions. Those observations included:

- Locating what was believed to be the exact rock gulley where, in 1853, the foremost Victorian marine naturalist Philip Henry Gosse found, new to science, the nationally scarce scarlet and gold star coral. In September 2011, approximately 208 were present in the same hollow (K. Hiscock, own observations).
- Gosse had dredge-sampled areas off Teignmouth and south to Torbay, England in 1864. Re-sampling the area during a single day in 2011, the dredge, together with material collected by divers, found most of the species that Gosse (1865) described as well as many others that he did not mention. They did not find the 'rough ground' that Gosse described – perhaps, when that ground is located, the rest of Gosse's species will be found (K. Hiscock, own observations).

- In 1953, Robert Forster commenced a series of underwater observations at locations around Plymouth, England, using the then novel self-contained underwater breathing apparatus (SCUBA). One of the locations that he described was Hilsea Point Rock, and, 50 years later, it was surveyed again with the conclusion that the overall appearance of the fauna and flora was much as described in the 1950s; although some species were not refound while other species were added to the lists (Hiscock, 2005).
- In 2008, a team of marine biologists visited Lundy, England to resurvey the rocky shores that had been censused by Leslie and Clare Harvey in the late 1940s. They found almost all of the species that the Harveys had listed and several more (Hiscock, 2008a and in preparation unpublished).
- In June 2010, St Catherine's Island at Tenby, Wales was surveyed 156 years to the day after Gosse visited the caverns there. The similarity with the 1854 description was remarkable and the shores amazingly rich (Hiscock, 2012).

It should not surprise us that many marine biological features are persistent on decadal if not century-long timescales. The environmental conditions that determine the habitat and its associated community of species have, within normal variability, been unchanging. Also, many marine species are very long-lived, slow growing and recruit very close to their parents. A prime example is the stagshorn sponge *Axinella dissimilis* (Plate 20) which is a species frequently found on some reef habitats in the north-east Atlantic. Measurements of the growth of this species over five years at Lundy (Fowler and Laffoley, 1993), including of large and small individuals, detected some slight increases and some decreases. Conservatively, growth rate was less than 1mm a year – and they grow to over 300mm in height. They are a species which has been observed to survive severe winter storms but which is very susceptible to towed heavy fishing gear. Amongst the algae, maerl (calcified seaweed that forms unattached twig-like growths 10–20mm across: Plate 21) is also very slow growing – the three most abundant maerl species in Europe grow about 1mm (0.5–1.5mm) per tip per year in length (Blake and Maggs, 2003). The age of individuals of *Lithothamnion crassiusculum* has been recorded as up to 100 years (Frantz *et al.*, 2000). Beds of maerl have a rich associated community but appear to have very specialised requirements for growth; the most extensive live bed known in England is in Falmouth Harbour where it has been known since the mid 1960s, though it has doubtless been there much longer.

Nevertheless, there are changes that occur in abundance of species and presence of biotopes, examples of which are the subject of most of this chapter.

Types of natural change

Seasonal change

Changes that occur from winter to summer and on into autumn are often well known (and therefore predictable) to those who use and observe the sea, but many may not be documented in peer-reviewed publications. Understanding that seasonal changes occur and what those changes are is essential in identifying when change is unexpected and therefore may 'matter' (from the point of view of biodiversity conservation). Understanding seasonal change is also important when planning comparative surveys and annual monitoring events. Some seasonal changes are likely to be recruitment events that might shift according to oceanic processes and to climate change (especially warming), and this might

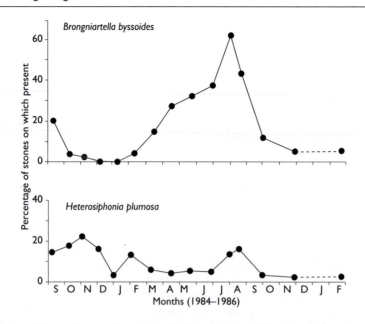

Figure 4.2 Seasonal fluctuations can be very marked. In the records for two algal species from stones at Skomer, Wales, *Brongniartella byssoides* has particularly large seasonal changes in abundance.

Source: Redrawn from Hiscock (1986).

be important background information for separating what are long-term trends from one-off events. There may even be 'mismatches' between seasonal food availability and species that need that food at a specific time (for instance when larvae have been released).

Often, a species is present throughout the year at a location but abundance (as numbers or biomass) varies through the year. Such changes were observed by Beukema (1974) at a location in the Wadden Sea where the species living in an intertidal flat showed maximal amounts during July to September and minimal amounts during December to March – a typical cycle in the northern hemisphere. In spring, increase in biomass was attributed to fast growth of animals already present in winter whilst declines during autumn were attributed to both decrease in numbers and to individual weight losses.

Seasonal fluctuations in occurrence and abundance may be in response to water temperature; light intensity and day length (especially for ephemeral benthic algae); disturbance by storms (especially the 'washing-out' of benthos); changes in salinity in estuaries; seasonal occurrence of predators or prey; or just because annual species have settled, thrived, grown old and died. Juvenile or 'resting' stages or alternate life history stages (algae mainly) may be present but not visible at some times of the year. Sessile species are likely to always be present in some form through the year but mobile species may migrate from one location to another.

'Appearances' and 'disappearances'

Some species, mainly ones that live in the water column and are subject to the vagaries of oceanic currents, may not be seen for many years and then occur in high abundances. They include species such as the Portugese man-of-war *Physalia physalis* and the by-the-wind sailor *Velella velella*, both hydrozoans. Other species that are native to a biogeographical region may be swept further than usual as larvae and, if present in sufficient numbers to reproduce, become established in an area, at least for many years. One such species in the north-east Atlantic is the barnacle *Solidobalanus fallax* which was first found in British

Box 4.1 'Appearances' and 'disappearances'

Species can have 'good' and 'bad' years – often documented in the fauna lists of marine stations and sometimes in papers. Here are some examples:

- In San Francisco Bay, the common amphipod *Ampelisca abdita* apparently moves from shallow to deep water, or from up-estuary to down-estuary locations, coincident with periods of high river run-off in winter (Nichols and Thompson, 1985).
- Population collapses are often linked to overfishing, as was the case for basking sharks (*Cetorhinus maximus*) at Achill Island in north-west Ireland. Although large numbers of sharks were indeed killed there, Sims and Reid (2002) found that, over a 27-year period, both the numbers of sharks caught at Achill and copepod (their food) abundance in the region showed downward trends that were positively correlated. They suggest that the decline in basking sharks may have been due to a distributional shift of sharks to more productive areas rather than a localised stock that was over-exploited. Basking sharks have 'good years' and 'bad years', most likely associated with the location and depth of their food.
- Recruitment to populations of the European eel, *Anguilla anguilla*, have declined since the early 1980s. Recruits migrate from the Sargasso Sea, and Baltazar-Soares *et al.* (2014) showed that regional, atmospherically driven ocean current variations in the Sargasso Sea were the major driver of the onset of the sharp decline in eel recruitment.
- Mussels, *Mytilus edulis*, can persist at a location for many years as dense beds until consumed by 'hoards' of the starfish *Asterias rubens*. The beds are replaced by other species until there is a large settlement of mussels which again dominate the rocks. (K. Hiscock, own observations. See also Sloan and Aldridge, 1981.)
- The crown of thorns starfish (*Acanthaster planchi*), which feeds on corals, has 'outbreaks' every few decades that can destroy coral reefs. Houk and Raubani (2010) identified positive correlations between wind stress, chlorophyll-a and upwelling corresponding with coral-eating starfish occurrences in Vanuatu, South Pacific during January–February 2009.
- In June 1966, there was a mass stranding of hyperiid amphipods on the Yorkshire coast of England (Gray and McHardy, 1967). A similar mass stranding happened again in May 2009.
- Sea slugs are well known for their sporadic occurrences and, although individuals must persist somewhere, a species may disappear from an entire region as seems to have happened to the orange and blue-spotted slug *Greilada elegans*, last seen in 1986 at Lundy and other parts of south-west Britain (Hiscock, 1994 and continuing observations).

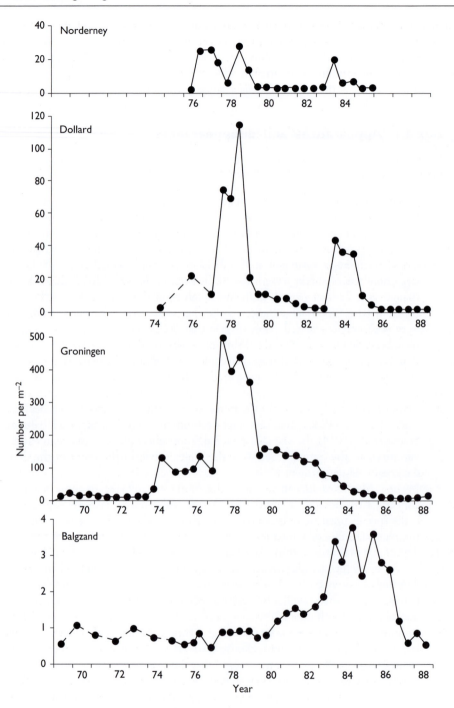

Figure 4.3 Some species show large annual changes in abundance and may even 'disappear' from a
location only to reappear in later years. Long-term changes in numerical densities of the
bivalve *Scrobicularia plana* at sites in the Wadden Sea.

Source: Redrawn from Essink *et al.* (1991).

waters from samples collected in 1988 (Southward et al., 2004). S. fallax is still present in Britain. However, another species, the hermit crab Clibanarius erythropus, recorded in south-west Britain for the first time during the winter 1959/60 has not been recorded from British waters since 1985 (Southward and Southward, 1988). The authors suggest that populations were being maintained via recruitment by favourable currents from Brittany but had most likely succumbed to the combined effect of age and declining temperatures.

Results of 'severe events' and the longevity of change

The amount of resistance (stability) and recoverability (resilience) potential that a species, community or habitat has determines its persistence in the event of changed conditions.

The stresses that affect ecosystem processes are many and complex. We assess the impacts of those stresses through field experiments and through observation and measurement when disaster strikes. Estimating how far an ecosystem can change before it collapses (and what it will change to) is, however, more likely to be based on expert judgement than through some mathematical calculation because of non-linearity of marine systems.

Changes in the ecology of an area and, perhaps, in the presence and abundance of valued species happen as a result of severe natural and anthropogenic impacts. One of the first systematic accounts of a natural event that caused high mortalities of intertidal and shallow subtidal species was of the extremely cold winter of 1962/3 in the British Isles. Professor Denis Crisp contacted colleagues all around Britain and in western Ireland to ask them what they had observed and collated their communications (Crisp, 1964). By separating species into biogeographical types, he was able to summarise effects: of 21 'southern' species, 57 per cent showed severe mortality, 34 per cent indicated less severe mortality and 19 per cent appeared unaffected; for 36 'Celtic' species (those where the western approaches to the British Isles are their main area of occurrence), the figures were 39 per cent, 47 per cent and 14 per cent respectively; and for 26 'Arctic' species, the figures were 0 per cent, 15 per cent and 85 per cent respectively. Moving to tropical habitats and the effects of elevated temperatures, coral reef bleaching events seem to have become increasingly frequent in recent years. Van Woesik et al. (2012) reviewed the topic in their introduction to a paper on bleaching events in Palau, Micronesia. Corals become pale because of the ejection or mortality of associated symbiotic algae when water temperatures are elevated 1–2°C above the seasonal average. When those elevated temperatures are sustained for a week or more, bleaching occurs; and mortality of the corals may follow, most likely as a result of starvation, having lost their symbiotic algae.

A key question for a manager might be: how long will this change last? The question may be asked after a severe winter or a hot summer, or after a disease event. Some of those questions are addressed in Chapter 11 ('Recovery, restoration and replacement of habitats and species'). In this chapter, natural, or what appear to be natural, fluctuations are addressed.

Some communities (represented by the ball in Figure 4.4) may switch to other communities after large-scale disturbance but may return to their original state (or another alternative state) after a period of environmental stability. For instance, communities on cobbles on the open coast may develop to a stable assemblage of species but become 'turned-over' and destroyed after a major storm that might happen only every few years. The community that develops will depend on the larvae present for colonisation during the period after the storm damage. There are studies that demonstrate fluctuations in the abundance of sessile or low-mobility species, some of which constitute alternative locally stable states (for instance: Dethier, 1984 for tide pools on the Pacific coast of the USA; Sebens, 1985 for temperate rock wall communities, and Hagen, 1987 for switches between urchin-dominated and kelp-dominated communities). Our understanding of multiple stable points in the marine environment is reviewed in Knowlton (2004) who concludes: 'preserving the resilience of ecosystems should be an essential component of all conservation strategies, since the disturbances that provoke departures from stable states or transitions between states cannot always be prevented' (p394).

Some communities (represented by the ball in Figure 4.5) may persist over long periods of time with only minor variation in composition. After normal disturbance their resilience will permit a return to the previous state; i.e. they are able to withstand shocks and to re-build themselves if damage has occurred. However, some species may not recover after being destroyed by an abnormal disturbance, perhaps because of the longevity of individuals and unlikely recruitment or because a different species now occupies the relevant niche. Such events may result in extinction of that community and colonisation by some different and persistent community (creating a 'regime shift': see 'Changing from one state to another', p56. For instance, fishing that removes a predator (such as spiny lobsters or snapper) of sea urchins will allow the urchins to thrive, destroying kelp forests. The urchins resist any recovery because they graze the kelp sporlings.

From the point of view of managing human activities for the benefit of biodiversity, Hughes *et al.* (2005, p382) observe that:

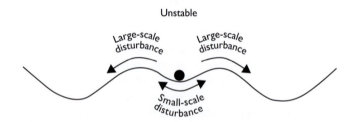

Figure 4.4 Some communities are inherently fragile and may be expected not to persist in the face of even small-scale disturbance. Small-scale disturbance makes small changes to the community (illustrated as a ball that may move within the limits of the hollow it is in) but the community returns to the entity it was previously. Large-scale disturbances are likely to change the community to something different, although return to the previous community is possible.

Source: Adapted from Gray (1977).

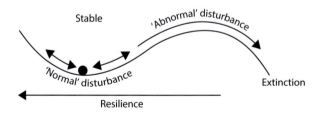

Figure 4.5 Abnormal disturbance may destroy species and communities that are not able to resist or recover; for instance those that are characterised by long-lived, slow-growing species.

Source: Adapted from Gray (1977).

Some systems have changed to the extent that they can effectively no longer converge to the original assemblage. From a complex systems perspective, they have crossed a threshold into a new state or domain of attraction that precludes return to the original state. The consequences for management are profound: it is easier to sustain a resilient ecosystem than to repair it after a phase shift has occurred.

It is important to try to understand how communities will respond directly to disturbances or to associated changes. The following are the sorts of questions that a marine biologist with environmental management experience probably goes through when delivering an expert judgement on the likely effect of an event or activity:

1   What environmental factors will the event or activities influence?
2   How strong is the effect of the changing factor?
3   Is there any synergy with other change occurring?
4   Will one factor change another (knock-on effects)?
5   How long has the changed factor lasted or is likely to last?
6   Will any key structural or functional (trophic cascade) species be significantly reduced in abundance or exterminated?
7   How long can the community resist change (is there redundancy in structural and functional species)?
8   Is a regime shift likely as a result of the changes taking place?
9   How quickly, if at all, can the community recover (will the community be replaced by a different stable community, has the physical and chemical habitat reverted to a previous state, etc.)?

Long-term fluctuations

There are few data sets that are of long enough duration to allow decadal-scale fluctuations in the same ecosystem to be revealed. But such fluctuations might be of great importance in accounting for 'feast and famine' situations that lead to sporadic recruitments followed by declines until the next suite of favourable conditions occur (Plate 23). Such data sets do exist for the western English Channel (Southward et al., 2005) and there has been much analysis of this data to try to establish patterns and reasons. One earlier account that summarises what seemed to be happening in this location was that of Cushing and Dickson (1976):

> Phosphorous, macroplankton and summer spawners were reduced in 1930/1 and they recovered forty years later in 1970/1. The spring spawners declined in 1935, five years after the initial change and they recovered in 1965, five years before the reversal. There were extensive distributional changes in 1930/1 and 1970/1. There were consequential changes involving the benthos.

Those changes were named 'the Russell Cycle' after Sir Frederick Russell who undertook much of the research. Cushing and Dickson further observed that '[t]he same cause . . . must have penetrated all the nooks and crannies of the ecosystem' (p 109). Whatever the cause, it proved difficult to pin down; but it did seem that there was some essential factor that was lacking in the water characterised by *Parasagitta elegans* (see Figure 4.6) (Southward, 1980; Southward et al., 2005). Furthermore, Southward et al. (2005) point out that the changes

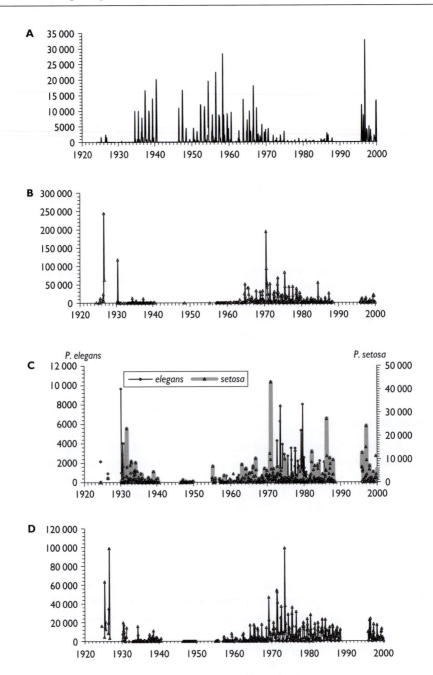

Figure 4.6 Examples of long-term data on mesozooplankton off Plymouth, UK, as monthly means per haul corrected to 4,000 m³ water. A = eggs of pilchard *Sardina pilchardus* (a warm water species); B = the copepod *Calanus helgolandicus* (more common in cooler periods); C = the arrow worm *Parasagitta elegans* (cold water, northern form) and *Parasagitta setosa* (intermediate and warm water species); D = larval stages of decapod crustaceans.

Source: Southward *et al.* (2005).

were not a straightforward periodic shift in species occurring at predictable frequencies and rates. Identifying predictable patterns of change may not be possible, but the fact that change may happen over decadal timescales – and trying to discover what drives those changes – is important if we are to learn to separate what is natural change from what is brought about by human activities.

Such long-term observations as those undertaken off Plymouth from the early part of the twentieth century and continuing today are rare. They do not, or have not in the past, attracted the open-ended funding that is needed to sustain them. The value of such observations in interpreting change resulting from human activities is illustrated by the Continuous Plankton Recorder (CPR) surveys undertaken since 1931 by the Sir Alister Hardy Foundation for Ocean Science (www.sahfos.ac.uk). The Foundation's data set provides a wide range of environmental and climatic indicators and is used by marine scientists and policymakers to address marine environmental management issues such as harmful algal blooms, pollution, climate change and fisheries. In recent years, information from the CPR has demonstrated a northward shift in warm water plankton by about 1,000km in the north Atlantic (Beaugrand et al., 2002). No doubt, as statutory monitoring that includes biological measures is increased, the pool of information about long-term natural change as well as impacts of human activities will begin to build.

Warming – 'events', 'trends' and 'shifts'

Warming (and cooling) sometimes occurs because oceanic currents shift, bringing warmer or colder water to a region perhaps for a few months or perhaps for a longer period. However, warming of the atmosphere and consequently of the seas is an impact of emissions from human activities. Whatever the reason, warming will cause change in the distribution and abundance of species and may exacerbate adverse effects of localised human activities including eutrophication and introduction of non-native species. Separating what might be 'events' from 'trends' and identifying 'shifts' may be difficult, and understanding change resulting from warming that is 'natural' and warming resulting from 'human activities' is often difficult. However, where we can make those separations, we can learn from events what to expect, in the long term, from global change. The key questions for biodiversity conservation are 'will it matter?' and 'can we do anything about it?' This chapter addresses natural warming events but, inevitably, may not separate them from warming brought about by human activities; examples of the latter are given in Chapter 5.

Whatever examples are used, it is important to try to separate 'events' from 'trends'. Events include particularly warm summers (as happened with significant consequences for seabed marine life in the Ligurian Sea, north-west Italy, in 1999, 2003 and 2007: Garrabou et al., 2009) or shifts in oceanic currents bringing warmer waters (as happened in south-eastern and western Australia, causing significant impacts on algal populations in particular: Ling et al., 2009; Smale and Wernberg, 2013; Plates 25 and 26). Trends and shifts are recognisable after decades of observation.

Disease

Disease and parasite outbreaks cause change. Those outbreaks may be entirely natural, may result from compromised immune systems brought about by contamination, may be due to such factors as temperature increases, high turbidity events or pollution (Harvell et al.,

1999), or may even result from increased densities of a species after conservation measures have been successful (see, for instance, Wootton *et al.*, 2012). There is some evidence that incidence of disease in at least some groups of marine species is on the increase (Ward and Lafferty, 2004) although the reasons are equivocal and may not be due to human activities. Indeed, contaminants may adversely affect parasites more than their hosts (Lafferty, 1997). Furthermore, Lafferty and Holt (2003) point out that stressors which depress host population density may reduce density-dependent transmission of host-specific infectious disease by reducing contact rates between infected and uninfected individuals.

The incidence of nematode parasites that adversely affected populations of sea urchins in Norway is mentioned later in the section on 'Kelp forests' (p58). Another source of infection and consequent mortality is from bacteria. In the Ligurian Sea in 1999 and 2003, *Vibrio* bacterial infections caused mass mortalities of seabed invertebrates (Garrabou *et al.*, 2009; Vezzulli *et al.*, 2010; Plate 27). The *Vibrio* infections were linked to warming events, these authors finding a sharp increase in vibrios abundance when the seawater temperature was at or above 22°C. *Vibrio* infections have also caused disease in sea fans *Eunicella verrucosa* in south-west England during 2003–06 with many colonies killed and others partially killed (Hall-Spencer *et al.*, 2007), although there was no evidence of elevated seawater temperatures at the time. Such an event may also have occurred in the region of Plymouth, England in late summer 1924 when, as cited in Box 8.2: 'Captain Lord reported that a great amount of *Eunicella* brought up was dead; many colonies brought in were partially dead, none in such good condition as in the previous July' (Marine Biological Association, 1957, p62). Perhaps disease outbreaks are a natural event and happen in a cyclical way or at random times, especially when organisms are stressed in some way and have poor resistance. Some plankton species may also act as vectors of disease (see Lipp *et al.*, 2002) and a change in their distribution or a season of high abundance may bring vibrios to benthic species. In the summer of 2008 and 2009, there were extensive die-offs of sponge species in the western Mediterranean. That die-off and previous massive sponge mortality events in the Mediterranean were related to high temperatures (Cebrian *et al.*, 2011). It might be that conspicuous events such as die-off of sea fans or sponges is a sign of more extensive damage that is unnoticed. Whatever the cause and extent of a die-off, the marine biologist is challenged with a difficult piece of detective work to establish the cause and the cause of the cause.

Changing from one state to another

Introduction

Where shifts in the community structure of a location – especially in regional seas – have occurred and result from large-scale hydrographic and climatic changes, the term 'regime shift' has been applied (Scheffer and Carpenter, 2003; Collie *et al.*, 2004). However, the term has also been used to refer to situations where it is almost certainly human activities that have caused the changes in local or regional environmental conditions that have caused shifts in dominant species. Evidence for regime shifts in the sea was reviewed by Kraberg *et al.* (2011) who cite papers describing regime shifts that have been driven by climatic changes which can occur on basin-wide scales, and smaller-scale shifts due, for instance, to overfishing or the introduction of alien species. Regime shifts have also been described in productive systems such as estuaries or other enclosed seas where they can be the result of coastal hypoxia events caused by eutrophication; i.e. excessive nutrient inputs (for instance, in the northern Adriatic: Giani *et al.*, 2012). Most often, regime shifts are characterised in the literature by changes in plankton and fish populations because long-term data is mostly available for those groups. Here, examples are given of shifts in community structure that may or may not be *sensu stricto* regime shifts but which demonstrate how change can occur from historical data describing the characteristics of a location.

Knowledge of regime shifts and their causes for benthic communities has been focussed on kelp forests, seagrass beds and coral reefs and the reasons for observed changes have often been tested through experimental studies (e.g. Steneck *et al.*, 2002 for kelps; Eklof *et al.*, 2008 for seagrass; Hughes *et al.*, 2007 for corals). Switches or 'catastrophic changes' are often the result of some change in consumer pressure but the interactions are complex. For instance, in the case of kelp forests destroyed by urchin grazing, why did the sea urchins increase in abundance? Further examples of change and the reasons for those changes are given next.

The following case studies are from a range of habitats and communities and provide examples only of the sorts of shift changes recorded in the literature. The examples may reflect natural fluctuations but may also be the result of human activities: there is uncertainty. Ecological shifts that have been brought about by human activities are exemplified in case studies given in Chapter 5.

Intertidal communities in the Wadden Sea, Germany

When large-scale change happens, it is usually because key structural features have changed (resulting in different habitats) or key functional species have changed in abundance (resulting in a trophic cascade that affects many other species). Reise and Schubert (1987) describe major differences in the subtidal Wadden Sea, Germany between 1925/26 and 1985/86. Those changes (Figure 4.7) were driven by loss of major structural features (beds of oysters and reefs of ross worm *Sabellaria spinulosa*) and colonisation, in some areas, by another key structural species, the mussel *Mytilus edulis*. Those changes could have been natural although the 'losses' are explained as most likely due to bottom trawling and the 'gains' to eutrophication. The total number of species present in both periods was about the same. In the more enclosed and geographically restricted intertidal Bay of Königshafen, Reise *et al.* (2008) compared vegetation maps and macrobenthic survey results from the 1920s and 1930s with the results of surveys conducted from 1988 to 2006. They observed striking changes in the biota that they concluded were not merely interannual fluctuations but represented a transition to a new ecological state which they attributed to a combination of four processes:

- introduced species of exotic origin have added to local species richness;
- extreme weather events initiated the loss of mussels with attached fucoid algae;
- eutrophication gave rise to massive green algal mats which affected most infauna and seagrass, and initiated high patch dynamics; and
- sea level rise, particularly at high tidal and storm surge levels, is most likely responsible for sand accretion smothering cyanobacterial mats at the salt marsh edge; and for sandiness at the expense of mud in the tidal zone, inhibiting *Corophium volutator* and facilitating *Arenicola marina*.

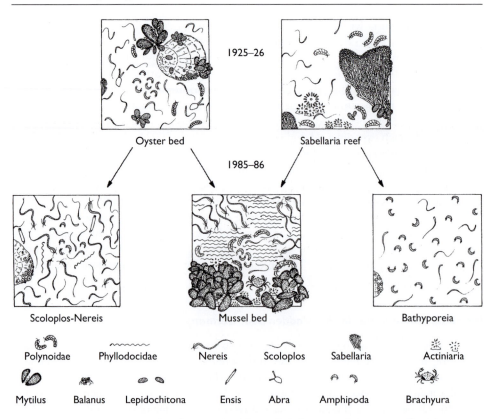

Figure 4.7 In the German Wadden Sea, oyster beds and ross worm reefs of the 1920s were substituted within 60 years by mussel beds, a polychaete assemblage, or an amphipod assemblage. The number of symbols reflects abundance.

Source: Reise and Schubert (1987).

Subtidal seabeds in enclosed areas

There have been very significant changes in the natural seabed habitats and other communities in enclosed areas that are accounted for by human activities mainly causing eutrophication, introduction of non-native species and habitat alteration. Examples of change that are likely to be due to natural influences are difficult to find and none are identified here. Chapter 5 describes those changes that are considered to have been brought about by human influences.

Kelp forests

Kelp forests are a good example of a habitat where structural species dominate. The kelps themselves make up the physical habitat that provides, amongst much else, shelter for fish, food for herbivores and an attachment sites for the eggs of invertebrates. Sea urchins are key structural species because they graze on the kelps and, in high enough densities, have the power to decimate areas of the kelp forests. Many temperate kelp habitats are characterised by a balance between the kelps and sea urchins. This relationship has been studied in many countries (Steneck *et al.*, 2002). In Norway, the green sea urchin (*Strongylocentrotus droebachiensis*) is a significant grazer of the sugar kelp *Saccharina latissima* (was *Laminaria saccharina*) and oarweed *Laminaria hyperborea* (also a kelp) (see Plate 28). High population densities of sea urchins have left some areas completely devoid of macroalgae for decades (Christie *et al.*, 1995). Such 'urchin barrens' are dominated by encrusting coralline algae, which the urchins do not consume.

High mortalities of the green sea urchin during the 1990s (Hagen, 1987) linked the falling abundance of *Strongylocentrotus droebachiensis* in northern Norway to prevalence of a nematode endoparasite *Echinomermella matsi* and made it possible to study the dynamics of the habitat without one of the keystone species. Christie *et al.* (1995) note that at sites where there had been a significant decline in the numbers of sea urchins there were dense stands of *Laminaria saccharina* (now *Saccharina latissima*) within a few months. Experimental removal of urchins led to similar effects (Leinaas and Christie, 1996). At first, small filamentous algae and a few kelp recruits were observed. Luxuriant stands of *Laminaria saccharina* were established within a few months and the long-lived *Laminaria hyperborea* dominated after two to three years. Urchin barrens have considerable resistance (Leinaas and Christie, 1996) and it would appear that it is changes in urchin populations rather than kelp populations that lead to balance shifts in kelp habitats.

In most examples of variability in urchin populations causing shifts in kelp-dominated habitats, it is human factors that have been the cause; see examples in Chapter 5.

Multiple stressors

Introduction

Identifying the reason(s) for change is not always easy, and this may be because there are multiple factors that have caused the change. Similarly, predicting likely change in biology as a result of change in one environmental factor may be confounded because other factors have also changed. Synergism can cause 'ecological surprises', where unexpected regime shifts occur quickly because a tipping point is exceeded (Crain *et al.*, 2008). Many authors warn about taking a simplistic one-factor view of the reasons for change, and some place the idea of multiple factors into the context of what can be done to prevent or reduce undesirable change. Russell *et al.* (2009, p2153), investigating the effects of climate and nutrient stressors on subtidal algal communities, make the point that

> global and local stressors need to be assessed in meaningful combinations so that the anticipated effects of climate change do not create the false impression that, however complex, climate change will produce smaller effects than reality. These findings empower local managers because they show that policies of reducing local stressors (e.g. nutrient pollution) can reduce the effects of global stressors not under their governance (e.g. ocean acidification).

Bearing in mind the importance of multiple stressors comes into prominence when the species or habitat being considered is of economic importance or identified as a key habitat for ecosystem productivity; examples are oysters and seagrass beds – included in this chapter because, although human activities have been involved in change, so, most likely, have natural factors.

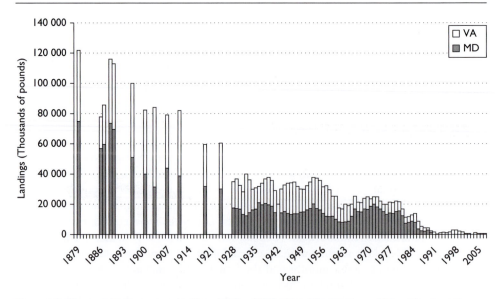

Figure 4.8 Chesapeake Bay oyster landings 1880 – 2008. VA = Virginia State; MD = Maryland State.
Source: www.oysterva.com/oyster-landings.html (accessed 6 December 2013).

Oysters in Chesapeake Bay

Chesapeake Bay, eastern USA has historically been the home to large biogenic oyster (*Crassostrea virginia*) reefs containing numerous other suspension feeders. Kirby and Miller (2005) report that growth of oysters increased after eutrophication began in the late eighteenth century; but, after 1860, growth decreased, perhaps reflecting the negative effects of hypoxia, harmful algal blooms, disease and fishing. There has been a 50-fold decline in the oyster population in the Maryland area of Chesapeake Bay since the early part of the twentieth century, which Rothschild *et al.* (1994) attribute mainly to the mechanical destruction of the beds and stock overfishing. The use of large oyster dredgers and hydraulic-powered patent tongs has further meant that many formerly productive areas are now covered in silt. With the deterioration of oyster reef habitat, the important suspension feeding function in the Chesapeake Bay ecosystem has also been lost, further contributing to increased turbidity. The loss of filtration by oysters and the biogenic habitat that they create is suspected to be the reason for increasing eutrophication and alteration of food webs in Chesapeake Bay (Luckenbach, 2002) and the increasing frequency, magnitude and duration of dinoflagellate blooms in the bay (Luckenbach *et al.*, 1993). Restoration of oyster populations in Chesapeake Bay is included in Chapter 11.

Decline of seagrass beds (Zostera marina) in the north Atlantic

The extent of *Zostera marina* beds has greatly decreased since the 'wasting disease' which decimated seagrasses on both sides of the Atlantic during the 1920s and 1930s (Nybakken, 2001). Early investigations led to the conclusion that *Labyrinthula macrocystis*, an infectious slime mold protist, was the organism responsible. Although this theory lost

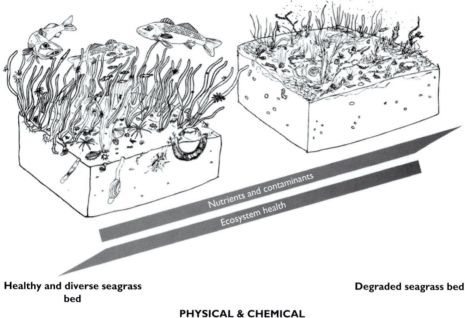

Healthy and diverse seagrass bed		Degraded seagrass bed

PHYSICAL & CHEMICAL FACTORS

Low	←	Mechanical disturbance	→ High
Moderate	←	Water flow rate	→ Low/stagnant
Low	←	Turbidity	→ High
Very low	←	Siltation	→ High
Optimum	←	Temperature	→ High
Low	←	Dissolved nutrients	→ High
Low	←	Chemical contaminants	→ High
High/variable	←	Salinity	→ Low

BIOLOGICAL FACTORS

Low	←	Disease	→ High
Low	←	Epiphytes	→ High
High	←	Small grazers (snails etc.)	→ Low
Low	←	Large grazers (birds)	→ High

Figure 4.9 Factors likely to determine the health of a seagrass (*Zostera marina*) bed. Drawing: Jack Sewell.

Source: Hiscock *et al.* (2006).

credibility when *Labyrinthula* were found in large numbers on otherwise healthy plants, Short *et al.* (1988) suggest that there were two forms, only one of which was pathogenic. The source of the disease remains unclear but 'disease' is one of the factors likely to affect seagrass.

Figure 4.9 highlights some of the biological, chemical and physical parameters underpinning the health of seagrass beds and that might represent multiple stressors.

Shifting baselines

Whilst there are areas that seem to be much as they were more than a hundred years ago (see the earlier section on 'Change, what change?'), conservation scientists are concerned that the marine communities they are looking at now may have changed from some previous and perhaps more natural state. If that is the case, then identifying targets for recovery to some unknown previous state will be difficult. 'Shifting baselines' are generally related to the impacts of human activities (see Chapter 5), and finding information that might point to natural shifts is confused by the suspicion that human activities must have at least contributed to that change. Chapter 3 includes a description of the change that results from a major oceanic current, the East Australian Current, which has increased in strength bringing warmer and saltier water south to the coast of Tasmania and resulting in major shifts in the character of seabed ecosystems (Ridgway and Hill, 2009; Ling et al., 2009). A different shift in the character of seabed communities resulting from changes in the strength of currents bringing warmer water to parts of western Australia is reported by Smale and Wernberg (2013) (Plates 25 and 26). Often, it is possible to find information from the past 50 years or so. For instance, the data set collected by Holme (1961, 1966) on the soft sediment benthos of the English Channel during the 1950s and 1960s provided a reference point of community composition with which to compare present day patterns. Resurveying the sites off Plymouth, Hinz et al. (2011) found a large change in community composition with a clear decline in infaunal biomass and an increase in polychaete dominance. However, they conclude that such changes are consistent with the effects of demersal fishing pressure and that the assemblage had changed but not, as the researchers might have expected, in relation to climate change but due to physical disturbance. Further examples of change and of the establishment of 'new' species assemblages are described in the section on climate change in Chapter 5.

Cause and effect or coincidental change?

In trying to account for change, there is a danger that some changes or trends may link together in an apparent cause and effect scenario but are, in fact, coincidental: for instance, loss of kelp at the same time as increase in sea surface temperatures, when the kelp may have been lost due to winter storms, disease or a cohort of recruitment dying naturally. Storms and disease may not have been noticed if they occurred for a period when observers were not in the water. Some changes might result from 'invisible' factors at the same time as visible factors that may be blamed. For instance, Díez et al. (2012) observed that although changes in seaweed assemblages in northern Spain were attributed to sea temperature rise, there were changes that could not be attributed to temperature rise alone. Those factors were possibly nutrient concentrations and water transparency. Often, it is the experience and common sense of a naturalist that identifies the reasons for change. Those experienced naturalists are not going to (did not) live forever. It is important that the historical knowledge that exists in publications such as books on marine life and in regional marine fauna lists is preserved, and that the knowledge from the wide range of marine life reporting schemes which now exist is recorded so that it is accessible next time a species disappears or appears in great abundance. Some such information is included in the species and biotope pages of the MarLIN programme (www.marlin.ac.uk/bacs.php). The issue of recording information on fluctuations in abundance of species, alternative community types, etc. needs to be urgently addressed by those who are disseminating information that seems to stop at taxonomy and geographical distribution of species.

Conclusions

The picture of change and the reasons (setting aside change unequivocally resulting from human activities) for change are complicated and may be confusing. On the one hand, many locations seem to have the same species and communities that were recorded there more than 100 years ago. On the other hand, there are changes occurring that are substantial and may be due to weather events, natural shifts in oceanic currents or outbreaks of disease. That change is important to understand but so is identifying the reason for that change – and the reason for the reason.

The following points are listed to help the manager or policy advisor answer the questions: 'Is the change natural?', 'Does the change matter?' and 'Can we do anything about it?'

1 Natural change is inevitable but is generally within limits that mean that the same characterising and 'special' species can be found at a location from year to year, although in abundances that vary.
2 Seasonal change in abundance and occurrence are to be expected in many pelagic and benthic species and communities. On the seabed, those seasonal changes are especially conspicuous in plants.
3 When large-scale change in communities happens, it is usually because some key structural or functional species has changed in abundance and it is often trophic cascade(s) that have resulted in the large change.
4 'Regime shifts', in which the dominant species create a change from one assemblage to another, may be natural and caused by, for instance, change in oceanic circulation or may be brought about by human activities. The reasons for change may be difficult to identify but the 'changed' ecosystem will persist for many years and it is unlikely that management action to reverse the change will be possible.
5 Finding patterns in long-term change requires long-term data sets but there are few examples that will help the manager to put change they might be seeing into context.
6 Experimental studies that manipulate natural communities in a way that simulates change that might occur as a result of natural events and human activities helps to predict consequences but not necessarily solutions.
7 Parallel changes in environmental conditions or human activities and marine species abundances or community composition may be coincidental and not necessarily to do with cause and effect.
8 Historical knowledge of change in the abundance of particular species or in community composition is important; that knowledge often resides with experienced naturalists but also needs to be registered in accessible databases and their information portals.

Policy advisors and environmental managers are likely to have to interpret observed changes in species and habitats and decide if that change is natural, if it matters, whether action is needed and if it is possible to address that change. The following decision tree (Figure 4.10) may help:

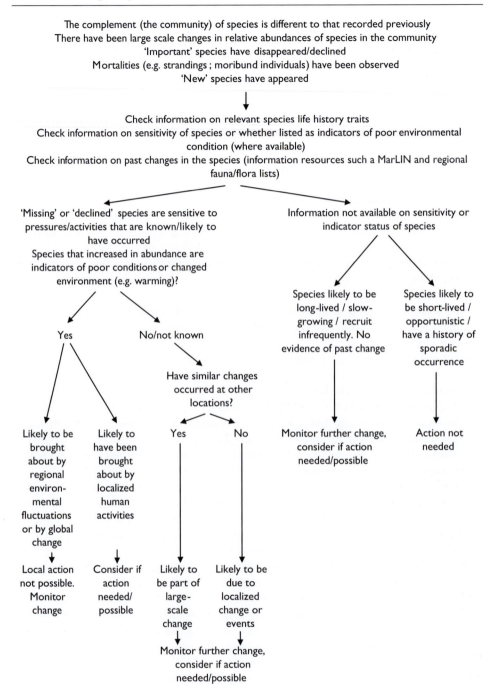

The complement (the community) of species is different to that recorded previously
There have been large scale changes in relative abundances of species in the community
'Important' species have disappeared/declined
Mortalities (e.g. strandings ; moribund individuals) have been observed
'New' species have appeared

↓

Check information on relevant species life history traits
Check information on sensitivity of species or whether listed as indicators of poor environmental
condition (where available)
Check information on past changes in the species (information resources such a MarLIN and regional
fauna/flora lists)

'Missing' or 'declined' species are sensitive to
pressures/activities that are known/likely to
have occurred
Species that increased in abundance are
indicators of poor conditions or changed
environment (e.g. warming)?

Information not available on sensitivity or
indicator status of species

Yes   No/not known

Species likely to be
long-lived / slow-
growing / recruit
infrequently. No
evidence of past change

Species likely to
be short-lived /
opportunistic /
have a history of
sporadic
occurrence

Have similar changes
occurred at other
locations?

Likely to be
brought
about by
regional
environ-
mental
fluctuations
or by global
change

Likely to
have been
brought
about by
localized
human
activities

Yes   No

Monitor further change,
consider if action
needed/possible

Action not
needed

Local action
not possible.
Monitor
change

Consider if
action
needed/
possible

Likely to
be part of
large-
scale
change

Likely to be
due to
localized
change or
events

Monitor further change,
consider if action
needed/possible

Figure 4.10 A decision tree to identify significance of change and need for, or possibility of, action.
Change needs to be obvious or within the limits of survey accuracy.

Chapter 5

Impacts of human activities on ecosystem composition, structure and function

Introduction

'Impact' refers to man-induced modification to the physics, chemistry and biology of a system. This chapter provides examples of the adverse effects of human activities on the marine environment. Those impacts 'matter' if they:

- destroy or degrade resources (food, recreation, natural heritage); and/or
- prevent other activities taking place (gathering food, accessing cultural resources).

Impacts especially matter if recovery from effects is not possible or will take a long time (probably human generations).

This chapter can only identify a small number of examples of human impacts. A more thorough analysis would require another book.

Human impacts on biodiversity are likely to range from complete destruction of habitats (for instance, land claim that covers mudflats and possibly includes subtidal areas), through alteration of habitats producing communities that are very different to what had been present (for instance, through agricultural run-off or domestic effluents that increase nutrient load and cause eutrophication or through the introduction of non-native species), to situations where biodiversity is considered to be enhanced (for instance, where oil rigs or offshore wind farms provide hard substratum habitats where previously only sediments had been present). In between, there are many localised incidents from oil spills or chemical discharges, or there may be more subtle effects from contaminants that we have difficulty detecting. Cataloguing the effects of pollution and of other impacts from human activities is covered in a wide range of textbooks, notably Kaiser *et al.* (2011) and Clark (2001). Although many degraded areas cannot be recovered, Lotze *et al.* (2006) and Lotze *et al.* (2011) do indicate some signs of recovery and it should be noted that many of the examples given in this chapter are from developed countries and may be historical: regulation and clean-up mean that damaging activities no longer occur or are restricted in occurrence. However, those historical examples remain as warnings of the consequences if activities are not properly regulated and controlled.

Destroying or modifying the structure of habitats or biological communities, impairing ecosystem functioning and interfering with natural processes will have consequences for the 'services' that the sea supplies as well as for maintaining the 'naturalness' that is widely valued on aesthetic and ethical grounds. Understanding the degree to which different human activities may impact on biodiversity and ecosystem structure and functioning is important in the development of conservation priorities. Whether or not action is taken will be a societal choice.

This chapter provides a catalogue of the types of human activities that are likely to affect marine ecosystems and how that impact is likely to occur. It is based on understanding the 'D', 'P' and 'I' of the DPSIR (Drivers – Pressures – State Change – Impact – Response) approach to management (Chapter 6; Atkins *et al.*, 2011). The information given here should be read with the contents of Chapter 4 (covering State Change – the 'S' in DPSIR – as natural change) especially as there is often a combination of natural and anthropogenic reasons for change. Impacts of human activities on marine ecosystems are also described in Chapter 11 in the context of recovery or restoration (the 'R' in DPSIR) after the damaging activity has ceased.

Which of those activities is likely to have most impact is difficult to rank and depends on whether short-term or long-term/permanent impacts are being considered and the degree of impact (from small changes in community composition to complete loss of communities and species). What is certain is that not all human activities necessarily damage marine life. Mapping all human activities in a region is therefore no indication of impact on ecology.

The complexities of assessing impact based on activity is described as a part of the MarLIN programme (Hiscock and Tyler-Walters, 2006) via www.marlin.ac.uk/marinenaturaleffects. php.

It is most practical here to identify generic pressures with examples of the causative activities. They are listed very approximately in the order of likely severity including extent of impact on biodiversity on a localised scale and taking account of likely persistence of effects:

- coastal developments (e.g. coastal defence; land claim; ports and marinas; mangrove forest clearance);
- physical disturbance (benthic trawling and dredging);
- eutrophication (e.g. nutrient enrichment via agriculture and sewage disposal);
- disruption of food webs (e.g. depletion of top predators);
- introduction of non-native species (e.g. via shipping and aquaculture);
- pollution by chemicals (e.g. via industrial discharge; land run-off; use of biocides);
- selective extraction (e.g. via fishing – traps; fishing – recreational);
- food production (e.g. aquaculture including creation of ponds);
- oil pollution (e.g. oil exploration/production platforms; oil tankers; oil terminals);
- sediment extraction (port dredging; sand and gravel extraction);
- dumping (non-toxic, e.g. from navigational dredging);
- offshore constructions (e.g. wind farms; pipelines; oil/gas rigs);
- littering;
- warm water (power stations cooling water effluent);
- collecting (scientific; educational; curio; souvenir);
- radioactive discharge (power stations).

Overarching all of the above is the actual (already expressed) impact of production of greenhouse gases with effects on climate including air and sea temperature rise and the likely (there are few examples in the open sea yet) impact of ocean acidification.

Coastal developments

The construction of harbours, breakwaters and coastal defences (Plates 29 and 30) not only obliterates existing habitats but creates new ones. Hard substratum (in the form of pilings, walls and various forms of boulder tumble) replaces sediments and the protection provided by those structures changes exposed coast habitats to sheltered habitats, perhaps now of mud rather than coarse sediments. The usual scenario in coastal defences is that the land is pushed outwards towards the sea and, acting together with sea level rise, the extent of the seashore is reduced ('coastal squeeze'). If hard substratum in the form of concrete walls replaces structurally heterogeneous natural rock, the communities of species that develop on the concrete walls will be much less diverse than what occurs on natural bedrock (see, for instance, Chapman, 2003; reviewed in Dugan *et al.*, 2011). The construction and maintenance of harbours often requires dredging of the seabed (Plate 31), changing the habitat and making it a transitory location for the development of communities. In developed regions of the world, the extent of coastal development is remarkable. Airoldi and Beck (2007) calculate that 22,000km^2 of the European coast is now covered in concrete or asphalt. Figures are given in Dugan *et al.* (2011) for the extent of coastal development around the world. They list and describe the likely environmental effects: alteration of coastal processes; loss of habitat; alteration of ecological structure, function and integrity. Furthermore, hard substrata placed where previously only sediments were present are likely to act as 'stepping stones' for the dispersal of species beyond their normal range including, perhaps, providing an 'escape route' for sessile species threatened by climate change. For native species, this may not be considered a problem, but, for non-native species that are invasive, spread to new areas may be accelerated.

Physical disturbance (benthic trawling and dredging)

Physical disturbance of the seabed by mobile fishing gear that causes long-term or permanent change to biology has been widespread since the nineteenth century and has extended to the deep ocean and to remote locations such as seamounts since about the 1980s. Also, powerful vessels and robust gear allow heavy trawls and dredges to not only fish over reef habitats but to remove or break those reefs. Stable hard substrata in the form of boulders can even be seen on fish quays prior to disposal (Plate 32). Mobile fishing gear that 'hops' over bedrock is likely to break or remove attached species. Structurally complex habitats that harbour high biodiversity are reduced to rubble. Long-lived species, such as corals over a hundred years old, are damaged or broken and removed or tangled in netting (Plate 33). Beds of maerl and reefs of horse mussels, *Modiolus modiolus*, may be severely damaged (Plate 34). The difficulty for scientists studying such impacts is finding historical data that describes pristine habitats that are now subject to trawling. By the time that scientific studies were being undertaken to describe the communities present on sediments in particular, the baseline had shifted because modification as a result of fishing was already under way. However, there is some historical evidence that can be used and there are reviews of that evidence. Robinson and Frid (2008) report that, over the long term in the North Sea, a common pattern emerges of the loss of epifauna and large and long-lived organisms such as burrowing bivalves, sea pens and reef-building sabellid polychaetes. Examples are given here and are also incorporated into the summary table of impacts of fishing given in the section on 'Selective extraction' (p 80).

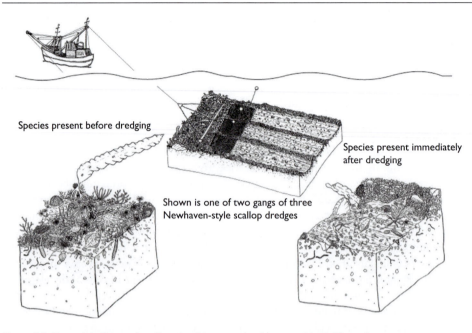

Species present before dredging

Species present immediately after dredging

Shown is one of two gangs of three Newhaven-style scallop dredges

Figure 5.1 Potential effects of scallop dredging on a healthy maerl bed. These images are representations and species shown are more densely grouped than in real life. Drawing: Jack Sewell.

Source: Sewell and Hiscock (2005) (where a detailed description of the biota represented can be found).

A number of effects on the seabed habitats result from dredging. The following text is based on Sewell and Hiscock (2005) where source references can be found. Tracks are created on the seabed, fine sediments are lifted into suspension and large rocks can be overturned. A mound of sediment may be carried in front of the dredge bar and deposited around the sides in distinct ridges, most obviously in the case of the spring-loaded scallop dredges. Investigations into the effects of oyster dredging and the use of modified oyster dredges to harvest clams have shown that the top 10–15cm may be removed by the action of the dredge, sediment plumes created, and tracks made on the seabed. The gravel fraction in the sediment can be reduced and sediments become more anoxic after dredging. The suspended sediment may also have an indirect effect on species some distance from the dredging operation if they are smothered and there can be detrimental effects on eelgrass beds. In common with other forms of dredging, predatory fish, whelks, hermit crabs, scavenging starfish and brittlestars are attracted to the track to feed on damaged and exposed animals. For this reason, numbers of scavengers generally increase at recently dredged sites. In the case of maerl (nodules of living calcified seaweed), long-lived beds of live maerl may be reduced to a few scattered nodules (see Hall-Spencer and Moore, 2000). A large trench is formed, with sculpted ridges of debris. Large boulders are overturned and bottom features are removed. Maerl is broken into small fragments, removed or buried. Large algae, especially sugar kelp *Saccharina latissma*, are shredded and dislodged by the trawl. File shell, *Limaria hians*, nests are removed and individuals are left damaged and exposed to predators. Many large echinoderms, bivalves and flatfish are either caught in or damaged by the dredge. Toothed dredges,

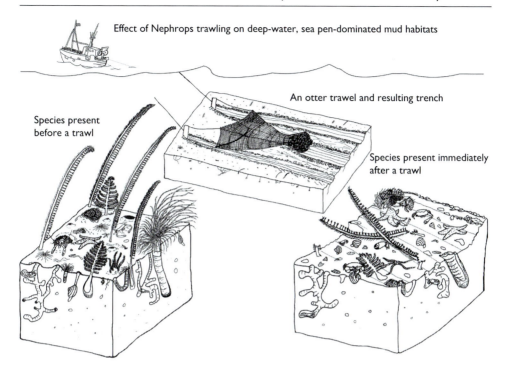

Effect of Nephrops trawling on deep-water, sea pen-dominated mud habitats

An otter trawel and resulting trench

Species present
before a trawl

Species present immediately
after a trawl

Figure 5.2 Diagrammatic cross sections of sediment with infauna and the likely impact of otter trawling for *Nephrops norvegicus* (scampi). These are representations and the sediment fauna is shown more crowded than in real life. Close-up sections are of trenches created by trawl doors or the heavy cod end. Drawing: Jack Sewell.

Source: Sewell and Hiscock (2005) (where a detailed description of the fauna represented can be found).

including 'rapido' dredges (used in the Mediterranean) and Newhaven-style dredges may pierce and kill large, fragile organisms, particularly the fan mussel *Atrina fragilis* (Plate 35).

Whilst fishermen will usually try to avoid reef areas, damage to such areas can be high when they are encountered. For instance, in north-western Australia, it was found that in an area of mixed substrata, on each tow of a trawl, 15.5 per cent of benthic organisms (mainly gorgonians, sponges and soft corals) that stood higher than 20cm off the seabed were removed (Moran and Stephenson, 2000). There has been a clear and significant impact from deep-water trawling on reefs of the coral *Lophelia pertusa* and on other deep-water organisms since the 1980s. Koslow *et al.* (2001) report that, on seamounts deeper than 1,400m, the benthic biomass of samples from unfished seamounts was 106 per cent greater than from heavily fished seamounts and the number of species per sample was 46 per cent greater. Impacts of trawling are further documented by Freiwald *et al.* (2004). The types of species that colonise seamounts and deep-water coral reefs include colonial hard corals, gorgonians, soft corals, hydroids, sponges and various echinoderms. The anthozoans and sponges, especially, are likely to be very old: Freiwald *et al.* (2004) cite 100–200 years for some mature coral colonies. Those fragile colonies, once broken, are unlikely to survive and the whole community may take hundreds of years to regenerate (Clark *et al.*, 2010). On areas of sedimentary seabed, trawls will disturb the upper few centimeters of sediment and may break or remove species that live at the surface. Typically, tracks from otter trawls may still be visible in muddy sediments in sheltered areas after 18 months (Lindeboom and deGroot, 1998).

Eutrophication

Introduction

Nutrient enrichment is a major factor in causing change and is due to combinations of agricultural run-off, sewage disposal and some industrial processes such as paper production. Fish farming in enclosed areas may cause eutrophication through waste food and through faeces of fish and affect marine life, especially in the vicinity of the cages that are used (Plate 36). Increase in nutrients may encourage dense algal growth in both plankton and benthos; although often of fast-growing seabed species that may smother other life. Decay of excessive growth depletes oxygen levels and may cause mortality due to deoxygenation. Eutrophication has been the cause or a contributing cause to habitat degradation documented in many parts of the world. Only a few examples are given next and some more in Chapter 11 where recovery is described.

Seagrass

Eutrophication has often been suggested as a common factor in the loss of seagrass beds worldwide, although often in combination with other factors (see 'Decline of seagrass beds (*Zostera marina*) in the north Atlantic', Chapter 4, p 60). Based on 35 seagrass studies, Hughes *et al*. (2004) report that nutrient enrichment in the water column, and an associated increase in epiphytes, had a strong negative effect on seagrass biomass. Algal epiphytes can limit light and nutrients getting to the seagrass blades, to their detriment. Den Hartog (1994) reports the growth of a dense blanket of *Ulva* [as *Enteromorpha*] *radiata* in Langstone Harbour, England in 1991 that resulted in the loss of 10ha of *Zostera marina* and *Zostera noltii*. The fast growing filamentous algae completely smothered the seagrass, leading to the decay of the underlying algae and subsequent deposition of sulphurous material on the sediment. By the following summer, the *Zostera* sp. were completely absent, although this may have been exacerbated by grazing by Brent geese.

Oysters

Oysters may benefit from eutrophication as the supply of phytoplankton food is increased – see Kirby and Miller, 2005 in relation to *Crassostrea virginica* in Chesapeake Bay; but following over-exploitation of oysters and continued eutrophication in the bay, there was increasing frequency, magnitude and duration of dinoflagellate blooms due, at least in part, to the loss of filtration by oysters (see Luckenbach *et al*., 1993).

Algal beds

The enhanced growth of foliose algae, especially green algae, is often conspicuous around sewage outfalls. Kraufvelin *et al*. (2006) experimentally enhanced nutrient concentrations over intertidal algal communities in mesocosms and demonstrated increased abundance of opportunistic algae, although only after three years during which algal grazing had resisted adverse effects. Kelp forests may be susceptible to eutrophication through the increased nutrients that favour growth of turf-forming algae that block the settlement of kelp spores. Gorman and Connell (2009), working in the area of Gulf St Vincent in South Australia, describe how loss of kelp forests can be associated with urban development. They conclude that natural seasonal contraction of turf covers (i.e. during winter months) does not occur under conditions (i.e. experimental) and locations (i.e. urban) with sustained levels of elevated nutrients and that such turf-dominated habitats inhibit canopy recruitment.

Seabed habitats

Eutrophication can cause a switch in the communities that characterise an area. In 1911 and 1912, C. G. J. Petersen undertook quantitative grab sampling surveys of the seabed in the Kattegat between Denmark and Sweden. Pearson *et al.* (1985) re-sampled those same locations and found that community composition had changed markedly over the area with

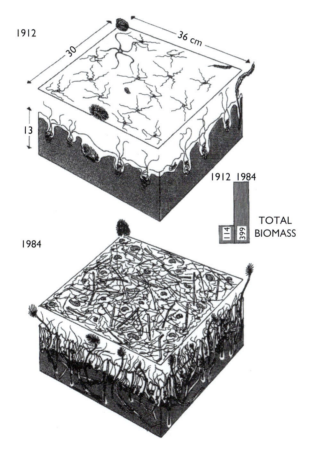

Figure 5.3 Pictorial representation of seabed communities in the Kattegat between Denmark and Sweden from the same location sampled 72 years apart.

Source: Pearson *et al.* (1985).

only approximately 30 per cent similarity of species between 1911/12 and 1984 at most stations. The significant differences in the communities found were attributed mainly to the effects of eutrophication. Such changed communities are likely to persist if the enhanced levels of nutrients persist but may be reversed back to, or at least move towards, the communities that existed before excessive nutrients pervaded the area. An example might be the northern Adriatic where large-scale deoxygenation events and subsequent mortality of seabed species was ascribed to a combination of a gradual increase in eutrophication pressure during the 1970s to the mid 1980s; this was followed by a reversal of the trend, especially marked in the 2000s, attributed to reduced phosphate input but also lower precipitation and therefore reduced riverine input (Giani et al., 2012). However, many changes persisted because of other factors such as increasing numbers of non-native species and seawater warming.

Whole ecosystems

Eutrophication may affect very large areas, especially of enclosed seas, with large catchments from urban and agricultural areas. Such areas include the Baltic Sea and the Black Sea. The Black Sea is a well-studied example with eutrophication as one of the reasons for change, the others being fishing and the introduction of non-native pest species. Langmead et al. (2007) observe that the eutrophication of the north-western shelf of the Black Sea was the result of nutrient enrichment, largely from the Danube and other rivers but aggravated by the loss of nutrient-retaining wetlands. Those nutrients stimulated algal growth and benefited pelagic rather than benthic ecosystems. Although impacts on higher trophic levels may have occurred, they were confounded by overfishing and invasion by species such as the non-native comb jelly *Mnemopsis leidyi*. Nevertheless, it was clear that enhanced phytoplankton productivity had resulted in reduced light penetration affecting an assemblage associated with the red alga *Phyllophora nervosa*. Furthermore, deposition of organic matter from the enriched water column created extended periods of hypoxia, resulting in the loss of more than 5,000km² of bivalves. Two thresholds of resilience had been exceeded (Figure 5.4) (Langmead et al., 2007).

Disruption of food webs

Removal (by fishing) of top predators in particular is likely to have a significant cascade of effects on other parts of the ecosystem. Jackson et al. (2001, p629) observe that 'Severe overfishing drives species to ecological extinction because over-fished populations no longer interact significantly with other species in the community'. Their simplified 'before' and 'after' food webs illustrate how dominant species have changed as a result of human activities, especially fishing.

The dramatic decline of fish stocks as a result of overfishing has been widely described (for instance, Pauly et al., 1998; Thurstan and Roberts, 2010). Figure 5.5 is an example from the Firth of Clyde, Scotland. What is often unclear is what the knock-on effects of removal of predatory species are on other parts of the ecosystem. Although Jackson et al. (2001) identify a variety of changes, care has to be taken in interpreting what might be coincidental. For instance, Pauly et al.'s (1998) article 'Fishing down marine food webs' is illustrated by artwork that shows what were fisheries for large fish become fisheries for small fish as stocks of the larger fish are exhausted. However, any apparently corresponding decline in

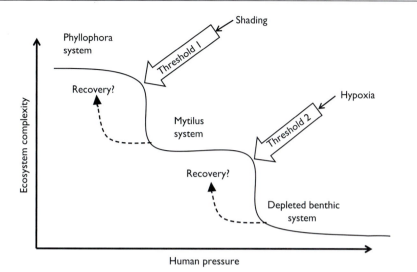

Figure 5.4 Eutrophication together with overfishing led to stepwise changes in the complexity and character of Black Sea ecosystems from the 1980s.

Source: Revised from Langmead *et al.* (2007).

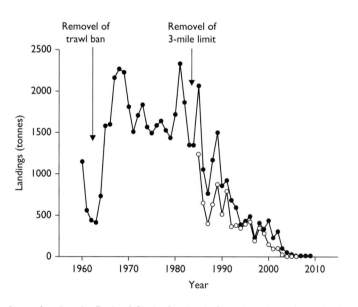

Figure 5.5 Landings of cod in the Firth of Clyde, Scotland. Closed circles indicate landings from the Wider Firth of Clyde and open circles, landings from the Inner Firth of Clyde.

Source: Thurstan and Roberts (2010).

benthos, especially of structural species, is most likely due to physical disturbance of the seabed by mobile gear and not loss of large predatory species. Reorganisations of food webs is, however, bound to occur, and Llope *et al.* (2011) suggest that removal of apex predators is a key element in terms of loss of resilience that inevitably leads to a reorganisation of the ecosystem. One example (of many) is the collapse of what had been highly productive pelagic fisheries off south-west Africa in the 1960s. Many apex predators relied on sardines (which are plankton feeders) for food, but populations of sardines had collapsed due to overfishing and environmental change. Although it seemed that jellyfish (considered a 'trophic dead end') had increased in abundance to become a main predator, presumably of sardine food, the jellyfish were in fact eaten by bearded gobies, *Sufflogobius bibarbatus*. Many higher trophic animals, including predatory seabirds, mammals and fish, switched from sardines to feeding almost exclusively on the bearded goby (Utne-Palm *et al.*, 2010). Care is needed. Whilst food web effects are doubtless occurring widely, as a result of fishing in particular, many conclusions about knock-on effects are based on simulations or conjecture, and what happens in the environment is confused by concomitant changes in such variables as eutrophication, seabed disturbance and occurrence of non-native species.

The removal of any key structural or functional species is likely to cause a cascade of effects on the ecosystem and eventually a phase/regime shift in the ecosystem. Loss of such species can be due to natural events, such as disease outbreaks (see Chapter 4), but also to human impacts. Some of the most commonly cited impacts concern sea urchin grazing and the very significant changes that are likely to occur when sea urchin predators are removed (see, for example, Estes *et al.*, 2010). In the case of a targeted fishery for urchins, *Strongylocentrotus droebachiensis*, in the Gulf of Maine, Vadas and Steneck (1995) proposed that urchin barrens in nearshore areas there existed as a result of the overfishing of large predatory fish that would previously have fed on urchins, crabs and lobsters. Areas that would have supported large stands of macroalgae had been replaced by urchins, crustaceans and encrusting coralline algae. Next, a fishery for urchins increased massively and urchin numbers tumbled resulting in a return to algal-dominated communities (Steneck *et al.*, 2013; Figure 5.6). Re-introduction of urchins failed due to predation by a crab, *Cancer borealis*, which had become abundant (possibly because the algae provided nursery habitat): a new apex predator had arisen and the community dominated by algae would persist.

Introduction of non-native species

Significant impacts from the transportation of species across the world have been with us since the days of world travel in the sixteenth century. Some species considered native to an area may in fact have been brought in so long ago that there was no catalogue of the native marine life already present and, so, they are listed as native (see Carlton, 2009).

Many non-native species that arrive in a new location may be considered benign – they fit in and do not displace native species or bring disease with them. But, others will aggressively out-compete native species, bring disease that affects native species or are toxic to native species. Some effects of non-native species may be less obvious: for instance, affecting food webs. Byrnes *et al.* (2007) suggest that the combined effects of loss of species (usually top predators and other carnivores) due to human activities and species gain (usually from lower trophic levels) will move food webs from a trophic pyramid capped by a diverse array of predators and consumers to a shorter, squatter configuration dominated by filter feeders and scavengers. Whatever practical impacts occur or do not occur, 'naturalness' is greatly valued in nature

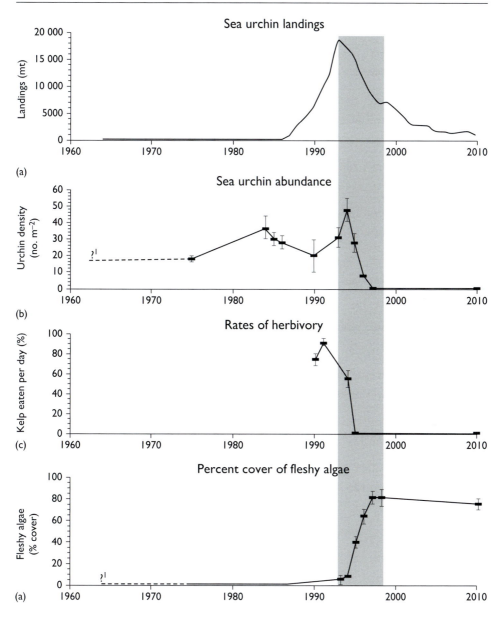

Figure 5.6 Fifty-year trends in sea urchin fishery landings, sea urchin abundance, rates of herbivory and percent cover of foliose algae. The grey bar indicates the phase shift period coinciding with the maximum harvest of sea urchins.

Source: Steneck *et al.* (2013).

conservation and that naturalness is compromised by the presence of non-native species. Most introductions are accidental – they arrive on the hulls of ships or in ballast water – but some introductions are deliberate, particularly in the case of mariculture. Not only may introduced species become abundant and change natural ecosystems (for instance, the kelp

Undaria pinnatifida and the Pacific oyster *Crassostrea gigas*: Plates 37 and 38) but they may also bring 'hitch-hikers' (for instance, the slipper limpet *Crepidula fornicata* and the brown alga *Sargassum muticum* in Europe). Some introductions result from what might be described as clumsiness – for instance, the aggressive aquarium variety of the alga *Caulerpa taxifolia* (Plate 39) was released from the aquarium at Monaco (Rilov and Galil, 2009) and, for a while, could have been exterminated in the wild but was not; it is now dominant in some areas of seagrass in the Mediterranean. The tropical Indo-Pacific lionfish, *Pterois volitans* and *P. miles* (Plate 40), were first reported from the coast of Florida in 1985 and have now spread throughout the Caribbean, feasting on native fish and having no natural predators (Albins and Hixon, 2008). The main concern is that the loss of herbivorous fish that are their prey will reduce algal grazing in an ecosystem that is already overfished and moving towards algal domination. Lionfish are a popular aquarium species and it is most likely that the unwelcome invaders originated from discarded or escaped captive fish. Some species will have arrived via ballast water in shipping and are mainly planktonic. Some are a nuisance – for instance, the diatom *Coscinodiscus wailesii* (a native of the Pacific and Indian Oceans, now present in the North Atlantic) creates mucus that can clog fishing nets – but others have had significant consequences for native marine life. There are many examples. An early one is the common European periwinkle *Littorina littorea* which was first recorded on the east coast of North America in 1840 (Chapman *et al.*, 2007). Periwinkles graze algae and invertebrates and are key functional species, altering shore communities significantly. The comb jelly *Mnemiopsis leidyiI*, which most likely arrived in ships' ballast water, has changed the Black Sea food web by feeding on larval fish. The dinoflagellate *Karenia mikimotoi*, another likely ballast water species, is toxic to invertebrates. In high abundances, dead and decaying cells from blooms may lead to reduced oxygen levels with consequent invertebrate and fish kills. Disease introduction is also a significant concern. American lobsters, *Homarus americanus*, have been introduced to European waters via the restaurant trade. They may carry a bacterial disease, gaffkaemia, that is lethal to other *Homarus* spp. This disease has resulted in the closing of parts of the North American lobster fishery, and its impact on European lobster populations/fisheries could be equally severe (Stebbing *et al.*, 2012).

Many non-native species have been 'picked up' by shipping whilst in sheltered harbours (Plate 41) and may remain in that preferred habitat and not spread widely to the open coast. However, this is bad news for the native biota in sheltered areas. For instance, Cloern and Jassby (2012, p11) observe that:

> San Francisco Bay stands out as a coastal ecosystem transformed by introduced species that contribute up to 97% of the individuals and 99% of the biomass of some communities. The rate of biological invasions is accelerating and estimated at one new species introduced to the San Francisco Bay–Delta system every 14 weeks from 1961 through 1995 (Cohen and Carlton, 1998).

Whilst San Francisco Bay might be 'the most invaded estuary and possibly the most invaded aquatic ecosystem in the world' (Cohen and Carlton, 1998, p556), there are other embayments, harbours and estuaries that are now greatly changed from their native state. For instance, Hewitt *et al.* (2004) suggest that Port Phillip Bay in southern Australia is one of the most invaded marine ecosystems in the Southern Hemisphere. One-hundred and-sixty introduced (99) and cryptogenic (61) species were identified, representing over 13% of the recorded species in the embayment (Figure 5.7). In the Mediterranean Sea, introductions result from the connection with the Red Sea through the Suez Canal as well as via more

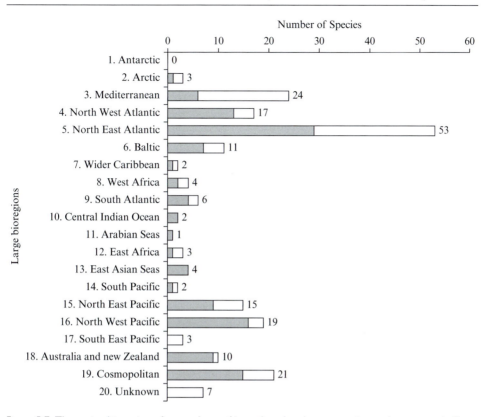

Figure 5.7 The native bioregions for numbers of introduced and cryptogenic species present in Port Phillip Bay, southern Australia.

Source: Hewitt *et al.* (2004).

common vectors such as shipping and aquaculture. Rilov and Galil (2009) describe and illustrate the cumulative numbers and origins of invasive fish, molluscs and crustaceans in the Mediterranean.

Whilst non-native species may completely change the natural character of an area, the arrival of some non-native species may not be considered 'bad news'. For instance, filter-feeding molluscs may provide ecosystem services by filtering water, removing impurities and clearing suspended matter, allowing greater light penetration and algal growth. Species that are structurally complex may provide substratum and shelter for a rich variety of associated (native) species. In the naturally impoverished eastern Mediterranean, the arrival of Red Sea species through the Suez Canal has dramatically increased the total number of species including of some colourful reef fish (Rilov and Galil, 2009). Nevertheless, the risks associated with non-native species mean that biosecurity measures are needed to prevent the arrival of *who knows what* because that arrival might be a highly invasive species that displaces or damages native biota. Removing non-native species populations is virtually impossible (see Chapter 11).

Pollution by chemicals

Many enclosed areas – especially estuaries that are, or have been, industrialised – have been grossly polluted. Waste from chemical plants or processes that discharge chemicals together with run-off from mines and waste tips, agricultural run-off and leachates from antifouling paints on vessels all contribute, or have contributed, to diffuse pollution that has adversely affected marine life. More localised impacts have been seen due to the chemicals used to disperse oil in the 1960s and 1970s (see, for instance, Smith, 1968), but the chemicals used now are of lower toxicity. Similarly, oil drilling once used diesel-based lubricants and their negative effects on seabed marine life were often clearly seen near to exploration platforms (for instance, Figure 13 in Levell *et al.*, 1989). The most toxic and persistent chemical contaminant to affect marine life in recent years has been Tributyltin (TBT), used in antifouling paints and to soak nets and timber to resist colonisation. The chemical is now banned from international shipping and its use is illegal in most countries. The use of TBT brought about one of the greatest 'disasters' to hit marine life, at least in enclosed areas of coast (see, for example, Bryan *et al.*, 1986). Possible 'signals' that the ecosystem was suffering in some way (for instance, the lack of late-stage oyster larvae in the plankton, imposex or localised extinction of the dog whelk) (Plate 42) were not spotted and investigations commenced only when severe impacts occurred, such as shell thickening in oysters. What scientists failed to realise was that TBT was having a widespread and disastrous impact on benthic biodiversity with a large number of species adversely affected, especially at their larval stage. In the upper Crouch estuary, over the ten years following the banning of use of TBT on small vessels, the number of seabed species present doubled (Rees *et al.*, 2001). Although TBT is now banned, it persists in sediments as a result of hull cleaning and paint spillage. The problems of such reservoirs of persistent chemicals are reviewed in Steyl *et al.* (2013). A new generation of less toxic antifouling paints are now used on the hulls of vessels although the levels of copper derived from antifoulants may still be at levels high enough to cause observed toxicities. For instance, in Shelter Island yacht basin, San Diego, USA, Neira *et al.* (2011) observed that, at some sites, copper in sediment had exceeded a threshold for 'self defence' mechanisms; and macrobenthic communities were not only less diverse but also their total biomass and body size were reduced compared to sites with lower copper concentrations. Copper-based antifouling paints may incorporate additional 'booster' biocide compounds (see Guardiola *et al.*, 2012, for a review of biocides and their related toxicities). Behavioural effects, such as decreased fecundity or reduced growth, are more difficult to assess than acute toxicity; and extrapolation from laboratory studies to what happens in the environment is difficult and often unwise. However, it seems likely that biocides present in the water column and incorporated into sediments will have an impact in enclosed areas of coast.

Point source discharges often demonstrate severe effects immediately adjacent to the effluent and provide the opportunity to identify which sessile or sedentary organisms are most sensitive to whatever is being discharged or what disturbance is occurring and, therefore, those species that might be indicators of poor conditions. However, the habitat characteristics need to be consistent with increasing distance from the point source. Two examples are given here in Figure 5.8 (which shows the elevated levels of cirratulid and capitellid polychaetes with increasing distance from disturbance, chemical contamination and oil at an oil rig) and Figure 5.9 (which shows the intertidal and subtidal reef species adversely affected by, and tolerant of, an acidified halogenated effluent from a bromine extraction plant).

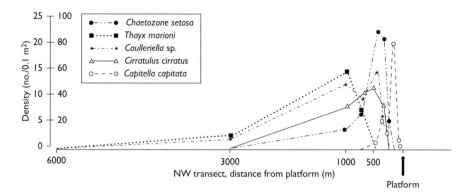

Figure 5.8 Elevated levels of species characteristic of a disturbed or polluted situation along a transect extending north-west from the Thistle oilfield platform.

Source: Levell *et al.* (1989). (Their source, Hannam 1987, could not be found in the cited volume.)

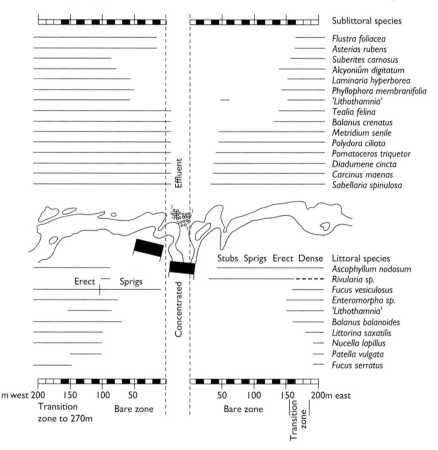

Figure 5.9 Distribution of conspicuous intertidal and subtidal species for a distance 200m west and east of an acidified halogenated effluent. The coastline is depicted horizontally in the middle of the drawing. One of the few studies that identifies hard substratum species intolerant of, or favoured by, a human factor.

Source: Redrawn from Hoare and Hiscock (1974).

Selective extraction

Selective extraction includes targeting particular species, especially shellfish, but also angling for specific fish together with recreational activities including collection of bait and collection of fish and invertebrates for aquaria. The numbers of selected species (for instance, crab, lobster, scallops, whelks, bait worms, tropical fish, anemones) are often depleted to the point where the fishery collapses, but there may also be knock-on effects on associated biota. For instance, bait digging brings buried cobbles and pebbles to the surface of what had been mud or sand and changes the habitat for species (Edwards and Garwood, 1992). Turning boulders while searching for bait or for recreational curiosity or for education, where the boulders are not turned back, will expose species that live under boulders to the light and desiccation that their habitat had previously protected them from. Mechanical harvesting of bait species is likely to cause extensive and long term change including loss of target and associated species. For instance, mechanical lugworm dredgers operating in the Wadden Sea caused a decline in total intertidal zoobenthos biomass, and the population of gaper clams, *Mya arenaria*, almost reached extinction and took five years to recover (Beukema, 1995).

Some of the effects of benthic trawling and dredging for fish have been outlined in the first category of impacts described in this chapter. There is a very large literature associated with the impacts of the gathering of fish, invertebrates and seaweeds for human consumption. Only a very small proportion can be summarised here. Table 5.1 is based on a summary in Sewell and Hiscock (2005) which, in turn, was based on a review by Gubbay and Knapman (1999). That information has continued, in the UK, to be added to and applied to the management of MPAs and to spatial planning via tables of sensitivity of different habitats (as biotopes) to different forms of fishing (but not including angling). A recent example is the study by Eno *et al.* (2013) which resulted in maps of seabed sensitivity in Welsh waters for combinations of 31 habitat types and 14 fishing activity types. Other countries may have similar management aids.

Food production (e.g. aquaculture including creation of ponds)

Food production can significantly change habitats through the removal of natural habitat (such as mangroves) and creation of artificial habitats (such as ponds for finfish or crustacean shellfish), smothering existing intertidal areas (for instance, oyster trays), introducing hard substrata (cages, rafts), producing waste (farmed fish faeces and waste food), and introducing non-native species (both the farmed species and 'hitchhikers') and disease. Many of the potential problems for native species and habitats can be minimised by careful siting of aquaculture facilities and through biosecurity measures, and managers should learn from problems that have occurred. However, destruction of natural habitats may still take place, and the granting of permission for developments should be a societal choice expressed through licensing rather than, as is more likely, happening as a result of commercial pressures.

Likely impacts that also require checklists for decisions about licensing of aquaculture activities include:

- loss or degradation of natural habitat;
- introduction of non-native aquaculture species that may escape and affect natural communities;

Table 5.1 Some potential impacts of gathering fish and shellfish for human consumption. Based on Appendix 2 in Sewell and Hiscock (2005) (where source references can be found) and relevant to the NE Atlantic

Potential impact	Types of fishing including mariculture
Biogenic reefs and associated fauna and flora damaged or destroyed	• Scallop dredging • Demersal fin fish trawling: beam trawling
Many large fragile organisms killed	• Scallop dredging • Demersal fin fish trawling: beam trawling
Some fragile organisms damaged or destroyed	• Crustacean fisheries: pots / creels / traps
Significant reduction in biomass of target and non target species	• Scallop dredging • Demersal fin fish trawling: beam trawling • Demersal fin fish trawling: otter trawling • Cockle & clam: towed tractor dredging
Significant reduction in abundance of target species	• Hand gathering
Significant reduction in species diversity and richness	• Scallop dredging • Crustacean shellfish: otter trawling
Maerl crushed, smothered and buried.	• Scallop dredging • Demersal fin fish trawling: beam trawling • Demersal fin fish trawling: otter trawling
Loss of large sediment epifauna species such as sea pens and anemones	• Crustacean shellfish (refers especially to Norway lobster *Nephrops norvegicusl*): otter trawling • Demersal fin fish trawling: beam trawling • Demersal fin fish trawling: otter trawling
Physical damage to soft or friable rocky outcrops which reduces structural complexity for associated biota	• Scallop dredging • Hand gathering by breaking rocks (for rock-boring molluscs)
Change in benthic community structure, favouring more mobile species, rapid colonisers and juvenile stages	• Demersal fin fish trawling: beam trawling • Scallop dredging • Cockle & clam: towed tractor dredging
Non-target organisms caught and die as discards	• Demersal fin fish trawling: beam trawling • Demersal fin fish trawling: otter trawling • Bait digging
Deep-water coral reefs crushed reducing structural complexity and species diversity	• Demersal fin fish trawling: beam trawling • Demersal fin fish trawling: otter trawling
Eel-grass beds damaged perhaps leading to sediment de-stabilization	• Demersal fin fish trawling: beam trawling • Demersal fin fish trawling: otter trawling • Cockle & clam: towed tractor dredging • Cockle & clam: hand gathering including raking
Sediment re-distributed so that coarse material brought to the surface with associated changes in community structure	• Bait digging
Death of underboulder fauna	• Bait collection • [Also recreational and scientific sampling/ observation]
Incidental catch of marine life including marine mammals and birds	• Demersal and pelagic fish: fixed or drift (gill) nets • Mariculture: finfish farming in cages (via anti-predator nets)
'Ghost fishing' by lost gear, dependent on condition of gear	• Demersal and pelagic fish: fixed or drift nets • Crustacean fisheries: pots / creels / traps
Damage to deep water fragile coral	• Demersal fin fish trawling: otter trawling

Table 5.1 (continued)

Potential impact	Types of fishing including mariculture
Smothering of benthic communities with faeces and waste food	• Mariculture: finfish farming in cages
Localised anoxic conditions	• Mariculture: finfish farming in cages
Sublethal effects of chemical treatments on benthic fauna	• Mariculture: finfish farming in cages (treatment of disease and sea lice)
Deliberate (oysters) and accidental introduction of alien species	• Mariculture: oysters • Mariculture: mussel cultivation (seeded beds)
New habitat created	• Mariculture: oysters • Mariculture: mussel cultivation (seeded beds)

- introduction of non-native species accidentally with aquaculture species;
- introduction of disease, with non-natives, that will spread to native species;
- stocking density that leads to disease or parasite 'hotspots' that spread to native species and wild populations;
- death of mammals and birds (entanglement in predator defences);
- addition of habitat not previously present;
- pollution from organic waste;
- pollution from pharmaceutical products;
- pollution from antifouling chemicals on nets;
- genetic alteration of wild stocks from cultivated stocks;
- introduction of species that are predators on native biota.

Habitat destruction to accommodate aquaculture facilities is conspicuous and may have unexpected consequences: for instance, destruction of mangroves that had previously protected a coastline from damaging wave action. Less obvious, in the case of mangroves, would be the loss of habitat for species that rely on the mangroves as nursery areas. High-density finfish farming is likely to cause several environmental problems including: acting as a hotspot for fish lice infestation that spreads to wild salmon migrating out of rivers (see Krkošek *et al.*, 2012); attracting the use of medicines that affect wild stocks; and, in areas with restricted water flow, accumulating organic material below the farms causing deoxygenation and a 'classic' organic enrichment gradient (Figure 5.10).

The production of food for farmed finfish also requires the use of wild-caught fish, further depleting stocks.

Oil pollution (e.g. oil exploration/production platforms, oil tankers, oil terminals)

Oil pollution has attracted a great deal of research, although most is published in limited-circulation reports. The impacts from oil pollution separate broadly into those resulting from accidental spills from shipping (Plate 43) and exploration/production rig accidents, and those resulting from chronic discharges such as oil refinery effluents or production water from oil rigs. Oil pollution, especially from spills, is very conspicuous, and it causes alarm amongst the public and damage to fisheries, to wildlife and to recreational activities. Distress and mortality to vertebrates, especially birds, may occur, and animal welfare

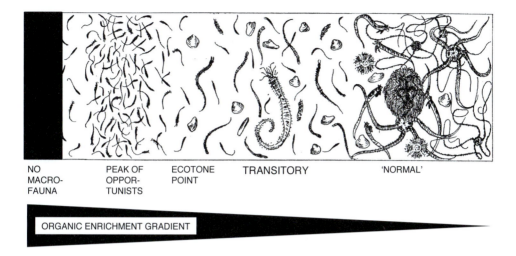

NO   PEAK OF   ECOTONE   TRANSITORY   'NORMAL'
MACRO-   OPPOR-   POINT
FAUNA   TUNISTS

ORGANIC ENRICHMENT GRADIENT

Figure 5.10 Diagrammatic representation of changes in abundance and species types along a
generalised organic enrichment gradient.

Source: Pearson and Rosenberg (1978).

issues come to the fore – but need to be separated from conservation concerns (Plate
44 shows an oiled seal pup). Mortality of organisms depends on the type and age of the
oil or petroleum product and the amount spilled (Plate 45 shows the results of a spill of
petroleum). Weathered crude oil may have little effect, whilst a spill of lighter oil including volatile fractions may decimate shore populations, especially when confined to small
areas. Also, oil floating on the surface is unlikely to have a toxic effect more than a few
centimetres below unless wave action or chemical dispersants spread the oil through the
water column. Oil can become incorporated into sediments, especially intertidally but also
through adhering to sediment particles that are subsumed into subtidal sediments providing a chronic source of pollution for many years, including in salt marshes and mangroves.
Thick or weathered oil may become incorporated into coarse sediments and remain as
an 'asphalt pavement' on the shore, reducing recolonisation potential. Certain species
are especially sensitive and when key functional species such as limpets are killed, there
will be conspicuous knock-on effects in terms of algal growth. In the case of mangroves,
the 'breathing roots' (pneumatophores) may become clogged, resulting in death of the
mangroves and denial of habitat for a wide range of species. Tainting of food species is
also an issue.

From the point of view of biodiversity conservation, it is important to know where are
the locations that might suffer most as a result of an oil spill and to have in place plans to
protect those locations should a spill occur. Time of year may also be important as some
species occur seasonally. That protection will depend especially on weather conditions at
the time of the spill and the extent of the spill.

IPIECA (1991) summarise ecological impacts of oil spills for different groups of species
as follows:

Group	Comments
Mammals	It has been rare for whales, dolphins, seals and sea lions to be affected following a spill. Sea otters are more vulnerable both because of their way of life, and their fur structure.
Birds	Birds using the water-air interface are at risk, particularly auks and divers. Badly oiled birds usually die. Treatment requires specialist expertise and the right facilities – amateur attempts can distress the birds even more. Recovery of populations depends either on the existence of a reservoir of young non-breeding adults from which breeding colonies can be replenished (e.g. guillemots) or a high reproductive rate (e.g. ducks). There is no evidence so far that any oil spill has permanently damaged a seabird population, but the populations of species with very local distributions could be at risk in exceptional circumstances.
Fish	Eggs and larvae in shallow bays may suffer heavy mortalities under slicks, particularly if dispersants are used. Adult fish tend to swim away from oil. There is no evidence so far that any oil spill has significantly affected adult fish populations in the open sea. Even when many larvae have been killed, this has not been subsequently detected in adult populations, possibly because the survivors had a competitive advantage (more food, and less vulnerable to predators). Adult fish in fish farm pens may be killed, or at least made unmarketable because of tainting.
Invertebrates	Invertebrates include shellfish (both molluscs and crustaceans), worms of various kinds, sea urchins and corals. All these groups may suffer heavy casualties if coated with fresh crude oil. In contrast, it is quite common to see barnacles, winkles and limpets living on rocks in the presence of residual weathered oil.
Planktonic	Serious effects on plankton have not been observed in the open sea. This is probably because high reproductive rates and immigration from outside the affected area counteract short-term reductions in numbers caused by the oil.
Larger algae	Oil does not always stick to the larger algae because of their mucilaginous coating. When oil does stick to dry fronds on the shore, they can become overweight and subject to breakage by the waves. Intertidal areas denuded of algae are usually readily repopulated once the oil has been substantially removed. Many algae are of economic importance either directly as food or for products such as agar. Algae cultured for this purpose lose their commercial value if tainted.
Marsh plants	Some species of plant are more susceptible to oil than others. Perennials with robust underground stems and rootstocks tend to be more resistant than annuals and shallow rooted plants. If, however, perennials such as the grass *Spartina* are killed, the first plants to recolonise the area are likely to be annuals such as the glasswort, *Salicornia*. This is because such annuals produce large numbers of tidally dispersed seeds.
Mangroves	The term 'mangrove' applies to several species of tree and bush. They have a variety of forms of aerial 'breathing root' which adapts them for living in fine, poorly oxygenated mud. They are very sensitive to oil, partly because oil films on the breathing roots inhibit the supply of oxygen to the underground root systems.

Coral reefs would seem likely to be particularly sensitive to oil spills. Haapkylä *et al.* (2007) confirm this sensitivity in relation to scleractinian (stony) corals and provide a review.

Chronic oil pollution usually occurs from point source discharges, and effects may be detectable near to the discharge but not far away. 'Near' usually means a few tens of metres, but, in the case of a refinery effluent in Southampton Water, UK, discharges during the 1950s and 1960s caused an area of salt marsh about 1km in extent to be killed (Dicks, 1976). For coral reefs, Loya and Rinkevich (1980) showed that steady, chronic discharge of oil from oil terminal operations caused effects which included decreased colonisation, decreased coral viability, coral mortality, damage to reproductive systems and many other changes. Bak (1987) describes, for the region of a refinery at Aruba in the Caribbean, chronic pollution effects that were clearly discernible over a distance of 10 to 15km along the reef. Historical data, which is by far the most abundant, may not be a guide to likely impacts today in view of much improved effluent quality standards. For instance, the effects of operational discharges from oil platforms off Norway have recently been reviewed by Bakke *et al.* (2012) who concluded that 'components of produced water can cause a number of negative effects that have consequences for the health, functions and reproduction of individual fish and invertebrate animals. Particular emphasis has been placed on possible endocrine effects, but other types of effects, such as genetic damage, oxidative stress, growth and reproduction, have also been found' (p27); and 'that the potential for environmental harm is generally moderate, and the concentrations that have produced effects do not normally occur more than around one kilometre from the discharge points' (p29).

Oil spills are often treated with dispersants that, in the case of the *Torrey Canyon* oil spill in 1967, may have caused more damage than the oil. However, toxicity of dispersants is now enormously reduced and, used properly, can prevent damage from the oil.

Sediment extraction (port dredging; sand and gravel extraction)

Sediments may be removed for port development and maintenance. Here, communities may be well developed and include long-lived species. Likely impacts are illustrated in Cattrijsse *et al.* (2002).

Sands and gravel extraction (Plate 46) is undertaken for the construction industry but also for beach replenishment (see, for instance, Newell and Woodcock, 2013). Such 'aggregates' are usually found in dynamic environments where natural disturbance occurs and so any communities present are likely to be dominated by fast-growing and short-lived species. There have been extensive studies in the UK of impacts of aggregate extraction. Dredging will remove organisms and change the nature of the remaining substratum, potentially affecting ecosystem structure and functioning and food availability for fish stocks. Most studies on the impact of dredging on marine benthic fauna show that dredging can result in a 40–95 per cent reduction in the number and biomass of organisms and a 30–70 per cent reduction in the number of species (Hill *et al.*, 2011).

There is an important exception to the statement that most aggregate-living species are fast growing and short-lived: maerl (calcified seaweed), extracted for use as a soil conditioner. Maerl (for instance, *Phymatolithon calcareum*) grows at a rate of about 1mm a year (Blake and Maggs, 2003). Maerl beds may be several thousand years old (the maximum

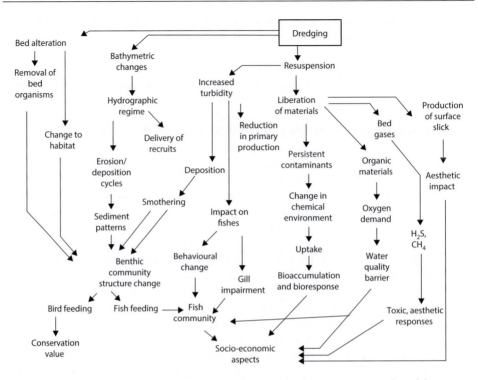

Figure 5.11 The potential environmental impacts of marine dredging – a conceptual model.

Source: Redrawn from M. Elliott, unpublished, in Cattrijsse *et al.* (2002).

age of the St Mawes Bank, Falmouth, UK is calculated to be 4,000 years: Bosence and Wilson, 2003). Live maerl is unlikely to be replaced and, overall, dead maerl beds have been reported to have a reduced epiflora and vagile epifauna compared to live maerl beds and are less attractive as nursery areas for juvenile scallops and probably other juvenile bivalves (see, for instance, Hall-Spencer, 1998). Impacts on live maerl beds from dredging are likely to be permanent, and loss of live maerl will prevent continued growth of the bed.

Recovery from sand and gravel extraction is addressed in Chapter 11.

Dumping (non-toxic, e.g. from navigational dredging)

Dredge spoil from harbour construction or maintenance and from some offshore construction has to be disposed of. That material might need to be decontaminated (if levels of substances exceed permitted concentrations) before disposal, then might go to landfill; but much will go offshore to be dumped. Many dump sites are historical – created before consideration was given to damaging effects on biodiversity. Impacts can be direct, where the sediment hits the seabed and smothers whatever is underneath, or indirect, via sediment plumes that are carried by currents. Whilst careful selection of dump sites might ensure that the location being smothered is not considered of high importance, unexpected effects may reveal themselves on distant locations that might be in MPAs or other sensitive areas.

If the sediments being disposed of still contain contaminants, this may also have an effect away from the dump site. Results from monitoring studies range from those that demonstrated large differences (>80 per cent dissimilarity) between disposal and reference sites in some areas to those that showed much smaller differences in others (Bolam *et al.*, 2006).

Some others studies also suggest very small or no effects. For instance, in the Solitary Island Marine Park, New South Wales, Australia, Smith and Rule (2001) report that dredge spoil dumping had no detectable effect on either the structure of the invertebrate community or the physical characteristics of sediments at the receiving site. In New England, following 35 years of research, it was reported that ocean disposal of dredged material has minimal environmental impact when carefully managed (Fredette and French, 2004). Indeed, Bolam *et al.* (2006, p424) observe:

> One notable feature of the results obtained here is the fact that dredged material disposal in the coastal environment does not result in large areas of seabed devoid of life. In many instances, one or more attributes within the disposal site appeared to indicate a 'healthier' situation relative to the reference site.

Offshore constructions (e.g. wind farms, pipelines, oil/gas platforms)

Offshore constructions and the operation of oil and gas platforms in particular may cause adverse effects on marine biodiversity ranging from those caused by chemical contamination, including oil pollution to sediment disturbance during construction or as a result of scour around structures, through to concerns that marine mammals and birds may avoid such structures (Plate 47 is an oil rig). The major effects of those structures that remain above the seabed are to act as artificial reefs for the colonisation of hard substratum species and to attract fish where previously only sediment communities may have existed. A secondary, and often welcome, effect is that areas with such structures become 'no go' for mobile fishing gear and, therefore, protect seabed communities from the damaging physical disturbance that occurs during fishing. Lindeboom *et al.* (2011, p1) comment on the impacts of an offshore wind farm in Dutch waters: '[t]he results indicate no short-term effects on the benthos in the sandy area between the generators, while the new hard substratum of the monopiles and the scouring protection led to the establishment of new species and new fauna communities.' However, the geographical distribution of many species is restricted by barriers such as areas of substratum that are unsuitable for settlement. Offshore constructions may provide 'stepping stones', including for the spread of non-native species. In the Northern Gulf of Mexico, approximately 4,000 oil and gas platforms have enhanced the dispersal of coral populations into areas where, previously, they were naturally absent (Sammarco *et al.*, 2004).

Littering

Littering, especially the disposal of plastic waste, is a concern especially for the conservation of many species that may ingest the plastic. Floating plastic may aid the spread of non-native species as well as the extension of native benthic species distributions across what would otherwise be barriers of open sea. An example of such might be the north-east Atlantic barnacle *Solidobalanus fallax* which, having previously been recorded from Portugal, Spain and France, was first found in British waters from samples collected in 1988 and has since become well established, populating organic surfaces such as kelp holdfasts and dead skeletons of sea fans; however, it is also found on floating plastic bags and on monofilament nets (Southward *et al.*, 2004). There may be other species that 'raft' on debris and may find their way across oceans. Microplastics – tiny plastic granules used as scrubbers in cosmetics and in air blasting, or breakdown products from macroplastics – are a particular concern as they can adsorb contaminants onto their surface and are injested by a wide range of marine organisms (Cole *et al.*, 2011).

What some might consider a rather extreme form of littering is the placement of artificial structures onto natural seabed. These might range from bereavement balls to naval vessels and oil rigs. The impact of such structures are similar to those described for offshore constructions. Some litter may provide a habitat or shelter for both attached and mobile species, including sometimes rare or scarce species (Plate 48), and introduces a dilemma for those wishing to clean up unsightly garbage.

Warm water (power stations cooling water effluent)

Warming seawater temperatures above ambient as a result of input of cooling water may occur especially in sheltered waters where effluent dispersal is limited. Pulses of warm water are unlikely to affect intertidal or shallow subtidal organisms, which are often subject to such changes due to insolation. Organisms passing through filters may be killed by very high temperatures within a power station, although industrial plants are also likely to introduce biocides to the water to prevent fouling and they alone might be the lethal factor. Continuous exposure to warm temperatures may be attractive to mobile species such as fish and may encourage species naturally more characteristic of warmer waters (including, perhaps, some non-native species) to flourish. Warmer water can also result in lowered oxygen saturation of the water. UNEP (1984) reviewed the effects of thermal discharges on marine life. They describe some apparent effects in temperate regions, but the results of studies are equivocal. In subtropical and tropical waters, field studies have shown damage to seagrass, coral reefs and benthic communities where temperatures have been raised by 3–5°C; and, in one case where temperature increases exceeded 5°C, macrobenthic organisms were totally excluded and fish diversity halved. Often, damage can be prevented by ensuring that the effluent is directed to high energy areas and away from shallow sheltered areas.

Collecting (scientific, educational, curio, souvenir)

Whilst education and recreation are important services provided by biodiversity, care is needed to ensure that those activities do not damage, or do not damage excessively, the features that are valued. Some impacts are obvious, such as when boulders on the shore are overturned while looking for crabs or unusual species but not turned back. The sessile organisms living under the boulders are highly sensitive to desiccation and will die. Others are less obvious, such as the crushing of organisms when boulders are turned back. Buckets of crabs and fish that are left to heat up in the sun and the water become deoxygenated with consequent mortality. Collecting specimens for taxonomy or for classification of rare species may adversely affect the population as a whole. Destructive sampling methods such as using dredges on fragile communities may remove long-lived species that will not come back. Quantification of such impacts is difficult but there is no doubt that they occur.

Radioactive discharge (power stations)

Except for experimental studies where levels of radioactivity are raised to several thousand times those found near to effluents of nuclear power stations, no adverse effects of radioactivity have been found on marine organisms in the field. However, seaweeds absorb and accumulate radioactive elements and, where that occurs, may be harmful to human health if consumed.

Impacts resulting from multiple stressors

Cause and effect are rarely simple to establish. Disastrous declines, such as those already mentioned in this chapter occurring in the Black Sea, have been determined as being due to several human factors – mainly nutrient loading, overfishing and non-native species. Others, used in Chapters 4 and 11, are due to mixed factors, including natural and human. Few species or biotopes have been studied sufficiently thoroughly to identify the range of factors that might have caused decline. However, Waycott *et al.* (2009), in a worldwide review, identified evidence of causes of decline in seagrasses in 77 of 128 sites where decline had occurred, concluding two major causes of seagrass loss: (*i*) direct impacts from coastal development and dredging activities (21 sites), and (*ii*) indirect impacts from declining water quality (35 sites). They conclude (2009, p12379) that (in addition to disease):

> Destructive fishing practices, boat propellers, coastal engineering, cyclones, and tsunamis also cause direct and immediate seagrass loss. More indirect and potentially more damaging are the impacts of water quality degradation resulting from increased nutrient additions and sediment run-off in human-altered watersheds. In addition, the indirect effects of aquaculture and invasive species have been observed to affect seagrasses. Other indirect effects from overfishing have caused the loss of predators, which can cascade down the food web and lead to the loss of the herbivores that clean seagrasses of fouling algae, resulting in seagrass loss. Lastly, global climate change is predicted to have deleterious effects on seagrasses and is emerging as a pressing challenge for coastal management.

Box 5.1 gives one further example of a mixture of human and natural factors that have caused substantial change.

Global impacts – climate change and ocean acidification

Introduction

Some changes are global in extent and, whilst they are likely to have an impact on a local scale, need to be addressed globally. 'The carbon dioxide problem', which refers to the increase in CO_2 in the atmosphere and oceans as a result of the burning of fossil fuels, is one such change and expresses itself through climate change and ocean acidification. McQuatters-Gollop (2012, p5636) observes:

Unprecedented basin-scale ecological changes are occurring in our seas. As temperature and carbon dioxide concentrations increase, the extent of sea ice is decreasing, stratification and nutrient regimes are changing and pH is decreasing. These unparalleled changes present new challenges for managing our seas, as we are only just beginning to understand the ecological manifestations of these climate alterations.

That introductory statement was given in the context of a European Union (EU) Directive requiring each EU Member State to set environmental targets to achieve 'Good Environmental Status' and pointing out that, in order to do so, an understanding of large-scale ecological change in the marine ecosystem is necessary.

Climate change – warming

Climate change expresses itself in several ways including increased storminess, increased frequency of extreme events and the possibility that large-scale oceanic processes such as the north Atlantic oceanic current (the 'Gulf Stream') may slow. The most conspicuous effect and the one that is likely to cause greatest change in the short term is warming of both the atmosphere and the seas. Setting aside what appear to be natural changes in oceanic circulation (for instance the warming events in Australia resulting from changes in currents: Ridgway and Hill, 2009; Smale and Wernberg, 2013), plankton and fish (i.e. mobile species that change their distributional patterns rapidly in response to warming) have shown change. Such species that are highly mobile or that have larvae that are planktonic and long-lived, are likely to show distributional changes that result from global warming now. Others, that have low mobility and are either adversely affected or favoured by higher air and seawater temperatures are also likely to show effects in terms of decreased or increased abundances, although not necessarily distributional shifts. The evidence for shifts in the distribution of highly mobile species is particularly marked in the north Atlantic where, for instance, Beaugrand et al. (2002) showed that planktonic copepods had moved northwards by 10 degrees of latitude (1,000km) within 50 years and colder water plankton had retreated in the same direction. For fish around Scotland, Beare et al. (2003, p1) report that 'the northern North Sea is currently experiencing waves of immigration by exotic, southern species (e.g. red mullet, anchovy and pilchard) which are unprecedented in the context of the 79-year history of our extensive databases'. For benthos, range expansions have been described in California (Barry et al., 1995), the British Isles (Hawkins et al., 2009), the Bering Sea (Grebmeier et al., 2006) and the Antarctic Peninsula (Clarke et al., 2005). However, Reid et al. (2009) observe that there is minimal information to indicate whether tropical and subtropical species, other than possibly corals on the eastern margin of Florida, are expanding poleward. Poloczanska et al. (2013) summarise the global imprint of climate change on marine life.

Hiscock et al. (2004) are cautious about the likely impacts of warming on seabed marine life around the British Isles. Using information on the life history characteristics of species, their present distribution and other factors, they produced a key supported by a decision tree to identify 'types' of organism according to their likely response to temperature rise. Many species were shown as likely to increase their range northwards and become more abundant in current locations. In contrast, fewer would decline in abundance and extent in the north. Hiscock et al. (2004) also predict likely changes in some biotopes that characterise seabed areas around Britain. Although range extensions northwards of benthic southern species in

Box 5.1 Phase shift in Caribbean coral reefs

'The coral reefs in the Caribbean region have undergone a dramatic transition over the past two to three decades, from hard coral to fleshy algae dominance . . . The factors behind this change are not completely understood but it reflects a combination of natural (hurricanes and disease) and anthropogenic (overfishing and nutrient increase) disturbances acting in synergy. By the late 1960s, fish biomass had been heavily reduced, and by the late 1970s the reefs around Jamaica were extensively damaged, resulting from direct and indirect effects of overfishing . . . Because large predatory fish were continuously overfished, herbivorous fish became the new target species. When the number of herbivorous fish declined, the sea urchin *Diadema*

Elkhorn coral off Paradise Island, Bahamas in 1983.

antillarium was able to increase in abundance, because the two groups shared the same algal resources . . . *Diadema* subsequently became the keystone herbivore. In 1981, Hurricane Allen struck the area and most of the branching coral species were killed or damaged, resulting in new open substratum becoming available for colonisation by fast growing algae. Despite high levels of nutrients, the density of benthic algae was kept low by the efficient grazing *Diadema*, and coral recolonisation took place. However, in 1982 and 1983, the sea urchin population suffered from a species-specific pathogen that reduced the population by 99% in some areas. Because all major grazers were then low in numbers, they were not able to prevent the establishment of algae, resulting in a dramatic change in the abundance ratio between coral and benthic algae . . . Brown fleshy algae became overwhelmingly abundant and prevented coral larvae settlement. Even large old coral colonies were out-competed by the fast growing macroalgae. This case demonstrates how the loss of diversity within the functional group of herbivores resulted in reduced resilience. A disturbance that could previously be buffered by a diverse functional group of herbivores, became the trigger that caused an ecosystem with reduced resilience to shift from a coral-dominated state to one dominated by algae. The extent to which this phase shift is irreversible is still unclear.'

Source: (Nyström *et al.*, 2000, p414)

the northern hemisphere are being reported, the examples are patchy. However, the sorts of changes that might be expected are exemplified in, for instance, Kortsch *et al.* (2012) (Box 5.2) for Arctic regions and Barry *et al.* (1995) for temperate regions.

Species that are at the extremes of temperature (in the tropics and in the polar regions) are likely to have most difficulty migrating to cooler locations and may have the lowest ability to adapt (acclimate) to changing temperature. Peck *et al.* (2014, p1) observe that 'both Antarctic and tropical species were less resistant to elevated temperatures in experiments and thus had lower warming allowances . . . or warming resistance, than temperate species' (Plate 49). Warming is likely to matter most if key structural or functional species are affected (including increases or decreases). Kelp forests are key structural features of cold temperate ecosystems, and loss due to warming is likely to have significant effects on associated richness and on the role that kelp forests play in, for instance, providing nursery areas. Smale *et al.* (2013, p1) observe: '[r]ecent evidence unequivocally demonstrates that the structure of kelp forests in the NE Atlantic is changing in response to climate and non-climate related stressors, which will have major implications for the structure and functioning of coastal ecosystems'. That evidence included a decline in approximately 1,400ha of kelp forest and increases in the abundance of warm temperate understory algae linked to rise in sea surface temperature in 2007 in north-western Spain with an associated decline in kelp-associated commercial species (Voerman *et al.*, 2013) and changes in seaweed assemblages in north-eastern Spain (Díez *et al.*, 2012). A decline in some canopy-forming intertidal algae in the region – especially *Himanthalia elongata* and to a lesser extent *Fucus serratus* – has also been observed (Duarte *et al.*, 2013).

There are other likely effects of warming such as increased incidence of disease (Harvell *et al.*, 2002) and parasites: for instance, the geographic range of the oyster parasite *Perkinsus marinus* extending 500km north owing to an increase in average winter low temperatures (Ford, 1996).

Ocean acidification

Average global surface ocean pH has already fallen from a pre-industrial value of 8.2 to 8.1, corresponding to an increase in acidity of about 30 per cent. Values of 7.8–7.9 are expected by 2100, representing a doubling of acidity. The damaging impacts of ocean acidification at present seem localised (e.g. to the Pacific Northwest oyster farming industry) or remote (e.g. to Southern Ocean pteropods); but in fact, all around the world, vast areas of the seabed are becoming exposed to waters that are corrosive to calcium carbonate (IGBP, IOC, SCOR, 2013). The damaging impacts of ocean acidification may seem a long time (decades to centuries) in the future but what might happen is demonstrated, in a few naturally occurring seeps of CO_2, by experimental studies and what are believed to be early effects of widespread acidification on a few species. Increased levels of carbonic acid in the sea are likely to have complex effects that depend on the type of calcified skeleton that organisms have (whether aragonite or calcite) and such further complexities as the depth below which aragonite dissolves (the aragonite saturation horizon, which becomes shallower as acidification increases) and synergistic effects of seawater warming. The following studies are examples that inform us about the possible effects of ocean acidification.

Box 5.2 A climate-driven regime shift in Arctic marine benthos

A. Time series of macroalgal cover at Kongsfjord. The dotted line shows the sample mean for the two regimes and the lower grey line shows the posterior mean.

B. Time series of selected dominant/characteristic macrofauna at Kongsfjord. The left axis is abundance of the sea anemone *Urticina felina* (Urtic) and the right axis, abundance of the sea urchin *Strongylocentrotus droebachiensis* (Strong) and the ascidian *Halocynthia pyriformis* (Haloc).

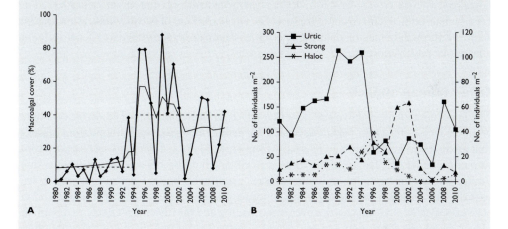

A 30-year data set from rocky subtidal habitats in Svalbard has enabled Norwegian scientists to identify an increase in benthic algae, including an abrupt eightfold increase at one site in 1995, and changes in benthic invertebrates that coincide with an increase in seawater temperature of 0.5°C and decreasing sea ice cover over the period of study. The authors suggest that the regime shift is likely to promote the 'borealisation' of Arctic marine communities in coming years.

Source: Kortsch *et al.* (2012).

- In natural CO_2 seeps on the island of Ischia, Italy, calcification of encrusting bryozoans is inhibited and seagrass fouling is reduced, favouring seagrass growth (Hall-Spencer *et al.*, 2008).
- In the same location, the shells of limpets become increasingly weak and are more easily damaged the closer to the seeps that they occur (Hall-Spencer *et al.*, 2008).
- Corals, coccolithophore algae, coralline algae, foraminifera, shellfish and pteropods experience reduced calcification or enhanced dissolution when exposed to elevated CO_2 (IGBP, IOC, SCOR, 2013).
- Studying coral reefs in the region of natural CO_2 seeps in Papua New Guinea, Fabricius *et al.* (2014) conclude that the densities of many groups and the number of taxa (classes

and phyla) of macroinvertebrates were significantly reduced at sites with elevated CO_2 compared to control sites.

In the studies that have been done, there seems to be a consistent pattern of biodiversity loss as CO_2 levels rise which causes radical changes in the ecology of the studied systems at around pH 7.8. Long-term ocean acidification could exceed the tolerance limits of marine species that live in coastal waters, even though they may have evolved strategies to deal with fluctuating pH on the short timescales typical of coastal environments (where the daily and seasonal changes in seawater pH are much greater than in the open ocean). Kroeker et al. (2013, p1890) observe that, 'in general, heavily calcified organisms, including calcified algae, corals, mollusks, and the larval stages of echinoderms, are the most negatively impacted, whereas crustaceans, fish, fleshy algae, seagrasses and diatoms are less affected or even benefit from acidification'. Offsetting the adverse effects of ocean acidification may be achieved through managing damaging activities that can be controlled at a local scale, or may not be possible locally.

Other human impacts

The impacts catalogued above are those that affect, in particular, seabed biodiversity. There will be adverse effects on pelagic species from persistent organic pollutants, from plastics that are ingested by oceanic wanderers and from artificial noise. Pollutants such as polychlorinated biphenyls (PCBs) are of particular concern and have been associated with endocrine disruption, immunotoxicity and cancers (see: http://wildwhales.org/conservation/threats/toxins). The oceans have become a much noisier place with the sounds of shipping and of activities such as mooring chain movements, drilling and pile driving all likely to disturb or reduce communications between cetaceans in particular. Strandings of cetaceans are often observed during or soon after military exercises and high-intensity sonar is blamed (Parsons et al., 2008). Those effects may not just be limited to vertebrates, and cephalopods may be affected (André et al., 2011).

Future problems

Whilst many future problems for marine biodiversity resulting from human activities are unknown, we can expect that they may result from new products that find their way into the marine environment or synergies between existing and/or new products. Nanoparticulates and new pharmaceutical products are two areas that come to mind. Deep-sea mining is another.

Conclusions

1   Identifying when human activities have a harmful impact on nature ranges from the problem being so large and the reason for it so obvious that demanding 'evidence' could only be a delaying tactic for action, to the sort of long-term decline or sudden loss that defies explanation and may be due to a multitude of factors working together or just some part of a long-term variability not yet recorded.
2   Changes, including degradations, will persist as long as the cause persists, including through the presence of contaminants, elevation of nutrients, physical disturbance and constructions.

3   Many of the impacts from human activities on biodiversity, particularly in coastal habitats, are because of construction and land claim and are unlikely to be reversed.

4   Three impacts from human activities rank high (after construction) in changing ecosystems: fishing (especially bottom fishing), eutrophication and the introduction of non-native species. Where all three occur, and adding warming to the mix, change will often occur. That change may constitute a regime shift and return to previous conditions is unlikely.

5   Contaminants have an insidious effect that is difficult to detect and separate from natural change.

6   Short-term impacts (for instance oils spills, extreme weather events, short-term disease) may result in large-scale change to the biology of a location, but recovery normally occurs within a few (<5) years unless structural features or species that are long-lived, slow growing and recruit infrequently/locally have been damaged.

7   One of the greatest problems that we face in identifying the extent and character of change brought about by human activities is that of 'shifting baselines' – our reference point for making comparisons may be of a community that has already been vastly changed by human activities but which had not been documented in earlier states.

Chapter 6

The application of science to management: introduction

Introduction

The rest of this volume is dedicated to the application of scientific approaches to biodiversity conservation. Science is seen here as knowledge derived from a body of facts systematically arranged and gained by observation and experiment (various sources, see http://dictionary.reference.com/browse/science?s=t). Science is used in a structured way to provide the evidence that justifies management measures and that tracks the changes occurring as a result of those measures. The DPSIR (Drivers – Pressures – State Change – Impact – Response) framework is well established (see, for instance, Atkins *et al.*, 2011) and provides a link from societal activities through scientific knowledge to response that gives a logical progression to appropriate action for conservation. Whatever that action is, it will be linked to the 'ecosystem approach' (see Chapter 1) meaning that we have to protect and maintain natural ecological characteristics while at the same time delivering the services and benefits required by society (Elliott, 2011).

Figure 6.1 illustrates one cycle of the DPSIR approach that might be applied to one 'Pressure' (for instance aggregate extraction, bottom trawling, non-native pest species, contaminants – see Chapter 5). Where there are several different activities that might affect biodiversity and require management action, there will be multiple DPSIR cycles under way in the management regime.

The application of science to management spans conservation action from global to local: from understanding and addressing the causes and consequences of climate change and ocean acidification to protecting the habitats of rare species.

To apply science to management, the manager will need to have access to information and to tools (checklists, criteria to assess 'importance', methods for monitoring, analytical software to help interpret complex data, decision trees, etc.). That information and those tools should help the manager to answer, from the point of view of biodiversity conservation, the 'will it matter if . . .?' and 'does it matter that . . .?' questions in relation to the results of Environmental Impact Assessments and of monitoring following development or events (see Chapter 10). The tools should also help in identifying how to prevent, mitigate or compensate for adverse effects.

Managers that have to assess 'quality' or 'state' and then take action to protect the marine environment or restore what has been damaged will benefit from having quantitative indicators of undesirable change or condition. Those indicators may be in terms of multi-metric indices that identify the character of a community, which may be of a healthy through to a damaged nature. There will also be species whose life history traits suggest

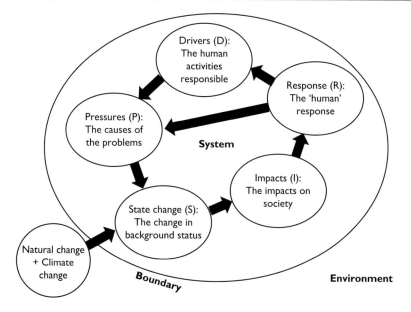

Figure 6.1 The DPSIR approach as a cycle and system in the environment. The diagram recognises that there may be natural change occurring as well as changes brought about by human activities.

Source: Redrawn from Atkins *et al.* (2011).

undisturbed through to disturbed habitats ('indicator species': see Chapter 10 'Indicators', p185). Ecologists advising policy will need to be able to differentiate between accurate data and information and that which is flawed or limited in value: often through some measure of confidence. All too often, inexperienced policy advisors accept scientifically flawed approaches or information that is attractive but inaccurate. The cascade of approaches starts with measures with high confidence via reasonable certainty to those with low confidence (but all that is available). The most difficult concept for policy advisors to accept is expert judgement: that mix of knowledge and experience with common sense which will help to interpret survey results or events through what is known as 'wisdom'.

The DPSIR approach

The nature of 'threats': Drivers and Pressures

'Drivers' are the demands that society makes of the environment. They include such requirements as transportation, food, recreation, energy, living space and dealing with waste. Those demands in turn generate activities which create 'Pressures' on the environment. Those Pressures can lead to 'Impacts'. A list of human activities that may affect marine life and ecosystems was given in Table 1.1. Several Pressures may act together to create Impacts (see Figure 2 in Atkins *et al.*, 2011). In order to undertake research to identify likely effects of human activities and the Pressures they create, there has to be a link to the environmental 'factors' that will change. A checklist of environmental factors likely to cause change (from www.marlin.ac.uk) follows:

Physical factors

- Substratum loss;
- Smothering;
- Suspended sediment;
- Desiccation;
- Changes in emergence regime;
- Changes in water flow rate;
- Changes in temperature;
- Changes in turbidity;
- Changes in wave exposure;
- Noise disturbance;
- Visual presence;
- Physical disturbance and abrasion;
- Displacement.

Chemical factors

- Synthetic compound contamination;
- Heavy metals contamination;
- Hydrocarbon contamination;
- Radionuclide contamination;
- Changes in nutrient levels;
- Changes in salinity;
- Changes in oxygenation.

Biological factors

- Introduction of microbial pathogens/parasites;
- Introduction of non-native species;
- Selective extraction of this species;
- Selective extraction of other species.

Drivers and Pressures are unlikely to express themselves in a simple single-factor event. There will be several factors acting at the same time and sometimes synergistically. The reason(s) for change may be obvious but, even then, proof or evidence is likely to be demanded (for instance, loss of biogenic reefs where scallop dredgers have been operating may obviously be the result of the dredging but the fishing industry will still demand evidence and suggest that surely it could have been eutrophication or climate change etc.). The experienced scientist might be able to work out what is driving change, and computer software may identify the environmental factors that are most likely driving shifts in the character of samples and the species that are most important in the separation of different sample clusters (for instance, PRIMER: Clarke and Gorley, 2006). Those analytical techniques are not described here but are very important in helping the scientist to recognise the source of change and the possible reasons behind it. Predicting the likely impacts of multiple drivers is the subject of research projects such as MEECE (Marine Ecosystems Evolution in a Changing Environment: www.meece.eu) that are developing decision support tools for managers.

State change

State change refers to the changes that occur as a result of Pressures (and sometimes due to or contributed to by natural change). Those changes may be in the state of environmental factors listed above and/or in the state of biological characteristics such as the composition of benthos or abundance of fish populations. Any change in state needs to be assessed in relation to the concept that change may be natural and, as far as information on natural change is available, separating change that is brought about by human activities from change brought about by seasons, variable recruitment, etc. Outside of any such 'envelope' of change, there may be severe events such as hurricanes that will be natural and not elicit management action. Chapter 4 includes examples of such changes.

Impact

Chapter 5 summarised examples of undesirable human impacts. However, impacts may be considered positive or negative. For instance, introduction of hard substrata where none existed before (which would happen in a wind farm development) may be considered a positive impact, whereas the same hard substratum providing 'stepping stones' for the spread of non-native species may be considered a negative impact for biodiversity conservation. The relationship between an activity taking place and the likelihood of an adverse effect on biodiversity or sustainable use is not simple, and the character of the receiving environment, the duration, magnitude, frequency and extent of the activity or event are all important to take into account. Some of these factors are explored in Hiscock and Tyler-Walters (2006) and in more detail on the MarLIN website (www.marlin.ac.uk).

Response

When an undesirable impact has been identified, the next step for management is to determine if action is needed and what the response should be. It might be that a particular Pressure (via the activity that created it and perhaps the Driver that created the activity) needs to be reduced or extinguished. Once that action is taken, recovery may follow or, if not, consideration given to whether recovery can be given a nudge by human intervention. If recovery does not occur and seems not to be possible, there may be compensatory measures that can be taken. The principles of 'giving nature a nudge' (restoration) or introducing compensatory measures (replacement or biodiversity offsetting) are explored in Chapter 11.

Bringing the science together to inform management

The DPSIR approach is informed by the topics in subsequent chapters and is invoked where management action is needed to protect species and habitats. Although this volume focuses on the way in which science underpins biodiversity conservation, the scientist should not lose sight of the importance of socio-economic drivers and engaging with those sectors of society that might be able to inform or might be affected by solutions. Engaging with stakeholders is an essential part of the practice of nature conservation.

Conclusions

1   Understanding how threats to biodiversity come about is an important starting point for deciding what measures might be needed to improve prospects for nature conservation and sustainable use. They are the Drivers and Pressures in the DPSIR system and the human activities that cause those pressures.

2   Wherever sufficient information exists, changes from a pre-existing state (State Change) (but taking account of what might be natural variability) and the Impacts that have occurred as a result of Drivers and Pressures, together with the 'does it matter?' and the 'can we do anything about it?', questions will shape Response.

3   The background information that we need to understand, and to organise what we understand, is provided in preceding chapters. The information that we need to take action and the mechanisms for taking action are in subsequent chapters.

4   A 'toolbox' of decision aids can be assembled from material in this volume but socio-economic and political considerations will often drive what action is (or is not) taken.

Chapter 7

'Threatened' and 'sensitive' species and habitats

Introduction

Drawing attention to species and habitats that are vulnerable to human activities is an essential part of seeking action to protect what is threatened. This chapter describes 'traditional' measures of degree of threat and how – using information on life history traits of species, including those that are critical components of habitats – we can begin to identify species and habitats that are threatened but would fall into a 'data deficient' category using traditional measures.

Identifying which are 'threatened' or 'vulnerable' species for protection has, for many years, relied on quantitative measures of rarity, decline, area of occupancy and total known population. That quantitative information is available for many charismatic species and for commercially exploited species but seldom for unexploited species and especially the biodiversity that exists in seabed habitats. Another measure is needed and that is 'sensitivity'. Sensitivity refers to the intolerance of a species or habitat to an activity or environmental factor and the degree to which recovery is likely. Some assessments of sensitivity refer to 'resistance' rather than 'intolerance' of species to a factor. In such studies, 'High' intolerance becomes 'Low' resistance. 'Sensitive' species and habitats (as biotopes) are important to protect but may also be used (through their presence/absence or abundance) as indicators of degree of disturbance, or more accurately, lack of disturbance. Undamaged examples of habitats may have large numbers of species that are sensitive to damaging activities.

Knowing what are the species and habitats in an area that are likely to be adversely affected by an activity (they are sensitive to the activity) or that, if lost, would 'matter' (they are rare, scarce, in decline or threatened with decline) is a key part of an environmental assessment, including consideration of where MPAs might be beneficial and whether or not a development or new activity should go ahead. Also, knowing where those sensitive or important species and habitats are enables response planning in the event of localised pollution, especially an oil spill. Relevant information can be mapped and used as a basis for spatial planning; but there will be gaps in information, and, before any development commences or restrictive measures are proposed, appropriate survey should inventory the species and biotopes present, enabling, as far as current knowledge allows, identification of any rare, scarce, in decline or threatened with decline (including sensitive) species and habitats.

Sensitivity is not the same as vulnerability. A species or habitat is only 'vulnerable' if it is exposed or likely to be exposed to potentially damaging activities, events, disease or contaminants. In many cases, an assessment that a species or habitat is sensitive to a particular factor will be irrelevant because that factor and the changes that it causes do not exist in the vicinity of the feature being considered.

Degree of threat – IUCN Red Lists

Species

'Degree of threat' for species is assessed using criteria that have been developed for well-studied species for which there is quantitative information on rarity, decline, area of occupancy or total known population. The outcomes of assessment are summarised as 'threat categories' (IUCN, 2001) in the IUCN Red List (Figure 7.1).

The criteria for Critically Endangered, Endangered and Vulnerable species are summarised in Figure 7.2. Those criteria rely on measurements that are rarely available for most marine species or habitats although, notably, accommodate some degree of estimation and expert judgement where precise figures are not available. Dulvy (2013) considers that great progress has been made in incorporating marine species to the Red List although continuing to cite mainly cetaceans, turtles, fish, reef-building corals and some molluscs, echinoderms and seagrasses (Plate 50 is one of those charismatic species). There were 792 marine species or subpopulations (100 listed as Critically Endangered, 155 listed as Endangered and 537 as Vulnerable) listed by IUCN in November 2013 (http://marinebio.org/oceans/red-list-species.asp).

Habitats and ecosystems

Although degree of threat criteria are well established for species, there are currently no such international criteria for habitats or ecosystems. Nevertheless, Keith *et al.* (2013)

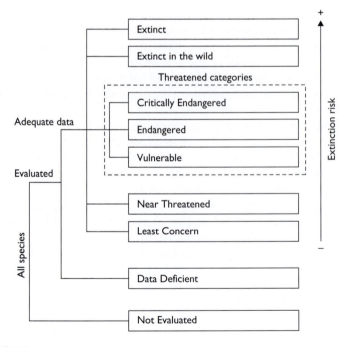

Figure 7.1 IUCN Red List categories.

Source: IUCN (2001), available from: www.iucnredlist.org/technical-documents/
categories-and-criteria/2001-categories-criteria

A. Population size reduction. Population reduction (measured over the longer of 10 years or 3 generations) based on any of A1 to A4

	Critically Endangered	Endangered	Vulnerable
A1	≥ 90%	≥ 70%	≥ 50%
A2, A3 & A4	≥ 80%	≥ 50%	≥ 30%

A1 Population reduction observed, estimated, inferred, or suspected in the past where the causes of the reduction are clearly reversible AND understood AND have ceased. **A2** Population reduction observed, estimated, inferred, or suspected in the past where the causes of reduction may not have ceased OR may not be understood OR may not be reversible. **A3** Population reduction projected, inferred or suspected to be met in the future (up to a maximum of 100 years) *[(a) cannot be used for A3]*. **A4** An observed, estimated, inferred, projected or suspected population reduction where the time period must include both the past and the future (up to a max. of 100 years in future), and where the causes of reduction may not have ceased OR may not be understood OR may not be reversible.	*based on any of the following:* (a) direct observation *[except A3]* (b) an index of abundance appropriate to the taxon (c) a decline in area of occupancy (AOO), extent of occurrence (EOO) and/or habitat quality (d) actual or potential levels of exploitation (e) effects of introduced taxa, hybridization, pathogens, pollutants, competitors or parasites.

B. Geographic range in the form of either B1 (extent of occurrence) AND/OR B2 (area of occupancy)

	Critically Endangered	Endangered	Vulnerable
B1. Extent of occurrence (EOO)	< 100 km²	< 5,000 km²	< 20,000 km²
B2. Area of occupancy (AOO)	< 10 km²	< 500 km²	< 2,000 km²

AND at least 2 of the following 3 conditions:

(a) Severely fragmented OR Number of locations	= 1	≤ 5	≤ 10

(b) Continuing decline observed, estimated, inferred or projected in any of: (i) extent of occurrence; (ii) area of occupancy; (iii) area, extent and/or quality of habitat; (iv) number of locations or subpopulations; (v) number of mature individuals

(c) Extreme fluctuations in any of: (i) extent of occurrence; (ii) area of occupancy; (iii) number of locations or subpopulations; (iv) number of mature individuals

C. Small population size and decline

	Critically Endangered	Endangered	Vulnerable
Number of mature individuals	< 250	< 2,500	< 10,000

AND at least one of C1 or C2

C1. An observed, estimated or projected continuing decline of at least (up to a max. of 100 years in future):	25% in 3 years or 1 generation (whichever is longer)	20% in 5 years or 2 generations (whichever is longer)	10% in 10 years or 3 generations (whichever is longer)

C2. An observed, estimated, projected or inferred continuing decline AND at least 1 of the following 3 conditions:

(a) (i) Number of mature individuals in each subpopulation	≤ 50	≤ 250	≤ 1,000
(ii) % of mature individuals in one subpopulation =	90–100%	95–100%	100%

(b) Extreme fluctuations in the number of mature individuals

D. Very small or restricted population

	Critically Endangered	Endangered	Vulnerable
D. Number of mature individuals	< 50	< 250	**D1.** < 1,000
D2. *Only applies to the VU category* Restricted area of occupancy or number of locations with a plausible future threat that could drive the taxon to CR or EX in a very short time.	-	-	**D2.** typically: AOO < 20 km² or number of locations ≤ 5

E. Quantitative Analysis

	Critically Endangered	Endangered	Vulnerable
Indicating the probability of extinction in the wild to be:	≥ 50% in 10 years or 3 generations, whichever is longer (100 years max.)	≥ 20% in 20 years or 5 generations, whichever is longer (100 years max.)	≥ 10% in 100 years

Figure 7.2 Summary of the five criteria (A–E) used to evaluate if a taxon belongs in an IUCN Red List Threatened category (Critically Endangered, Endangered, Vulnerable). Reference to the full document is essential for explanation of terms and concepts.

Source: IUCN (2001), available from: www.iucnredlist.org/technical-documents/categories-and-criteria/2001-categories-criteria

propose an approach to identifying Red List ecosystems that uses criteria similar to those in Figure 7.2. Their model identifies four distributional and functional symptoms of ecosystem risk as a basis for assessment criteria:

A. rates of decline in ecosystem distribution;
B. restricted distributions with continuing declines or threats;
C. rates of environmental (abiotic) degradation; and
D. rates of disruption to biotic processes.

A fifth criterion, (E.) quantitative estimates of the risk of ecosystem collapse, enables integrated assessment of multiple processes and provides a conceptual anchor for the other criteria.

Work to develop and populate the Red List for ecosystems including marine ecosystems is under way in 2014.

Degree of threat: considerations for marine species and habitats

Endemicity in the marine environment

That a species is 'only known to occur in a restricted location' is a particularly important consideration when identifying species for protection. Most species have a wide geographical distribution but some are restricted to limited areas or even, in the case of some cave-dwelling species, to one location (see, for example, Iliffe and Kornicker, 2009). Plate 51 is of *Cryptocorynetes longulus*, one of three known species in the genus belonging to a class of the Crustacea that was first described as recently as 1981 from cave systems in the Bahamas (Yager, 1981). Isolated island archipelagos are likely to have a high endemicity and, around the Galapagos Islands, nearly 20 per cent of marine species are endemic (www. galapagos.org) (Plate 52 is one of those species). On a much larger scale, Costello *et al.* (2010) recorded that 51 per cent of New Zealand species are endemic whilst only 2 per cent of Baltic species are endemic to those regions, with endemicity in other regional seas falling between those two extremes. Wherever a species is endemic to a region or a large proportion of the world's population of that species is found there, the relevant state(s) have a high responsibility for its protection. However, high levels of localised endemism are unusual in the marine environment where connectivity through the water column is good and geographical barriers, few – even seamounts now seem not to be the isolated habitats with a high level of endemism that they were once thought to be (Clark *et al.*, 2012).

Rarity of marine species and habitats

Rarity is a part of 'degree of threat' but has a particular resonance with the public and with policymakers. Rarity is a difficult concept to define. Many species and habitats are naturally 'rare' – they have only ever occurred in small numbers and/or at a few locations. Furthermore, some large species, such as some whales, are never going to reach populations of more than a few tens of thousands. A species may be known from only a few specimens when it is first described as new to science, but that does not necessarily mean that it will not, in the longer term, become known as widespread.

Table 7.1 Application of area of occupancy criteria to assess rarity

Regionally rare (sessile or of restricted mobility) species	Species occurring in less than 2 per cent of the 50km × 50km UTM* grid squares of the following bathymetric zones in the region (e.g. North East Atlantic): littoral/sublittoral/bathyal, abyssal
Nationally rare species	Species occurring in less than 0.5 per cent of the 10km × 10km squares within the study area
Nationally scarce species	Species occurring in less than 3.5 per cent of the 10km × 10km squares within the study area
Regionally rare habitat	Habitat type occurring in less than 2 per cent of the 50km × 50km UTM grid squares of the following bathymetric zones in the region (e.g. North East Atlantic): littoral/sublittoral/bathyal, abyssal
Nationally rare habitat	Habitat type restricted to a limited number of locations in territorial waters

Source: Based on Sanderson (1996) and Derous (2007).

Note: * Universal Transverse Mercator system (of cartography)

The 'area of occupancy' concept can be used as a proxy to assess the rarity of species within a biogeographical or geopolitical region. This is the approach adopted by Sanderson (1996) for Great Britain, and rare species are included as one of the features that identify 'national importance' (see Box 7.2). Derous *et al.* (2007) took Sandersons's area of occupancy criteria and adjusted them to be used to identify regionally as well as nationally rare or scarce species and habitats (Table 7.1).

The percentage of UTM grid squares that are translated into a species being rare or scarce was based on those percentages used for terrestrial species but applied to the sort of area that might be under the influence of coastal processes and where survey intensity was considered sufficient to provide meaningful comparisons. In Britain, that was taken as about three nautical miles from the coast (a now defunct territorial seas limit) which included 'bay closures'. The criteria developed by Sanderson (1996) further identified measurements for 'Nationally scarce' and 'Nationally uncommon' species which may also be influential terms to use in environmental assessments and in speaking to policymakers. It should be born in mind that a species or habitat may be assessed as 'rare' in a particular country or, perhaps, a regional sea but may be widespread outside of that region. That consideration may not be relevant as the rare species will be valued and protected in the governance area where it is being considered. However, there are significant limitations to systems of assessing rarity that are based on the percentage of grid squares the species occur in – not least that there may be one individual of a species or millions in one square but the contribution to rarity assessment is the same.

A system that relies on percentage occurrence in grid squares cannot be used for large mobile species because, during its lifetime, one individual will be reported in many grid squares. Often, it is an estimate of the total world population that is used to track change in abundance of large, highly mobile species (see, for instance, Gerber *et al.*, 2007 for bowhead whales) and this is one of the measures used in the IUCN Red List categories. Not having measures of rarity, and therefore not being able to identify measures of 'decline', was a problem when considering recovery of populations of cetaceans listed in directives, conventions and statutes when Hiscock *et al.* (2013) investigated measures of recovery. A scoring system was developed and the terminology used in Sanderson (1996) retained (Box 7.1).

Box 7.1 Assessing rarity in highly dispersed mobile species. A score-based system developed by Clare Lacey and Eilis Cox in Hiscock *et al.* (2013) (redrawn) and used to assess rarity for English waters

1 Population size   Using the best available population estimates; calculate the percentage of the worldwide stock of animals that resides in the area of interest.

Percentage	Score (max 25 available)	Worked example – harbour seal
Endemic species – 100%	25	A European subspecies – *Phoca*
81–99%	22	*vitulina vitulina* – will be considered as
61–80%	20	the total population for this exercise.
41–60%	17	Approximately 4% of European
26–40%	12	harbour seals are found in England
Unknown or 5–25%	10	(SCOS 2009). **So, population size**
1–4%	8	**scores 8.**
0.05–1%	5	
<0.05%	3	

2 Occurrence   This section refers only to occurrence within the area of interest. Occurrence is classified as falling into one of five categories, and then a score is assigned accordingly.

Distribution category	Score (max 25 available)	Worked example – harbour seal
Continuous (found all around the coast)	6	Harbour seal haul out sites are
Almost continuous (a few isolated areas where they aren't found)	8	concentrated in approximately 5 main locations and additional
Multiple patches (found in multiple patches around the coast)	10	smaller sites. This is occurrence in occasional patches. **So,**
Occasional patches (found in 5–10 patches around the coast)	17	**occurrence scores 17.**
Isolated (found only in very few isolated areas (less than 5)	25	
Unknown	12	

3 Trophic level   As apex predators are naturally rarer than primary producers, it was thought that some measure of this should be accounted for within these criteria.

Trophic level	Score (max 10 available)	Worked example – harbour seal
Apex predator	10	Harbour seals are mid-level predators,
Mid-level predator	7	feeding on fish and crustaceans but also falling
Planktivore	5	prey to killer whales elsewhere in their range.
Primary producer	3	**So, trophic level scores 7.**

4 Final Scores Add up all of the scores for each section to get a final score out of 60. Compare to the table below:

Score (out of 60)	Assigned criteria	Worked example – harbour seal
41–60+	Nationally rare	Harbour seal total score = 8 + 17 + 7 =
31–40	Nationally scarce	32 = **Nationally scarce.**
15–30	Nationally uncommon	
<15	Widespread	

With regard to habitats, some have always been restricted in extent and occurrence but some are now very restricted in occurrence where once they were widespread. They include loss of areas of mudflat due to port construction, loss of mangroves due to shrimp farming and loss of biogenic reefs due to trawling. Some habitats may have declined following disease (for instance, seagrass and oyster beds) although what role humans had in those events is unclear. Rare or scarce habitats should be protected but identification of quantitative measures to label physiographic types, broadscale habitats and biotopes as rare or scarce has not, it seems, been done. Documenting habitat loss and the extent of remaining examples is often an important part of influencing for conservation measures. Quantifying what is a 'rare' or 'scarce' habitat has not been addressed, but the work started by Keith *et al.* (2013) to produce an IUCN Red List of ecosystems should help.

Bringing measures together

To stand a chance of identifying species of invertebrates and algae that may be threatened, something that avoids or supplements the requirement for quantitative information on decline is needed. Measures that can be applied to the sort of information available for such marine species and habitats have been developed as criteria for identifying 'Nationally Important Marine Features' in the UK (Lieberknecht *et al.*, 2004). The criteria are summarised in Box 7.2.

Whatever terms are used to describe degree of threat, they must be easily understood by non-scientists who just need to know that there is a scientifically objective measurement behind them. However, more work is needed on rarity concepts especially to accommodate species where area of occupancy may not be relevant and to identify habitats and ecosystems that are threatened and would benefit from protection.

Sensitivity of species and habitats

Introduction

Understanding the basic biology and ecology of species is the starting point to understanding their sensitivity. In turn, that understanding allows us to identify species that are, or might be, under threat. The presence of sensitive species and the biotopes that they occur in may also provide an indication of 'good quality', and they may therefore be identified as indicator species. Sensitivity of a species is identified via knowledge of biological traits: the particular

Box 7.2 Criteria developed in the UK to identify Nationally Important Marine Features from a biodiversity conservation point of view. Summarised from Lieberknecht et *al.* (2004)

CRITERION 1: Proportional importance   A high proportion of the marine landscape, habitat, or population of a species (at any time of its life cycle) occurs within the UK. This may be related to either the global or regional extent of the feature.

Features are categorised as follows:

Globally important: a high proportion of the global extent of a marine landscape or habitat or a high proportion of the global population of a species (at some stage in its life cycle) occurs within the UK. 'High proportion' is considered to be more than 20 per cent.
Regionally important: a high proportion of the regional extent of a marine landscape or habitat, or a high proportion of the regional population of a species (at some stage in its life cycle) occurs within the UK. 'Regional' refers to the north-east Atlantic (OSPAR) area. 'High proportion' is considered to be more than 30 per cent.

CRITERION 2: Rarity   Marine landscapes, habitats and species that are sessile or of restricted mobility (at any time in their life cycle) are considered nationally rare if their distribution is restricted to a limited number of locations.

Rarity is assessed as follows:

The feature occurs in fewer than 0.5 per cent of the total number of 10km × 10km squares in UK waters (eight or less 10km squares within the three-mile territorial seas limit of UK waters).
    A mobile species qualifies as nationally rare if the total population size is known, inferred or suspected to be fewer than 250 mature individuals. Vagrant species should not be considered under this criterion.

CRITERION 3: Decline   An observed, estimated, inferred or suspected significant decline (exceeding expected or known natural fluctuations) in numbers, extent or quality of a marine landscape, habitat or a species in the UK (for species, quality refers to life history parameters). The decline may be historic, recent or current. Alternatively, a decline at a global or regional level, where there is cause for concern that the proportional importance criterion will be met within the foreseeable future. (Further quantitative guidance is provided.)

CRITERION 4: Threat of significant decline   It is estimated, inferred or suspected that the feature will suffer significant decline (as defined under the 'decline' criterion) in the foreseeable future as a result of human activity. This assessment will need to take into account the inherent sensitivity of the feature and its expected degree of exposure to the effects of human activity.
    A feature may also qualify under this criterion if there is real cause for concern that it will fulfil the proportional importance criterion in the near future due to the threat of global or regional decline.

features that a species has of a character or attribute. For instance, all species grow (an attribute) but the 'trait' describes the growth rate. Biological traits are described for such features as adult mobility, growth rate, adult dispersal potential, larval/propagule dispersal potential, sociability, feeding method, longevity and fragility. Ecological traits are related to habitat preferences such as in relation to salinity, depth (light regime), wave exposure, strength of tidal flow, environmental position (whether pelagic, infaunal, epifaunal, etc.), temperature, tolerance to organic pollution, biogeographic distribution, etc. Knowing traits information for the key structural or functional species in a biotope enables their use as surrogates for the sensitivity of the biotope. The important traits are those that predispose the species to damage by factors. However, information on traits may be lacking for many of the species that are listed for protection – often because they are rare and research has not been carried out to identify such key traits as longevity, dispersal potential and fragility. For instance, Tyler *et al.* (2012) found that full data on eight fundamental biological traits existed for only 9 per cent (*n* = 88) of the UK demersal marine fauna, and 20 per cent of species completely lacked data. Knowledge of species traits is essential to understanding ecosystem structure, functioning and viability (Chapter 3) and to assessing whether change 'matters' in terms of, for instance, the loss of a species (see 'Understanding change', Chapter 4). Whether or not a species is of 'conservation concern' may depend on its biological traits.

Natural history and ecology

Much of our knowledge of biological traits comes from natural history observations. Recording those observations started in Greece with the work of Aristotle in about 350 BC and continues today. With added information from experimental studies, catalogues of biological traits for species provide a foundation for assessing intolerance and recovery potential which, together, identify likely sensitivity of organisms to environmental change including pressures and activities. Natural history observations that advise us about traits can be 'mined' from a wide range of publications extending back to the Greeks 2,300 years ago, but also, more practically, from nineteenth-century monographs, the fauna and flora lists from marine stations and from such publications as Yonge's (1949) *The Seashore*.

Whilst a knowledge of 'natural history' through fieldwork may seem old-fashioned to some and not 'scientific', it is the starting point from which we begin to understand the world around us, how it is structured, how it 'works', how to break it and, perhaps, how to mend it. Natural history is the study of species and their habitats. Undertaken in a structured and objective way, it is 'science'. Science is simply knowledge gained through systematic observation and experimentation. It may involve careful chemical analysis or complex sample/experimental designs with impressive statistical analysis of results, but it also includes systematic accumulation and application of simple facts. Indeed, the term 'scientist' has only been in use since 1833. Before William Whewell coined the name, readers of this volume would most likely have been called 'natural philosophers'.

Experimental observations

Much of the literature that identifies biological traits of species, if it is not from natural history, is from experimental studies. Those experiments might be natural and unplanned, including such observations as are made (if the marine biologist is quick enough) following storms, cold or warm weather events, harmful algal blooms, etc. Such observations are also made during events caused by humans, such as oil spills or on inspecting the contents of a scallop dredge. Organised and controlled experiments that manipulate species and communities or introduce contaminants known or suspected to affect them inform knowledge of intolerance and recovery.

Assessing the sensitivity of species

Biological traits information is of core importance in assessing 'sensitivity' of species and, through those species, of the biotopes in which they are key structural or functional features. Identifying sensitivity and creating a tool for marine environmental managers to use is exemplified by the MarLIN programme instituted at the Marine Biological Association of the UK in 1999 (Hiscock and Tyler-Walters, 2006). That information on sensitivity can be used to identify likely indicator species of disturbance or lack of disturbance and to determine whether a location has sensitive features and needs protection. However, for many species, as already outlined, there will not be sufficient information on traits to assess likely sensitivity to an activity or factor. In such cases, surrogates (a species with similar characteristics – perhaps a different species of the same genus) might inform the traits for the species under consideration. For many habitats, the presence of sensitive (indicator) species should not be expected – many habitats are naturally characterised by species found in disturbed situations and their 'quality' needs to be assessed against undisturbed examples in similar environmental conditions (Table 7.2).

Figure 7.3 Experimental studies are important in understanding impacts on species and biotopes in relation to changes in the environment. Here, nutrient levels have been increased over rocky shore communities at Solbergstrand, Norway, revealing a delay of about three years before significant effects of increased abundance of opportunistic algae were observed. The delay was because existing ecosystem processes such as grazing resisted the ascendancy of the opportunistic algae (Kraufvelin *et al.*, 2006).

Source (image): Hartvig Christie.

Table 7.2 Life history characteristics of opportunistic species (likely to have low or moderate sensitivity to disturbance because of rapid recovery potential) and climax species (may have high or very high sensitivity to disturbance because of slow or no recovery potential)

Opportunistic species – r – selected	Climax species – K – selected
Dominant in disturbed habitats	Generally occur in stable habitats
Small body size	Large body size, often mobile
Short lifespan, normally <1 year	Long lifespan, >1 to many years
Early and frequent reproduction	Delayed and less frequent reproduction
Rapid growth to maturity	Slow growth
High rates of natural mortality	Low rates of natural mortality
Population size fluctuates	Population sizes relatively stable

Concepts for developing sensitivity rankings developed from the mid 1990s onwards. MacDonald *et al.* (1996) put forward a way of assessing sensitivity in relation to fishing, while Hiscock (1999) looked at the importance of life cycles of species in identifying sensitive areas. The core work in the first ten years of the MarLIN programme was identification of the sensitivity of species and biotopes, especially those that were designated in some way for protection or action (Hiscock and Tyler-Walters, 2006). Those approaches and assessments have, in the UK, been widely developed and used in prioritising species for action.

The assessment rationale developed in the MarLIN programme involves judging the intolerance of a species to change in an external factor arising from human activities or natural events. The rationale then assesses the likely recoverability of the species following cessation of the human activity or natural event. Intolerance and recoverability are then combined to provide a meaningful assessment of their overall sensitivity to environmental change. Examples of species that rank as 'Very high' and 'Low' sensitivity are shown in Plates 53 and 54. The process provides a structured way of assessing sensitivity that can be used in environmental assessments, in the identification of sensitive features for protection and in the assessment of 'quality' (the more sensitive features present, the less disturbed the habitat is likely to be).

The process is described on the MarLIN website (www.marlin.ac.uk/sensitivityrationale. php), where examples of the assessed sensitivity of species and biotopes can also be accessed (www.marlin.ac.uk/bacs.php). Table 7.3 shows the matrix of intolerance against recoverability rankings that identifies sensitivity levels.

The likely intolerance of a species is assessed with respect to a specified magnitude and duration of change ('benchmarks') for the 24 separate environmental factors listed in the 'checklist of environmental factors likely to cause change' in Chapter 6, p 98–99.

'Intolerance' is assessed against the following definitions (intolerance is expressed in relation to change in a specific factor):

Rank	Definition
High	The species population is likely to be killed/destroyed by the factor under consideration.
Intermediate	Some individuals of the species may be killed/destroyed by the factor under consideration and the viability of a species population may be reduced.
Low	The species population will not be killed/destroyed by the factor under consideration. However, the viability of a species population will be reduced.

Rank	Definition
Tolerant	The factor does not have a detectable effect on survival or viability of a species or structure and functioning of a biotope.
Tolerant*	Population of a species may increase in abundance or biomass as a result of the factor.
Not relevant	The rating applies to species where the factor is not relevant because they are protected from the factor (for instance, through a burrowing habit), or can move away from the factor.

'Recoverability' is assessed against the following definitions:

Rank	Definition
None	Recovery is not possible.
Very low/none	Partial recovery is only likely to occur after about 10 years and full recovery may take over 25 years or never occur.
Low	Only partial recovery is likely within 10 years and full recovery is likely to take 25 years.
Moderate	Only partial recovery is likely within 5 years and full recovery is likely to take up to 10 years.
High	Full recovery will occur but will take many months (or more likely years), but should be complete within about 5 years.
Very high	Full recovery is likely within a few weeks or, at most, 6 months.
Immediate	Recovery immediate or within a few days.
Not relevant	For when 'sensitivity' is not relevant or cannot be assessed. Recoverability cannot have a value if there is no sensitivity and is thus 'Not relevant'.

Table 7.3 Combining 'intolerance' and 'recoverability' assessments to determine 'sensitivity'

		Recoverability						
		None	Very low	Low	Moderate	High	Very high	Immediate
			(>25 yr.)	(>10–25 yr.)	(>5–10 yr.)	(1–5 yr.)	(<1 yr.)	(<1 week)
Intolerance	High	Very high	Very high	High	Moderate	Moderate	Low	Very low
	Intermediate	Very high	High	High	Moderate	Low	Low	Very low
	Low	High	Moderate	Moderate	Low	Low	Very low	Not sensitive
	Tolerant	Not sensitive	Not sensitive	Not sensitive	Not sensitive	Not sensitive	Not sensitive	Not sensitive
	Tolerant*	Not sensitive*	Not sensitive*	Not sensitive*	Not sensitive*	Not sensitive*	Not sensitive*	Not sensitive*
	Not relevant	Not relevant	Not relevant	Not relevant	Not relevant	Not relevant	Not relevant	Not relevant

Source: www.marlin.ac.uk/sensitivityrationale.php

Note: * likely increase.

Assessing the sensitivity of habitats

To assess the sensitivity of habitats (as biotopes), we take key structural, key functional and characterising species that have sensitivity assessments and use those species to identify sensitivity of a biotope.

Using sensitivity assessments to identify conservation action

Sensitivity assessments are a time-consuming process. In the MarLIN programme, it took about five days of research per species to identify sources of information on traits, experimental studies or case histories, etc. that were relevant to a particular species and to populate the database that is behind the website. So, the programme concentrated on species that were UK Biodiversity Action Plan species and on key structural or functional species and species that were dominant in biotopes of conservation concern. The resource that is now available on the MarLIN website can inform a wide range of decision-making regarding likelihood of damage to features as a part of environmental assessments. Information on sensitivity of species and habitats can be tabulated and mapped to provide aids to spatial planning. The information can also help to assess why a change (usually a decline) might have occurred. The way that the information can be used in decision-making is illustrated in Figure 7.4.

Sensitivity and 'indicator' species

It would seem easy, based on a knowledge of intolerance and recovery potential, to identify species that are indicators of specific damaging activities including input of contaminants. However, species may have considerable resistance to adverse factors, especially once they have settled and grown. A long-lived species may 'tough it out' in a compromised habitat and only show signs of reduced abundance when older individuals die and are not replaced by new recruits. That reduction in numbers might also be due to poor reproductive outputs in times of famine that result from natural long-term fluctuations in food sources, i.e. not a reaction to damaging activities. Attributing cause to effect will also be confused by the multiplicity of stressors that are likely to be affecting a location and by natural change. Furthermore, subtle effects are unlikely to be observed and, when effects are gross, it may be too late to take action. All in all, the concept that indicator species can be identified not only to tell us that something has 'gone wrong' but to suggest what has caused that 'something' should be treated with caution. Zettler *et al.* (2013, p1), having identified coincidental reasons for changes in species abundances along gradients, concluded:

> the following points have to be carefully considered when applying static indicator based quality indices: (1) species tolerances and preferences may change along environmental gradients and between different biogeographic regions, (2) as environment modifies species autecology, there is a need to adjust indicator species lists along major environmental gradients and (3) there is a risk of including sibling or cryptic species in calculating the index value of a species.

Traits-based information, especially where that has been translated into an assessment of sensitivity in relation to different factors, should enable the identification of species and habitats that are under threat (are 'vulnerable') if an activity is permitted in an area. Some of those species and habitats may also be rare or scarce and, altogether, signal that an activity should not be permitted in an area. The absence of relevant traits information is a problem for taking such action but, often, knowledge of the biology of similar species may be used as surrogate information.

All too often, even though the likely dire consequences (for biodiversity) of an activity are clear from our knowledge of the sensitivity of species and biotopes that occur in a location,

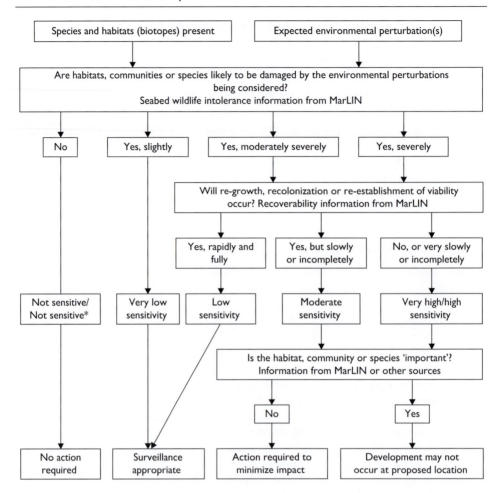

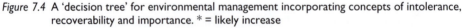

Figure 7.4 A 'decision tree' for environmental management incorporating concepts of intolerance, recoverability and importance. * = likely increase

Source: Redrawn from Hiscock and Tyler-Walters (2006).

those activities continue to be permitted. The obvious examples are historical whaling and the impact of mobile fishing gear on habitats such as coral gardens on seamounts, shellfish reefs and maerl beds. Examples have already been given in Chapter 5. However, no matter how good the science and how experienced the scientists, policymakers, often spurred on by commercial interests, demand evidence. Experimental studies are extremely valuable in producing that evidence. For instance, reefs of horse mussels, *Modiolus modiolus*, in the north-east Atlantic are ranked (by MarLIN), based on the biological traits of component species, as having 'Very high' sensitivity to substratum loss with recovery potential ranked as 'Very low/none' and an expected 'Major decline' in species richness. Many areas of horse mussel reefs have been destroyed and are not recovering (see 'Physical disturbance (benthic trawling and dredging)', Chapter 5, p67) at locations around the UK. In order to test what should have been reliable information based on experience in Northern Ireland especially and on traits-based assessment, Cook *et al.* (2013) undertook experimental trawling and scallop dredging once through beds of horse mussels. The trawls, in particular, dramatically reduced species richness and removed the key structural species. Having undertaken what, for ethical reasons, had to be a limited experimental study, they concluded (2013, p8):

> Calls for evidence-based conservation have acknowledged that conservation science lacks the resources to deliver meta-analyses in the same way as medical science, but limited scientific knowledge has long been used, for example, as an excuse to hinder the development of marine reserves.

Nevertheless, policy advisors can get it wrong and give science a bad name. For instance, reefs of the tube-building worm *Sabellaria spinulosa* in the north-east Atlantic are ephemeral and regrow very quickly after disturbance if the underlying habitat remains. They are a component of a sometimes rich community that develops on stable cobbles and sediments. But they are a 'biogenic reef' and these, which include coral reefs, are universally considered threatened. Anyone who looks at traits-based information on the species and the component species of the habitat will see that the *Sabellaria spinulosa* reefs are not threatened by single or short-term impacts and the conclusion must be that development which adversely affects (usually for a short while) the reefs is acceptable. Developers, however, have been required to divert pipelines and to remove and replace reefs (really clumps) of tube worms at great expense. Next time, when a development produces damage that really matters, the scientists may have difficulty making their case!

Conclusion: bringing measures of 'degree of threat', 'importance' and 'sensitivity' together

1 Protecting rare, declining or threatened species or habitats where they occur naturally is the most practical approach to ensuring their survival and viability.
2 Using terms such as 'rare' and 'scarce' or 'important for conservation' can be useful when speaking with policymakers and seeking support from the public, but they need to be based on meaningful (for conservation) science.
3 Established criteria can identify which are threatened species and habitats providing that there is quantitative information on their rarity or their historical decline: they are the species that are listed in directives, conventions and statutes. It is much more difficult to identify which are threatened species and habitats without quantitative information; but their 'sensitivity' to human activities – where sufficient information on relevant life history traits exists for species, including key functional or structural species in habitats – provides another way of identifying the need for conservation action.
4 Researching and cataloguing life history traits of a much larger number of species, especially key functional and structural species as well as rare and declining species, is an essential pre-requisite for identifying their sensitivity and the sensitivity of the biotopes that they occur in to human activities.
5 By bringing together measures of rarity, decline and sensitivity of species and habitats, decisions can be made about whether an activity or event being considered will 'matter' from the point of view of protecting biodiversity. The best course of action for protection will depend on the particular factors that a species or biotope is sensitive to. Figure 7.5 may help.

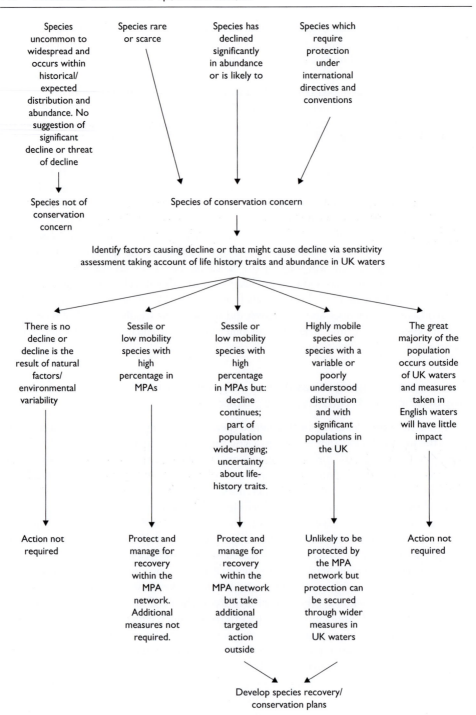

| Species uncommon to widespread and occurs within historical/ expected distribution and abundance. No suggestion of significant decline or threat of decline | Species rare or scarce | Species has declined significantly in abundance or is likely to | Species which require protection under international directives and conventions |

Species not of conservation concern

Species of conservation concern

Identify factors causing decline or that might cause decline via sensitivity assessment taking account of life history traits and abundance in UK waters

| There is no decline or decline is the result of natural factors/ environmental variability | Sessile or low mobility species with high percentage in MPAs | Sessile or low mobility species with high percentage in MPAs but: decline continues; part of population wide-ranging; uncertainty about life-history traits. | Highly mobile species or species with a variable or poorly understood distribution and with significant populations in the UK | The great majority of the population occurs outside of UK waters and measures taken in English waters will have little impact |

| Action not required | Protect and manage for recovery within the MPA network. Additional measures not required. | Protect and manage for recovery within the MPA network but take additional targeted action outside | Unlikely to be protected by the MPA network but protection can be secured through wider measures in UK waters | Action not required |

Develop species recovery/ conservation plans

Figure 7.5 A decision tree for the identification of species for conservation action including recovery measures.

Source: Based on Hiscock *et al.* (2013).

Plate 1. Aesthetic values. Colourful marine communities enrich our lives but may need protection. Corals, sponges and bryozoans. Portofino MPA, Italy.

Plate 2. Information and awareness. MPAs provide opportunities for education. The Marine Warden on Lundy, UK leading a snorkel safari.

Plate 3. Recreation and tourism. Symbolic and aesthetic values. Rich coral reefs are a major source of tourist income and public enjoyment. Maldives.

Plate 4. Food provision. 'Biodiversity' provides and supports a wide range of food including finfish, shellfish and algae. Valencia fish market, Spain.

Plate 5. Respect for nature (cognitive values). Coral community on a deep seamount where some individuals may be hundreds of years old but highly susceptible to bottom fishing (see Clark et al., 2010). Source: Ifremer Victor 6000/ German-French ARK-XIX/3a cruise.

Plate 6. Coastal protection and life cycle maintenance. Some habitats such as seagrass beds are critical as nurseries and for the food of some threatened species as well as consolidating sediments enhancing diversity and providing coastal protection. Eleuthera, Bahamas.

Plate 7. 'What is where' needs a vocabulary to name similar entities. Biotope classifications provide that vocabulary in a hierarchical way. See Connor *et al.* (2004). The biotope *Eunicella verrucosa* and *Pentapora foliacea* on wave-exposed circalittoral rock (CR.HCR.XFa.ByErSp.Eun) at Stoke Point, southern England. See Figure 2.3.

Plate 8. The UK National Biodiversity Network (http://data.nbn.org.uk) collates and disseminates information on species distributions and abundances. Here, the recorded distribution of a UK Biodiversity Action Plan species, the pink sea fan *Eunicella verrucosa*, and the locations of two types of MPA in south-west England have been brought together to demonstrate coincidence of protected areas and a protected species. *Source*: UK National Biodiversity Network.

Plate 9. Historic records provide reference data and help understand change. Rarely recorded clumps of *Serpula vermicularis* can still be found in Torbay, UK from where they were first sampled (and illustrated) in 1856. *Source:* Gosse (1865).

Plate 10. Surveys that involve large vessels with offshore capability are expensive but necessary. Here, a Hamon grab is being deployed from FRV *Cefas Endeavour* to collect samples in an area subject to spoil disposal. The records of species present add to our knowledge of biodiversity.

Plate 11. Quantitative *in situ* marine biological surveys may require complex logistical and safety considerations as well as experienced personnel. Preparing to dive on a monitoring site in Milford Haven, Wales.

Plate 12. 'Bioblitz' surveys engage professional and volunteer recorders to inventory the flora and fauna of an area over, usually, 24 hours, providing a reference point for future surveys. *Source:* Jack Sewell.

Plate 13. Kelp forests include key structural species that provide shelter and habitat to support rich communities in temperate to polar regions. Here, at Akselsundet in Svalbard.

Plate 14. Plants and animals offer refuges to other species. Sea anemones and clown fish in the Maldives.

Plate 15. The crown of thorns starfish is a key functional species that feeds on coral and has occasional outbursts (see Timmers et al., 2012) causing mortality and loss of reef. Daedelus Reef, Red Sea.

Plate 16. Burrowing sea urchins, Echinocardium cordatum, enhance oxygen transport in sediments and cycle nutrients but are susceptible to mobile fishing gear (see Osinga et al., 1995).

Plate 17. A solitary gooseneck barnacle, Pollicipes pollicipes, in south-west England: one of very few individuals probably brought by occasional strong currents from mainland Europe and that are not viable populations.

Plate 18. A grey trigger fish, Balistes capriscus, in a marina in south-west England. They 'arrive' from May onwards but many are cast up dead in mid-winter. They are a vagrant in Britain that does not, apparently, breed.

Plate 19. The yellow cluster anemone, *Parazoanthus axinellae*, persists where they occur but in variable abundance, demonstrating 'intermediate' levels of stability (see Burton *et al.*, 2014 and Figure 4.1).

Plate 20. The stagshorn sponge *Axinella dissimilis* grows at a rate of less than 1mm a year (see Fowler and Laffoley, 1993). Individuals may persist for hundreds of years and natural change in abundance would not be expected.

Plate 21. Maerl beds (this is *Phymatolithon calcareum*) are very long-lived and persist over hundreds of years. Growth of each branch is about 0.5 to 1.5mm a year (see Blake and Maggs, 2003).

Plate 22. Storms cause occasional 'wash outs' of fauna that are not, therefore, the results of human activities causing change.

Plate 23. Standard plankton hauls reveal years in which plankton (mainly copepod Crustacea and pilchard eggs here) are abundant and many in between where they are scarce, creating 'feast and famine' for species that feed on plankton (see Southward *et al.*, 2005). *Source:* Alan Southward.

Plate 24. Changing physical processes outside of enclosed inlets is unusual but, here, a solid causeway prevents water flow between islands. Eriskay, Outer Hebrides, Scotland. *Source:* Sue Scott.

Plates 25 and 26. Impact of a warming event on shallow algal communities in Western Australia. (a) Prior to warming, a closed canopy of *Scytothalia dorycarpa* and *Ecklonia radiata* and (b) after warming showing large gaps where *S. dorycarpa* was eradicated. See Smale and Wernberg (2013). *Source:* Thomas Wernberg.

Plate 27. Dead *Paramuricea clavata* in the Portofino MPA after a disease event (see Garrabou *et al.*, 2009). Such events may be natural and happen every few decades but may be exacerbated by warming and/or eutrophication.

Plate 28. Many shallow water temperate habitats are characterised by a balance between algae and sea urchins that may change naturally from time to time. Hammerfest, Norway. See Christie *et al.* (1995). *Source:* Hartvig Christie.

HUMAN IMPACTS

Plate 29. Part of Gothenburg Port in Sweden. Harbour developments have covered over extensive intertidal habitats. *Source:* Harvey Tyler-Walters.

Plate 30. Coastal defences cover over natural habitats and create new ones. Le Lavandou, France. See Dugan *et al.* (2011) for the extent and impacts of coastal development around the world.

Plate 31. Capital and maintenance dredging in ports is a source of habitat loss and continued habitat disturbance. Here, in Plymouth Sound MPA, a rocky reef is being deepened to accommodate a new ferry route.

Plate 32. Structurally complex features of the seabed (that support high species diversity) have been lost as a result of mobile fishing gear. A boulder with encrusting marine life waiting for disposal at Plymouth fish market, UK.

Plate 33. Deep water coral community tangled in discarded fishing gear. See: Clark *et al.* (2010). *Source:* Ifremer Victor 6000/German-French ARK-XIX/3a cruise.

Plate 34. Track of a scallop dredge through a bed of maerl causing loss of biogenic habitat and smothering (see Hall-Spencer and Moore, 2000). *Source*: Jason Hall-Spencer.

Plate 35. Fan mussels, *Atrina fragilis*, impaled on a Rapido Dredge (see Pranovi *et al.*, 2000). Dredges that penetrate the seabed are highly destructive. *Source*: Jason Hall-Spencer.

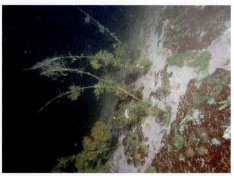

Plate 36. Dead and fouled sea whips, *Primnoella chilensis*, near a fish farm north of Punto Llonosa in Comau Fjord, Chile. Fish farming contaminates the environment through waste food, fish faeces and pharmaceutical products.

Plate 37. Listed as one of the top 100 invasive species in the world (see Lowe *et al.*, 2000), *Undaria pinnatifida* (wakame) was discovered for the first time near Plymouth, England in 2003 and is now widespread there.

Plate 38. Rock (Pacific) oysters, *Crassostrea gigas*, settle on shores especially near to oyster farms and can become dominant, displacing native species. Noss Mayo, south-west England.

Plate 39. The aggressive aquarium variety of the alga *Caulerpa taxifolia* was released from the aquarium at Monaco and is now widespread in the Mediterranean (see Rilov and Galil, 2009). Zante, Greece.

Plate 40. Indo-Pacific lionfish (*Pterois volitans* and *P. miles*), were first reported in the Caribbean in 1985, probably from aquarium releases. They feast on native fish and have no natural predators (see Albins and Hixon, 2008). Daraha, Red Sea.

Plate 41. The non-native bryozoan *Tricellaria inopinata* attached to a recreational vessel that will travel from marina to marina spreading its occurrence and dominating some communities.

Plate 42. The anti-fouling paint Tri-butyl Tin (now widely banned) caused imposex in dogwhelks (see Bryan *et al.* 1986), preventing egg laying, but also caused widespread depletion of other species (see Rees *et al.*, 2001).

Plate 43. The Sea Empress oil spill in February 1996 released 72,000 tons of crude oil into the sea around the Pembrokeshire (Wales) National Park resulting in extensive changes to shore life. *Source*: Blaise Bullimore.

Plate 44. The Christos Bitas oil spill in 1978 resulted in deaths of wildlife including birds and seals. Animal welfare issues come to the fore in such events but recovery of those vertebrate populations will be in a few years.

Plate 45. The results of a spill of refined products in Milford Haven, west Wales. Bleached algae and limpet scars are visible. However, recovery from oil spills may occur within less than five years (see Southward, 1979; Moore, 2006).

Plate 46. Sand and gravel extraction: the dredged sediment may be screened to preferentially load particular grades of aggregate. Biological recovery of dredged seabed may take from 5 to 12 years (see Foden *et al.*, 2009). *Source*: British Marine Aggregate Producers Association.

Plate 47. Offshore structures act as artificial reefs for colonisation of hard substratum species and attract fish where previously only sediment communities may have existed. Is that 'good' for biodiversity?

Plate 48. The nationally scarce (in Britain) coral *Caryophyllia inornata* present inside a wreck at Lundy, UK. Wrecks and other artificial substrata seem a preferred habitat and 'clean-up' may present a dilemma for conservation.

'THREATENED' AND 'SENSITIVE' SPECIES AND HABITATS

Plate 49. Species living in polar and tropical regions are likely to be most sensitive to ocean warming because of poor acclimation to change (see Peck *et al.*, 2014). Seabed community, Antarctic Peninsula.

Plate 50. The IUCN Red List currently includes mainly vertebrate and coral reef species. The hawksbill turtle *Eretmochelys imbricata* is listed as 'Critically Endangered' (see www.iucnredlist.org). Maldives.

Plate 51. *Cryptocorynetes longulus*, one of three known species in the genus belonging to a class of Crustacea first described from cave systems in the Bahamas as recently as 1981 (Yager, 1981). See Wollermann *et al.* (2007). Marine species endemic to isolated locations are unusual and their habitats important to protect. *Source:* Tom Iliffe.

Plate 52. *Tambja mullineri*, a sea slug endemic to the Galapagos Islands where nearly 20% of marine species are endemic to the archipelago. Such endemicity gives a special responsibility to governing authorities. See www.galapagos. org and www.seaslugforum.net/find/tambmull.

Plate 53. *Leptopsammia pruvoti* is a solitary coral that is nationally rare in Britain with localised populations, some of which recruit infrequently. It has 'Very High' sensitivity to physical disturbance (www.marlin.ac.uk) and may need special measures to protect populations.

Plate 54. Honeycomb worm, *Sabellaria alveolata*, reefs are a type of biogenic reef and are listed as of conservation importance in the UK. They have 'Low' sensitivity to physical disturbance (www.marlin.ac.uk) and special measures to protect reefs may not be needed.

SAMPLING AND RECORDING

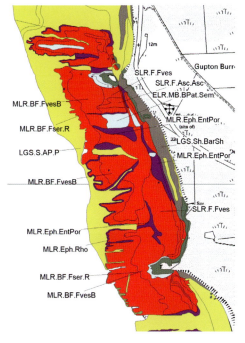

Plate 55. One of the starting points for Phase 1 intertidal survey – an aerial photograph (see Wyn *et al.*, 2006).
Source: Natural Resources Wales.

Plate 56. After survey – the map provides information on the location and extent of biotopes (see Wyn *et al.*, 2006). *Source*: Natural Resources Wales. Map: © Crown copyright 2014. Ordnance Survey Licence Number 100055079.

Plate 57. Citizen science can play a large role in marine conservation. A recreational diver recording habitats and marine life during a Phase 1 Seasearch survey (www.seasearch.org.uk) dive. *Source*: Richard Morton/Seasearch.

Plate 58. Towed video arrays provide the opportunity to image extensive areas for survey and monitoring. This rig is used to survey areas now closed to scallop dredging in Lyme Bay, UK (see Sheehan *et al.*, 2013a). *Source*: Colin Munro.

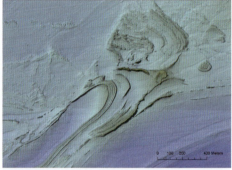

Plate 59. Autonomous Underwater Vehicles may provide a rapid way of surveying habitats underwater. Here, off south-eastern Australia (see http://imos.org.au/auv.html). *Source*: Stefan Williams.

Plate 60. Multibeam image of the seabed. Acoustic survey can identify reef areas for targeted survey and for mobile fishing gear exclusion zones (see Sheehan *et al.*, 2013a). Here, in Lyme Bay, south-west England. *Source*: Natural England.

Plate 61. Phase 2 surveys document the abundance of species at a location and require experienced personnel. Here, surveying algae at Lundy, UK.

Plate 62. Taking stereo pairs of photographs as a part of a study following changes in rock wall communities in Sweden in 1980. Such studies help to understand natural fluctuations and longevity of communities (see Lundälv, 1985).

Plate 63. Selection of MPAs involves the application of 'ecological' criteria such as representativeness, naturalness, rarity, diversity and sensitivity and socio-economic considerations that are brought together by stakeholder groups. *Source:* Peter Jones.

Plate 64. Cuttlefish, *Sepia officinalis*, are one of very few invertebrates that have distinct breeding and resting areas and therefore direct 'connectivity' (often a MPA design criterion) between two locations (see Pawson, 1995). Female and two males in Torbay, south-west England.

Plate 65. A rich community of sponges with anthozoans and bryozoans that 'shouts' 'biodiversity hotspot' to the experienced observer. The location included several nationally rare and scarce species, a new record for Britain and a species only known from six locations in the world. The biotope occurs within the Isles of Scilly Special Area of Conservation.

Plate 66. Enforcement of regulations is essential if MPAs are to be successful. That enforcement might mean patrols and reacting to calls from the public. Here, a patrol boat in the first marine park in Europe at Port Cros, France, in 2013, 50 years after establishment.

Plate 67. Monitoring is needed to assess the success of conservation measures. The abundance and size of lobsters and their movements have been studied in the No-Take Zone at Lundy since its establishment in 2003 (see Hoskin *et al.*, 2011). *Source:* Devon and Severn Inshore Fisheries and Conservation Authority.

RECOVERY, RESTORATION AND REPLACEMENT

Plate 68. Artificial reefs colonise quickly and provide information on likely recovery rates of damaged habitats but do not mimic natural habitats (see Hiscock *et al.*, 2010). Ex-*HMS Scylla* near Plymouth, UK.

Plate 69. Colonisation on new surfaces can be very rapid but in this case (a sunken warship with TBT antifouling paint at least 25 years old) has only occurred on surfaces with non-toxic paint or where corrosion has occurred.

Plate 70. Urchin barrens in the vicinity of the marine reserve at Leigh, New Zealand a few years after the reserve was created in 1975 and before snapper populations had recovered (see Leleu *et al.*, 2012). *Source*: Roger Grace.

Plate 71. When populations of snapper (and spiny lobsters) recovered and individuals were large enough to eat urchins within the now strictly protected reserve, the kelp forest recovered (see Leleu *et al.*, 2012). *Source*: Roger Grace.

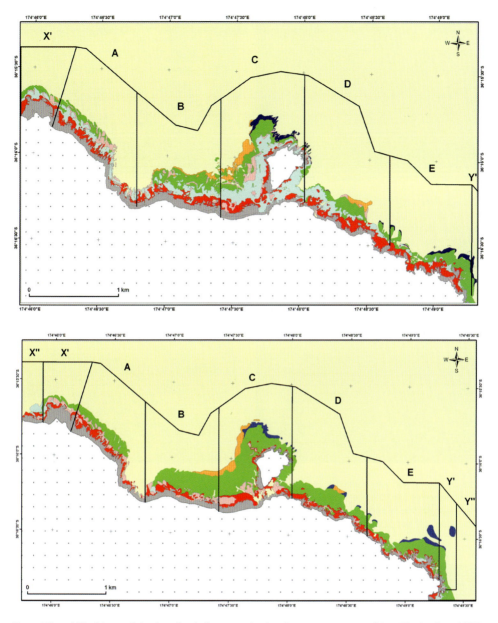

Plates 72 and 73. Maps of the benthic habitats in the Leigh marine reserve (New Zealand) in 1977 (upper) and 2006 (lower). Land is stippled. Sediment (sand, gravel, cobble) is yellow; deep-reef is dark blue; sponge garden is orange; kelp is green; urchin barren is pale blue; crustose algae are pink; mixed algal turf and *Carpophyllum* are red, and intertidal areas are grey. The urchin barrens have been replaced by kelp forest following protection. *Source:* Leleu *et al.* (2012).

Plate 74. The pink sea fan *Eunicella verrucosa* did not settle on ex-*HMS Scylla* until the fourth year after it had been sunk in 2004, perhaps reflecting sporadic recruitment events in a colonisation process. Image taken in October 2013 (see Hiscock *et al.*, 2010).

Plate 75. The scarlet and gold star coral *Balanophyllia regia* occurs in isolated groups that appear to be self-recruiting. Some locations for the coral have been known for more than 100 years (see Hiscock, 2012). Recovery, if whole colonies are lost, seems unlikely.

Plate 76. Diver carrying out routine maintenance of corals being reared on trays in a floating nursery and to be transplanted to damaged reef (see Edwards, 2010). *Source*: Shai Shafir.

Plate 77. Coastal defences can be designed to be more 'friendly' to nature (see Firth *et al.*, 2013). *Source*: Louise Firth.

Plates 78 and 79. Harbour constructions can incorporate features that will be colonised by species that require submerged intertidal habitats. Sydney Harbour (see Chapman and Underwood, 2011). *Source*: Gee Chapman.

Chapter 8

Sampling and recording

Introduction and overarching issues

Sampling and recording are essential activities for characterising the biodiversity of a location, identifying distinctly different assemblages of species and establishing where there are rare or threatened species and habitats. This chapter gives examples of the hierarchical way in which surveys may be undertaken and the methods that may be used, but it is critical of some techniques that may be cherished but do not deliver the information or evidence required for conservation. It finishes by providing examples of matching survey methods to conservation objectives. The surveys described in this chapter are descriptive surveys and, although they can be repeated to identify change, are not the monitoring studies described in Chapter 10. Neither is this chapter about the technical application of equipment or the identification of methods according to the statistics that are used to analyse data. That information can be found in volumes such as Eleftheriou (2013).

The chapter emphasises that what is sampled and recorded will depend on the aims and objectives of the work, and the objectives have to be clear – they will drive the techniques that are used, the skills required of the personnel and the equipment that is needed. This chapter is, or tries to be, realistic about the particular difficulties of working in the marine environment where almost all of the nature conservation resource is out of sight and that which is accessible from land is often inundated by the tide every 12 hours or so.

There are advantages and disadvantages to all techniques and there are compromises to be made that hinge on size of budget, skills of personnel and the equipment available. There are also stepwise approaches to collecting information that start with gathering coarse data and then homing in on the acquisition of finer, more targeted data wherever possible in ways that are accurate and/or statistically robust. Equipment available to undertake survey work is constantly developing, especially remotely operated visualisation equipment.

'Citizen science' is a relevant and often highly productive way of collecting information. Such activities include reporting schemes (both for occurrence records and for observations of seasonal change, behaviour, etc.) and public engagement/education schemes that encourage sea users and everyone who has an interest in the sea not only to collect data and information but to show a duty of care to the marine environment and the species in it. Reporting schemes also include survey – both by volunteers and by professional marine biologists undertaking *in situ* survey and monitoring. They range from regional schemes such as the Big Sea Survey (www.bigseasurvey.co.uk) to international projects such as Reef Check (www.reefcheck.org).

Common standards are important. Surveyors need to 'speak the same language' so that results can be compared effectively. The same language includes for the naming of species and, at least on a regional basis, for biotopes (see the section on 'Biotopes' in Chapter 2, p13). If descriptive surveys and some monitoring surveys are to use scales of abundance, then one scale needs to be agreed. Ensuring data quality requires training, experience and discipline. Validation systems are important for observations that may be used in site description or interpreting change. To make most use of the data that are collected during surveys, there is great benefit in adopting a common data standard and a common data entry platform at least on a national level.

Manuals that include checklists of equipment needed, the skill level of surveyors required and procedures to be followed will be available, linked to survey, surveillance and monitoring imperatives in many countries. In the UK, the procedural guidelines associated with the Marine Monitoring Handbook (Davies *et al.*, 2001) are, to an extent, kept up to date and can be found at: http://jncc.defra.gov.uk/page-2430. In California, monitoring protocols for rocky intertidal areas have been developed (Engle, 2008). Worldwide, the NaGISA protocol (http://nagisa.cbm.usb.ve/cms) was developed to inventory biodiversity in coastal habitats as a part of the Census of Marine Life.

Survey and surveillance

Introduction

There are three major areas of activity in relation to biodiversity conservation that involve sampling and recording: survey, surveillance and monitoring. Those three activities may be interpreted in different ways in different directives, conventions and statutes and in the minds of different policy advisors and scientists. It would not be productive to review those viewpoints. The meanings given in this volume are:

- Survey is undertaken as a single event at a particular location with the objective of describing the character of that area, site or feature (original definition).
- Surveillance is a continued programme of biological surveys, systematically undertaken to provide a series of observations in time (Davies *et al.*, 2001).
- Monitoring is surveillance undertaken to ensure that formulated standards are being maintained (Davies *et al.*, 2001).

The monitoring referred to here is of the state of the environment and not of the performance of management measures.

Survey (including structured observation) has several potential aims; for instance:

- identifying the broad biological and physical characteristics of an area;
- measuring 'richness' and 'diversity' (which can be of habitats or of species);
- identifying degree of change in a community or the abundance of certain species;
- providing the information necessary to report on whether good ecological/environmental status of an area has been achieved, including meeting targets;
- documenting events that help us to understand 'change' (for instance, reproductive events including mass settlements; disease events including mass mortalities; impacts from human activities).

Those broad aims need to be converted into objectives that identify how the aims are going to be achieved via specific actions. Those objectives need to be 'SMART' (Specific, Measurable, Attainable, Relevant/Realistic and Time-bound). 'Time-bound' usually refers to completion by a certain time or according to a particular frequency, and will be determined by the nature of the work, from (for instance) answering questions about seasonal occurrence in an academic study through to achieving the reporting schedule required by a regulatory authority. In conservation (rather than academic or curiosity-led) research, the measures used and the results obtained need to tell management something: they are driven by 'operational objectives'.

Is survey or surveillance needed to inform management?

Survey, including repeat survey for monitoring, is potentially very expensive, especially in the marine environment. In terms of informing marine conservation, answering the following questions may help to keep both policy advisors and surveyors on track:

- What are the policy objectives to be addressed?
- What are the conservation objectives to be addressed?
- Can those policy and conservation objectives be answered without survey and/or monitoring?
- Can those policy and conservation objectives be addressed by accessing/analysing existing data and information?
- Are there support tools (lists of indicator species, methodological guidelines, etc.) that can be matched to policy and conservation objectives and used in survey?
- What are the methodological options for survey and/or monitoring (including frequency of survey and longevity)?
- What is the likely accuracy of outputs from the different methodological options?
- Can the techniques used provide some net gain for conservation (improving conservation science, creating educational material, wider application including cost savings in the future, etc.)?
- Are the skills (personnel) and equipment available to undertake survey and/or monitoring?
- What is the cost of each of the methodological options?

Information on what habitats are where and how extensive they are can sometimes be obtained without new survey – existing aerial photographs and detailed maps or charts may provide the necessary information. Often, asking fishermen or divers or rock poolers will point to where particular features are. When assessing impacts of human activities, the likely impact is obvious to any experienced ecologist: for instance, if you drag a heavy sharp dredge over a reef colonised by erect fragile species, those species will be destroyed and management action will be necessary. But, even in such obvious examples of applying common sense and experience, 'evidence' of the effects of the activity is likely to be demanded. Such evidence will be worthwhile as it will identify the degree of damage, what is being damaged and the prospects for recovery (see, for instance, Hall-Spencer and Moore, 2000; Boulcott and Howell, 2011; Cook et al., 2013; Sheehan et al., 2013). Follow-up studies may be important to record and possibly inform recovery: an unlikely commitment in studies which are frequently undertaken as a part of a PhD lasting three years or, often, in statutory bodies with changing personnel. There may also be sufficient evidence from past observational studies or chance observations which will be sufficient to feed into management for conservation. Such observations are often dismissed as 'anecdotal' but – backed up by knowledge that the individuals making the observation are reliable – are valid. Some examples of time and money wasted are difficult to understand: for instance, undertaking expensive acoustic survey to establish whether erect rock reefs are still occupying the same area in locations unaffected by potentially damaging activities.

Survey

Introduction

The significance of understanding 'what is where' was outlined in Chapter 2. Establishing what is where relies on gathering together existing data and, wherever possible, filling gaps in knowledge with new survey work. The data and information gathered together for biodiversity conservation needs to inform:

- the location and extent of broadscale habitats ('Level 3' biotopes in the example classification given in Figure 2.4);
- the location and, for intertidal areas at least, extent of Level 5 biotopes, especially in MPAs;
- the character (composition, abundance of characterising species) of Level 5–7 biotopes present in an area, for instance, an enclosed area of coast, a prospective MPA;
- the occurrence of any special features such as rare or fragile habitats and species, including their abundance and distribution.

Survey that is going to be used to identify the possible location of a series of MPAs is usually divided into parts of the coastline that represent distinctly different physiographic features and biogeographical areas within which representative MPAs will be located (see Figures 2.2 and 9.2). In the case of the Marine Nature Conservation Review of Great Britain (MNCR) (Hiscock, 1996), there were 15 coastal sectors for the 19,000km of coastline and inshore waters of England, Scotland and Wales.

Phase 1 survey – habitats

Surveys that map habitat types are often described as 'Phase 1' surveys and provide the information needed to target more detailed 'Phase 2' surveys that will inventory the species present in different habitats. Knowing where the broadscale habitats are acts as a means of identifying representative locations for conservation; although the finer the classification that can be used, the more thorough is the representation in any series of MPAs. However, there is rarely a national coverage of survey data available to identify the characteristics of any but a few well-studied locations. Using environmental variables as indirect surrogates for biodiversity is being developed (see, for instance, Pitcher *et al.*, 2012) but is fraught with difficulties and often ends up with very low confidence results. Often, it is the experienced naturalist who can describe what habitats are where.

On the shore, the possibility of mapping broadscale or more fine-scale habitats is made possible with the help of aerial survey followed by ground truthing when the tide is out. In

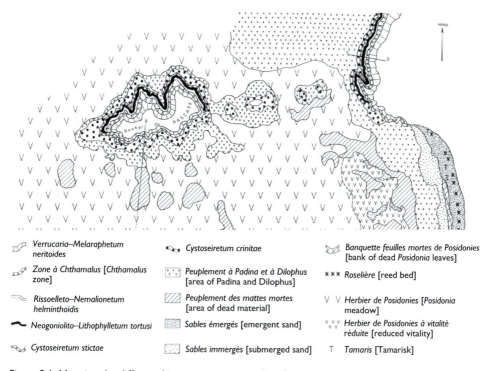

Verrucaria–Melaraphetum neritoides

Zone à Chthamalus [Chthamalus zone]

Rissoelleto–Nemalionetum helminthoidis

Neogoniolito–Lithophylletum tortusi

Cystoseiretum stictae

Cystoseiretum crinitae

Peuplement à Padina et à Dilophus [area of Padina and Dilophus]

Peuplement des mattes mortes [area of dead material]

Sables émergés [emergent sand]

Sables immergés [submerged sand]

Banquette feuilles mortes de Posidonies [bank of dead Posidonia leaves]

Roselière [reed bed]

Herbier de Posidonies [Posidonia meadow]

Herbier de Posidonies à vitalitè rèduite [reduced vitality]

Tamaris [Tamarisk]

Figure 8.1 Mapping the different biotopes in an area identifies their extent (including that of rare ones that might need protection), identifies representative locations for more detailed inventory of species and provides a reference point for future surveys to identify change. One of the earliest areas with a marine component to be identified as a national park was at Port-Cros off the Mediterranean coast of France. Part of a map of biotopes (as biocénoses) from the north coast of Port-Cros. The naming of biocénoses uses a phytosociological nomenclature.

Source: Reformatted from Augier and Boudouresque (1967).

locations where the water is clear, such aerial survey can also be used for shallow subtidal habitats although ground truthing is, again, very important. Phase 1 survey for intertidal areas is exemplified in temperate regions with tidal excursions by work undertaken in Wales (Wyn *et al.*, 2006). There will be many other examples including of subtidal areas using divers in temperate (for instance, Figure 8.1) and tropical areas. However, working underwater is difficult and mapping can usually only be done in clear warm waters and with some reliable way of position fixing. More often, phase 1 survey will be by spot dives searching a carefully georeferenced area and often by volunteer divers (for instance, Plate 57).

Mapping subtidal habitats, especially deeper than snorkeling depths or in poor underwater visibility or where it is desired to map a large area, is best undertaken by remote sampling which means taking grab or dredge samples for sediment habitats or using remote operated vehicles (ROVs), automated underwater vehicles, drop-down video or towed video for sediments and hard substrata (Plates 58 and 59). In shallow tropical waters especially, divers can be used providing that accurate position fixing is possible. The cost of *in situ* sampling (grab sampling, drop-down video, diver surveys) may be high and the results difficult to extrapolate to a large area. Those problems have led to more extensive use of

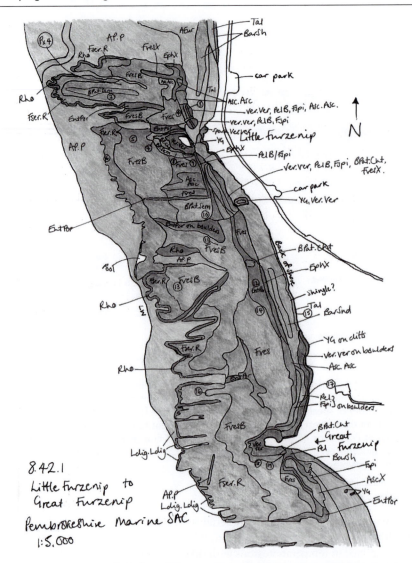

Figure 8.2 Phase 1 survey results before GIS output for a part of the coast of Wales showing codes for biotopes (Connor *et al.*, 2004). The surveyors had outlines of major shore cover types derived from aerial photographs as a starting point. The aerial photograph and coloured biotope map are shown in Plates 55 and 56.

Source: Wyn *et al.* (2006).

acoustic survey techniques since the 1990s. The results from multibeam sonar (Plate 60) are impressive for topographically complex habitats such as reefs and enable targeted *in situ* survey (by drop-down video, ROV, towed video sledges or diving) to identify reef biotopes and, often, damage caused to biodiversity by human activities. However, the results from using backscatter data from multibeam sonar or using acoustic ground discrimination sonar (AGDS) to identify physical characteristics of the seabed, let alone their biology, may be relatively poor and highly variable (Wilding *et al.*, 2003), and they need to be treated with caution unless thoroughly ground truthed and interpreted by skilled operators. Nevertheless, Quintino *et al.* (2010, p602) mention several surveys as having 'shown the ability of the single-beam AGDS QTC VIEW Series V used in this work to distinguish different sediment types'. They used acoustic survey to obtain information on sediment grain size and on algal biomass in muddy and sandy sediments, including vegetated and non-vegetated seabed. However, unless ground truthed, the different signals obtained by AGDS cannot be mapped as 'biotopes'. Following a study that mapped fish habitats in the English Channel, van der Kooij *et al.* (2011, pp10–11) observe that: 'the tool should be used with caution. For accurate acoustic representation of the seabed, all influences on the echoes except those of the seabed sediments need to be excluded from the data.' All in all, the message from many studies is to treat with caution any interpretation of AGDS or backscatter data from multibeam sonar. Direct observation and sampling is the best way of obtaining scientifically robust results.

Phase 2 survey – species and biotopes

The purpose of a 'phase 2' survey ranges from identifying the occurrence and extent of a particular single species through to cataloguing the abundance of all of the species that can be sampled in a specific habitat (for instance, underboulder habitats) in a reasonable length of time. Phase 2 surveys (Plate 61) provide one type of survey data that can establish a baseline against which future change can be assessed. The full range of different levels of survey between those two extremes may all have their role in biodiversity conservation. The single-species survey may be of a plant or animal that is rare, scarce, in decline or that is indicating some change in condition (for instance a non-native species or a species sensitive to a human activity) of the area. The sampling of 'everything' may be a curiosity-driven study or, more likely, to establish the character of an area in terms of how rich the complement of species is there (for instance, in terms of biodiversity hotspots) or the quality of an area according to measures of species diversity or the presence of indicator species that may tell a manager about the existence of adverse pressures. An increasingly popular way of creating an inventory of the biodiversity in a prescribed small area (a bay, an island, etc.) is the 'bioblitz'. During the 24 hours of a bioblitz, experts in various groups of organisms together with sampling teams will record or collect for identification every species they find in the prescribed area.

Survey to describe the biological characteristics of an area has been undertaken for more than a hundred years – most often to establish ecological principles but sometimes to inventory the species in an area in a way that could be repeated to document change. In Ireland, the Royal Irish Academy's Clare Island Survey included 'the first detailed account of the algal associations of any areas of the British Isles' (Cotton, 1912, p12), whilst Southern (1915) described the fauna, including the account of 30 main types of habitat and association. Although the intention of the original survey may not have been to provide a reference point to record change, such surveys have often been repeated in recent years. For the Clare Island survey, Rindi and Guirey (2004) reported that they had recorded 223 species of algae compared to 224 recorded in the survey of 1910 and that 'the benthic algal assemblages of Clare Island still have basically the same structure and distribution as in 1910' (p471). In 1913, Petersen (1914) described the animal communities of the seabed in the semi-enclosed waters of the Kattegat off Denmark. Communities were characterised by the conspicuous organisms, particularly molluscs and echinoderms, present in samples.

However, in the resurvey of Petersen's stations by Pearson *et al.* (1985), the communities were very different to those sampled 70 years earlier: the result, it was believed, of eutrophication. There are examples of such 'foundation' and 'follow-up' surveys from all over the world. They help to characterise locations and to document change where it has occurred. Although simple lists of species present in such surveys are informative, quantitative or semi-quantitative survey methods are important to characterise different assemblages and, although not the reason for using them, to provide a better basis for later resurvey of sites that would identify the degree to which, if at all, they were different.

Phase 2 survey to provide information for the identification of MPAs is exemplified by the work of the MNCR which was commenced in 1987 by the Nature Conservancy Council with the objectives of:

- extending our knowledge of benthic marine habitats, communities and species in Great Britain, particularly through description of their characteristics, distribution and extent;
- identifying sites and species of nature conservation importance.

The MNCR finished in 1998 but the methods developed (see Hiscock, 1996, which includes recording forms, abundance scales, guidance on completion of forms and examples relevant to temperate and subtropical areas) continue to be used for descriptive survey and some monitoring today. Outputs from such surveys include the development of the Britain and Ireland biotopes classification, which provided the foundation for the marine part of the EUNIS classification (Davies *et al.*, 2004, maintained on: http://eunis.eea.europa.eu/habitats.jsp). The work was undertaken using experienced surveyors on the shore and, for reef habitats, divers in the shallow sublittoral. Excavation, core, grab and dredge sampling were used to characterise sediment habitats. The work was aimed at describing the range of inshore habitats and associated communities present around England, Scotland and Wales although the results from each survey site can be used as a reference point against which to identify change.

A significant problem with using a variety of techniques (grab sampling, video, *in situ* diver survey, etc.) and having species that occur as countable entities (density) and species that express themselves as cover, lies in bringing all of that disparate data together in a comparable way. Finding such measures is essential if survey data is to be analysed to identify biotopes. Producing a comparable scale will be fraught with difficulties of size of organisms (large organisms will never occur in such high densities as very small organisms) and inherent rarity (some species are never present in high densities: that is their nature). Also, in reducing detailed data to a comparable scale, the often valuable detail of exact counts of numbers is lost.

For surveys to support marine conservation and especially to compare locations and to identify biotopes, the most practical solution has been the abundance scale. Such scales started life after fieldworkers had been challenged to say what they meant by 'abundant', 'frequent', 'not uncommon', etc. It seems that the first abundance scales (for animals) in Britain were those of Crisp and Southward (1958). Similar scales, with algae, were used for characterising shores of different exposure (Ballantine, 1961) and, although really designed for student exercises studying zonation on shores, came to be used for surveillance of rocky shores in oil terminals (Crapp, 1973). There were more iterations over the years, including adding scales for sublittoral rocky areas, until 1990 when the MNCR settled on a scale; that scale (Table 8.1) was still in use in 2013 and, in Great Britain, should be continued for continuity.

Table 8.1 An abundance scale for application to survey data and that is comparable across different measures. Species named are examples only. S = Superabundant, A = Abundant, C = Common, F = Frequent, O = Occasional, R = Rare. From Hiscock (1996)

GROWTH FORM			SIZE OF INDIVIDUALS / COLONIES				
% COVER	CRUST / MEADOW	MASSIVE / TURF	< 1 cm	1–3 cm	3–15 cm	> 15 cm	DENSITY
> 80%	S	S	S				> 1 / 0.001 m^2
40–79%	A	A	A				1–9 / 0.001 m^2
20–39%	C	C	C				1–9 / 0.01 m^2
10–19%	F	F	F			S	1–9 / 0.1 m^2
5–9%	O	O	O			A	1–9 / m^2
1–5% or density	R	R	R			C	1–9 / 10 m^2
< 1% or density						F	1–9 / 100 m^2
						O	1–9 / 1000 m^2
						R	<1 / 1000 m^2
PORIFERA	Crusts *Halichondria*	Massive spp. *Pachymatisma*		Sml solitary *Grantia*	Lge solitary *Stelligera*		
HYDROZOA		Turf species *Tubularia* *Abietinaria*		Small clumps *Sarsia* *Aglaophenia*	Solitary *Corymorpha* *Nemertesia*		
ANTHOZOA	*Corynactis*	*Alcyonium*		Sml solitary *Epizoanthus* *Caryophyllia*	Med. solitary *Virgularia* *Cerianthus* *Urticina*	Large solitary *Eunicella* *Funiculina* *Pachycerianthus*	
ANNELIDA	*Sabellaria spinulosa*	*Sabellaria alveolata*	*Spirorbis*	Scale worms *Nephtys* *Pomatoceros*	*Chaetopterus* *Arenicola* *Sabella*		
CRUSTACEA	Barnacles Tube-dwelling amphipods		*Semibalanus* Amphipods	*B. balanus* *Anapagurus* *Pisidia*	*Pagurus* *Galathea* Small crabs	*Homarus* *Nephrops* *Hyas araneus*	
MOLLUSCA			Sml gastropod *L. neritoides*	Chitons Med. gastropods *Patella*	Lge gastropod *Buccinum*		

Table 8.1 (continued)

	GROWTH FORM		SIZE OF INDIVIDUALS / COLONIES				
% COVER	CRUST / MEADOW	MASSIVE / TURF	< 1 cm	1–3 cm	3–15 cm	> 15 cm	DENSITY
	Mytilus Modiolus		Sml bivalves Nucula	L. littorea Turritella Med. bivalves Mytilus Pododesmus Neocrania	Lge bivalves Mya Pecten Arctica		
BRACHIOPODA BRYOZOA	Crusts	Pentapora Bugula Flustra			Alcyonidium Porella		
ECHINODER- MATA				Echinocyamus Ocnus	Antedon Sml starfish Brittlestars Echinocardium Aslia Thyone	Large starfish Echinus Holothuria	
ASCIDIACEA	Colonial Dendrodoa			Sml solitary Dendrodoa	Lge solitary Ascidia Ciona	Diazona	
PISCES					Gobies Blennies	Dogfish Wrasse	
PLANTS	Crusts Maerl Audouinella Fucoids/Kelp Desmarestia	Foliose Filamentous			Zostera	Kelp Halidrys Chorda Himanthalia	

Abundance scale descriptive surveys are sometimes used to detect change by repeating the survey at the same location. Detecting change using data from surveys carried out by different people at different times is rarely straightforward. Whilst fully quantitative data – in which all organisms are carefully counted within sampling units such as quadrats – produces numbers that can be entered directly into a numerical or statistical analysis, the actual numbers recorded reflect many components of variability, ranging from unconscious observer bias to the complex interplay between environmental and biological heterogeneity in space and time, biological processes and interactions, and chance. It is often the case that, in order to carry out statistical analyses, the numbers have to be transformed to make them fit the assumptions of the particular test being carried out. Using an abundance scale is equivalent to transforming the numbers during the recording phase rather than during the analysis phase. The focus of disquiet with such data tends to be on recorder bias rather than factors influencing perceived abundances in the field. Although such bias may be controlled if the observers have the opportunity to cross-calibrate records or if an object that can be reanalysed, such as a photograph, underpins each sample, such controls are difficult to apply if the surveys being compared are widely separated in time or space. There are caveats associated with any sort of data – just be aware of them.

Surveillance

Programmes of biological surveys systematically undertaken to provide a series of observations in time may be academic studies aimed at understanding natural fluctuations including seasonal or longer-term changes, or they may be linked to regulatory regimes where the aim is to identify any unusual changes that might be associated with human activity. Such studies provide valuable background information for monitoring, perhaps allowing natural change (which does not require management action for biodiversity conservation) to be separated from human-induced change (which may require management action). So, although studies are often academic, they are still highly relevant to biodiversity conservation.

   In terms of the methods used, surveillance studies range from inspection (asking the question 'has anything changed?') through semi-quantitative studies using abundance scales, to fully quantitative sampling using fixed sites through to random sampling designs. Some examples of change identified by surveillance programmes are given in Chapter 4. The MarClim project (www.marclim.co.uk) is an example of a survey programme that uses a standard methodology to track climate change impacts in rocky intertidal habitats around the UK and Europe and provide long-term time-series data on biodiversity that is used by UK conservation agencies to track natural versus human-driven changes around the coastline. MarClim uses the SACFOR (Superabundant, Abundant, Common, Frequent, Occasional, Rare) scale (see Table 8.1) to assess abundance of seventy-five species of warm water, cold water and invasive origins, as well as replicated quadrat surveys of keystone limpet and barnacles, and replicated timed searches for climate indicator species of top shells. The data allow range shifts in response to climate change to be quantified and enables monitoring of population fluctuations and success of both habitat-forming and rare species across years and decades (Mieszkowska et al., 2006).

   Table 8.2 identifies surveillance objectives and links them to the sorts of methods that might be used to achieve those objectives. Reliable information obtained from surveillance feeds into 'adaptive management' (see Chapter 9).

Selection of methods

To ensure that the most meaningful and accurate information is obtained to support conservation, care is needed in deciding what methods are most feasible, statistically reliable and informative. Some techniques such as grab sampling and rocky shore and subtidal abundance scale surveys have well-established equipment and techniques. Others, such as acoustic survey, continue to develop.

At the end of the survey, reporting forms will need to be completed. If they are pre-existing standard forms, it is wise to make sure that you know what is in those forms before you design your programme!

'Attainable' (the 'A' in SMART) is important and encompasses practicality from an economical as well as a technical point of view. It is no use identifying a programme of stratified random sampling using quadrats if the number required to produce statistically meaningful results will be impossible to achieve within the constraints of time and budget.

Box 8.1 Determining appropriate methods

Fixed quadrat locations ensure that the same community and, if they are long-lived, the same individuals of a species are being recorded in surveillance or monitoring studies, but they suffer from concerns that they are not statistically representative of the whole community.

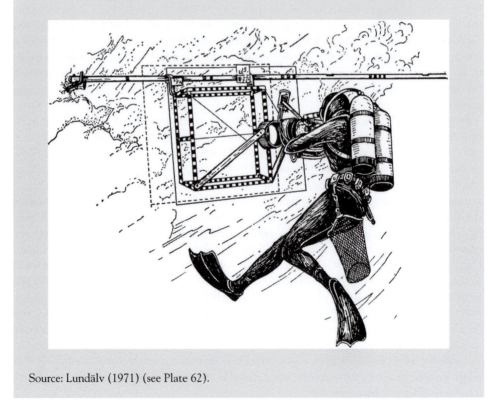

Source: Lundälv (1971) (see Plate 62).

Also, certain techniques have desirable advantages that outweigh the disadvantages. For instance, photographs of fixed quadrats (Plate 62) or viewpoint photographs may not have the statistical robustness of random quadrats but will show if the same individuals of a species are persistent, may show growth rates and may help with validation of identifications. If there are fixed quadrats at several locations all showing the same changes, that change is likely to be widespread; but fixed quadrats do have the disadvantage that they are representative just of that quadrat.

The taxonomic skills of survey personnel are very important. Whilst matching biotopes according to conspicuous species may be reasonably easy, identifying species in phase 2 survey or analysing samples to record species richness, calculate diversity indices, etc. requires a high level of knowledge and experience. Quality assurance measures are necessary during survey and in training exercises to ensure that results are sound and accurate. What should not happen though is selection of low level of survey so that it is within the skills of the operatives when the results will not provide meaningful information for conservation measures or reporting.

Matching methods to objectives

This chapter has already emphasised the importance of having SMART objectives and of matching survey methods to conservation objectives. That matching is done via establishing survey objectives, which may include targets. Identifying specific targets within objectives is challenging. Those targets may be to maintain the status quo or may be to return to some previous, undamaged state. In an environment where we often do not know if the current state is representative of what would be expected in the absence of human activities or what communities composition and species abundance were in past times, targets may be either very generalised or aspirational. In situations where the damage to be repaired is clear, targets can relate to recovery or restoration of habitats and species (see Chapter 11).

The very large number of likely conservation (policy) objectives linked to the achievement of the aims in directives, conventions and statutes means that only a very few examples of how survey methods might be linked to objectives can be given here. Table 8.2 is based on a similar table in Hiscock (1998b). Procedural guidelines for each method are not included in this volume but are available as a part of the Marine Monitoring Handbook on the JNCC (Joint Nature Conservation Committee, UK) website (www.jncc.defra.gov.uk/page-2430).

Interpreting results: cause and effect

It is a great frustration to scientists recording change that it is often difficult to establish the cause. Nevertheless, there are ways:

- Has such a biological change or event happened before and was the cause established?
- Was there an obvious environmental event that might have triggered the change? For instance, have there been enhanced seawater temperatures or a very cold winter?
- Were there parallel changes in other species?

Table 8.2 Example of matching methods objectives for a specific habitat type and method

Conservation objective	Survey/monitoring objective	Habitat type	Method	Advantages	Disadvantages/Limitations
Ensure that major habitat types retain or restore (where damaged) their area	Map/remap extent of major substratum features including major biotope complexes	Intertidal rock and sediment	Aerial photography at 1:10,000 plus ground truthing to draw biotope maps in GIS	• The maps show which are extensive and which are restricted biotopes (that might need conservation measures) • Phase 2 survey can be targeted on mapped examples of biotopes • The maps provide a reference point for surveys to detect future change • Data stored in a GIS can be presented and interrogated in a variety of ways, providing a flexible tool • The maps can be used for education	• Many shore species and communities occur along a continuum and therefore biotope boundaries are often artificial and subjective • Mapping biotopes with strict adherence to a national classification may not take account of regional characteristics • Small features or species of interest may be overlooked where a large area is being studied • Any seasonal changes may affect representivity of maps for different times • Mapping biotopes does not indicate the quality of those biotopes • An important biotope may not be a mapable unit resolved by the aerial photograph
Maintain or increase the species richness in the biotope and/or abundance of key (rare, fragile,	Census/re-census of the species which are present in biotopes at a site, including their abundance	Intertidal/subtidal rock or hard substratum	Abundance scale, Checklist and Exact location (ACE) surveys	• Records are obtained rapidly and, if significant change is suggested, a check can be undertaken immediately for possible reasons • More species can be discerned *in situ* than by video or photograph	• Abundance scale results are not amenable to statistical analysis • Worker variability can be high using this technique • There is no video film (but there may be still photographs) to check back to if change is suggested and results need validation

Management objective	Biotope	Monitoring purpose	Method	Advantages	Disadvantages
declining, representative or damaged) species in biotopes				• The records are sufficiently detailed to be analysed against other biotope records in order to assess species richness or the presence of unusual features or rare/scarce species	
Maintain or increase the species richness in the biotope and/or abundance of key (rare, fragile, declining, representative) species in biotopes	Subtidal sediments	Establish the species present in biotopes and their density within statistical limits	Quantitative sampling using diver-operated cores or grab/box core samples remotely at defined location; samples sieved and preserved for sorting, identification and enumeration; number of cores required to sample species richness and to separate differences in quantity of individuals caused by temporal rather than spatial variability is determined by pilot study	• Quantifiable results which are open to statistical analysis and interpretation • Produce replicable data to a common standard (if using the same sampling gear) • Provide data to which statistical limits may be applied, thus allowing better determination of measurable change • Provide data from which biotopes may be quantitatively determined using multivariate analysis	• Natural patchiness may require intense sampling to account for variation, due to the 'blind' nature of sample collection • The choice of which gear to use relies on having information about sediment type • Analysis of sediment samples for fauna can be costly and time consuming • Larger and more mobile epifauna tends to be undersampled • Data produced for epifauna and infauna may be in different formats
Maintain or increase the abundance of key structural or key functional species including rare, fragile or declining species in biotopes	Subtidal rock and other hard substrata	Establish the abundance of specified species present in examples of biotopes. Measure size and growth rates of specified species	Photographic recording of marked locations to a scale suitable for the species being surveyed	• Non-destructive • Enables surveillance of specific individuals, colonies, communities, etc. over time • Enables collection of large volumes of data per unit time underwater • Provides a permanent record • Enables accurate quantification of organism abundance, cover, size, etc.	• Dependency on reasonable water clarity • Significant time requirement for laboratory analysis of photographs • Potentially unsuitable for communities dominated by tall and overhanging organisms (e.g. kelp forest) • Taxonomic voucher specimens are not acquired

Table 8.2 (continued)

Conservation objective	Survey/ monitoring objective	Habitat type	Method	Advantages	Disadvantages/Limitations
				• Enables checks to be made in case of mistaken identifications, etc. • Relatively low cost • Divers may not need taxonomic expertise	• Cryptic fauna are not sampled • Equipment relatively cumbersome • Initial capital equipment costs high • Results are of change in those quadrats and may not be representative of wider-scale change
Establish degree of likely sensitivity of a population through gaining an understanding of longevity and growth rate of the species	Measure growth and longevity of a population	Intertidal/ subtidal rock or hard substratum	Identify individuals of each species and ensure they can be re-identified on future occasions For growth studies, measure appropriate dimensions of identified individuals or use photography against a scale	• Quick, providing individuals being monitored are easily found • Permanent record	• Individuals being monitored may disappear • Individuals being monitored may have reached a maximum size and so growth rate measurements are irrelevant • Individuals being monitored may be obscured in some years or sampling events by silt or overgrowth

Source: The advantages/disadvantages text uses material from the Procedural Guidelines in Davies (2001) but is abbreviated and changed in places.

Box 8.2 The value of recording 'events'

The pink sea fan *Eunicella verrucosa* is listed in the IUCN Red List (IUCN, 2013) as 'Vulnerable' and, in the UK, it is a protected species.

The first observation that 'something was wrong' with the sea fans in the Marine Nature Reserve at Lundy came from a diver in 2000. Observations, including from monitoring studies, documented a decline in condition and high levels of mortality in sea fans from 2000 to 2003. Analysis of tissue samples revealed that the problem was being caused by a bacterium of the *Vibrio* genus. The bacterium was found to have affected sea fans throughout most of south-west England (Hall-Spencer *et al.*, 2007).

A pink sea fan, *Eunicella verrucosa*, dying from a *Vibrio* infection in the Marine Nature Reserve at Lundy, UK. Some parts of the sea fan are already colonised by fouling organisms.

The *Eunicella verrucosa* event was the first recorded instance of a disease being found in a coral species growing in cold temperate waters, but just how worrying was the event? Disease is maybe something that randomly strikes sea fan populations with many years between events; and, although we should identify causes, we can usually do nothing about such losses. This conclusion is reinforced by an entry in the Plymouth Marine Fauna (Marine Biological Association, 1957, p62) which notes that in the 'latter half Aug. and first half of Sept. 1924; Captain Lord reported that a great amount of *Eunicella* brought up was dead; many colonies brought in were partially dead, none in such good condition as in the previous July'.

Maintaining observation of past 'events' helps to interpret the seriousness and likely importance of human activities in new events – but where and how will that information be held?

Ideally, relevant environmental factors are being monitored and it may be possible to see a peak or trough in a potential reason for change. Often, an event might occur and go unnoticed – for instance, a scallop dredge being towed over reefs, especially if at night; a particularly long swell that penetrated to depths where wave action is not normally felt; an angling competition that cleared territorial fish; release of toxic chemicals that dispersed quickly. Learning from the study of events that are recorded is important and several examples are given in Chapter 4 of natural events and events brought about by human activities that start to provide case studies that might explain something new. The care to be taken lies in whether the environmental change is to be treated as causative or coincidental, and experimental studies may be needed to establish cause and effect.

Many of the most valuable pieces of information that help to understand marine ecosystems and whether a change 'matters' come from casual or serendipitous observations of events such as spawning, disease and recreational impact. Those observations are free and sea users like to make them. Scientists just have to work out how to record them in a meaningful and accessible way. One 'meaningful and accessible way', pre computer databases, was the traditional marine fauna and flora lists for a geographical area, maintained over many years and published as books. For each species, details were given of occurrences, events such as spawning and years in which high abundances occurred. Those paper volumes have still not been replaced by an internet-based resource although websites, such as that of MarLIN (www.marlin.ac.uk), often add interesting facts.

Conclusions

1   Having clear objectives is an essential starting point for identifying the most suitable techniques to provide information needed.
2   The marine environment is difficult and potentially very expensive to work in.
3   Often, it is necessary to undertake rapid outline (phase 1) surveys including by remote methods such as aerial photography, multibeam sonar and video to identify extent of different habitats and to target more detailed work.
4   *In situ* survey and/or sampling is important for many habitats that cannot be identified or characterised by remote methods and to catalogue species present or to measure change.
5   For many purposes related to conservation, targeted surveys of species or habitats of conservation importance can be undertaken. This means that only a restricted number of habitat features or species need to be searched for and, often, volunteer recorders can undertake such work.
6   Sampling and recording 'indicators' and 'targets' may be of central importance to many studies. Those measures will have been identified by statutory authorities in response to directives, conventions and statutes.
7   Some types of repeat survey may be a waste of time and money if they investigate features which reconnaissance surveys or common sense indicate are not changing or are unlikely to change.
8   Sample design is very important, especially for monitoring. Identifying suitably robust statistical techniques that will be used should, in an ideal situation, precede survey. However, more pragmatic techniques are commonly used, given that it is often not possible to satisfy the rigours of statistical tests because of the impossible number of samples that would be required.

9   Equipment available for survey, including biodiversity monitoring, is developing rapidly – especially imaging and image analysis technology – but needs careful and appropriate application to avoid impressive but misleading results.

10 Whatever methods are used, it is important to know their limitations and to be sure of the accuracy of results.

Chapter 9

Selection, design and management of marine protected areas

Introduction

Designated conservation areas are one of the measures that can be used to protect marine biodiversity. They are especially identified to protect representative examples of habitats and to protect species and habitats that are in decline or threatened with decline, particularly as a result of human activities. This chapter takes the knowledge that we have, or can obtain, of what is where and what is representative or threatened (covered in previous chapters) and describes the criteria for selection of areas for protection and the considerations needed to manage those areas.

Identifying the location of meaningful Marine Protected Areas (MPAs) can be achieved by the application of 'ecological' criteria to this knowledge. Less easy is determining the size of areas and their distance apart that will be effective for conservation and have the greatest benefit for the wider marine environment. Achieving 'viability' within and 'connectivity' between MPAs are both scientific minefields: they are 'design' criteria. There will also be 'practical' criteria to consider by collaborating with stakeholders (Plate 63), including: minimising impacts on commerce, respecting or taking into account cultural traditions, maintaining educational activities, maintaining recreational opportunities and maintaining aesthetic qualities. It is the ecological considerations that are mainly addressed here.

Directives, conventions and statutes often 'drive' the identification and establishment of MPAs, but practising marine conservationists need to interpret the sometimes poorly thought through objectives in those imperatives. The major international drivers (for politicians) for the establishment of MPAs are:

- 'the establishment of marine protected areas consistent with international law and based on scientific information, including representative networks by 2012' (The World Summit on Sustainable Development, Johannesburg, 2002. See, for instance, UNEP-WCMC, 2008, p13).
- '[t]he establishment and maintenance by 2010 for terrestrial and by 2012 for marine areas of comprehensive, effectively managed, and ecologically representative national and regional systems of protected areas that collectively, *inter alia* through a global network, contribute to achieving the three objectives of the Convention and the 2010 target to significantly reduce the current rate of biodiversity loss at the global, regional, national and sub-national levels and contribute to poverty reduction and the pursuit of sustainable development' (www.cbd.int/decision/cop/?id=7765, item 18: Convention on Biological Diversity, Conference of Parties in 2004).

- '[t]he OSPAR Network of Marine Protected Areas and to ensure that by 2010 it is an ecologically coherent network of well-managed marine protected areas' (OSPAR Recommendation 2003/3 adopted by OSPAR 2003: OSPAR 03/17/1, Annex 9: see www.ospar.org).

The words in those directives and conventions and in any statutes that a country puts into place will be picked over to try to determine just how the requirements can be implemented – and it is at this point that the science that we have needs to be identified to try to meet those environmental and political aspirations.

What are Marine Protected Areas supposed to do?

MPAs do many different things, ranging from fish stock protection through maintenance of biodiversity to providing recreational or educational opportunities. When MPAs for biodiversity conservation were first suggested and a few were established (in the late 1960s and early 1970s), the reasons for creating those areas were often linked to the increasing economic activities of man at sea with the most serious (in relation to damaging marine habitats) listed as pollution, dumping and dredging (Björklund, 1974). Increased human activities in the form of spearfishing and SCUBA diving were also very visible and often considered damaging. Interestingly, fishing was rarely mentioned in those early days. Identification of potential sites for protection was most likely intuitive or based on practical considerations of areas already important for recreation or scientific study. In the 1970s, the Law of the Sea Conference was seen as taking a lead in international moves towards marine conservation (Björklund, 1974) but that expectation moved on to the International Union for the Conservation of Nature and Natural Resources (IUCN). The IUCN World Commission on Protected Areas defines a protected area as: '[a] clearly defined geographical space, recognised, dedicated and managed, through legal or other effective means, to achieve the long-term conservation of nature with associated ecosystem services and cultural values' (Dudley, 2008, p 60).

By 2012, it was estimated that 5.3 million km^2 or 1.6 per cent of the world's oceans were designated as some form of protected area (Trathan et al., 2012); but their effectiveness for conservation was being questioned and it was felt that selection was being done (in part it is assumed) on the basis of 'get what you can where you can annoy as few people as possible' (Dulvey, 2013, p.359). That meant establishing very large MPAs in remote areas so that percentage targets for protection of the world's oceans were being approached without too much pain. In the article by Trathan et al. (2012, p.4), Mark Spalding of The Nature Conservancy is quoted as saying: 'We really need MPAs in places where marine biodiversity is struggling. Those sites are generally going to be small, expensive, and hard to manage.' The picture is, however, much more complicated than targeting areas where biodiversity is struggling. Protecting large areas effectively can produce benefits such as acting as reservoirs of diversity from which recovery of damaged areas can occur. Both large and small areas are relevant.

The different types of MPAs are catalogued and described for IUCN in Day et al. (2012) who further excluded some sites that may previously have been considered MPAs. Those sites are ones where nature conservation is not the primary objective of establishing the area, such as locations solely for recreation, fish stock management, sustainable extraction of marine resources, wind farms, military training areas, etc. The primary definitions of IUCN categories of MPAs are given in Box 9.1.

Box 9.1 Primary definitions of IUCN categories of MPAs

Category Ia

. . . [S]trictly protected areas set aside to protect biodiversity and also possibly geological/geomorphological features, where human visitation use and impacts are strictly controlled and limited to ensure protection of the conservation values. Such protected areas can serve as indispensable reference areas for scientific research and monitoring.

Category Ib

. . . [U]sually large unmodified or slightly modified areas, retaining their natural character and influence, without permanent or significant human habitation, which are protected and managed so as to preserve their natural condition.

Category II

. . . [L]arge natural or near natural areas set aside to protect large-scale ecological processes, along with the complement of species and ecosystems characteristic of the area, which also provide a foundation for environmentally and culturally compatible spiritual, scientific, educational, recreational and visitor opportunities.

Category III

. . . [S]et aside to protect a specific natural monument, which can be a landform, seamount, submarine cavern, geological feature such as a cave or even a living component such as a specific coralline feature. They are generally quite small protected areas and often have high visitor value.

Category IV

. . . [A]im to protect particular species or habitats and management reflects this priority. Many category IV protected areas will need regular, active interventions to address the requirements of particular species or to maintain habitats, but this is not a requirement of the category.

Category V

. . . [A]reas where the interaction of people and nature over time has produced an area of distinct character with significant ecological, biological, cultural and scenic value: and where safeguarding the integrity of this interaction is vital to protecting and sustaining the area and its associated nature conservation and other values.

Category VI

. . . [A]reas that conserve ecosystems and habitats, together with associated cultural values and traditional natural resource management systems. They are generally large, with most of the area in a natural condition, where a proportion is under low-level non-industrial sustainable natural resource management and where such use of natural resources compatible with nature conservation is seen as one of the main aims of the area.

Source: (Dudley, 2008, summarised in Day et al., 2012, pp 9–10)

The categories can be applied to whole MPAs or can be zones within MPAs (see Figure 9.8).

Identifying and managing MPAs: from aspirations to realities

Introduction

Whether starting from scratch or enhancing an existing series of MPAs, relevant information needs to be brought together so that agreed criteria can be applied. A systematic conservation planning approach is described by Margules and Pressey (2000) for terrestrial areas, and most is relevant to the marine environment:

1   Compile biodiversity data in the region of concern. This includes collating existing data along with collecting new data if necessary, and if time and funds permit. Where biodiversity data, such as habitat maps and species distributions, are limited, more readily available biophysical data may be used that reflect variation in biodiversity, such as mean annual rainfall or soil type.
2   Identify conservation goals for the region, including setting conservation targets for species and habitats, and principles for protected area design, such as maximising connectivity and minimising the edge-to-area ratio.
3   Review existing conservation areas, including determining the extent to which they already meet quantitative targets and mitigate threats.
4   Select additional conservation areas in the region using systematic conservation planning software.
5   Implement conservation action, including decisions on the most appropriate form of management to be applied.
6   Maintain the required values of the conservation areas. This includes setting conservation goals and monitoring key indicators that will reflect the success of management.

This sequential approach is adopted, with some modifications, in the following sections.

Compiling biodiversity data

Information about what species and habitats are where is the starting point to identifying locations that are representative of the range of habitats in a region and of special habitats and species. Each country will have a different system for maintaining, and making accessible, data and information. Ideally, data holders will have agreed to supply their data to a central database. Also, contracts that use public money should at least require that data is, after validation, submitted to a central and accessible database. The problem of finding data is, in part, because journals do not publish the results of yet another survey and, so, the results reside, inevitably, in the grey literature. Also, even if the results of a survey are published in a scientific journal, the detailed species lists that are needed are often not published (that situation is changing with the ability to place supplementary material on a journal website). Although much of recent survey literature is now posted on websites, it was not always thus, and old-fashioned library searches may still be needed. Indeed, if those searches are not undertaken, your site dossiers will not pass review by experienced marine ecologists; and policy advisors will not pursue those sites for designation until they pass review.

   Figure 9.1 shows a process, relevant to Great Britain, for ensuring that all scientific data sources are identified and accessed. It does not encompass data from industry or volunteers that might inform knowledge of what is where. Neither does it include data on usage and

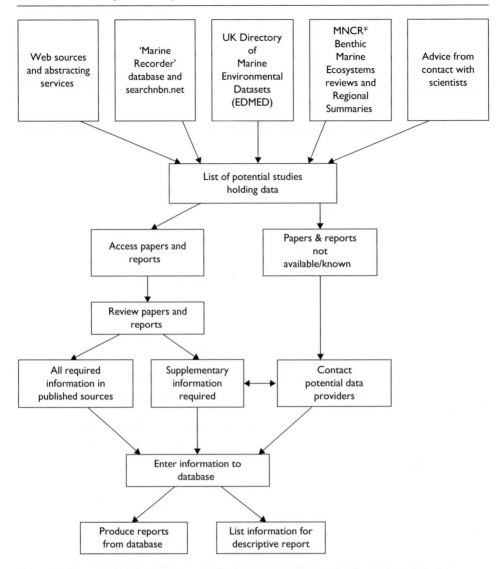

Figure 9.1 The process of accessing scientific data sources to provide information relevant to compiling biodiversity data. Using that information to identify biotopes, the location of scheduled species, the location of biodiversity hotspots, etc. are later stages. *MNCR = Marine Nature Conservation Review of Great Britain.

commercial value of resources, those are part of a different stage in the selection and design process.

The hope must be that data has already been brought together in some national or regional scheme and is readily available. More often, data and information on what is where is in a wide range of publications from peer-reviewed papers to survey results from studies commissioned for commercial reasons and that may be considered confidential. The requirement to 'Use available data' (see Hiscock, 1997), often part of research contracts, is challenging and frustrating if data has not been brought together. Programmes such as the MNCR (Hiscock, 1996) gathered together existing data and collected new survey information to provide a database that has been of critical importance in various exercises in England, Scotland and Wales to identify MPAs. The MNCR database was the foundation of the Marine Recorder database which provides one example of a system for collation of marine biodiversity data (http://jncc.defra.gov.uk/page-1599).

Remote sensing data is unlikely to be accurate unless extensively validated. Surrogates for biodiversity data (Margules and Pressey, 2000 mention rainfall and soil type for terrestrial systems) may be relevant in the case of bottom types, salinity, depth and exposure to waves and tidal streams in marine systems, providing that data has been collected *in situ* and the seabed types have not been predicted using algorithms. Unfortunately, recent history demonstrates how willing policy advisors are to embrace coloured maps that look impressive but that are likely to be ridiculed by fishermen and field ecologists who 'know' a particular area. Such algorithms have been used in the programme UKSeaMap (http://jncc.defra.gov.uk/ukseamap) but have proved very unreliable (Marine Ecological Surveys Ltd *et al.*, 2011).

Involving stakeholders and compiling socio-economic data

Whether or not we have MPAs is a societal choice, and society needs to be involved in the selection, design and management of MPAs. Involving society means that people understand what is being proposed and what are the likely consequences for them but also takes advantage of the knowledge that they have. Identifying where are the most suitable locations for MPAs needs the collaboration of those who own or license activities in the areas being considered, who know the character of the areas being considered and who use the areas being considered. Dudley (2008) identifies 'primary stakeholders' who are: (a) those needed for permission, approval and financial support; and (b) those who are directly affected by the activities of the organisation or project. Secondary stakeholders are those who are indirectly affected. Tertiary stakeholders are those who are not affected or involved but who can influence opinions either for or against. Likely financial consequences of MPA establishment and management need to be taken into account and may prioritise areas that have least impact on commercial activities and most benefit for scientific or recreational activities. The dilemma for planners is what to do first. If the ecologists are asked to first apply selection criteria to identify potential areas for protection and the user-stakeholders are called in after that, there will be suspicion and mistrust amongst some users who feel they are being kept in the dark and are about to receive some unpleasant surprise. Some sectors may build angry opposition to something they do not know about, able only to allow their imaginations to assume the worse. On the other hand, if the user-stakeholders are brought in first, they will have the opportunity to unreasonably identify no-go areas and to thwart efforts to take suitable sites forward. What is really needed is a situation where those who know about the particular features of a candidate area (scientists, divers, fishermen, etc.) can come together to share the information that they have and identify goals that align with those of the user-stakeholders. Look for a diplomat!

Identifying conservation goals

'Goals' are statements of intent (aims) and are put into practice though 'objectives' which are measurable.

Box 9.2 The goals of California's Marine Life Protection Act (MLPA)

The goals of California's Marine Life Protection Act (MLPA) are given (from Kirlin *et al.*, 2013, p.4) as:

Goal 1. To protect the natural diversity and abundance of marine life, and the structure, function, and integrity of marine ecosystems.

Goal 2. To help sustain, conserve, and protect marine life populations, including those of economic value, and rebuild those that are depleted.

Goal 3. To improve recreational, educational, and study opportunities provided by marine ecosystems that are subject to minimal human disturbance, and to manage these uses in a manner consistent with protecting biodiversity.

Goal 4. To protect marine natural heritage, including protection of representative and unique marine life habitats in California waters for their intrinsic value.

Goal 5. To ensure that California's MPAs have clearly defined objectives, effective management measures, and adequate enforcement, and are based on sound scientific guidelines.

Goal 6. To ensure that the MPAs are designed and managed, to the extent possible, as a component of a statewide network.

Clear goals and selection guidelines should help the process of agreeing on the location and extent of a series of MPAs in a particular region or country. Looking for 'success stories' is useful for influencing others and giving clues about the process to be adopted, the role of science and the likely cost. One such success story is from California where, after many years of planning and negotiation, the designation of approximately 16 per cent of state waters in 126 MPAs is reported in a special issue of *Ocean & Coastal Management* (introduced by Gleason *et al.*, 2013). Saarman *et al.* (2013, p 48) indicate that:

The MPA design guidelines used in California were effective because they were simple, scientifically credible, and directly related to the conservation based MLPA [Marine Life Protection Act] goals. They also provided a logical and rigorous means of comparing MPA network proposals and assessing likelihood that they would meet the goals of the MLPA legislation. The use of simple 'rules of thumb' or guiding principles for MPA design gave stakeholders and decision-makers a way to incorporate science more directly into their planning, while still acknowledging the underlying complexities of natural and human systems.

There are, of course, many success stories and, hopefully, many lined up to become success stories. Only some can be mentioned in this chapter.

Conservation goals are often a 'given' in broad terms. They are the aspirations in directives, conventions and statutes that scientists need to translate so that they will be meaningful for the conservation of biodiversity and practical to achieve. They are achieved

Table 9.1 Principles and secondary goals expressed in the Guidelines (Agreed by the Ministers of the Australian and New Zealand Environment and Conservation Council, 1998)

Principles	Secondary goals
1 Regional framework 2 Comprehensiveness 3 Adequacy 4 Representativeness 5 Highly protected areas 6 Precautionary principle 7 Public consultation 8 Indigenous involvement 9 Equitable decision making	1 To promote the development of MPAs within the framework of integrated ecosystem management. 2 To provide a formal management framework for a broad spectrum of human activities, including recreation, tourism, shipping and the use or extraction of resources, the impacts of which are compatible with the primary goal. 3 To provide scientific reference sites. 4 To provide for the special needs of rare, threatened or depleted species and threatened ecological communities. 5 To provide for the conservation of special groups of organisms, e.g. species with complex habitat requirements or mobile or migratory species, or species vulnerable to disturbance which may depend on reservation for their conservation. 6 To protect areas of high conservation value including those containing high species diversity, natural refugia for flora and fauna and centres of endemism. 7 To provide for the recreational, aesthetic and cultural needs of indigenous and non-indigenous people.

Source: www.environment.gov.au/resource/guidelines-establishing-national-representative-system-marine-protected-areas

through the selection and design criteria and management measures that are described later. Conservation goals are often mixed with goals concerned with education, recreation and sustainable fisheries. As a further example, in Australia, the initial imperative for a National Representative System of Marine Protected Areas (NRSMPA) states that:

> The primary goal of the NRSMPA is to establish and manage a comprehensive, adequate and representative system of MPAs to contribute to the long-term ecological viability of marine and estuarine systems, to maintain ecological processes and systems, and to protect Australia's biological diversity at all levels.
>
> (ANZECC TFMPA, 1998, p5)

The 'primary goal' is expanded through nine principles and seven secondary goals (Table 9.1).

Halpern (2003, pS130) observes: 'Finally, it is paramount that we explicitly state our goals when creating marine reserves. These goals help guide the design of reserves and are critical for assessing whether or not a reserve has functioned successfully.'

Reviewing existing conservation areas

The identification of MPAs rarely starts from scratch. Protected areas may already be in place and range from voluntary areas established by local interests through to MPAs established under a previous measure, perhaps for an objective different from current intentions. Indeed, if there are to be 'layers' of protection, it would be hoped that any new measures required will be designed to compensate for the shortcomings of the previous measure(s). Such a situation has happened in Europe where the requirements of the Habitats Directive of 1991 were written around terrestrial 'threatened' habitats and marine sections were poorly drafted in terms of the habitats and species identified for protection and the criteria for identifying sites (see, for instance, Von Nordheim *et al.*, 2006). In particular, there was no properly constructed classification of marine habitats to provide a catalogue for identifying and characterising threatened habitats: that came much later. It was in 1997 that a Britain and Ireland biotopes classification emerged that would provide the starting point for a European classification. The classification was originally developed by the MNCR as part of the European Commission (EC) Life Nature-funded BioMar project. The most recent version is given in Connor *et al.* (2004). Some imagination is also needed. Areas established for protection of some other feature – such as fish stocks or *de facto* protected areas such as locations used to dump munitions or where there are wind farms – may also protect biodiversity, although whether they can be described as MPAs is doubted by Day *et al.* (2012).

Selecting and designing conservation areas

Introduction

Protected areas have been identified for more than a hundred years – often opportunistically and often based on the personal knowledge and experience of the naturalists who suggested where they should be. That was very much the case in Great Britain at the start of the second half of the twentieth century when National Nature Reserves and Sites of Special Scientific Interest were being designated. When the naturalists had to explain in a systematic way why a location had been selected, criteria were developed and the process became more objective and more defensible. The development of those criteria also meant that new and less experienced personnel could, if they were properly trained, use them to take conservation forward. However, it was clear that terrestrial criteria didn't translate directly to marine conservation and early work 'marinised' those terrestrial criteria (Mitchell, 1987). Those ecological and practical criteria were straightforward although often the information to address them was incomplete. Moving into a new century, policy advisors stretched their rhetoric into areas that would prove difficult to tie to scientific knowledge and our understanding of how marine ecosystems 'work': the design criteria. The process of selection and design has become mechanistic and knowledge of natural history, that was so important in the early days of conservation, has been left behind.

Ecological/scientific criteria relevant to marine biodiversity are reviewed and catalogued (as 'biological valuation criteria') in Derous *et al.* (2007); and, in Roff and Zacharias (2011), they are listed and, where relevant, synonymised with those biological valuation criteria. Whilst scientific or ecological criteria to select suitable locations could be addressed using the scientific knowledge available on rarity, degree of threat, diversity, sensitivity, etc. (see Chapter 7), 'design' of a series or network of MPAs was much more difficult. Concepts such as viability, adequacy and connectivity were not only poorly understood but were easily applied in a naive way. Applying such design criteria needed the heuristic ('rule of thumb') approach, and that reality was reflected in Ardron (2008a) and in Partnership for Interdisciplinary Studies of Coastal Oceans (PISCO):

> MPAs should encompass a variety of marine habitats across a range of depths and environmental gradients [. . .]

MPAs should be large enough that adult marine organisms do not move out of them too frequently and become vulnerable to fishing [. . .]

MPAs should be close enough together that sufficient larvae can disperse from one to the next.

(www.piscoweb.org/policy/marine-protected-areas/marine-protected-area-design)

The marine conservation practitioner now has a long list of criteria that can be applied to selection and design of MPAs. The following sections seek to tease out the most practical and meaningful.

Selection

INTRODUCTION

Recent approaches to identifying locations of MPAs are summarised in Hiscock (2008b), whilst Hiscock (2010) identifies some of the gaps between policy and science that can make meaningful action for conservation difficult. Examples of the scientific or ecological criteria that have been indentified for the selection of MPAs are given in Table 9.2.

Derous *et al.* (2007) provide a detailed list of the main criteria that have been proposed and applied to MPA selection.

The criteria or principles in Table 9.2 beg many questions, for instance:

- What are the species that should be considered as 'threatened and/or declining'? The quantitative criteria developed to identify them (by IUCN, 2013) can only be applied to a few well-studied species.
- How should rarity be assessed? Some species and habitats are naturally very restricted in occurrence. Is a species rare if it occurs in a very restricted geographical area but its numbers are in millions?
- At what level of a hierarchical habitats classification should representativeness be considered?
- How can naturalness be assessed when human activities have had such a large effect in some areas a long time ago?
- How do we identify sensitivity (for species and biotopes) when that depends on having knowledge of life history traits that are unknown for many species?
- How do we know what is 'high natural biodiversity'?
- Should 'distinctiveness' be a criterion? Distinctive locations are atypical of their sur-roundings (Roff and Evans, 2002).

The various sets of criteria that are listed in Table 9.2 have many similarities and a few differences. Most criteria are self-explanatory although will need quantification (size, numbers) and catalogues (biotope classifications, rarity/threat listings) in order for them to be applied. Some are not self-explanatory and need reference to the original paper. Sometimes, 'representativeness' or 'representativity' is included in design rather than in selection criteria. No one set of scientific or ecological criteria stands out as 'the one to use': all have relevant additions and peculiar omissions. All have been used to inform what is hoped here to be a relevant set of criteria for assessing the scientific or ecological merits of locations that will assist in the identification of the most meaningful MPAs for biodiversity conservation. The

Table 9.2 'Scientific' or 'ecological' criteria used in the identification of marine protected areas

Mitchell (1987) and Hiscock and Mitchell (1989)	Roberts et al. (2003) (includes 'design' criteria)	OSPAR Ecological criteria / considerations (2003)[1]	Derous et al. (2007) Biological Valuation Criteria; also in Roff and Zacharias (2011)	Convention on Biodiversity 'scientific criteria' (2008)[2]
• Naturalness • Representativeness • Rarity • Diversity • Fragility • Size	**Prerequisite criteria** • Biogeographic representation • Habitat representation and heterogeneity **Excluding criteria** • Human threats • Natural catastrophes/ threats **Modifying criteria** • Size • Connectivity • Vulnerable habitats • Vulnerable life stages • Species and populations of special interest • Exploitable species • Ecosystem linkages • Ecological services for humans	• Threatened or declining species and habitats/ biotopes • 'Important' species and habitats/ biotopes • Ecological significance • High natural biological diversity • Representativity • Sensitivity • Naturalness	**First Order Criteria** • Rarity • Aggregation • Fitness consequences **Modifying criteria** • Naturalness • Proportional importance	• Uniqueness or rarity • Special importance for life history stages of species • Importance for threatened, endangered or declining species and/or habitats • Vulnerability, fragility, sensitivity or slow recovery • Biological productivity • Biological diversity • Naturalness

Notes:
[1] 'Guidelines for the identification and selection of marine protected areas in the OSPAR Maritime Area' (Reference number: 2003–17). See www.ospar.org
[2] Convention on Biodiversity. COP Decision 9 IX/20, Bonn, 19–30 May, 2008. See www.cbd.int/conventions

most practical criteria to describe here are those that are included as part of international conventions and directives or defined by international bodies. Those criteria, based mainly on those outlined by OSPAR in 2003 and by the Convention on Biodiversity in 2008, are given next.

THREATENED OR DECLINING SPECIES AND HABITATS/BIOTOPES

Chapter 7 addresses the character of: '"Threatened" and "sensitive" species and habitats'. Most often, this criterion is linked to 'Red Lists' that have used quantitative information on decline to identify species or habitats for protection. Internationally, IUCN maintain their Red List of Threatened Species (IUCN, 2013). Countries or regions may have their own lists of threatened or declining species and habitats including, for instance, in Great Britain

(Biodiversity Action Plan priority species and habitats: http://jncc.defra.gov.uk/page-5705) and for the north-east Atlantic (OSPAR, 2008). However, for marine species, the required quantitative information is often only available for charismatic megafauna whereas identifying species that are sensitive according to their life history traits and threatened because of damaging human activities where they occur is more meaningful.

Threatened habitats or ecosystems are not currently listed by IUCN but that work was under way at the time of writing (Keith *et al.*, 2013). Any such assessment will rely on having a catalogue of ecosystems or habitats, knowing where they occur, how large they are and quantitative information on decline. Such measures are likely to be readily found for such habitats as mudflats, mangroves and shallow coral reefs but will be difficult to quantify for, for instance, seamounts and similar structures that have deep water communities on hard substrata. So, in addition to those habitats where quantification is possible, there will be ones where expert judgement comes to bear; and that is accommodated by IUCN guidelines for species where '[a]n observed, estimated, inferred, projected or suspected population reduction' (IUCN, 2001, p 26) is a part of the criteria used to identify threatened species.

UNIQUENESS AND RARITY

'Uniqueness' is a strong consideration. If a particular habitat type or species occurs uniquely in a particular country or small geographical feature, then strong measures need to be taken to protect that habitat or species: for example, cave systems that hold populations of species known from nowhere else. 'Rarity' is a key criterion for the selection of MPAs but is often difficult to define (see Chapter 2, 'How much of it is there? Assessing "rarity"', p19). Nevertheless, uniqueness and rarity have strong political force when supporting calls for conservation.

Within the geographic limits of a particular state, a species that is considered 'rare' may be much more abundant elsewhere in the world. Experienced naturalists will have a 'feel' for what is rare but developing quantitative criteria for marine species has some way to go. Whether that geographical rarity 'matters' for that country needs to be considered. Some rare species may occur serendipitously in a country or at a location and may not 'count' as worthy of special protection measures. An example in Britain is the gooseneck barnacle *Pollicipes pollicipes* which is abundant at some wave-exposed locations in continental Europe and which occurs very rarely in southwest England – the result of long-distance larval dispersal – but does not form viable colonies.

Species that are listed, for example in Biodiversity Action Plans or on Red Lists or similar lists of rare and threatened species, can often be protected if their habitats are included in MPAs – there is no special need to identify MPAs for particular species although they will be a qualifying feature. However, those habitats will not be the broadscale habitats used to achieve representivity, they will be based on a much finer level of differentiation which identifies specific and easily separated biotopes. There is likely to be a residue of species that do not occur in protected habitats or sites and they will need their own measures. Those measures may be to identify an MPA to protect them or may be to schedule that species for protection wherever it occurs.

REPRESENTATIVENESS

Representing the range of habitats and associated communities of species within a particular biogeographical province needs the starting points of:

1   a biogeographical classification of the region under consideration; and
2   a classification of habitats and their associated communities.

Marine biogeographic realms of the planet have been identified for oceanic to coastal areas (see UNESCO, 2009). The role of broadscale ecosystem classification systems in conservation is described in Chapter 2 ('Structuring what we know about species and habitats', p12) and the ecoregions identified by Spalding *et al.* (2007) for coastal and shelf regions are shown in Figure 9.2.

Within each of the main ecoregions, representative examples of the major habitat types should be identified for an MPA series. Those could be within physiographic features (for instance, estuaries, inlets and bays, fjords, atolls, lagoons, open coast, offshore level seabed) or according to broadscale biotopes (for instance, intertidal bedrock, intertidal sediment, subtidal algal-dominated rock, subtidal animal-dominated rock, coral reef, subtidal sediments). Those examples are not a complete list and, anyway, there will be subdivisions such as different types of lagoons in the case of physiographic features and different exposures of open coast bedrock in the case of biotopes.

From a practical point of view, it will be difficult to identify, for instance, locations that encompass examples of all of the approximately 350 biotopes that constitute Level 4 of the EUNIS classification (see Chapter 2, Figure 2.4) and it is most likely that Level 3, which has about 25 types, is more practical. Twenty-three broadscale habitats were used to identify representative MPAs in English waters (Natural England and Joint Nature Conservation Committee, 2010). Furthermore, Rondinini (2010) undertook an analysis of survey data from England to identify the amount of each habitat type that was needed to be representative, concluding that 'the IUCN target of protecting 12% of a habitat type would result in the representation of 57–72% of the species that it contains' (p4). However, there was wide variation between habitat types with 20 per cent of habitat type A1.1 expected to represent approximately 60 per cent of its species, while 20 per cent of habitat type A6.2 was expected to contain approximately 80 per cent of its species. Those figures could be bettered if rich (for biotopes and species) areas are selected and could be more meaningful for conservation if examples with rare and scarce species were chosen, reflecting the comment:

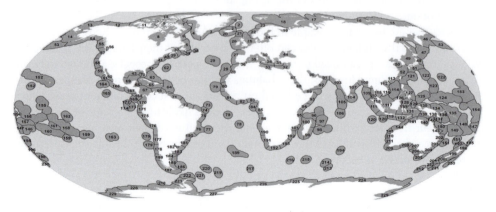

Figure 9.2 Ecoregions defined for coastal and shelf regions of the world.
Source: Spalding *et al.* (2007).

targeting habitat types to represent a given proportion of species may result in the over-protection of common species and under-protection of rare species, in particular of rare species restricted to one habitat type. For this reason, targets on habitat types should be regarded as coarse-filter targets on overall biodiversity (of which species richness is only one and incomplete indicator), and should complemented by species-level targets.

(Rondinini, 2010, p 20)

ECOLOGICAL SIGNIFICANCE/IMPORTANCE FOR LIFE HISTORY STAGES

For the protection of populations of a species, it may be essential to identify locations that are known to be important for breeding, feeding, as nurseries or for resting. Often, such areas, when they become known, immediately attract exploitation whereas in many cases they should attract protection.

BIOLOGICAL DIVERSITY

'High natural biodiversity' (from the OSPAR guidelines) is often a very important consideration in selecting areas for protection and may be considered as getting 'best value for money'. Diverse communities can provide resilience to environmental perturbations (Petchey and Gaston, 2009), and the identification and protection of areas of high marine biodiversity should contribute to the ecosystem-based approach to the management of our seas through identifying which are the most valuable areas for biodiversity and where protection will yield benefits for the maintenance of ecosystem structure and functioning including the biotic processes that drive them (Hiscock and Breckles, 2007). Identifying areas with high biodiversity may also improve the efficiency of a series of MPAs by capturing a greater number of species and habitats of conservation importance within individual sites (Langmead and Jackson, 2010). 'Biodiversity' can be measured in terms of the number of habitats within an area or in terms of numbers of species and, of course, the more different habitats identified, the more species are likely to be supported in them. And, ideally, not just 'any' species are included but species that are rare, scarce, in decline or threatened with decline.

There may be a temptation to try to predict where biodiversity hotspots might occur through identifying ocean processes and the characteristics of water quality that might encourage presence of a high diversity of species perhaps including rare or sensitive species. Roff and Evans (2002) draw attention to such distinctive habitats which they believe are typically associated with elevated resources at some trophic level. Areas of oceanic upwelling may attract conspicuous aggregations of birds, fish and cetaceans although how important they are for the biodiversity on the seabed below is unclear. An experienced ecologist can use their knowledge to target areas for survey that often yield rich communities and rare species. Trying to make that knowledge and experience into an algorithm applied by a laboratory-based researcher should only be done if the results are followed by survey.

In reality, whatever measures or algorithms are used and whatever indices are produced, it is often knowledge and experience that inform where the biodiversity hotspots are. We go back full circle to the mid-twentieth-century naturalists who identified the first protected areas based on what they had seen and that they 'knew' a place was special because of its diversity or the unusual species that were present there. Plate 65 is a rich community of

Box 9.3 Importance for life history stages

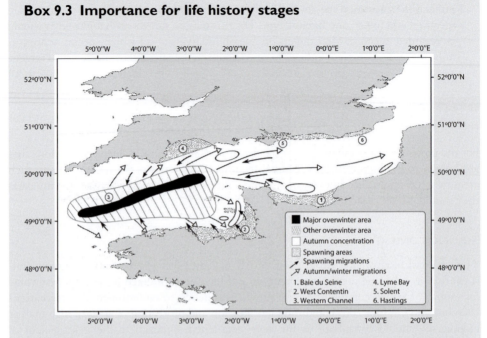

Cuttlefish, *Sepia officinalis*, in the north-east Atlantic have well-known locations where they breed and lay their eggs (Plate 64) and some knowledge of where they overwinter. Breeding areas attract the use of traps to catch the cuttlefish. Overwintering areas attract trawling. In the case of breeding areas, the cuttlefish enter the traps, breed and lay their eggs on the traps. Ideally, such breeding areas should be protected but, after breeding, cuttlefish die and so harm is limited providing the traps are left in the water until eggs have hatched. Much greater damage may be done to the populations by fisheries that target overwintering populations – and their locations are well known (Pawson, 1995).

Source: diagram redrawn by Isobel Bloor for the English Channel from Legrande (unpublished) in Pawson (1995).

species in the Isles of Scilly, UK that included nationally rare and scarce species and that, when seen by an experienced naturalist, shouted 'biodiversity hotspot'.

Richness is also important in the case of biotopes. If, for instance, a location can be found that has a wide range of Level 4, 5, and 6 biotopes, we get the most bang for our bucks by selecting the location within the Level 3 biotope used to identify representativeness.

SENSITIVITY (VULNERABILITY, FRAGILITY OR SLOW RECOVERY)

Chapter 7 describes the concept of sensitivity and the ways of assessing 'species and habitat sensitivity'. The value of understanding sensitivity is for much more than identifying protected sites and so is not described in detail in this chapter. However, what needs explaining

Box 9.4 Mangroves and connectivity

Mangroves are well known as nursery areas for fish. In a study of reef fish in the Caribbean (Mumby, 2006), it was found that biomass of several species more than doubled when the reefs were connected to rich mangrove resources. Algorithms were used to generate a connectivity matrix among coral reefs and mangroves that facilitated the identification of connected corridors of habitats. The work helped to identify priority sites for mangrove restoration. Image: an area of mangroves in North Island, New Zealand.

here is that sensitivity is a result of intolerance to a pressure ('fragility') and the likely rate of recovery ('slow recovery'). Vulnerability refers to the likelihood that a damaging pressure or activity that causes that pressure will occur at the site.

NATURALNESS

Perhaps the most difficult ecological criterion for selection is 'naturalness'. We are all aware of the concept of 'Shifting baselines' (see Chapter 4) and that we may not know what is 'natural' at a location. Nevertheless, there is occasionally historical data, and there is knowledge and experience from, often retired, naturalists to use. Sometimes a site might be considered 'natural' if very long-lived and slow-growing species are present. Often, we have to settle for believing that a location is close to natural if it appears undamaged and there is no known adverse activity or source of contamination nearby. Naturalness is close to the highest ranking of 'quality' in such measures as the Marine Strategy Framework Directive in Europe (see reference in Chapter 10, Environmental Impact Assessments, to 'baselines').

'Design'

INTRODUCTION

'Design' identifies the 'how many?', 'how large?' and 'how far apart?' questions. Design also takes account of practical matters such as incorporating an MPA into or adjacent to existing protected areas (thus making management easier) or choosing areas where, wherever possible, there will be a minimal impact on socio-economic activities (thus avoiding conflict and loss of income).

Designing MPAs that 'work' is not like a civil engineering project where size and strength as well as the infrastructure needed can all be calculated and built in. The 'how big?' and 'how far apart?' of MPAs is a much more rule of thumb affair. Hoping that design can be calculated in some objective, parameter-based methodology may be just that – an aspiration rather than a reality.

IUCN-WCPA (2008, Chapter 5) identify 'Five ecological guidelines for designing resilient MPA networks':

1   Include the full range of biodiversity present in the biogeographic region (representation; replication; resilience and resistance characteristics).
2   Ensure ecologically significant areas are incorporated (protection of unique or vulnerable habitats; protection of foraging or breeding grounds; protection of source populations).
3   Maintain long-term protection (consider spillover; adaptive management).
4   Ensure ecological linkages (connectivity; adult movement patterns; larval dispersal).
5   Ensure maximum contribution of individual MPAs to the network (size, spacing, shape).

The following eight criteria are identified as design criteria (IUCN-WCPA, 2008):

- representativeness;
- replication;
- viability;
- precautionary design;
- permanence;
- maximum connectivity;
- resilience; and
- size and shape.

Connectivity, representativity, replication and adequacy/viability are the four agreed-upon OSPAR criteria for ecological coherence (OSPAR, 2007).

The IUCN and OSPAR design criteria beg many questions, including:

- What level of replication is needed?
- What is 'adequate' or 'viable'?
- Does 'precautionary' cover for inadequate scientific knowledge or does it relate to size?
- Is connectivity relevant in such a well-connected environment?
- Resilience depends on many factors – are any under management control?

- Size and shape relate to adequacy/viability measures, but are practical considerations of shape and boundary location more important?

Many of the design criteria are overlapping or interactive with each other. Many will be clarified if the objectives of establishing MPAs in a location are clear. IUCN (2007) suggest that, at the very outset, designers must clearly define objectives in three broad areas:

- Ecological objectives seek to protect, manage and/or restore marine ecosystems and their components.
- Economic objectives determine how the region will benefit from the network, and who may suffer negative economic impacts.
- Sociocultural objectives include the full range of benefits that biodiversity provides, especially those that directly affect human health and well-being.

Once the objectives are clear, there is science that can be applied to inform the process of design for biodiversity conservation. Some of that science concerns ecosystem structure, functioning and viability, addressed in the introduction to Chapter 3 (p22).

Representativeness, replication, viability or adequacy and connectivity are the major design considerations together with size and shape.

REPRESENTATIVENESS

Representativeness is included as a criterion in both lists of selection and design criteria. It is relevant to both and has been addressed in the section on selection criteria (see p147).

REPLICATION

Designating multiple MPAs with similar characteristics is considered by some as an 'insurance policy' – if one site is damaged, the other(s) still exist. More scientifically, multiple sites of the same character enable comparisons to be made of changes occurring and whether there is consistency across more than one location. If particular features are rare and/or fragile or a country has a large proportion of the world representation of that feature then multiple sites are also justified. There is no simple formula to identify how many replicates are needed or can be justified.

VIABILITY

Concepts of viability are described in Chapter 3 (see p41). Design of MPAs may incorporate the concept of a 'minimum viable area', which refers to the minimum area of a habitat that it is considered necessary to protect in order to ensure as far as possible that it is self-sufficient and therefore will persist over time (Salm et al., 2000; Roberts et al., 2010). Part of that self-sufficiency must be concerned with the requirements of component species. Parnell et al. (2006, p946) observe that '[r]eserves need to be large enough to include and sustain the important populations that spend most of their time within the immediate area'. Two key factors are important when considering species: how far the species moves once it has settled in an area, and how far its larvae or propagules go during dispersal phases. When considering the protection of habitats, a 'viable area' may be the extent of the particular habitat taking account of the dispersal capabilities of the species that populate it. Habitats particularly require the maintenance of the physical and chemical characteristics that support their presence and determine the species that will thrive there. So, the extent of those particular characteristics needs to be taken into account. Small areas can be viable because larval supply or the migration of adults is either very localised or happens through the water column and not the seabed, where barriers may occur.

Those species that are sessile or sedentary or that are territorial or spend a significant part of their life cycle in a particular location can benefit from protection in MPAs. Those that are entirely pelagic or have a nomadic lifestyle are unlikely to benefit unless locations that are critical to their life cycle (such as breeding or feeding areas) can be identified. However, the area that is viable for one group of species or a particular habitat may not be for another and so misunderstanding occurs along with inappropriate or over-simplistic quantitative guidelines or criteria (see Box 9.5). Fish and larger crustaceans may need a minimum area to forage but that area will be different for different species. A viable area for a species with short-lived larvae or propagules is likely to be small – perhaps only a few metres across. On the other hand, it is futile to use dispersal capability to work out a viable area for limited-mobility species by reference to species with long-lived larvae or other dispersal mechanisms that recruit from distant locations.

Gaines et al. (2010) mention that the fundamental factor for enhancing (presumably, biodiversity) conservation and fishery prosperity is that an isolated reserve must be 'self-persistent' and therefore must have a positive population growth. Persistence is a feature of viability, and valued communities or species can 'persist' in quite small areas (see Box 9.5). They may be self-recruiting with very short-lived larvae (for instance, some stony corals) or may propagate by asexual reproduction (for instance, seagrass beds) and occupy the same small area, perhaps just a few metres across, over many decades. Persistence can also occur where there is recruitment from outside of the reserve – but, of course, that recruitment has to be reliable as a net export of larvae or individuals will lead to decline. Nevertheless, emphasising persistence in two subtidal epifaunal communities in southern New England, USA, Osman and Whitlatch (1998) suggest that there is strong local control of recruitment that overrides any variability in larval production and that epifaunal communities are, anyway, often dominated by species producing short-lived larvae. Gaines et al. (2010) provide a simplified rule of thumb for reserve spacing: reserves should contribute sufficient larvae to and receive sufficient larvae from other reserves. However, larval recruitment could just as well come from within the reserve or from areas that are not protected and, except where all of the examples of a particular habitat type are protected, that rule of thumb doesn't seem to make sense.

The fact that viable areas for many benthic species can be very small will, no doubt, cause consternation to administrators working with tables of acceptable size limits based on generalities or, as is often the case, movements of fish species. Nevertheless, it may not just be the area occupied by a valued species that is needed to support it. Some species with foraging areas or needing a minimum population size to maintain genetic viability may need large areas to support them. Also, protecting small areas is impractical and doesn't provide the buffer zones that may be essential to avoid damage from nearby activities. Therefore, areas should be larger rather than smaller. Furthermore, protecting ecosystem properties and processes needs to be taken into account, including knowing the size of territories of constituent mobile species.

Box 9.5 How large is 'viable'?

The coral, *Balanophyllia regia*.

The rock fissure occupied by a population of scarlet and gold star corals (*Balanophyllia regia*) in Plymouth Sound, UK was noted so precisely from records made in 1906, that the 1957 edition of the Plymouth Marine Fauna records 'since then they can always be found in the same place about two dozen together' (Marine Biological Association, 1957). They were still there in 2014. *Balanophyllia regia* is known to have a very short-lived larva (Paul Tranter, pers. comm.) and it seems likely that those isolated populations are self-recruiting.

A viable population may occupy a very small area.

Seagrass, *Zostera marina*.

The selection of Marine Conservation Zones in Wales included the guidance: '*the minimum habitat patch size should be 500 m to 1 km diameter. For some of the important habitats (e.g. maerl beds, seagrass beds) it may be difficult to find areas that are large enough to reach these guidelines.*' Despite this reasonable guidance, a seagrass bed at Skomer Island was excluded as it did not reach the habitat indicative viability target area. The bed was first recorded in 1946, first mapped in 1979 and had been monitored regularly since 1997. During that time the bed had increased both in extent as well as density, which suggests that it is indeed viable.

A viable biotope may occupy a small area (smaller than guidelines that become rules suggest).

Angler fish /monk fish, *Lophius piscatorius*.

Roberts and Hawkins (2012) asking 'How much area should be protected?' in a report on fish stock recovery areas observed that 'Roberts *et al.* (2010) . . . examined movement distances of mature adults of 72 different species, including a wide range of taxa of commercial importance such as fish, crustaceans and molluscs. Thirty-one species (43% of the sample) did not move at all after settlement from the plankton, while a further 27 species (38% of the sample) typically moved less than 10 km after reaching maturity. On this basis, the authors recommended that for an English network the median size of reserves in territorial waters should be no less than 5 km in their minimum dimension' and, later in the report, suggested that protected areas 'should average 10–20 km in their minimum dimension' referring to relatively mobile species.

Large areas may be needed to maintain viable populations of highly mobile species

Although some species may need only a small area to maintain viable populations, MPAs that protect a range of habitats and species as well as being managed for water quality are likely to be more than 1km across. From a practical point of view, it is often whole estuaries, bays or islands or the full extent of a scheduled habitat type that are protected.

'CONNECTIVITY': DISPERSAL POTENTIALS AND ISOLATION

It is connectivity that creates a network of MPAs but it is important to recognise that 'connectivity' has many facets for the MPA designer and manager to explore. For species that are being protected or that are a critical structural or functional part of communities, design should consider:

- whether links between separate locations can be identified (i.e. connectedness);
- whether links between separate locations are unlikely because of short dispersal distances or adverse currents, etc., and
- whether the degree of isolation that exists at a location precipitates against any connectivity between locations (which generally refers to enclosed areas with little communication with the open sea or offshore islands).

Connectivity may be through movement of adults or settled individuals or via the dispersal of larvae and propagules. The MPA practitioner needs to be aware that:

- marine species have the possibility to disperse very well through the water column if they can swim or if their larvae or propagules are long-lived;
- recruitment to an MPA could come from another MPA or, often more likely, from a location that is not in a protected zone;
- recruitment of species between specific MPAs is only likely if the MPAs are of a similar ecological character;
- many species have short-lived larvae or propagules and therefore do not significantly disperse – they need to be looked after where they are.

Shanks et al. (2003) looked at dispersal distances of marine species and found a gap in frequency of type between 1km and 20km, leading to the conclusion that reserves needed to be large enough to contain short-distance dispersing propagules and be spaced far enough apart that long-distance dispersing propagules released from one reserve can settle in an adjacent reserve. They went further and suggested that a reserve 4.6km in diameter should be large enough to contain the larvae of short-distance dispersers and reserves 10–20km apart should be close enough to capture propagules released from adjacent reserves. Palumbi (2003) recommended 20–150km apart. What also needs to be taken into account is that the adjacent reserves being planned using connectivity distances need to be of the same character (e.g. high energy rocky reefs; deep mud; estuary) and have the same biotopes that are supposedly reinforcing each other by larval or propagule dispersal (e.g. seagrass beds; kelp forest habitats; mangroves).

Some early ideas that take account of connectivity in the design of a series of MPAs make it clear that an 'ecologically coherent network' is especially important for highly mobile species, such as certain birds, mammals and fish, to safeguard the critical stages and areas of their life cycles (such as breeding, nursery and feeding areas). For instance, in OSPAR

(2007), Principle 9 states: '[d]etailed connectivity issues should be considered only for those species where a specific path between identified places is known (e.g. critical areas of a life cycle)' (p44). If building in measures of connectivity to determine spacing between separate MPAs had been reserved for highly mobile marine species and 'special' places in their life cycle, then it could have been retained as a relevant consideration. But, generalised 'connectivity' measures between MPAs were extended to encompass a wide range of species and the concept became flawed scientifically but promoted nevertheless. The concept of enabling each separate MPA to support adjacent MPAs via some sort of direct connectivity (i.e. as a network) is very attractive but should not be adopted without applying scientific rigour to the aspiration.

The few papers that exist on the success or otherwise of designing in connectivity for biodiversity (rather than fisheries) conservation can only result in pessimism about the likely practicality of the concept. Pelc et al. (2010) observe that measurements of realised connectivity remain difficult to obtain whilst Claudet et al. (2008) conclude that the ecological effectiveness of well-enforced marine reserves in the north-west Mediterranean is not increased by the proximity of other reserves. Even for fish species, Planes et al. (2009), using DNA parentage analysis, found that 40 per cent of orange clownfish (Amphiprion perula – an exploited species) larvae recruiting into an MPA in Papua New Guinea were from parents resident in the reserve and that up to 10 per cent were from other island MPAs. The inference is that 50 per cent of recruitment was from the wider (unprotected) marine environment. Jones and Carpenter (2009) considered the larval dispersal potential of 31 rare/scare benthic invertebrates listed in UK Biodiversity Action Plans and found that over half had a low dispersal potential (<1km). They argued that the establishment of representative MPA networks may be a reachable objective whilst the aim of establishing ecologically coherent MPA networks may be 'a bridge too far' (p737). Furthermore, many locations are isolated by geographical barriers, such as unsuitable habitats for settlement, or closed by topographical features such as sills. Naturally occurring isolation is likely to occur between cave systems, between islands including seamounts, between separated estuaries or fjordic habitats and between isolated lagoons. These locations may hold unique species (known for cave systems) or genetic types. Whatever the case, if larvae cannot escape, then the populations of those species need to be looked after where they are as recovery is unlikely or, in the case of an adversely affected species only being found in such an isolated location, extinction is likely. The isolation of island populations is explored by Bell (2008) who concludes: '[l]ow levels of larval exchange [between island MPAs and the mainland] may limit the success of any protected area and may prevent multiple conservation objectives from being achieved' (p2807). Jessopp and McAllen (2007), sampling plankton from a semi-enclosed marine reserve with long water retention time, from bays with short water retention, and along open coastline, conclude that only limited larval exchange was occurring between reserve and non-reserve areas, despite species having potentially large dispersal distances. Strangely, it is often areas that are isolated that are biodiversity hotspots. Examples that spring to mind are the Galapagos Islands, Lough Hyne in Ireland and the Isles of Scilly off the south-west peninsula of England. Much more work is needed before the concept of designing for direct connections for non-fish species between MPAs is proved.

The word 'network' continues to be used here as it is so widespread in directives, conventions and statutes; but, unless the word 'network' has been redefined to simply mean a collection, set or series, many so-called 'networks' are, as pointed out by Roff and Zacharias (2011) and by Roff (2014), actually 'sets' of MPAs.

Setting aside connectivity between MPAs, MPAs are highly likely to improve larval supply of exploited species to the wider marine environment – protected or unprotected. Christie *et al.* (2010), in a paper misleadingly entitled 'Larval connectivity in an effective network of Marine Protected Areas', reported that observations of 'larval connectivity provide the first direct evidence of marine protected areas (MPAs) successfully seeding unprotected areas with larval fish' (p 7). Harrison *et al.* (2012) observed, for two exploited fish species on the Great Barrier Reef, that populations resident in three reserves exported 83 per cent (coral trout, *Plectropomus maculatus*) and 55 per cent (stripey snapper, *Lutjanus carponotatus*) of offspring to fished reefs, with the remainder having recruited to natal reserves or other reserves in the region. They estimated that reserves, which accounted for just 28 per cent of the local reef area, produced approximately half of all juvenile recruitment to both reserve and fished reefs within 30km. Such 'seeding' or 'spillover' is to be expected for species with long-lived larvae or propagules, and the wider environment together with other MPAs of the same character and within relevant distances are likely to benefit.

Occasional long-distance excursions by species that are normally part of self-recruiting populations most likely occur to establish a new population that will then become self-recruiting. Where the recruits settle will depend on where currents take them and their ability to choose a suitable habitat; but this will be serendipitous, meaning that, often, suitable habitats are not occupied by expected species. Such occasional and unpredictable events cannot be programmed into network design.

Given the knowledge that we have about the range of species dispersal distances, about where larvae and propagules go when they are released and about the very low probability that one MPA will in some way directly support recruitment in another, it is very surprising that the word 'network' has become so strongly entrenched in the vocabulary of policy advisors. Indeed, seeking to design a 'network' could delay very valuable, if apparently simplistic, work to create sets of MPAs that are representative of the range of habitats and species in a biogeographical region and that protect features that are rare, scarce, in decline or threatened with decline.

Furthermore, whilst emphasis has been placed in various MPA programmes on designing in connectivity by placing MPAs a measured minimum or range of distances apart, it is more likely the other side of the 'connectivity coin' that matters in management for biodiversity conservation. Species with short dispersal distances need to be looked after where they are because the prospects for recovery from some distant MPA are minimal.

SIZE AND SHAPE

The size of a particular MPA has been addressed in the section on 'viability' (p41). Shape may be dependant mainly on the extent of the habitat being protected – if it is long and thin then the MPA may be long and thin, and so on. Most often, the boundary of the MPA will follow the boundary of the habitat to be protected although, in the case of very extensive habitats, a representative area should be identified; whilst, in the case of patchy examples of a habitat (rock reefs for instance), a boundary may encompass all of the reefs but will include non-priority habitats such as sand.

Design software

Early work using software to 'design' a network of MPAs includes the exercise by Sala *et al.* (2002) to identify potential protected areas in the Gulf of California. They used optimisation algorithms and multiple levels of information on biodiversity and ecological processes (spawning, recruitment and larval connectivity), starting with a goal of identifying 20 per cent of representative habitats and 100 per cent of rare habitats. Although socio-economic considerations were included, the outcomes do not seem to have been discussed with stakeholders: the point at which everything becomes difficult! Taking so many different design criteria into account is intimidating and Fernandes *et al.* (2005) make the point that, with reference to reserve design software, '[f]inding minimum-impact, optimal solutions from such a large array would have been beyond manual calculation, and the software was useful in providing an efficient beginning point for developing a draft zoning plan' (p1739). That reserve design software, Marxan, was developed by Ian Ball and Hugh Possingham and provides decision support for the 'optimal' design of reserve systems based on explicit trade-offs (Ball *et al.*, 2009). A later development known as Marxan with Zones is designed to enhance Marxan by providing alternative multiple-use zoning options in geographical regions for conservation (Watts *et al.*, 2009). Marxan is a decision aid not a decision-maker as its mechanistic approach is very dependent on data availability and may fail to take account of local knowledge and complex socio-economic considerations. The location and extent of no-take areas in the Great Barrier Reef Marine Park, which implemented many of the theoretical design principles and included use of Marxan, is shown in Figure 9.3.

Other considerations

Factors outside of our control

Whilst size of protected areas has dominated consideration of the viability of the protected species and habitats, management needs to ensure that the ecological processes that support them are maintained (see Figure 3.6). Those processes are overwhelmingly important but usually occur on a very large scale and would be difficult to change. However, activities such as altering the seawater flooding regime of saline lagoons or building solid causeways that block tidal flow can mean that the new conditions compromise the processes that are needed to maintain viability. Also, when change occurs, the manager needs to be aware of the processes that may have caused that change.

MPAs are not enough

MPAs allow for site-based measures to be introduced for the benefit of biodiversity, fish stocks, recreation, education and research. However, all of the benefits of good management within an MPA may be overwhelmed by what is happening in the wider marine environment. MPAs are not protected from diffuse pollution, hydrographic regime shifts or nearby construction projects that alter ecological processes. For instance, on the Ligurian coast of Italy, Montefalcone *et al.* (2009) conclude that the establishment of MPAs had not been sufficient to mitigate regional ecological impacts and that ecosystems, specifically seagrass beds, within MPAs remain vulnerable to risks originating outside of their boundaries.

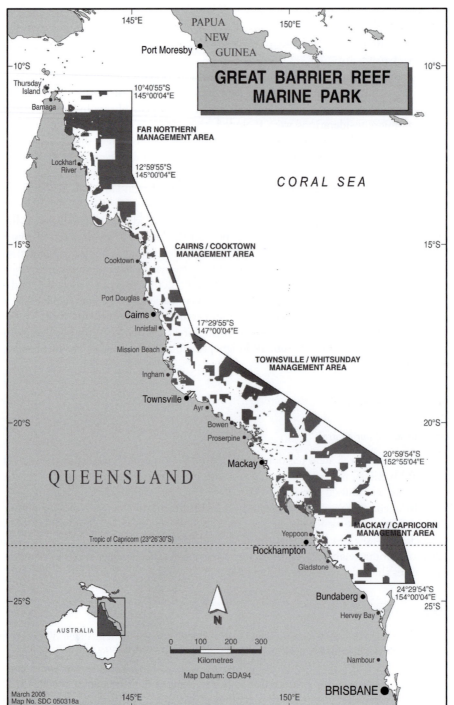

Figure 9.3 Location and extent of no-take areas in the Great Barrier Reef Marine Park.

Source: Fernandes *et al.* (2005).

That conclusion was emphasised by Parravicini *et al.* (2013) who found that, in the same area, the establishment of MPAs had been ineffective in halting degradation on rocky reef sessile communities due most likely to organic pollution but also possibly to a regime shift in the area after two warming events.

Socio-economic considerations

Taking account of socio-economic considerations is another aspect of design and is informed by knowledge of where activities occur or may occur in the future, often supported by spatial planning initiatives. Furthermore, the 'ecosystem approach' to environmental protection and management holds that human activities are a part of any consideration of management, making spatial planning an essential element of the ecosystem approach. There is a need though to get the elements of design in the 'right order', and that should mean first identifying where MPAs are needed or might best represent biodiversity. There is a likely conflict that is summed up in Roberts *et al.* (2003, p S215):

> Too often, socioeconomic criteria have dominated the process of reserve selection, potentially undermining their efficacy. We argue that application of biological criteria must precede and inform socioeconomic evaluation, since maintenance of ecosystem functioning is essential for meeting all of the goals for reserves.

Benefitting from the knowledge of stakeholders and working with them to accommodate, as far as possible, their legitimate needs and concerns is, however, an essential part of the MPA design process and is often a determinant of acceptability and success.

Getting the terminology right: 'networks' and 'sets' of MPAs and 'coherence'

'Networks' and 'sets' of MPAs

From early, fairly straightforward proposals to establish protected locations that were representative of different habitats and that would include threatened species and habitats, aspirations for MPAs became more and more ambitious. In particular, the idea of 'networks' of MPAs gained momentum from early proposals (for instance, Sala *et al.*, 2002) through to the word becoming extensively used in directives, conventions and statutes. Unfortunately, as already indicated, the word 'network' has been widely applied without thinking whether the connectivity that is inherent in a network is actually present in what are often, in reality, 'sets' of MPAs. The differences between 'networks' and 'sets' of MPAs are explored in Roff and Zacharias (2011). They are clear about the differences:

- A 'set' of MPAs is any group of protected areas within a geographic region or regions that collectively represent the components of marine biodiversity of that region.
- A 'coherent' set of MPAs is a set of MPAs within a defined region that collectively achieve a defined goal. For example, they may achieve a level of protection for 20 per cent of the region, and collectively represent all of the identifiable biotic and abiotic components of marine biodiversity within the region.
- 'Networks' of MPAs are '[a] collection of individual marine protected areas that operates cooperatively and synergistically at various spatial scales, and with a range of

protection levels, in order to fulfill ecological aims more effectively and comprehensively than individual sites could alone' (IUCN, 2007, p3).

Grorud-Colvert *et al.* categorise different types of marine reserve network although only one, the 'connectivity network' ('a set of multiple marine reserves connected by the dispersal of larvae and/or movement of juveniles, or adults (2011, p299): see also Planes *et al.*, 2009), come close to the common perception of a network – that is, a series of interconnected nodes. They go on to specify tests to establish if there is a significant overall network effect greater than the sum of individual reserve effects. Gaines *et al.* (2010), in their paper entitled 'Designing marine reserve networks for both conservation and fisheries management', describe the requirement to have minimum total areas either of large single MPAs or many smaller ones to be effective. Their 'network' is a grouping of MPAs with no indication of direct connections between each than is more than the general connectivity that occurs in the marine environment. However, they do draw attention to theoretical models that suggest that networks can have emergent benefits that make the network more than the sum of its parts (Neubert, 2003; Crowder *et al.*, 2000).

Roff and Zacharias (2011, Chapter 17) describe how an efficient multi-species network can be achieved but much of their approach requires knowledge that we are unlikely to have (especially on larval development times) or that is more complex than we think (larval development times do not equal, with residual current strength and direction, connections as larval behaviour is often unknown). The competent conservation scientist should check whether they have the knowledge to design a network or that they have indeed designed a network before casually using the term.

Ecological coherence

To compound the problems for scientists trying to apply scientifically difficult concepts of connectivity, in 2003 OSPAR introduced the phrase 'ecologically coherent' in addition to 'network'. Both terms suggest connective structures (see Ardron, 2008a) so, to make sense, 'coherent' must mean more than just population connectivity. Even as late as 2012, OSPAR had to declare that 'no specific definition for the term "ecological coherence" has yet been formally agreed upon internationally and only a few theoretical concepts and practical approaches have been developed for an assessment of the ecological coherence of a network of MPAs' (OSPAR, 2013, p32). However, according to OSPAR and HELCOM (cited in OSPAR, 2012), an ecologically coherent network of MPAs:

- interacts with and supports the wider environment;
- maintains the processes, functions, and structures of the intended protected features across their natural range; and
- functions synergistically as a whole, such that the individual protected sites benefit from each other to achieve the two objectives above;
- (additionally) the network may also be designed to be resilient to changing conditions (e.g. climate change).

Those goals are worthy but do not translate into design criteria.

OSPAR (2007) and Ardron (2008b) suggest that assessment of ecological coherence could be grouped under four general criteria: adequacy/viability, representativity, replication and connectivity. Those principles are widely accepted in MPA literature and, setting aside the fact that they do not together translate from the word 'coherent', they can be applied to MPA design. Those four characteristics are scientifically challenging to achieve and Ardron (2008a, p1527) observes that '[p]roper scientific assessment [of ecological coherence] is hampered by the current lack of detailed ecological data'. Added to that lack of detailed ecological data is our poor understanding of what are complex physical and biological processes that govern what occurs where and how it changes naturally. These problems led to the development of heuristic ('rule of thumb') measures that would assist in addressing viability (based on size of area) and connectivity (based on distance apart of areas). Ardron (2008a) supports such experience-based approaches and is critical of requirements for 'purely scientifically based assessments' (p1531) which, whilst preferable, may not always be possible.

It seems that what OSPAR were really aiming for were MPAs that were determined on ecological principles and, wherever possible, connected with other MPAs.

All in all, perhaps we are trying too hard to emulate the engineers who can design a bridge that will take 20 buses without collapsing (which they can do) in trying to design effective 'networks' (which we cannot do). Nevertheless, we can still ensure that sets of MPAs are representative, include threatened species and habitats, and function to protect the species and habitats that occur in them. Sloppy use of terminology has confused rather than clarified the process of designing a series of MPAs that is effective for marine conservation. Aspirational aims or goals that cannot be achieved with the science that we currently have are unnecessary and unhelpful.

What to expect

Recovery of numbers of previously exploited species is likely to be very rapid in highly protected MPAs and is described, together with associated changes in other species, in Chapter 11, 'Examples of recovery' (p198). A synthesis of a wide range of studies, but including mainly species that were previously exploited, is given in Lester et al. (2009) who describe higher levels of biomass and abundance of fish, invertebrates and, sometimes, algae in highly protected MPAs (Figure 9.4). They observe that 'reserves are more likely to lead to large positive effects for species that are fished, intentionally or incidentally, or that are otherwise harmed by activities occurring in unprotected waters' (Lester et al., p43). It is more difficult to find evidence for differences in abundance and variety of non-exploited species (the general 'biodiversity' of a location) between MPAs and non-MPAs.

In a study of rocky inshore areas across the Mediterranean, Sala et al. (2012) compared MPAs with various levels of protection and unprotected sites. They found much higher biomass of fish in well-protected areas (Figure 9.5) but 'did not find any effect of MPAs on benthic communities, and there was no clear pattern of the structure of benthic communities associated with the gradient in fish biomass' (p10). Nevertheless, they did observe:

> The only example of recovery of a Cystoseira canopy after protection comes from the Medes Islands Marine Reserve. The Medes Islands did not have sublittoral Cystoseira when they were protected in 1983, but Cystoseira sp. became abundant after 1992, suggesting that recovery of formerly abundant Cystoseira canopies in the

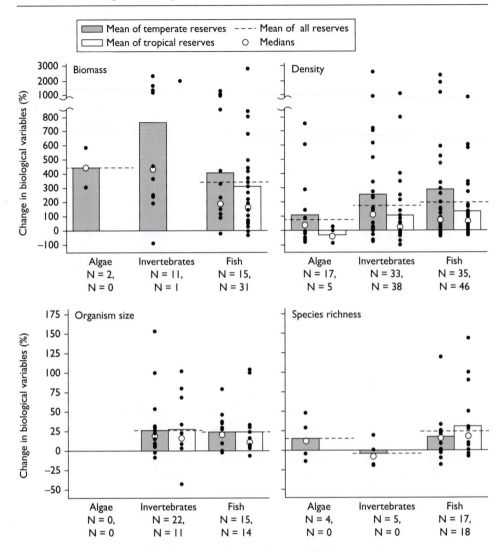

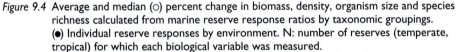

Figure 9.4 Average and median (o) percent change in biomass, density, organism size and species richness calculated from marine reserve response ratios by taxonomic groupings. (●) Individual reserve responses by environment. N: number of reserves (temperate, tropical) for which each biological variable was measured.

Source: Lester *et al.* (2009).

NW Mediterranean takes longer than recovery of fish assemblages. Since dispersion of *Cystoseira* appears to be very limited, the recovery of lost canopies in large areas may prove difficult.

(Sala *et al.*, 2012, p10)

'Rebalancing' from exploited to protected may create some surprises and some species may decline in abundance as a result. An example is the rise in abundance and size of spiny lobsters in the Leigh Marine Reserve so that the clam population became vulnerable and

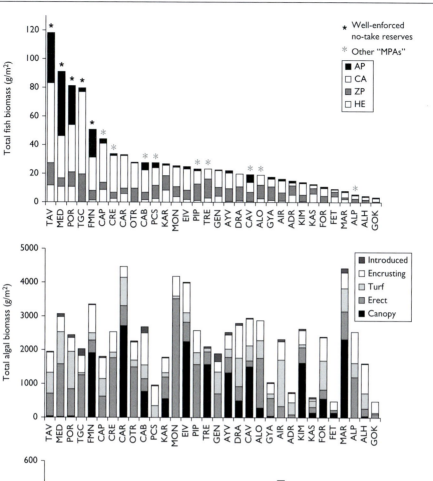

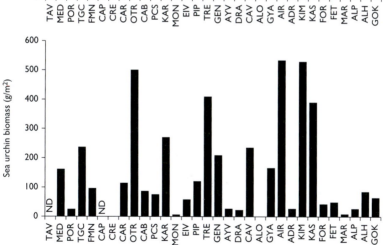

Figure 9.5 Biomass of fish, algae and sea urchins at 32 locations in the Mediterranean Sea. The sites are ordered according to the fish biomass where well-enforced MPAs have the greatest biomass, especially of apex predators. Algal and sea urchin biomass show no clear relationship with fish biomass or MPA status. AP = apex predators, CA = carnivores, ZP = (zoo)planktivores, HE = herbivores + detritivores.

Source: Sala *et al.* (2012) (where a key to the location codes can be found).

was depleted (e.g. Langlois *et al.*, 2006b). Work that has been under way at the only no-take area in the UK (4.3km² of the Lundy Marine Nature Reserve) since 2004 has identified a great increase in the abundance and size of lobsters, *Homarus gammarus*, within the protected area and with probable benefits to stocks outside. There are also initial indications that velvet swimming crabs, *Necora puber*, might be adversely affected by the rise in lobster numbers and their size (Hoskin *et al.*, 2011). In north-west Italy, Parravicini *et al.* (2013) report that fishing restrictions in MPAs may have contributed to an observed community shift. Large herbivorous fish, *Sarpa salpa*, were favoured by the fishing restrictions and their increased grazing was capable of driving algal assemblages towards a turf-dominated state (and thus decreasing structural complexity).

There may be disappointment when protected areas become degraded despite the measures taken to manage damaging activities within them. The reasons range from effects of diffuse pollutants to regime shifts resulting from natural oceanic changes (see 'Changing from one state to another', Chapter 4, p56).

Managing what we have

Introduction

Management actions involve reducing or removing damaging pressures and restricting or preventing the activities or inputs that cause those pressures. In some areas identified as part of a series of MPAs, active management may not be needed – they are in good condition and subject to natural fluctuations. In some areas, management will address characteristics of the wider marine environment that may be adversely affecting the features of the MPA (especially such matters as agricultural run-off, release of contaminants into the sea and action to prevent arrival of non-native species). Direct action will be against damaging activities within the protected areas such as aggregate extraction, bottom trawling, hand gathering of living resources. That management action is assisted by having ranked the degree of damage likely to be caused by different activities and is being undertaken in many countries as a part of spatial management initiatives (see, as an example, Figure 9.6). Management may be directed at increasing resilience of natural communities through the sorts of actions mentioned in Chapter 11 ('Prioritising action', p226). Sometimes, management is against a specific pest species such as the crown of thorn starfish on the Great Barrier Reef. The starfish consumes coral and is considered to have 'outbreaks' much more frequently than is natural because of land run-off that includes nutrients from artificial fertilisers. Starfish have been killed by injecting them with acid and, on the Great Barrier Reef, a control strategy is being developed (see www.gbrmpa.gov.au/about-the-reef/animals/crown-of-thorns-starfish/management-strategies, accessed 12 April 2014).

Goals, objectives and indicators

The MPA manager needs structures that inform what management is to achieve. Often, there are broad goals or statements rather than clear measurable objectives. Once objectives have been agreed, then indicators can be identified. Objectives should be SMART (Specific, Measurable, Achievable, Relevant and Time-bound).

Fishing gear type		Generic sub-features					
		Subtidal sand (high energy)	Subtidal gravel and sand	Subtidal muddy sand	Seagrass	Maerl	Mussel bed on boulder and cobble skears
Towed (demersal)	Beam trawl (whitefish)	A	A	A	R	R	A
	Beam trawl (shrimp)	A	A	A	R	R	A
	Beam trawl (pulse/wing)	A	A	A	R	R	A
	Heavy otter trawl	A	A	A	R	R	A
	Multi-rig trawls	A	A	A	R	R	A
	Light otter trawl	A	A	A	R	R	A
	Pair trawl	A	A	A	R	R	A
	Anchor seine	A	A	A	R	R	A
	Scottish/fly seine	A	A	A	R	R	A
Towed (pelagic)	Mid-water trawl (single)	NA	NA	NA	NA	NA	NA
	Mid-water trawl (pair)	NA	NA	NA	NA	NA	NA
	Industrial trawls	NA	NA	NA	NA	NA	NA
Dredges (towed)	Scallops	A	A	A	R	R	A
	Mussels, clams, oysters	A	A	A	R	R	A
	Pump scoop (cockles, clams)	A	A	A	R	R	NA
Dredges (other)	Suction (cockles)	A	A	A	R	R	NA
	Tractor	NA	NA	NA	R	NA	NA
Intertidal handwork	Hand work (access from vessel)	NA	NA	NA	R	NA	A
	Hand work (access from land)	NA	NA	NA	R	NA	A
Static - pots/traps	Pots/creels (crustacea/gastropods)	G	A	A	A	A	A
	Cuttle pots	G	A	A	A	A	A
	Fish traps	G	A	A	A	A	A
Static - fixed	Gill nets	G	A	A	A	A	A

Figure 9.6 Part of a tabulated summary of risk categories for fishery against habitat types present in Special Areas of Conservation (redrawn). (There are many more columns of habitat types.) Such matrices are an important touchstone for managers and policy advisors. They rely on assessments of sensitivity (see Chapter 7) and are here interpreted as a 'traffic light' system (but without the colours) easily understood by stakeholders and politicians. R = Red (it is clear that the conservation objective for a feature (or sub-feature) will not be achieved because of its sensitivity to a type of fishing); A = Amber (there is doubt as to whether conservation objectives for a feature (or sub-feature) will be achieved because of its sensitivity to a type of fishing); G = Green (it is clear that the achievement of the conservation objectives for a feature is highly unlikely to be affected by a type of fishing activity or activities); NA = not applicable (for gear types where there can be no feasible interaction). A further 17 fishing gear types have not been included in this example.

Source: Redrawn from the UK Marine Management Organisation with permission (www.marinemanagement. org.uk/protecting/conservation/ems_fisheries.htm).

Integrated management and marine spatial planning: MPAs in context

MPAs cannot be managed in isolation from all of the other activities that are happening in the coastal zone or further offshore. They are a part of Integrated Coastal Zone Management (ICZM) and of marine spatial planning (MSP) which works to ensure, as far as possible, that the many different uses of the sea and its fringing habitats do not interfere with each other. MSP is defined as 'the process of analysing and allocating parts of three-dimensional marine spaces to specific uses to achieve ecological, economic, and social objectives that are usually specified through the political process' (Ehler and Douvere, 2007, p13).

Spatial planning identifies areas preferred or allocated for different activities and a simplified map is shown in Box 9.6. Although geographically separated from an MPA, many of those activities may still adversely affect that MPA. Advice on best practice in spatial planning is available for different regional seas and catalogued by UNESCO's Marine Spatial Planning Initiative (www.unesco-ioc-marinesp.be). There are differences between policy initiatives that set out to protect biodiversity and those that are developing marine spatial plans. In the ecosystem approach, biodiversity conservation is an essential and integrated part needed to ensure 'Good Environmental Status', whilst in spatial planning, MPAs are just one of the uses of sea space (see Qui and Jones, 2013).

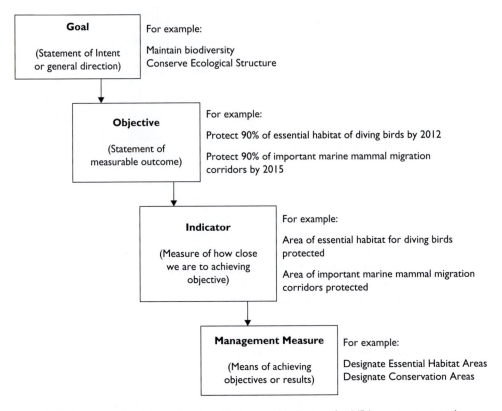

Figure 9.7 The connection between goals, objectives and indicators for MPA management and marine spatial planning.

Source: Douvere and Ehler (2011).

Box 9.6 Coastal Zone Management/Marine Spatial Planning

Simplified map of spatial planning zones in the Belgium Exclusive Economic Zone (EEZ). The length of coastline is approximately 65km. MPAs are the Birds and Habitats Directives Zones.

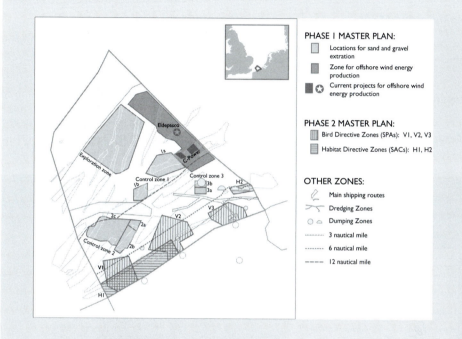

PHASE 1 MASTER PLAN:
- Locations for sand and gravel extration
- Zone for offshore wind energy production
- Current projects for offshore wind energy production

PHASE 2 MASTER PLAN:
- Bird Directive Zones (SPAs): V1, V2, V3
- Habitat Directive Zones (SACs): H1, H2

OTHER ZONES:
- Main shipping routes
- Dredging Zones
- Dumping Zones
- 3 nautical mile
- 6 nautical mile
- 12 nautical mile

Source: Douvere *et al.* (2007).

'Managing a nature reserve or marine park in isolation from surrounding land uses and peoples, and without wide cooperation from agencies, stakeholders and impacters, may not fully succeed. The reason is that protected areas alienated from a wider programme of coastal resources management exist as 'islands of protection' surrounded by uncontrolled areas of threat where pollution, habitat destruction and overfishing may exist. CZM provides an appropriate framework for incorporation of protected areas into a larger system of protection and a method of consensus building for their support.'

(Salm *et al.*, 2000, p 107)

The process of integrating management of all of the various activities, especially in inshore areas, is not easy, and understanding how one activity may adversely affect the quality of an MPA may be difficult to demonstrate and even more difficult to address in terms of management action. It is essential to apply our understanding of marine processes (see

Figure 3.6), to have information on what is where from a biodiversity point of view and to have knowledge of the sensitivity of species and habitats (Chapter 7, 'Sensitivity of species and habitats', p107) in the MPA, but that information is often incomplete.

Cicin-Sain and Belfiore (2005) suggest nine guiding principles for managing MPAs within an integrated coastal management context. They are based on governance regimes and the reader is referred to Jones (2014) for more information.

Zoning within MPAs

The categories of activities that are matched against what is and is not permitted are exemplified in Figure 9.8 and have been reviewed internationally by Day *et al.* (2012) (Figure 9.9).

Adaptive management

Once an MPA is established or, indeed, any conservation measure that protects species and habitats is implemented, monitoring should tell the manager what changes are occurring and how effective regulation and other measures are. Change might be ecological and the

ACTIVITIES GUIDE (see relevant *Zoning Plans* and *Regulations* for details)	General Use Zone	Habitat Protection Zone	Conservation Park Zone	Buffer Zone	Scientific Research Zone [2]	Marine National Park Zone	Preservation Zone	State Zoning Only	Estuarine Conservation Zone
Aquaculture	Permit	Permit	Permit[1]	×	×	×	×		Permit
Bait netting	✓	✓	✓	×	×	×	×		✓
Boating, driving, photography	✓	✓	✓	✓	✓[2]	✓	×		✓
Crabbing (trapping)	✓	✓	✓[3]	×	×	×	×		✓
Harvest fishing for aquarium fish, coral and beachworm	Permit	Permit	Permit[1]	×	×	×	×		×
Harvest fishing for sea cucumber, trochus, tropical rock lobster	Permit	Permit	×	×	×	×	×	State Zoning Only	×
Limited collecting	✓[4]	✓[4]	✓[4]	×	×	×	×		✓
Limited spearfishing (snorkel only)	✓	✓	✓[1]	×	×	×	×		✓
Line fishing	✓[5]	✓[5]	✓[6]	×	×	×	×		✓
Netting (other than bait netting)	✓	✓	×	×	×	×	×		✓
Research (other than limited impact research)	Permit	Permit	Permit	Permit	Permit	Permit	Permit		Permit
Shipping (other than in a designated shipping area)	✓	Permit	Permit	Permit	Permit	Permit	×		Permit
Tourism programme	Permit	Permit	Permit	Permit	Permit	Permit	×		Permit
Traditional use of marine resources	✓[7]	✓[7]	✓[7]	✓[7]	✓[7]	✓[7]	×		✓[7]
Trawling	✓	×	×	×	×	×	×		×
Trolling	✓[5]	✓[5]	✓[5]	✓[5,8]	×	×	×		✓

Figure 9.8 Zoning scheme for the Great Barrier Reef.

Source: www.gbrmpa.gov.au/__data/assets/pdf_file/0020/4358/IntroActiveGuide.pdf (accessed on 23 December, 2013).

Activities	IUCN types of MPAs						
	Ia	Ib	II	III	IV	V	VI
Research: non-extractive	Y*	Y	Y	Y	Y	Y	Y
Non-extractive traditional use	Y*	Y	Y	Y	Y	Y	Y
Restoration/enhancement for conservation (e.g. invasive species control, coral reintroduction)	Y*	*	Y	Y	Y	Y	Y
Traditional fishing/collection in accordance with cultural traditional and use	N	Y*	Y	Y	Y	Y	Y
Non-extractive recreation (e.g. diving)	N	*	Y	Y	Y	Y	Y
Large scale low intensity tourism	N	N	Y	Y	Y	Y	Y
Shipping (except as may be unavoidable under international maritime law)	N	N	Y*	Y*	Y	Y	Y
Problem wildlife management (e.g. shark control programmes)	N	N	Y*	Y*	Y*	Y	Y
Research: extractive	N*	N*	N*	N*	Y	Y	Y
Renewable energy generation	N	N	N	N	Y	Y	Y
Restoration/enhancement for other reasons (e.g. beach replenishment, fish aggregation, artificial reefs)	N	N	N*	N*	Y	Y	Y
Fishing/collection: recreational	N	N	N	N	*	Y	Y
Fishing/collection: long term and sustainable local fishing practices	N	N	N	N	*	Y	Y
Aquaculture	N	N	N	N	*	Y	Y
Works (e.g. harbour, ports, dredging)	N	N	N	N	*	Y	Y
Untreated waste discharge	N	N	N	N	N	Y	Y
Mining (seafloor as well as sub-seafloor)	N	N	N	N	N	Y*	Y*
Habitation	N	N*	N*	N*	N*	Y	N*

Figure 9.9 A matrix of activities that may be appropriate or not within each of the types of Marine Protected Areas specified by IUCN (see Box 9.1, p138). N = No; N* = Generally no, unless special circumstances apply; Y = Yes; Y* = Yes because no alternative exists, but special approval essential; * = Variable, depends on whether this activity can be managed in such a way that it is compatible with the MPA's objectives.

Source: Redrawn from Day et al. (2012).

result of natural fluctuations (see Chapter 4, 'Change, what change?', p45). Change can include improvement in understanding of conservation science so that we better understand how the system or species being protected 'works'. It may be that change has occurred in socio-economic perceptions and barriers to protection that had existed previously have been removed. Management should not be static but should adapt to experience and improved knowledge.

Adaptive management (Salafsky *et al.*, 2001: Figure 9.10) allows for not having got it right in the first place. That might mean, for instance, that the extent of a habitat has been under-recorded or that a precautionary boundary has included areas that are no longer required in a protected area.

Management measures must be effective and 'effectively managed' is a frequent part of the objectives of MPAs. If the pressures that are likely to damage biodiversity are not effectively managed, then situations arise such as concern regarding impacts of continued coastal development and water quality issues on the Great Barrier Reef Marine Park (UNESCO, 2013). UNESCO (2013, p22) note the outcomes of 'a number of important scientific and technical reports released during 2012, indicating significant loss of coral cover over the past 27 years resulting mainly from storm damage, climate change effects and crown of thorns starfish and concluding that reducing crown of thorn starfish outbreaks are a key factor in restoring the loss'. Although those factors are mainly unmanageable (although a campaign to destroy starfish was under way in 2013), it seems that insufficient action is being taken, to the extent that UNESCO (2013) suggested that the Great Barrier Reef World Heritage Site may be put on the List of World Heritage in Danger.

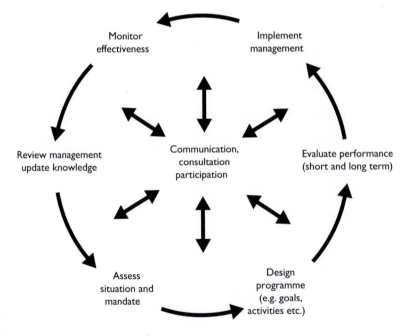

Figure 9.10 Adaptive management cycle.
Source: Redrawn from Salafsky *et al.* (2001).

Improving what we have

The preceding text has reflected where we are now with the best use of science and the knowledge that we have in selecting and establishing meaningful sets of MPAs. Understanding the effectiveness of those MPAs in delivering biodiversity conservation and in improving design and management is, inevitably, ongoing. The European Union has identified the following science needs and priorities to improve the effectiveness of their MPAs:

- Promote a coordinated, harmonised and open access approach to MPA-relevant data obtained through marine survey work;
- Refine habitat classifications using modeling distributions of critical or vulnerable marine ecosystem indicators at a scale relevant to both MPA planning and fisheries management;
- Promote systematic long-term monitoring of MPAs and their surrounding waters;
- Advance the understanding of ecological coherence gaps and critical components such as connectivity;
- Establish a core set of indicators to measure MPA network efficiency;
- Promote the incorporation of adaptive approaches and new and emerging issues such as climate resilience and blue carbon in MPA management;
- Provide legal clarity to establish clear guidelines for international bodies and Member States regarding cooperation in the high seas and implementation of stringent MPA management measures;
- Establish culturally appropriate guidance to promote stakeholder engagement and incorporate socio-economic issues;
- Develop policy-relevant guidance for systematic and harmonized MPA network development, management and review; and
- Promote cross-sector partnerships and develop pilot projects that link marine monitoring with maritime surveillance.

(Olsen *et al.*, 2013, p8)

There are problems with the application of selection and design criteria, possibly because of overenthusiasm to mimic the sort of precision that can be applied to engineering projects but more likely because of pressure from politicians driven by MPA opponents to quantify what we do. In conclusion, MPAs established for the conservation of biodiversity are representative of the range of marine habitats in a (bio)geographical area and they protect or should protect rare, sensitive and threatened habitats and species. Where selected locations are critical for life history stages of a species, they may protect connectivity nodes; but protecting species where they are now is more likely to succeed than identifying hypothetical networks. Furthermore, identifying sizes of areas and distance apart based on what is actually very empirical science has allowed bureaucrats to create rules and targets that lead to perfectly good sites failing to be selected. MPAs should also provide reference points for scientists investigating structure and functioning in communities, undertaking autecological studies and assessing the impacts of human activities in unprotected areas. MPAs should also be used to enable to the public to see rich and varied marine life.

Selection and design of MPAs should not be a 'black art' – the criteria and measures that we have are based on evidence and on sound science. They are justifiable to politicians and to doubters or to adversaries. However, those criteria and measures need to be used as guidance and not as a rule book. Experience, common sense and, especially in relation to taking account of socio-economic considerations, pragmatism are needed in application.

There are many problems of inadequacy or poor design and management in the MPAs that we have. Agardy *et al.* (2011) describe five shortcomings of MPAs summarised here as:

1   Many MPAs are too small to achieve their goals.
2   Many are inappropriately planned or managed.
3   Many fail due to degradation of the surrounding unprotected area.
4   Many do more harm than good due to displacement and unintended consequences of management.
5   MPAs may create a dangerous illusion of protection when in fact no protection is occurring.

Furthermore, MPAs, once established, need to be effectively managed with enforcement of the rules plus regular assessment to ensure that the objectives are being achieved (Toropova et al., 2010).

All of the above assumes that politicians and their advisors will apply criteria in a beneficial way to the protection of biodiversity that is representative and threatened. Unfortunately, and driven by quantitative targets that are often meaningless, it may appear that action has been taken when in fact meaningful action has not. There are now many examples of large areas being protected that were of little or no interest to fishermen or industry but which bump up the percentage of areas 'protected' to meet targets. As a specific example, in relation to north and north-west Australia, the Centre for Conservation Geography (2011, p5) report that:

> the proposed marine sanctuaries protect less than 3% of the shelf and upper slope where scientists report marine life to be most threatened. By comparison the proposed marine sanctuaries protect more than 80% of the abyssal plain where fishing and mining tends not to occur.

Conclusions

1   There are well-established criteria to identify the characteristics of areas that should be selected for protection. Inevitably, those areas are locations where we know what is there and where identifying 'representativeness', 'rarity', 'presence of threatened and/or declining species or habitats', 'sensitivity' and 'naturalness' are all important. Additionally, 'high natural diversity' may be applied and biodiversity hotspots identified.
2   Practical issues need to be considered when identifying potential MPAs. They include socio-economic effects (positive and negative), the likelihood of effective management being possible and whether there is potential for recovery. A negative economic or societal impact is likely to predicate against establishment whereas high intrinsic appeal is likely to encourage establishment.
3   Identifying management measures that will maintain and, if needed, recover the species and habitats in a MPA depend on identifying the purpose of the MPA and, in particular, what is damaging or has damaged features. Some MPAs will protect a sector of the inhabitants but some will be designed to be full reserves with all extractive and depositional activities prohibited.
4   MPAs are a part of Integrated Coastal Zone Management or Spatial Planning. An aim of integrated management is to ensure that MPAs are not adversely affected by activities in the wider marine environment.

5   Feedback on the effectiveness of measures within MPAs, knowledge of change occurring in the MPA and taking account of improved scientific knowledge, change of usage and evaluating public perceptions are all essential. They feed in to adaptive management.

6   The IUCN-WCPA (2008) guide to establishing resilient networks of MPAs has a self-assessment checklist (Box 9.7) to help the practitioner establish whether (or not) they have achieved their objectives.

Box 9.7 Self-assessment checklist for the establishment of resilient networks of MPAs. From IUCN-WCPA (2008).

The checklist is designed to help planners, managers and national and regional authorities assess current progress towards building effective MPA networks as well as to evaluate progress toward long-term network objectives. Each item is scored as 'Yes', 'No', 'Partially' or can be assessed on a defined scale.

BROADSCALE CONSIDERATIONS AND PLANNING POLICIES GUIDELINES

Scientific & information management considerations. Has all available scientific information and local knowledge of stakeholders been used to support planning and management, and is it is regularly updated and used for effective decision-making?

Use of best available science & precautionary design. Is the MPA network configured to take into consideration all or most of the scientific and socio-economic information and traditional knowledge within the area, while uncertainty and lack of information has not delayed decision-making?

Incorporate stakeholders. Has a wide range of stakeholders (including local and regional stakeholders) been directly involved in planning the network and assisting the managers by being involved in virtually all of the planning and management decisions for the network?

Clearly defined objectives. Is there a range of clear, achievable and measurable objectives (including ecological, social and economic objectives) defined for the MPA network and derived from the legislation?

Integrated management framework. Does the MPA network fit within a clear integrated and holistic framework, including both planning and management at differing scales (ranging from national planning frameworks, through to regional/local planning and site planning)?

Adaptive management. Is the MPA network readily able to incorporate changes such as new information from field experience or as a result of changing external circumstances?

Economic & social considerations. Does the design and implementation of the MPA network consider the economic and sociocultural setting, as well as the real benefits and costs of the network (including both tangible and intangible benefits and costs)?

Spatial & temporal considerations. Does the MPA network design include a wide range of spatial and temporal considerations, such as ecological processes, connectivity and external influences, and do managers continue to consider these factors as part of ongoing implementation?

Institutional & governance considerations. Does the MPA network have well-established mechanisms for horizontal integration among all levels of government and vertical integration among agencies with different mandates, as well as involving local communities, indigenous peoples and regional groups?

ECOLOGICAL GUIDELINES

Size. Has specific consideration been given to the size of the individual MPAs within the network to account for adult species movement ranges and larval dispersal distances to maximize the network's effectiveness in achieving its ecological objectives?

Shape. Has specific consideration been given to the shape of the individual MPAs within the network to account for edge effects and the enforceability of regularly shaped boundaries with clear delineation?

Replication. Does the MPA network include spatially separated replicates of no-take areas within the ecoregions to spread risk?

Long-term protection. Does the MPA network have an efficient combination of legislative instruments (statutes, laws, regulations) and/or administrative instruments (policies) at various levels (local/state/national), that collectively provide long-term protection for the MPA network and ensure its viability?

Full range of biodiversity in biogeographic region. Does the MPA network fully represent the region by capturing the full range of biodiviersity, ensure representation across depth ranges and biogeography, and ensure ecosystem integrity?

Ecological linkages. Is the MPA network purposefully designed to maximize all ecological processes (spatial and/or temporal) known to occur in the area?

IMPLEMENTATION GUIDELINES

Political will & leadership. Is there strong and effective leadership, commitment and support at both the political and agency levels, with a shared vision and capacity to achieve success?

Public education, communication & awareness. Is the community (including the local communities and the wider public) aware of the MPA network and the management agency(ies), through effective education outreach and communication plans?

Compliance & enforcement. Are feasible enforcement programs and methods to build compliance considered in the MPA network?

Monitoring & assessment. Does a monitoring and evaluation system exist showing progress against most, if not all, of the MPA network objectives being monitored regularly? Are the results widely disseminated and used in adaptive management?

Sustainable financing. Does the MPA network have a well-developed and periodically audited program of long-term funding (assessed, and, if necessary, increased against a recognized financial index) to meet both core and emerging costs?

Source: www.protectplanetocean.org/resources/docs/MPAnetworks-MakingItHappen.pdf

Chapter 10

Assessing likely impacts and monitoring change

Introduction

Society expects to obtain a wide variety of services from the marine environment but, at the same time, wants them protected for the future. This chapter explains what might be included in environmental (or ecological) impact assessments and the sorts of information that will inform those assessments. It emphasises that protection of the environment should be a fundamental part of *any* proposed development and not just a part of management measures for activities within MPAs. Protection (which incorporates an acceptance that change will happen) of the environment, including of biodiversity features, is the start of a process that continues into monitoring. Monitoring is both biological and regulatory. Biological monitoring is undertaken to establish if formulated standards are being maintained although will often document change that is natural and change that may be explainable or unexplainable. Monitoring must be designed to have the precision to separate apparent change brought about by the methods it has used or as a result of natural variability from change that is real and the result of human activities.

Environmental Impact Assessments

Environmental Impact Assessments (EIAs) have been a part of the planning process since the 1960s. They are intended to assess the likely impacts of a proposed plan, project or activity on environmental, social and economic matters. They often include proposals for mitigating adverse effects. They should provide an objective basis for deciding whether an activity is acceptable or not and whether there are measures that might reduce or prevent impacts on features that are important to biodiversity conservation. In terms of biodiversity conservation, the term 'Ecological Impact Assessment' (EcIA) may be more appropriate as it identifies the potential impacts of actions on ecosystems and their components.

What is legally required will vary from country to country. For an EcIA, IEEM (2010) suggest the stages identified in Box 10.1.

The EcIA should consider likely impacts on habitats and species and may use a checklist such as that in Table 10.1 although other categories may be relevant.

An early stage in any impact assessment is to establish what are the habitats and species present in the relevant area and whether any are identified as key structural or key functional species and whether any are scheduled for protection or valued in some other way (for cultural reasons or recreation). That requires access to existing information (Chapter 2)

Box 10.1 Stages of an Ecological Impact Assessment

An Ecological Impact Assessment (EcIA) should include the following stages:

1   **scoping**, involving consultation to ensure the most effective input to the definition of the scope of an EcIA (in practice, scoping is iterative throughout the EcIA process);

2   identification of the likely **zone of influence**, which may vary during the whole lifespan of the project;

3   identification and evaluation of **ecological features, resources and functions** likely to be affected by the project;

4   identification of the **drivers** of biophysical changes attributable to the project;

5   identification of the **biophysical changes** attributable to the project that are likely to affect **valued ecological features and resources**;

6   assessment of whether these biophysical changes are likely to give rise to a significant ecological impact, defined as an impact on the **integrity of a defined site or ecosystem** and/or the **conservation status of habitats or species within a given geographical area**, including cumulative and in-combination impacts;

7   refinement of the project to avoid or reduce identified negative impacts and incorporate **mitigation measures** and/or **compensation measures** for any residual significant negative impacts and **ecological enhancement measures** to improve the wider environment;

8   **assessment of the ecological impacts** of the refined project and **definition of the significance** of these impacts, including cumulative and in-combination impacts;

9   provision of advice on the **consequences for decision making** of the significant ecological impacts, based on the value of the resource, feature or function; and

10 provision for **monitoring** and following up the implementation and success of mitigation and compensation measures and **ecological outcomes**, including feedback in relation to predicted outcomes.

(IEEM, 2010, p4)

and probably new survey that will deliver accurate and relevant information (Chapter 8). The developers or those planning a project or currently undertaking a potentially damaging activity will need to identify the likely environmental effects, and that might involve modelling of physical and chemical factors as well as seeking out case studies and/or understanding some of the relevant principles of ecosystem structure and functioning. Having established the likely environmental changes, the effects on habitats and species of those changes will need to be assessed. If the assessor is fortunate, there will be tables that match biotopes and species to their intolerance and recovery potential to those environmental changes ('Sensitivity of species and habitats' in Chapter 7, p107). If not, some new research will be needed in relation to key structural or functional species and habitats, commercial

Table 10.1 Categories that might be considered in an EcIA. The categories are derived from those used to assess sensitivity to environmental factors in the MarLIN programme (www.marlin.ac.uk)

Is the proposed development likely to result in . . . ?	• Change in nutrient levels

Is the proposed development likely to result in . . . ?
• Substratum loss
• Smothering
• Increase in suspended sediment
• Desiccation
• Increase/decrease in emergence regime
• Increase/decrease in water flow rate
• Increase/decrease in temperature
• Increase/decrease in turbidity (light penetration)
• Increase/decrease in wave exposure
• Noise
• Visual disturbance
• Abrasion/physical disturbance
• Displacement
• Synthetic compound contamination
• Heavy metal contamination
• Hydrocarbon contamination
• Radionuclide contamination

• Change in nutrient levels
• Increase/decrease in salinity
• Increases/decreases in oxygenation
Is the proposed development likely to affect . . . ?
• Key structural or functional species
• Species that are valued because of their rarity, cultural importance or recreational appeal
• Locations that are used for feeding, shelter, breeding/spawning, migration of species
• Food sources for species
• Food webs
• Extent of habitats
• Frequency of habitat disturbance
• Use of the area for harvesting (from recreational to commercial)
Is the proposed development likely to introduce . . . ?
• Microbial pathogens/parasites
• Non-native species

species or those that are scheduled in some way for protection. Survival rates (for instance, of fish at power station intakes) and sublethal effects (for instance, adverse effects on growth or on fecundity including chemical castration or feminisation) need to be taken into account. In-combination effects (where more than one factor combine) may be particularly difficult to predict. Setting the baseline against which change will be assessed may also be problematic (see Figure 10.2). It may be appropriate to indicate confidence in the predicted effects. IEEM (2010, p35) suggest:

- Certain/near-Certain: probability estimated at 95% chance or higher.
- Probable: probability estimated above 50% but below 95%.
- Unlikely: probability estimated above 5% but less than 50%.
- Extremely Unlikely: probability estimated at less than 5%.

The 'unlikely' categories are relevant for species or habitats that are highly valued in a nature conservation context (for instance nationally rare species or habitats only represented in that location in the country). Alternatively, confidence in a sensitivity assessment can be given.

The impact assessment is likely to be a large document explaining the reasons for reaching conclusions about likely impacts and the confidence in those conclusions. Box 10.2 includes examples of the EIA summary tables for sensitivity of habitats and species for example activities that were part of a power station development in Pembrokeshire, Wales.

There will be many other examples of impact assessments worldwide that should help undertake a new one in similar locations and with similar proposed or ongoing activities.

Box 10.2 Summary tables from part of an impact assessment of the likely effects of construction including on the foreshore and in the shallow subtidal. The sensitivity assessment is derived from information found on the MarLIN website (www.marlin.ac.uk)

1   Sensitivity of intertidal biotopes to substratum loss, smothering, increase in sedimentation and turbidity and abrasion and physical disturbance as potential environmental effects of construction and dredging activities.

Biotope	Intolerance	Recover-ability	Sensitivity	Species richness	Evidence/confidence
LR.FLR.Lic.Ver. *Verrucaria maura* on littoral fringe rock	Low	Very high	Very low	Minor decline	Low
LR.FLR.Lic.YG. Yellow and grey lichens on supralittoral rock	Low	Very high	Very low	Minor decline	Low
LR.FLR.Eph.BlitX. Barnacles and *Littorina* spp on unstable eulittoral mixed substrata	Inter-mediate	Very high	Low	Minor decline	High
LS.LMp.Sm. Salt marsh	Inter-mediate	High	Low	Decline	Very low
LS.LMu.Smu. Sandy muddy shores	Low	Very high	Very low	Minor decline	Moderate
LS.LMu.UEst. Hed.Ol. *Hediste diversicolor* and oligochaetes in low salinity mud shores	Low	Very high	Very low	Minor decline	Moderate
LS.LCS.Sh.BarSh. Barren littoral shingle or gravel shores	Tolerant	Inter-mediate	Not sensitive	Not relevant	Low
LS.LMu.MEst. Hedmac. *Hediste diversicolor* and *Macoma balthica* in littoral sandy mud	Low	Very high	Very low	Minor decline	Moderate
LS.LMp.LSgr.Znol. *Zostera noltii* beds in littoral muddy sand	High	Low	High	Decline	High
LR.LLR. FVS. AscVS. *Ascophyllum nodosum* and *Fucus vesiculosus* on variable salinity mid eulittoral rock	Inter-mediate	High	Low	Decline	High

LS.LMu.UEst.Hed. Str. *Hediste diversicolor* and *Streblospio shrubsolii* in littoral sandy mud	Low	Very high	Very low	Minor decline	Moderate
LS.LMx/LR.FLR. Rkp.SwSed. *Mosaic shingle and algae [Littoral mixed sediment/ seaweed in sediment-floored eulittoral rockpools]*	Inter-mediate	High	Low	Decline	Low

2 Sensitivity of shellfish species to smothering

Common name	Scientific name	Intolerance	Recover-ability	Sensitivity	Evidence/ confidence
Common cockle	*Cerastoderma edule*	Intermediate	High	Low	Moderate
Common periwinkle	*Littorina littorea*	High	High	Moderate	High
Native oyster	*Ostrea edulis*	High	Very low	Very high	Low
Common shore crab	*Carcinus maenas*	Tolerant	Not relevant	Not sensitive	Low
Edible crab	*Cancer pagurus*	Low	Very high	Very low	High
Brown shrimp	*Crangon crangon*	Intermediate	Very high	Low	Low

Source: Based on Environmental Statements for the Pembroke Power Station (2007) (www.marinemanagement.org.uk/licensing/public_register/eia/ es_pembroke.htm) with permission. Biotope codes have been corrected from the original via http://jncc.defra.gov.uk/marine/biotopes/BiotopeSearch.aspx

Measures to alleviate impacts

The EcIA may identify areas that are habitats for scheduled species where populations of those species will be destroyed or damaged (described as 'valued ecological features and resources' in Box 10.1). That conclusion may mean the development cannot go ahead or, perhaps more often, that a little lateral thinking is needed. Perhaps the main construction can be moved to one side, perhaps the species can be moved to a new suitable location, perhaps they can be moved and then put back after the construction phase has finished. In the case of developments that alter physical processes, such as reducing wave action, there might be little that can be done – because reducing wave action was the whole idea of the development. In the case of road causeways originally planned to be solid, conduits can be introduced at locations along their length to allow water flow to continue. Very hot cooling water can be stored and the heat allowed to dissipate (perhaps to the benefit of the plant or the public) before being discharged. In a very few cases, it might be that compensatory measures can replace lost habitats: for instance, saline lagoons can be recreated elsewhere with the help of a mechanical digger, or what was previously farmland protected by coastal defences can be allowed to flood with seawater to create replacement salt marsh or mudflats (but that is for Chapter 11). Ecological enhancement measures (Box 10.1) are unlikely to be relevant in the marine environment unless the location has been previously adversely affected by human activities (for instance, there is contamination of sediments that can be removed).

When the development is complete

It is important, once a development or a new activity has been approved, to follow through by assessing whether the original assessment had been accurate and whether any measures to alleviate impacts or compensatory measures have been successful and, if not, why not. That is a part of monitoring.

Whilst the process described above seems logical and objective and is the preferred or primary approach, the advice given (and, perhaps, defended in a judicial process) is often finally based on the knowledge, experience and consequent opinion of seasoned ecologists.

Monitoring

Introduction

The definition that is used here is from the UK statutory nature conservation agencies Marine Monitoring Handbook (Davies *et al.*, 2001, p16):

- Surveillance is a continued programme of biological surveys systematically undertaken to provide a series of observations in time.
- Monitoring is surveillance undertaken to ensure that formulated standards are being maintained.

Monitoring programmes which produce quantified descriptions of real change and which are accountable in terms of their accuracy and significance of results are required for site management. It is through sound monitoring programmes that site managers can receive timely warnings of unacceptable change and see whether the measures they adopt are maintaining a site's features of interest. Targets or change limits will be identified against which monitoring is undertaken. General principles of monitoring and procedures for feedback to practical conservation are described here. The manager will need to know about the tools available to inform his or her work programme, and the field survey contractor will need to have the necessary training, skills and equipment to do the work.

Monitoring in relation to environmental protection spans a wide range of activities from census (presence/absence surveys) through such exercises as estimating the size of fish stocks, from measuring diversity of benthos to measuring levels of contaminants and identifying sublethal effects such as reproductive performance or growth. A list of 64 major biophysical categories that could be monitored is given in Roff and Zacharias (2011). Proposals for monitoring as part of implementation of the EU Marine Strategy Framework Directive in the UK include (for benthos excluding fish) 43 monitoring measures (HM Government, 2012). This section mentions a few examples of monitoring that might be undertaken in relation to seabed biodiversity conservation.

The results of monitoring further inform adaptive management but, often, their most important function for statutory agencies is to enable reporting against the requirements of the directives, conventions and statutes that government ministers are accountable to.

Those legislative 'drivers' are many. In Europe, a variety of directives from the EC (especially the Habitats Directive, the Water Framework Directive and the Marine Strategy Framework Directive) all require information on status and quality. Harmonising those various imperatives to ensure that there is a monitoring framework that will inform all of them is helped by regional forums and requirements to operate through regional conventions.

Monitoring for biodiversity conservation

Monitoring for biodiversity conservation has several potential aims:

1   To establish if the measures taken to protect the ecosystem and the habitats and communities of importance at a site are working:

    i.   Have the general characteristics of the protected/managed area been maintained?
    ii.   Have the special features identified been maintained/have they improved?
    iii. Is there any 'payoff' for commercial species exploitation – is there spill-out?
    iv. What are the knock-on effects of protection (changes in the balance between predators and prey, etc.)?

2   To understand what variability in biodiversity features is occurring in relation to natural or unmanaged change:

    i.   change resulting from natural environmental variability;
    ii.   change resulting from climate change (especially temperature rise);
    iii. change resulting from arrival of non-native species.

3   To set quotas for fisheries or to moderate scientific collecting or recreational activity.

Types of monitoring

Elliott (2011) identifies ten types of monitoring in relation to marine environmental protection and management. Four are noted here as particularly relevant to biodiversity conservation:

- Surveillance monitoring – a 'look-see' approach which begins without deciding what are the end-points followed by a post hoc detection (*a posteriori*) of trends and suggested management action.
- Condition monitoring – used by nature conservation bodies to determine the present status of an area; it could be linked to biological valuation.
- Operational monitoring – used by industry for business reasons (e.g. for a dredging scheme linked to aims for management and to determine if an area requires further dredging).
- Compliance monitoring – used by industry and linked to licence (or permit/authorization/consent) setting for effluent discharge, disposal at sea, etc.

(Elliott, 2011, p654)

'Surveillance monitoring' has been addressed in Chapter 8 as 'Surveillance' (p127). 'Condition monitoring' is the type of monitoring mainly considered here although it is linked

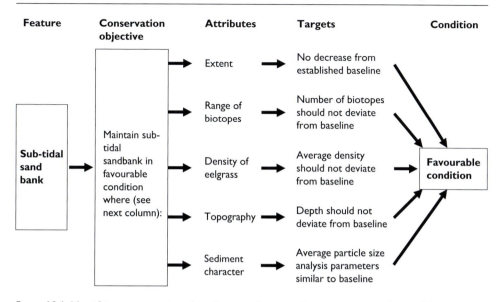

Figure 10.1 Identifying conservation objectives, attributes and targets to assess favourable conditions for one of the habitat specified in Annex 1 of the EU Habitats Directive.

Source: based on Figure 1-1 in Davies *et al.* (2001).

to 'Operational monitoring' in the sense that there is a feedback to management of the results of monitoring that advise if management action is required and if that action works.

The drivers for monitoring are often the words that are used in directives, conventions and statutes. For the EU Habitats Directive, there is a requirement to 'Maintain favourable conservation status'; for the EU Water Framework Directive, to 'Achieve good chemical and good ecological status', and for the EU Marine Strategy Framework Directive a requirement to maintain 'Good Environmental Status' (discussed in Borja *et al.*, 2013). Such imperatives need to be converted into indicators and targets for use in monitoring. An example is given in Figure 10.1.

Sometimes, the features (habitats and species) that will require monitoring are named in the directives and conventions, and sometimes they need to be identified. Those habitats and species are likely to be ones that are considered threatened and need to be 'looked after'. Alternatively, they are species and habitats that, should they change, will tell policy advisors and managers that environmental quality is improving or declining and/or that the measures they have taken are or are not working. Those are the 'indicators' described next.

Indicators

Identifying indicators of quality or change may provide a shortcut for monitoring and may be constructed to be understandable and relevant to politicians and the public whilst being scientifically robust. A significant problem is that marine scientists and policymakers are likely to have a different perception of what are 'biodiversity indicators' (explored in Heinke and Kowarwik, 2010). Here, an indicator is considered to be a variable which supplies information on other variables that are difficult to access. Ideally, indicator species are likely to be restricted in their occurrence to particular and narrow environmental

Table 10.2 The required properties of indicators and monitoring parameters for successful marine management

Property	Explanation
Anticipatory	Sufficient to allow the defence of the precautionary principle, as an early warning of change, capable of indicating deviation from that expected before irreversible damage occurs.
Biologically important	Focuses on species, biotopes, communities, etc. Important in maintaining a fully functioning ecological community.
Broadly applicable and integrative over space and time	Usable at many sites and over different time periods to give an holistic assessment which provides and summarises information from many environmental and biotic aspects; to allow comparisons with previous data to estimate variability and to define trends and breaches with guidelines or standards.
Concrete/results focused	We require indicators for directly observable and measurable properties rather than those which can only be estimated indirectly; concrete indicators are more readily interpretable by diverse stakeholders who contribute to management decision-making.
Continuity over time and space	Capable of being measured over appropriate ecological and human time and space scales to show recovery and restoration.
Cost-effective	Indicators and measurements should be cost-effective (financially non-prohibitive) given limited monitoring resources, i.e. with an ease/economy of monitoring. Monitoring should provide the greatest and quickest benefits to scientific understanding and interpretation, to society and sustainable development. This should produce an optimum and defensible sampling strategy and the most information possible.
Grounded in theory/ relevant and appropriate	Indicators should reflect features of ecosystems and human impacts that are relevant to achieving operational objectives; they should be scientifically sound and defensible and based on well-defined and validated theory. They should be relevant and appropriate to management initiatives and understood by managers.
Interpretable	Indicators should reflect the concerns of and be understood by stakeholders. Their understanding should be easy and equate to their technical meanings, especially for non-scientists and other users; some should have a general applicability and be capable of distinguishing acceptable from unacceptable conditions in a scientifically and legally defensive way.
Low redundancy	The indicators and monitoring should provide unique information compared to other measures.
Measurable	Indicators should be easily measurable in practice using existing instruments, monitoring programmes and analytical tools available in the relevant areas, to the required accuracy and precision, and on the timescales needed to support management. They should have minimum or known bias (error), and the desired signal should be distinguishable from noise or at least the noise (inherent variability in the data) should be quantified and explained; i.e. have a high signal to noise ratio. They need to be capable of being updated regularly, being operationally defined and measured, with accepted methods and Analytical/Quality Control/Quality Assurance and with defined detection limits.
Non-destructive	Methods used should cause minimal and acceptable damage to the ecosystem and should be legally permissible.
Realistic/attainable (achievable)	Indicators should be realistic in their structure and measurement and should provide information on a 'need to know' basis rather than a 'nice to know' basis. They should be attainable (achievable) within the management framework.

Table 10.2 (continued)

Property	Explanation
Responsive feedback to management	Indicators should be responsive to effective management action and regulation and provide rapid and reliable feedback on the findings. Such feedback loops should be determined and defined prior to using the indicator.
Sensitive to a known stressor or stressors	The trends in the indicators should be sensitive to changes in the ecosystem properties or impacts, to a stressor or stressors which the indicator is intended to measure and also to a manageable human activity; they should be based on an underlying conceptual model, without an all-or-none response to extreme or natural variability, hence potential for use in a diagnostic capacity.
Socially relevant	Understandable to stakeholders and the wider society or at least predictive of, or a surrogate for, a change important to society.
Specific	Indicators should respond to the properties they are intended to measure rather than to other factors, and/or it should be possible to disentangle the effects of other factors from the observed response (hence having a high reliability/specificity of response and relevance to the end point).
Time-bounded	The date of attaining a threshold/standard should be indicated in advance. They are likely to be based on existing time-series data to help set objectives and also based on readily available data and those showing temporal trends.
Timely	The indicators should be appropriate to management decisions relating to human activities and therefore they should be linked to that activity; thus providing real-time information for feedback into management giving remedial action to prevent further deterioration and to indicate the results of or need for any change in strategy.

Source: Elliott (2011).

conditions and are therefore typical or indicative of those conditions. They need to have a high inertia (they are difficult to shift) so that any change in them is likely to be in response to a major event. The main problem that arises seems to be when natural constraints affect a species but the change is considered to be an indicator of adverse effects from human activities. For instance, a species that cannot withstand high levels of turbidity from dredge spoil disposal (a human activity) will not anyway be present in areas with high turbidity due to the natural process of land run-off.

Elliott (2011) brings together various sources to produce a detailed list of monitoring properties (Table 10.2).

Benchmarks, attributes and targets

Identifying which are candidate indicators (habitat feature, species and indices based on species) inevitably becomes complicated, especially when life history traits and any history of adverse effects as a result of human activity are poorly known. Furthermore, the indicators need to be for specific pressures. Nevertheless, indicators and indices are being identified, including for the EU Water Framework and Marine Strategy Framework Directives (see, for instance, Borja *et al.*, 2000 (Box 10.3) and follow developments in the DEVelopment Of innovative Tools for understanding marine biodiversity and assessing good Environmental Status: www.devotes-project.eu).

Box 10.3 The AZTI Marine Biotic Index (AMBI)

Source: Borja *et al.* (2000).

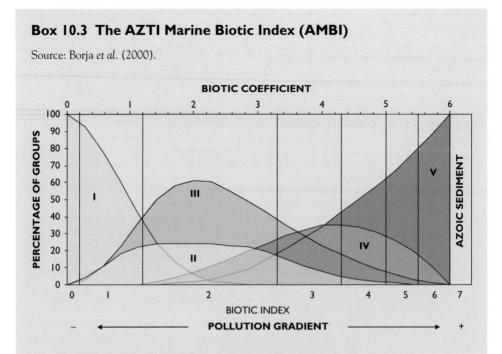

The AMBI is a biotic index which provides a 'pollution classification' of a particular site, representing benthic community 'health'. It is derived from European data from soft sediments and mainly in relation to organic enrichment. The result of analysing data is a number in a range of 0–6 (7 for azoic sediments) that can be simplified into five classes from undisturbed communities to extremely disturbed communities. Thresholds in the scale of the AMBI were based upon the distribution of the abundance of each species in relation to one of five ecological groups (sensitive to pollution, indifferent, tolerant, and second- and first-order opportunistic species). The figure is a theoretical model from Borja *et al.* (2000) based on various sources. I: Species very sensitive; II: Species indifferent; III: Species tolerant; IV: Second-order opportunistic species; V: First-order opportunistic species. The Biotic Coefficient is continuous. The relative proportion of abundance of each group in a sample is separated into eight levels (0–7): the Biotic Index.

'Benchmarks' or 'reference conditions' and targets are of central importance for monitoring to inform implementation of conservation measures. However, as with understanding change of any sort, knowing what should be present including how much and in what condition in a habitat unaffected by human activities is problematic (see Chapter 4, 'Shifting baselines', p62). Nevertheless, identifying reference conditions from pristine or least disturbed areas is at the core of relevant European directives and recommendations of the US Environmental Protection Agency. At its most basic, a monitoring objective will be to 'maintain' (knowing or assuming that what is present now is acceptable) or 'improve' (assuming or knowing that what is present now has been adversely affected by human activities). Understanding and taking account of uncertainty is important; but, once again, knowledge and experience will be valuable in determining what is an unimpacted state or, if not known, what is a reasonable point to start from, including what is a functioning and diverse status for that habitat. Borja *et al.* (2012) review the issue of identifying reference conditions concluding that rigidly defining a pristine system as having no significant human impact does not seem possible. The decision process in Figure 10.2 takes account of uncertainties although doesn't tell the policy advisor how to solve them. The 'Limit/threshold' in Figure 10.2 may be taken as an 'action threshold' but there will be several such points at which management actions are triggered – from the first signs that damage is likely to be caused by an activity to the triggering of restoration measures when damage has occurred. A problem in environmental protection is that, often, the early signs of damage are noticed, reported, refuted by those responsible for the damage and only admitted when damage is severe and unequivocal. The financial consequences of attempts at restoration and the loss of income in the case of commercial resources will be much more severe than if the early signs had been acted upon. Examples are many but include impacts of overfishing on the Grand Banks off Newfoundland, impacts of fishing on deep-water corals, impacts of scallop dredging on horse mussels in Strangford Lough, impacts and subsequent restoration following blast fishing on coral reefs.

Box 10.4 illustrates the sort of cascade of imperatives that will lead to survey and monitoring objectives.

Informing management

Effective reporting

Assessing the effectiveness (or failure) of conservation measures and reporting in a way that informs policy advisors and managers is essential if there is to be feedback on regulation and management and, if needed, adaptation of measures. Most examples are from fisheries conservation measures but the format could be applied to biodiversity conservation measures. An unpublished report by the Closed Area Working Group in the USA provides such a format. The Nantucket Lighthouse Closed Area was established to protect stocks of juvenile yellowtail flounder although the account of effects (positive and negative) looks at the wider marine environment (Table 10.3 is an example from one of the closed areas).

Evidence of change in parameters being measured may or may not be the result of human activities and may be an improvement in status or a decline in status.

Significance of observations

A next stage is to advise on the significance of observations of change. Such advice relies greatly on knowledge and experience but also on accessing information about the sorts of changes that have been observed in experimental studies or in academic surveillance or in situations where the impact of human activities is obvious (for instance where there is a gradient of adverse effect away from a point source). Being able to access information about species and biotopes in terms of sensitivity to human activities or natural events and about any historical record of change will help to indicate whether change may or may not be natural.

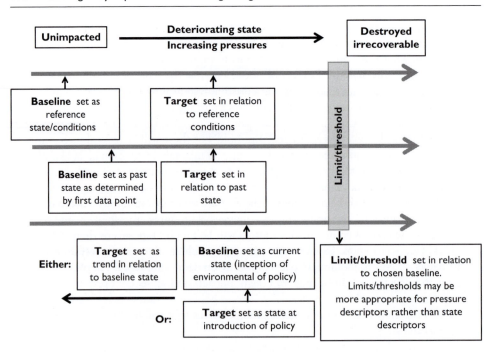

Figure 10.2 Choosing baselines, targets and limits or thresholds in environmental monitoring. The point chosen as a baseline or target depends in part on knowledge of past and current states and is a pragmatic decision. The limit or threshold levels may be set for status (biological, physical or chemical) or for pressure.

Source: Based on an unpublished outcome of the UK Marine Monitoring and Assessment Strategy (UKMMAS) (www.defra.gov.uk/mscc/groups/uk-marine-monitoring-and-assessment-strategy/).

Confidence in results

It may be necessary to indicate levels of confidence in the results of monitoring surveys. Those levels may relate to statistical levels or may be assessment based on experience such as that described in the section on 'Environmental Impact Assessments', p178.

Box 10.4 The European Union Marine Strategy Framework Directive

The European Union Marine Strategy Framework Directive requires the maintenance of 'Good Environmental Status' (GES) in EU seas by 2020. In the UK, that is interpreted as:

- ecologically diverse and dynamic seas which are clean, healthy and productive;
- use is at a sustainable level;
- fully functioning and resilient ecosystem;
- biodiversity decline is prevented, biodiversity is in balance and protected;
- hydro-morphological, physical and chemical state support the above;
- no pollution effects.

The descriptors against which those aims will be assessed are:

Biological diversity is maintained. The quality and occurrence of habitats and the distribution and abundance of species are in line with prevailing physiographic, geographic and climatic conditions . . .

Non-indigenous species (NIS) introduced by human activities are at levels that do not adversely alter the ecosystems . . .

Populations of all commercially exploited fish and shellfish are within safe biological limits, exhibiting a population age and size distribution that is indicative of a healthy stock . . .

All elements of the marine food webs, to the extent that they are known, occur at normal abundance and diversity and levels capable of ensuring the long-term abundance of the species and the retention of their full reproductive capacity . . .

Human-induced eutrophication is minimised, especially adverse effects thereof, such as losses in biodiversity, ecosystem degradation, harmful algae blooms and oxygen deficiency in bottom waters . . .

Sea floor integrity is at a level that ensures that the structure and functions of the ecosystems are safeguarded and benthic ecosystems, in particular, are not adversely affected . . .

Permanent alteration of hydrographical conditions does not adversely affect marine ecosystems . . .

Concentrations of contaminants are at levels not giving rise to pollution effects . . .

Contaminants in fish and other seafood for human consumption do not exceed levels established by Community legislation or other relevant standards . . .

Properties and quantities of marine litter do not cause harm to the coastal and marine environment . . .

Introduction of energy, including underwater noise, is at levels that do not adversely affect the marine environment.

Source: (HM Government, 2012, pp12–13)

For benthic habitats, the 'Biological diversity is maintained' descriptor for GES is interpreted as:

- Biodiversity loss has been halted and, where practicable, restoration is under way.
- The abundance, distribution and condition of species and habitats in UK waters are in line with prevailing environmental conditions as defined by specific targets for species and habitats.
- Marine ecosystems and their constituent species and habitats are not significantly impacted by human activities such that specific structures and functions for their long-term maintenance exist for the foreseeable future.
- Habitats and species identified as requiring protection under existing national or international agreements are conserved effectively through appropriate national and regional mechanisms.

There are 43 indicators and indicator targets for benthic habitats initially put forward in the UK.

A definition of the 11 descriptors (except 7, Hydrographical conditions) of Good Environmental Status can be found in Borja *et al.* (2013).

Source: HM Government, 2012: https://www.gov.uk/government/uploads/system/uploads/attachment_data/file/69632/pb13860-marine-strategy-part1–20121220.pdf

Table 10.3 Summary reporting that immediately informs a policy advisor or minister of the outcomes of conservation measures is essential. The example below is adapted from an unpublished report by the Closed Area Working Group in the USA, where references to the papers and reports that are the basis for conclusions can be found

Closed Area 2	Effect (+ or −)
Effects on Managed Species	
Haddock move in and out of closed areas; preliminary data suggest that more haddock are moving out of closed areas (spillover) than are moving in	+/−
No significant positive impacts of the closure were detected for haddock	+/−
After closure was implemented, increase in catch-per-tow of haddock was greater outside closure boundaries than inside	−
Overall area occupied by yellowtail flounder increased by a factor of 2 when abundance was high	+
Local density of yellowtail flounder increased in high-quality habitat closed to commercial fishing	+
Condition of YF females decline slightly at high abundance	−
Condition of YF males did not change with abundance	+/−
Improved recruitment survival for some groundfish stocks may be due to the protection of critical nursery habitats	+
After the closure, spawning-stock biomass increased and exploitation rates decreased for GB cod, haddock, and GB and SNE yellowtail flounder (only slightly for cod and SNE YF, but significantly for haddock and GB YF)	+
Revenues greater near closed area boundaries, but also more variable; can be more profitable, but also more risky to 'fish the edge'	+/−
Evidence of spillover effect from the fact that catches are higher at borders	+
Increases in scallops and sedentary finfish; 14-fold increase in scallop biomass	+
Little difference found for fish biomass and abundance inside vs. outside	+/−
Fishermen claimed to have seen growth of YF biomass within closed area	+
Habitat Effects	
Video and photographic evidence that colonial epifaunal species are much more abundant at undisturbed sites	+
Percent seabed cover increased for sponges	+
Increase in colonial epifauna used for juvenile cod refuge	+
Local density of yellowtail flounder increased disproportionately in high-quality habitat closed to commercial fishing (specifically stratum 1160 in southern portion of the closure)	+
Closure area confirmed as encompassing a large area of preferred habitat for yellowtail flounder	+
Improved recruitment survival for some groundfish stocks may be due to the protection of critical nursery habitats	+

Table 10.3 (continued)

Closed Area 2	Effect (+ or −)
Other Ecosystem Effects	
Biomass, abundance, and number of species increased	+
Species richness and abundance increased, but mean diversity decreased within closure	+/−
Increases in crabs, seastars, and mollusks	+
Greater than 10-fold increase in benthic megafaunal production, mainly from sea scallops and sea urchins	+
Increase in abundance of many prey species for juvenile cod	+

Source: www.nefmc.org/nemulti/closed%20area%20working%20group/121128/Doc%202%20Literature%20 Assessment.pdf

Conclusions

1 Monitoring biological change in protected areas should be capable of both detecting real change and the scale of change.

2 Monitoring is undertaken against objectives which may need to be defined in terms of quantitative measures or targets.

3 Monitoring abundance of species is likely to major on those that are identified as 'important' for biodiversity conservation but also on any indicator species that might identify 'quality' or a change in the abundance of key structural or functional species.

4 Monitoring for quality or to help establish cause and effect may also benefit from monitoring contaminant levels (in water, sediments and organisms) or indices of health in organisms.

5 Cause and effect are often difficult to establish but may be informed by the results of experimental studies or by knowing if similar changes that have occurred previously or elsewhere that can be related to an 'event'.

6 Monitoring the effectiveness of regulation is about whether enforcement is preventing the damaging pressures that have been identified as harmful to the features being protected.

7 The results of monitoring need to be presented to policy advisors and managers clearly.

Chapter 11

Recovery, restoration and replacement of habitats and species

Introduction

The purpose of this chapter is to give the reader an understanding of what we know about recovery of biodiversity, whether and how that recovery may be assisted and, if recovery or restoration is not possible, whether there are alternative habitats that will compensate for the loss. Action to enable or assist recovery of species and habitats may or may not be expensive and may or may not work. Also, loss of some species and habitats may be more critical than others to conservation and for the provision of ecosystem services. It is therefore important to consider how important, feasible and expensive it will be to take action to allow recovery to occur or to help it: prioritising action is a practical consideration.

A first question for the manager or policy advisor to ask is: has this habitat (or species) been adversely affected by human activities? That question may be difficult to answer because of our poor record of what was 'natural' before humans started to have a significant effect on ecosystems and because of our poor understanding of what might be natural change. However, in many cases, human impact is obvious or at least suspected and the conservation objective moves from 'maintain' to 'recover', 'restore' or 'replace'.

Where a habitat or the population of a valued species has been lost or damaged, conservation action needs to be informed by past experience of recovery from similar events and of the likely consequences of different actions that might aid recovery in the specific instance being considered. In many cases, 'action' means no action either because none is needed (recovery will occur naturally) or because the factors causing the change were so overwhelming that action to regain a pre-existing situation is not possible. Where action can be taken, it may be to facilitate recovery or it may be to replace something that has been lost forever.

Recovery is seen as a passive event that relies on recolonisation and regrowth of pre-existing species and an associated rebalancing of ecosystem structure and functioning. Marine species and habitats that have declined in abundance or are threatened with decline are most likely to benefit from removal of whatever pressure they are, or have been, under and the maintenance of a suitable environment in which to thrive. Recovery of some populations of exploited or damaged species is likely to occur after a few years of conservation action, but other species and the habitats they create may take decades to recover or may not recover at all.

Restoration (including 'regeneration') implies that some action other than just removing damaging pressures is undertaken. On the land, that might mean culling predators or grazers, introducing grazers, removing large trees, planting trees, etc. In the sea, interference with natural processes is rarely needed (or possible). On the other hand, species that have disappeared from an area because of human activities or have fallen below numbers needed for a viable population may benefit from reintroduction. In a small number of cases, lost habitats may be reintroduced – and that may even include removing a habitat about to be damaged by development and putting it back when the work is complete.

Replacement may be part of a plan to create positive (for biodiversity) benefits when change to natural systems is inevitable (for instance, construction of coastal defences or harbours). Replacement may also be considered when a natural habitat has been destroyed or radically altered by physical disturbance and particularly may occur where structurally complex hard substratum habitats have been destroyed by mobile fishing gear. However, artificial constructions rarely mimic natural habitats (Plate 68).

If predictions of likely recovery or of restoration action are to be successful, understanding life history traits is at the core of taking appropriate action and there are lessons to be learned from successes and failures that will inform strategies and targets if action is needed in the future.

Restoration and replacement are the 'Response' actions in the DPSIR approach.

Recovery

Introduction

Recovery may take a long time and go through several successional stages. That process may or may not lead to a community or the population of a species that would be expected without human disturbance. Since populations and communities vary naturally with time, it is most practical to seek unimpeded progress towards a sustained population or a diverse functioning community. However, if the habitat, including such features as water quality, has remained the same as that before disturbance, the recovered population or community should be considered 'close to natural' at a point where changes occurring are on a scale that is normal for that population or community. Recovery, but not necessarily back to an original state, is incorporated into a conceptual model by Tett *et al.* (2007). They indicate that, following the removal of whatever stress had caused change, recovery will occur but not necessarily along the same trajectory that decline occurred: the difference being termed 'hysteresis'. This concept is illustrated in Figure 11.1.

Objectives for 'recovery' (and 'restoration') are likely to range from the very general (related to the whole habitat or community) to the very specific (related to a much-valued species) and from highly descriptive to quantitative. Lotz *et al.* (2011) define types of recovery (Box 11.1) that could be converted to conservation or management objectives for the specific location, habitat or species being considered. Care is needed as some pragmatic measures (such as: recover to xx% of the number of species previously present) fail to recognise that the value of a location for biodiversity conservation is (or was) the population or populations of particular species and not just any species – having the same number of species in a 'recovered' habitat may be of an alternative community that is not as stable or valued as what was there before.

A conservation objective for recovery of a damaged habitat might be:

> The biological diversity of its characteristic communities is recovered such that the
> quality and occurrence of habitats and the composition and abundance of species in

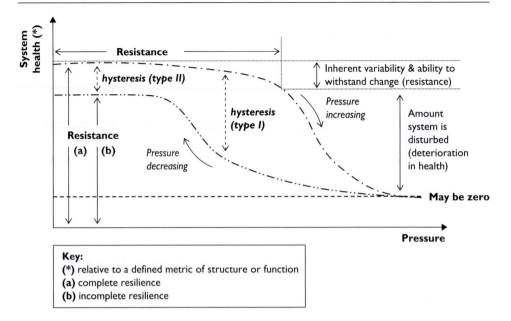

Figure 11.1 Conceptual model of recovery illustrating hysteresis. As a pressure is removed, Type I
hysteresis represents the lag in recovery. Status may not improve for some time after
the pressure is removed. Resilience is the degree of recovery. Complete resilience
results in a return to the original level, partial resilience is a return to some lower (or
higher) level, with Type II hysteresis being the difference between the two.

Source: Elliott *et al.* (2007) based on Tett *et al.* (2007).

those communities are at least as favourable as those characteristically found in the
prevailing physiographical, geographical and climatic conditions **in the absence of
significant anthropogenic impacts.**

(From part of an example Marine Conservation Zone designation order published in
2013 by the UK Department of the Environment (https://www.gov.uk/government/
uploads/system/uploads/attachment_data/file/82735/mcz-annex-g-121213.pdf). The
emboldened text is added here.)

Jones and Schmitz (2009) summarise recovery rates for different ecosystems and a variety of
pressures. Marine ecosystems generally recovered more rapidly than terrestrial systems and
the average recovery time for different ecosystems types ranged from 10 to 42 years, with slow
successional ecosystems taking longer than short-lived ones. Such generalities need to be
treated with caution as some activities such as clear-felling ancient forests or destroying structurally important corals that are hundreds of years old in highly stable environments, such
as on seamounts, may take much longer. Clark *et al.* (2010, p268) observe that '[b]ased on
the limited number of seamount studies and the knowledge gained by research from shallower shelf and slope areas, it is likely that recovery trajectories for benthic communities on
seamounts will span decades or centuries, especially for widely separated seamounts.'
    For the marine environment, Borja *et al.* (2010b) identify different sorts of recovery in a
large number of case studies from estuarine and coastal environments and observe (p1249):

Box 11.1 Definitions of 'Recovery'

Recovery of populations (e.g. in terms of abundance, distribution, size or age structure, or functional role) or ecosystems (e.g. in terms of diversity, habitat availability, food web structure or water quality) can be defined and measured in different ways, as detailed below.

Simple increase

A simple increase is a general increase or improvement in the specified response over time, ideally a reversal towards pre-disturbance conditions. This can be measured as a relative or absolute change since a disturbed state or other reference point . . . The trend can be linear, exponential or otherwise increasing or, for some parameters, decreasing (e.g. pollution levels). The trend could also be measured over a certain time period, such as the past 10 or 50 years, or since the implementation of an important management measure . . .

Standardized or scaled increase

If the purpose is to compare across different species or ecosystems, the measured improvement would ideally be scaled to, or standardized by, the life histories of the species involved (e.g. generation time or intrinsic growth rate, r_{max}) or rates of succession of different ecosystems to account for underlying differences in the timescale of responses . . .

Increase towards a specified target

Many conservation or management plans define distinct targets for population abundance or ecosystem parameters, for example the biomass at maximum sustainable yield (B_{MSY}) for assessed fish stocks . . . an optimum sustainable population level (OSP) for marine mammals or the maximum population size observed . . .

Increase to a historical or pristine level

Sometimes, the goal might be to recover a population or ecosystem to its 'natural' state before human disturbance. This requires the knowledge of its historical population level or ecosystem state (i.e. historical baseline) or an understanding of its carrying capacity (K) either under current or historical ecosystem conditions . . . Establishing such historical baselines is not easy and can be controversial if different data sources or reconstruction methods reveal different results . . . The goal could also be to recover a population to some proportion of its former level or carrying capacity (e.g. 50% K) or its pre-exploitation or virgin abundance (B_0).

Recovery of former structure or function

Under some circumstances, the recovery goal might not be an increase in certain parameters but a shift among different demographic, social or functional components within a population (e.g. juvenile:adult or male:female ratios) . . . or ecosystem (e.g. trophic levels, functional groups or habitat composition) . . . to restore a former, more robust natural or pristine structure.

Source: Box 1 in Lotze *et al.* (2011, p596).

. . . although in some cases recovery can take <5 years, especially for the short-lived and high-turnover biological components, full recovery of coastal marine and estuarine ecosystems from over a century of degradation can take a minimum of 15–25 years for attainment of the original biotic composition and diversity may lag far beyond that period.

Examples that exist of recovery in habitats and species are drawn from a wide range of sources that provide clues as to the likely rapidity and extent of recovery as a result of changes in environmental quality, protection from harmful activities and 'events' (such as oil spills, physical disturbance by fishing gear, warming events, etc.). The examples cited here include a high proportion of benthic habitats and species as there is a large literature concerning exploited species (see Lotze *et al.*, 2011) with much the same message: exploited species such as finfish and shellfish generally show rapid recovery at least in numbers (size of individuals and biomass will take longer) once the pressure that was adversely affecting them is removed. However, large and slow-growing species with low reproduction rates such as whales are likely to take much longer. Lotze *et al.* (2011) are optimistic in their review of recovery of mainly exploited large vertebrate species. They suggest that 15–50 per cent of species and ecosystems that had been depleted in numbers show some signs of recovery, but this is rarely to their former levels of abundance. They point out the problem of knowing how recovery should be assessed because of shifting (or 'sliding') baselines (see, for instance, Pauly, 1995; Dayton *et al.*, 1998; Chapter 4, p45).

Some change may not be reversible, especially where the habitat is now different to its original state – although that original state is often unknown. Obvious examples are where estuarine or sheltered habitats have been replaced by concrete jetties or where the shores of bays have been sheltered from wave action by breakwaters. In less obvious instances, intensive trawling will flatten areas of seabed, creating better habitat for fast-growing polychaetes and better ground for flatfish and their fisheries (Lindeboom and de Groot, 1998; Engel and Kvitek, 1998; van Denderen *et al.*, 2013), but also destroying three-dimensional geological structures and thereby reducing biodiversity. Once lost, such three-dimensional geological structures will not rebuild naturally.

Examples of recovery

Introduction

Where degradation has occurred at a location and the source of that degradation is clear and is localised, management action to remove that source is often possible. For recovery to occur, the physical habitat must be intact, the surrounding water quality good and ecosystem processes must be as they were before degradation occurred. Recovery following 'taking off the pressure' at specific locations is exemplified in many studies (for instance, Borja *et al.*, 2010b catalogue recovery times from 51 studies). Here, specific types of events and activities that cause changes are listed and examples given of the time taken for recovery and the character of recovery after their cessation. Such information is of key importance to making decisions regarding whether or not recovery can occur but also whether or not an activity causes significant damage in what might anyway be a dynamic habitat and/or a naturally changeable assemblage of species.

Natural events

Natural events are listed first because, although management action is not relevant, they provide examples of the time taken for recovery and provide background information on what to expect regarding speed and completeness of recovery. Destructive natural events include storms, cold winters, hot summers, 'red tides' and disease outbreaks. Warming events also cause change but whether or not they are considered 'natural' depends on the extent to which global effects of human activities are believed to be responsible.

Unusually severe storms may rip up seagrass beds, break up coral reefs, destroy intertidal algal beds, wash out burrowing species, etc. Recovery will most likely be within a few years though there is considerable variation; in the case of coral reefs broken up by storms, recovery may take only 2–5 years but may be up to 30 years (reviewed in Pearson, 1981). Whilst the effects of the cold winter of 1962/3 in Britain were well documented (Crisp, 1964), recovery was not. However, it seems that whilst most species that showed mortality recovered within a very few years, some may still not have returned to where they were previously present: for instance, the ascidian *Phallusia mammillata*, previously present in Plymouth Sound and along the coast east of Plymouth (Marine Biological Association, 1957), was still not recorded there more than 50 years after the 1962/3 winter (K. Hiscock own observations and Hiscock, 2005 for Hilsea Point Rock).

Dethier (1984) studied rock pools in the eastern USA that were dominated by different species often adversely affected by waves, excessive heat, wave-driven logs or rocks, and unusual influxes of predators and herbivores. Such natural disturbances did not generally remove all of the dominant species and recovery to original abundances required from three months to more than two years. If dominant species were removed entirely as an experiment, recovery time could be more than three years.

Underwood (1999) reports that, following a few weeks of severe storms in New South Wales, Australia in 1974, algal cover took about six to eight years to recover although other components of the assemblage had still not shown recovery by 1998.

Oil pollution

Recovery of intertidal communities following oil spills in temperate regions has been widely studied. Often, recovery, even from severe spills, is rapid, taking up to five years for the shore to have regained its previous appearance and abundance of structural and functional key species (Moore, 2006). However, disruption of dispersant-treated shore communities was reported to last at least 10 years and possibly as much as 15 years (long after the oil had disappeared) following the *Torrey Canyon* oil spill polluted shores in south-west England in 1967 (Hawkins and Southward, 1992). Moore (2006) observes that, where there was a longer-term impact (slower recovery), this was likely to be due to persistent oil, loss of slow-growing and keystone species, limited potential for recruitment and severe clean-up actions. Of these, by far the majority of long-term impact was caused by persistent oil (i.e. a residual toxic input to the environment) or severe clean-up actions (i.e. significant physical damage to habitats).

Chemical contaminants

Chemical water quality is important and much effort has been put into establishing 'maximum permissible levels' of contaminants and nutrients that are put into marine waters

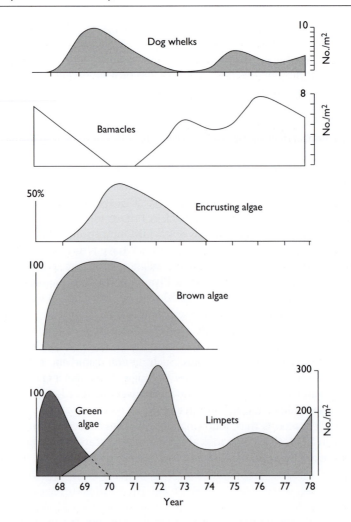

Figure 11.2 Changes in the abundance of some common shore species following the Torrey Canyon oil spill in March 1967.

Source: Redrawn from Southward (1979).

including the transitional waters of estuaries and other enclosed areas. Those levels may be based on experimental studies that can determine lethal concentrations but rarely identify what are sublethal concentrations affecting the ability of an organism to grow, reproduce and survive for a natural lifespan. Lethal and sublethal effects of contaminants were brought into sharp focus when Tributyltin antifouling paints were introduced in the 1980s (see, for example, Bryan *et al.*, 1986 and 'Pollution by chemicals' in Chapter 5, p78). In the upper Crouch estuary in the UK, over the ten years following the banning of use of TBT on small vessels, the number of seabed species present there doubled (Rees *et al.*, 2001). So, in that instance, removal of the pressure resulted in at least partial recovery.

Persistent contaminants are liable to have been incorporated into sediments and continue to be mobilised when there are storms or as a result of dredging or other disturbances.

The image in Plate 69 is of the hull of a now sunken ship coated in TBT paint which is still effective more than 25 years after it was applied – the same persistency is likely for flakes of such paint washed into sediments during hull refurbishment or as a result of spills. Continued effects of contaminants locked into sediments is very difficult to assess, but sensitive organisms may continue to be adversely affected and biodiversity not as high as it might have been in uncontaminated sediments. However, there are not the studies to quantify any such losses and conservation relies greatly on experimental studies to identify likely impacts and recovery rates from contamination.

Organic enrichment

Organic enrichment occurs widely in enclosed areas and near to centres of population. Such enrichment may arise from industrial activity such as from pulp mill effluents, from fish farms, from agriculture including from fertilisers and farm slurry that is released into the sea, or from discharge of human sewage including sewage that has been partially treated. The effects are well documented for point source discharges or disposal and the classic study by Pearson and Rosenberg (1978) illustrates impacts on benthos that can be applied to many different types of organic inputs (see Figure 5.10). A variety of papers give clues as to what might be expected in terms of recovery following cessation or reduction of the input. Rosenberg (1976) reported on recovery following closure of a pulp mill in a Swedish estuary, observing that '[t]he succession of the macrobenthic communities to a level where the recovery process was indistinguishable from annual fluctuations took about eight years' (p414). Borja et al. (2006) report that, in northern Spain, following progressive sewage effluent clean-up in the Nervión estuary, it took more than 13 years for the middle reaches to achieve the same richness and diversity as the outer reaches and 14 to 15 years for the inner reaches to achieve the same state as the middle reaches. They estimated that complete recovery would take a further 10 to 15 years, bringing the recovery period close to the 40 plus years suggested for the Mersey estuary in north-west England (Hawkins et al., 2002). In the same region, Díez et al. (2009) reported changes in intertidal macroalgal communities that occurred while the sewage input was ameliorated in the period 1984 to 2006. Progressive changes in algal occurrence were identified as five stages with increasing species richness being a major effect and with different species characterising different stages of recovery, thus providing measures of quality from 'extremely degraded' to 'slightly degraded' and 'control site' which is a reference stage (Figure 11.3). However, by the end of the study, none of the algal assemblages had reached a point where they could be classified as being at the reference stage although, it is noted here, their control site may have been on the open coast outside of the estuary and therefore of a different environmental character. Whereas organic input can be greatly reduced or stopped, many harmful substances including heavy metals, pesticides and antifouling paints stay in the sediments and may continue to have an effect so that recovery is partial. Recovery from such inputs is much less well studied than the resulting impacts themselves, and it seems likely that the long recovery period for some habitats affected most conspicuously by organic waste may be because of other pollutants that persist.

Aggregate extraction

Removal of sand and gravel from the seabed for the construction industry or for beach replenishment is widespread. Usually, it is non-living material that is extracted but,

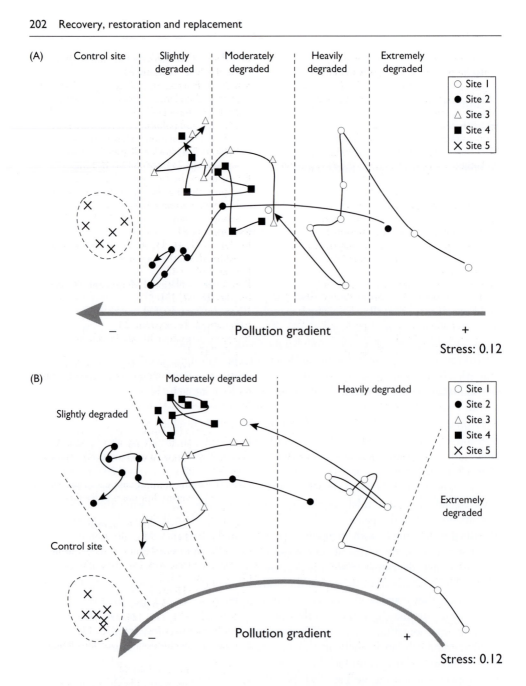

Figure 11.3 Trajectories of recovery/improvement in intertidal macroalgal communities at four sites in northern Spain during amelioration of sewage inputs 1984–2006. (A)= assemblages from 1.4m intertidal level; (B) = assemblages from 0.75m intertidal level. The non-metric multidimensional scaling ordinations are based on species abundance.

Source: Díez *et al.* (2009).

Physical recovery		Rapid recovery – resilient		Biological recovery	
Estuaries	1.5 years	↓	5 years	Estuaries	
Coarse sediments strong tidal stress				Coarse sediments strong tidal stress	
Sand plains				Sand plains	
Coarse sediments weak tidal stress				Coarse sediments moderate tidal stress	
Coarse sediments moderate tidal stress	20 years	Slow recovery-sensitive	12 years	Coarse sediments weak tidal stress	

Figure 11.4 Mean periods of recovery following cessation of aggregate extraction.

Source: Based on Foden *et al.* (2009), redrawn from a poster presentation.

inevitably, the organisms living in the sediment are also removed and killed. In the case of 'calcified seaweed' (taken for use as an agricultural soil conditioner) extraction may be of living material.

Ideally, dredging will not be permitted in areas designated for marine conservation but, particularly where those areas correspond to harbours, dredging may occur. A great deal of work has been undertaken to assess recovery following aggregate extraction in the UK and some work on methods to aid recovery. Recovery to something close to the community present in reference (undredged) areas may be from a few tidal cycles (highly mobile sand banks) to many years or decades (coarse sediments in moderate or weak tidal stress) or not at all where the remaining substratum is different to that previously present (Hill *et al.*, 2011). Although recovery to the same community that was present before dredging may not be possible, functional recovery with a different suite of species may be rapid (Cooper *et al.*, 2008). Foden *et al.* (2009) summarise the mean periods for physical and biological recovery from aggregate extraction in English waters (Figure 11.4).

However, measures of 'recovery' may be too simplistic in relation to conservation objectives, ignoring species that are of marine natural heritage importance and relying on such characteristics as species richness and abundance. Perversely, some species that may benefit from physical disturbance find their way into conservation directives, conventions and statutes and include, in the north-east Atlantic, reefs of the ross worm *Sabellaria spinulosa*.

Mobile bottom fishing gear

The potential for recovery of seabed habitats, species and communities from the physical impact of mobile fishing gear is dependent on the character of the seabed affected and whether pre-existing habitats remain after the activity ceases. For communities characterised by ephemeral or short-lived species or that colonise naturally disturbed habitats, recovery times are likely to be rapid and can be established by comparative or experimental studies (see, for instance, Dernie *et al.*, 2003). Some species may take a very long time to recover. González-Correa *et al.* (2005) describe how a deep bed of *Posidonia oceanica* showed only a few signs of recovery 100 years after trawing off southern Portugal. Where there is stable hard substrata that includes bedrock which has been disturbed, communities may take a long time to recover if long-lived and slow-growing species that previously

Table 11.1 Summary of typical conditions for impact and recovery

Rapid recovery (months–1 year)	Slow recovery (years–decades)
High tidal energy	Low or moderate energy
Fine sediments including sand	Coarse sediments
Disturbed community type	Stable community
r-selected species dominant	K-selected species dominant
Low-intensity dredging	High-intensity dredging
Sediment unchanged	Sediment changed
Small dredged area	Large dredged area

Source: Hill *et al.* (2011).

characterised them have been destroyed. However, where long-lived species were once present, it is unlikely that their presence was recorded and recovery may be 'celebrated' without knowing that significant species have been lost forever.

Most published information (for instance, Worm *et al.*, 2009) will emphasise the cascade of effects resulting from a rebalancing of predatory fish numbers (see 'Selective removal of species', p205). Studies that describe recovery of seabed communities following physical disturbance are many fewer but include, for instance, the following for areas subject to scallop dredging around the UK:

1   Hall-Spencer and Moore (2000) experimentally dredged live maerl, *Phymatolithon calcareum*, beds in the Firth of Clyde, Scotland. The percentage of live maerl was reduced dramatically (for instance from 25 to 15 live thalli per core sample) and did not recover over the subsequent four years. Although that specific study area was not further surveyed, an area that had been known as the richest maerl bed with extensive reefs of file shells, *Limaria hians*, in the Clyde (at Creag Gobhainn in Loch Fyne) was found in 2012 to have no *Limaria*, and maerl was represented only by scattered live rhodoliths with a maximum density of 1 per cent cover compared to a density of 25 per cent cover in 1999 (Moore *et al.*, 2013). The area was near to a registered scallop fishing ground although direct evidence of dredging was not found in 2012.

2   Bradshaw *et al.* (2001), comparing areas off the Isle of Man that were closed to fishing since 1989 with fished areas, demonstrated that that scallop dredging alters benthic communities and the closure of areas to commercial dredging may allow the development of (recovery to) more heterogeneous communities and permit the populations of some species to increase. In particular, upright species (mainly hydroids) were less abundant in dredged plots while encrusting species (bryozoans, sponges, small ascidians) flourished in dredged areas. If the cobbly substrata are left undisturbed, species that are structurally complex and attract a range of associated species (Bradshaw *et al.*, 2003) can recover and thrive.

3   Sciberas *et al.* (2013) demonstrated that changes in an area dredged for scallops in Cardigan Bay were primarily driven by seasonal fluctuations and that temporal changes in epibenthic community inside a permanently closed area were not related to recovery processes associated with the cessation of scallop dredging. They concluded that scallop dredging at the existing levels of fishing may have been insufficient to induce changes large enough to be detected in the presence of strong natural disturbance.

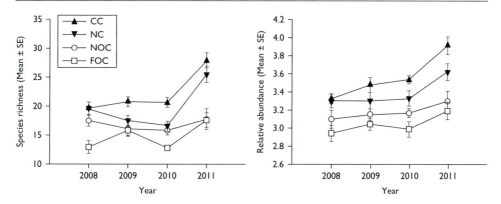

Figure 11.5 Recovery of species richness and relative abundance following closure of an area of Lyme Bay, south-west England, to scallop dredging. CC = Closed Control (▲); NC = New Control (▼); NOC = Near Open Control (open to fishing and adjacent to closed areas) (O); FOC = Far Open Control (open to fishing but far from closed areas) (□).

Source: Sheehan *et al.* (2013b).

4   In Lyme Bay, south-west England, scallop dredges were towed over bedrock and consolidated pebbles and cobbles that were colonised by attached species. Following closure of some areas in 2008, species richness and the abundance of certain fragile organisms increased significantly (Sheehan *et al.*, 2013a, 2013b). However, some species that colonise nearby unfished reefs are long-lived and slow growing and recolonisation of fished reefs may yet have some way to go.

Habitat alteration

Heavy mobile fishing gear may have created level seabeds of broken reef or removed large boulders deliberately to enable trawling but 'before and after' observations have not been made. It seems obvious that moving from stable rock reef to unstable rubble will lead to a change in community type at least and most likely a low species diversity. 'Blast fishing' on coral reefs breaks coral structures, leaving broken substrata unsuitable for coral recruitment (Fox *et al.*, 2003). Raymundo *et al.* (2007) observed no recovery of coral populations after 25 years or more but also cited Riegl and Luke (1998) who judge that recovery will take several hundred years.

Selective removal of species

Recovery of abundance and size of commercial species including fish, shellfish, echinoderms and algae following protection in MPAs is very well documented (see, for instance, Worm *et al.*, 2009; Roberts and Hawkins, 2012). Recovery of wide-ranging commercial species that are unlikely to be protected by MPAs is also well documented, including for fish and cetaceans (Lotze *et al.*, 2011). Often, recovery of numbers of the exploited species (although not necessarily to a pre-exploitation level) takes only a few years (for example, the implementation of a plan to reduce overfishing on Georges Bank in 1996 resulted in a strong increase of haddock *Melanogrammus aeglefinus* within five years: Rosenberg *et al.* 2006).

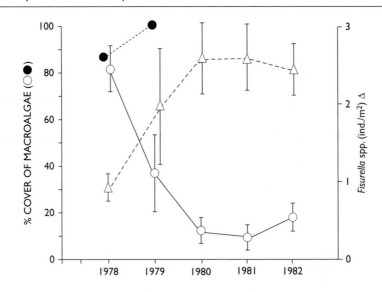

Figure 11.6 Change may be rapid after the removal of a damaging activity. Changes in percent cover of macroalgae (mean ± 1 SD, n = 3) and herbivore density (mean ± 1 SD, n = 3) subsequent to exclusion of harvesting on a rocky shore in Chile.

Source: Moreno *et al.* (1984).

However, in the case of the collapse of cod, *Gadus morhua*, populations due to overfishing, a fishing moratorium from 1990 in Atlantic Canada had not resulted in the expected full recovery more than 20 years later (Steneck *et al.*, 2013).

Traditional harvesting on rocky shores in Chile by 'mariscadores' removed algae and invertebrates for consumption. Exclusion of humans from a reserve in May 1978 saw a rapid increase in numbers of the herbivore that had been harvested and a corresponding reduction in the abundance of algae (Figure 11.6). Changes following protection are not usually so simple and the balance of many species will change and a more natural and different community develop (Figure 11.7)

Lobster harvesting

There are many studies worldwide that compare abundance and size of lobsters inside and outside of marine reserves that conclude that abundance and size are greater in an unexploited situation (for instance, Goñi *et al.*, 2010; Hoskin *et al.*, 2011; Kay *et al.*, 2012): there has been recovery towards a natural abundance and size structure. However, getting back to a natural or pristine situation is unlikely: recruitment almost certainly depends on production of larvae from unprotected areas and that may be much lower than in a universally unexploited situation. Such a poor supply of larvae may account for lack of recovery in populations of *Palinurus elephas* in parts of south-west England. Here, a diver could collect up to 20 spiny lobsters in one dive in the early 1970s but, now, seeing one is a great rarity. Most likely the lobsters that were taken were very old and recruitment infrequent even before widespread exploitation, and populations have not recovered.

In two cases at least, the preservation or recovery of lobster populations has been shown to have a significant effect on other parts of the ecosystem. For instance, in the Leigh marine

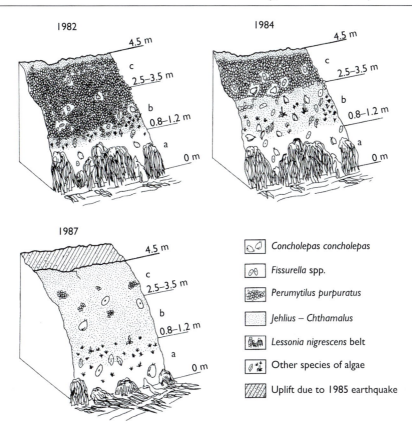

Figure 11.7 Change after removal of a damaging activity is likely to involve many species and losses as well as gains. Ecological changes on an exposed rocky shore at Las Cruces, Chile, following exclusion of collectors in late 1982. The gradual transition from a mussel- to a barnacle-dominated shoreline and increasing body dimensions of the mobile consumers *Fissurella* spp. and *Concholepas concholepas* are illustrated.

Source: Paine (1994) modified from Durán and Castilla (1989).

reserve in New Zealand, spiny lobster abundance increased rapidly within four years of reserve establishment, urchins (a prey species of spiny lobsters) decreased after 12 years, and kelp (which is grazed by urchins) increased after 15 years (Babcock *et al.*, 2010; Salomon *et al.*, 2010) (Plates 70 and 71). Urchins are also preyed upon by fish, especially large snapper. Leleu *et al.* (2012) quantified those observations by mapping cover of characteristic biotopes within the reserve area 30 years after the first such mapping, demonstrating how urchin barrens had become kelp forests (Plates 72 and 73). However, such obvious changes are unlikely to occur in habitats where key functional or structural species have not previously been exploited. Significantly, Leleu *et al.* (2012) report that deeper habitats (described as 'Deep reef' and 'Sponge flat') did not seem to have changed since 1977. Knock-on effects do not always happen or are not always clear. In the no-take zone at Lundy, England, lobster numbers and size had increased greatly in the eight years since the area was established (Hoskin *et al.*, 2011). However, Coleman *et al.* (2013) reported that there were no differences in how seabed assemblages changed over time between areas subject to potting and those not fished. Caution is needed when looking only or mainly at conspicuous epibiota. Leleu *et al.* (2012) observe that, in the Leigh Marine Reserve, less visually conspicuous communities not sampled in their mapping study may also have changed in response to the cessation of fishing in the reserve. These changes included a decreased abundance of large bivalves and heart urchins due to predation by lobsters, although no effect on smaller invertebrates (Langlois *et al.*, 2005, 2006a, 2006b) was observed.

Kelp harvesting

Kelp harvesting takes place in many parts of the world. In the Pacific, it is predominantly *Macrocystis pyrifera* that is harvested and, in the Atlantic, *Laminaria hyperborea* and *Laminaria digitata*. Kelp is also likely to be displaced by storms or by other forms of physical disturbance and may be susceptible to warming events. Experimental clearance of kelp and other species in the Isle of Man (Kain, 1975) demonstrated recovery to the same species and similar community as present in virgin forest within two-and-a-half years. Studies of recovery of populations following harvesting have mainly been directed at establishing when the next harvesting event can take place rather than recovery of species diversity in the habitat. In Norway, plants are harvested and the area is allowed to recover before re-harvesting. Christie *et al.* (1998) report that full recovery of the kelp forest biotope is likely to take more than five years. In particular, although kelp plants reached normal canopy height in three to five years and large numbers of organisms colonised the recovering kelp plants, the diversity of the holdfast fauna and stipe epiphytes did not reach the same level as in the natural kelp forest.

Loss of kelp due to environmental factors including seawater warming may result in long-term change and no recovery. In north-west Spain, Voerman *et al.* (2013) observed that four years after a decline there was still no kelp forest present, despite kelp being known for their fast recovery – in particular, *Laminaria ochroleuca* which was considered a thermophilic species.

Disease

Disease events strike marine species every so often. The results are usually only observed or reported in vertebrate species or in species that have some cultural importance or are valued for recreational enjoyment. Disease may continue to affect a species population for several years and recovery time can be very variable.

Seagrass beds often have very poor recovery after a pressure has ceased or may not recover at all. The wasting disease that affected *Zostera marina* in the north Atlantic in the 1930s decimated many beds and some areas completely lost their beds. Once a seagrass bed is lost, the sediment is no longer consolidated by the rhizomes and sediment loss, including loss of the seedbank, or disturbance may prevent recovery of the seagrass. Orth *et al.* (2006) observed natural recovery in the eastern USA in four bays with over 7,319ha reported in 2003 compared to 2,129ha in 1986. They considered that areas that had not recovered may have been too distant from sources of propagules to have been seeded. Often, it is increased nutrients that are considered the cause of decline and, once remediated, recovery occurs: for instance, the recovery of 27km^2 of seagrass beds in Tampa Bay, Florida (Greening and Janicki, 2006); recovery of 25ha in Mumford Cove, Connecticut (Vaudrey *et al.*, 2010); an increase from 0.02 to 1.6km^2 of seagrass from 1997 to 2002 following management actions to restore water quality and estuarine circulation and to reduce disturbance from fishing

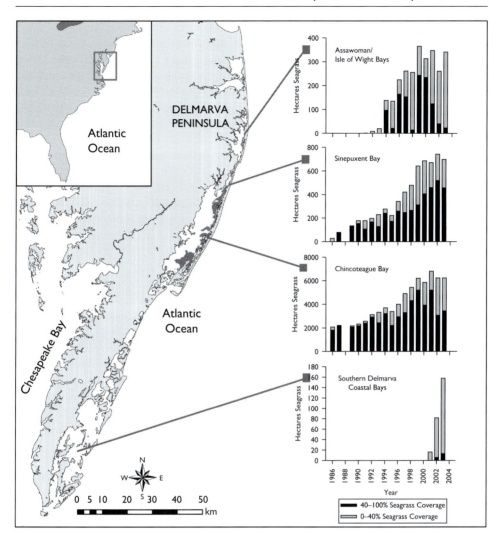

Figure 11.8 Map of the Delmarva Peninsula in the mid-Atlantic region of the United States showing the 2004 distribution of seagrass (dark shading), and graphs showing annual changes in seagrass coverage in two cover categories (sparse with 0–40 per cent coverage, and dense with 40–100 per cent cover) for each of the bays that had seagrass between 1986 and 2003.

Source: Orth *et al.* (2006).

practices in Mondego Bay, Portugal (Cardoso *et al.*, 2010); and a more than threefold increase in the extent of seagrass beds in the Northfrisian Wadden Sea, Germany from 1994–2006 (Reise and Kohlus, 2008). Olesen and Sand-Jensen (1994) reported that, in Danish waters, new *Zostera marina* beds took at least five years to become established and stable, and the survival and viability of the bed was strongly influenced by its size. Small patches with less than 32 shoots showed high mortality, but as the sizes and ages of the patches increased, mortality declined.

Sea fans are attractive parts of the submarine fauna and so disease events are noticed. In 1999, mortalities in *Paramuricea clavata* were recorded on the Ligurian coast of Italy (Plate 27). Cerrano *et al.* (2005) reported that, over a three-year period after the event, although the average size of colonies was reduced, their density as a result of successful recruitment had returned to pre-event levels. A similar disease event affected pink sea fans, *Eunicella verrucosa*, in south-west Britain in 2001–2003 and persisted to a small extent until 2006 (Hall-Spencer *et al.*, 2007). Populations were disease free after 2006 but numbers had not recovered in the MPA at Lundy by 2013, most likely because of poor recruitment (K. Hiscock, own observations). Such diseases are usually, it seems, the result of infection by *Vibrio* bacteria.

Seals are another conspicuous species and, in 1988 in north-west Europe, were greatly affected by an outbreak of phocine distemper. An estimated 18,000 seals died. Recovery occurred over subsequent years and, in the Wadden Sea, was from about 4,000 in 1989 to 17,000 in 2000. However, seals were again struck by disease in 2002 (Jensen *et al.*, 2002). In Britain, it was observed:

> Two outbreaks of phocine distemper virus (PDV) seriously affected the harbour seal population in eastern England with 50% dying in 1988 and 22% dying in 2002. In Scotland, an estimated 5% died in 1988 and far fewer in 2002. In marked contrast to populations elsewhere in Europe which showed an immediate and rapid recovery, harbour seals in eastern England took three years to recover from the 1988 outbreak and have yet to begin recovery following the 2002 outbreak. PDV outbreaks are likely to recur in the future but it is not possible to predict the proportion of the population that might be affected, which populations are most vulnerable (besides eastern England) or precisely when outbreaks will occur.
>
> (UKMMASC, 2010, p43)

Coral bleaching

It may be notable that Pearson (1981), reviewing recovery rates of coral reefs, does not mention bleaching, and, indeed, coral bleaching seems a fairly recent phenomenon. Bleaching happens when seawater temperatures are elevated 1–2°C or more above the seasonal average for several days. The symbiotic algae in the coral tissue, an important source of nutrition for the coral, are expelled or die and the host coral may die, most likely of starvation (for a review, see the introduction to van Woesik *et al.*, 2012). However, recovery is likely to be fairly rapid based on the findings of van Woesik *et al.* (2011). They repeatedly surveyed a coral assemblage that had experienced significant thermal stress events in 1998 and 2001 at Sesoko Island and found that (2011, p71) 'by 2007, species richness had recovered to about 13 species per m^2, which was similar to species richness in 1997,' and that 'hard coral cover increased from 3% in 2001 to 47% in 2010'. However, they found that 'species composition had undergone change', in that 'some species were thermally tolerant and increased in relative abundance through time', some 'increased in relative abundance through the thermal stress and remained constant thereafter' and some 'were neither winners nor losers through time.' Following a bleaching event in 1998, Golbuu *et al.* (2007) observed that coral cover recovered to previous levels in less than a decade. However, if warming events become more frequent, restructuring of the reef would be likely. Sheppard *et al.* (2008) also recorded recovery of corals in the Chagos archipelago which they considered more rapid than other reefs affected by the 1998 event because of lack of human disturbance there; they observe that their results illustrated the importance of reference sites that lack local direct impacts.

Recovery from multiple stressors

In many situations, there is at least a suspicion that more than one factor has caused change (see Chapter 5). Such 'cocktails' are difficult to separate so as to understand what has been the most important factor but, often, taking off the pressure(s) that can be managed may enable at least some recovery. For instance, in the northern Adriatic, Giani *et al.* (2012) mention eutrophication, increasing temperatures and overfishing as having caused changes to the benthos there; but, it was a reduction in nutrients (and increase in salinity) linked in part to lower rainfall and therefore river flow that has allowed significant reduction in anoxic events and recovery of benthos. In the Black Sea where eutrophication (caused by agricultural run-off) and damage caused by non-native species occurs (see, for instance, p17 in www.elme-eu.org/ELME_Results.pdf), wider environment effects can be addressed for agricultural run-off but not for non-native species. Recovery of long-lived and slow-growing species may be prolonged. Hughes *et al.* (2005) specify hunting, incidental netting and habitat degradation that need to be curbed to enable recovery of populations of sea cow, *Dugong dugong*, that had declined by 97 per cent over the past three decades along 1,000km of coastline in tropical Queensland, Australia. However, they suggest that recovery of this species back to the levels of the 1970s (which were already severely depleted) will take at least 120–160 years. Recovery of cetaceans from exploitation (whaling) is also slow but is occurring in many species (Lotze *et al.*, 2011). Nevertheless, there is concern that species at the top of the food chain are accumulating levels of contaminants such as PCBs that may compromise recovery.

Identifying recovery potential without case studies

The examples given above help the manager or policy advisor to estimate how long recovery will take in specific habitats and therefore to what extent damaged habitats will regain at least a self-sustaining character with diverse communities. However, for some habitats and species there is no information on which to estimate recovery time or recovery has never been observed in the years following damage or disappearance. Habitats for which information is not available are often remote and include the communities living in deep water on seamounts. Whatever the habitat, knowledge of the life history traits of the component species can be used to predict recovery, where that information is known or where a suitable surrogate exists. In the case of deep-water corals, it is known that larvae of *Lophelia pertusa* can travel long distances to colonise artificial structures but, for other species of coral or for species associated with deep-water coral reefs, there is little or no information that would suggest larval dispersal distances. In the case of maerl habitats, apparently destroyed in places on the west coast of Scotland by mobile fishing gear, growth rates of *Phymatolithon calcareum* are known to be less that 1mm a year, but likelihood of recruitment is not known. A maerl nodule 15mm across is therefore likely to be 15 plus years old, but infrequent recruitment would place recovery times at, say, 50 plus years after cessation of the damaging activity providing that water quality is good.

For species that decline in abundance without obvious cause, predicting whether they will reappear and after how long is problematic. What seems certain is that some species will disappear or decline in abundance for many years only to reappear decades later. These are often edge-of-range species or ones where multiple interacting forces (a 'perfect storm') are needed for reproduction and recruitment to be successful. The more knowledge that we accumulate on such species, the better placed we will be to understand when change 'matters' and when it is part of some natural cycle. Such knowledge is often held by elderly naturalists and needs to be recorded.

There are more and more examples of recovery after conservation measures have been taken. In the case of situations where impacts have been devastating, studies of colonisation of new surfaces such as on artificial reefs or new rock from volcanic activity can provide guidance on how rapidly recovery may occur. For instance, after the ex Royal Navy frigate *Scylla* was sunk near Plymouth UK in 2004, it took about two years before the initial fast-growing colonising species were replaced or supplemented by slower-growing and colonising species and a 'classic' steel-wreck biotope began to develop (Hiscock *et al.*, 2010) (Plate 68). However, it took much longer for populations of some fish to establish. For coral reef locations, Tomascik *et al.* (1997) found that five years after the 1988 volcanic eruption of Gunung Api, the sheltered lava flow supported a diverse coral community (124 species) with high coral cover.

Four biological traits are likely to determine recovery potential and rates:

- **Regrowth potential.** Organisms that grow from a stolon or holdfast or that are colonial and fixed to the seabed may be damaged by physical disturbance but regrow. They include algae that would normally lose their fronds at the end of the growing season, colonial hydrozoans, bryozoans and ascidians that grow by producing new zooids and sponges. Damage may be repaired although new growth may not be until the next growing season. Also, some sponges in particular may be very slow growing and have taken several decades to reach the size they were before damaged so that regrowth will be very slow.
- **Reproductive or recruitment frequency.** Most species reproduce once a year although some have a prolonged period when they reproduce. Recolonisation may therefore not occur until the relevant time of year. However, conditions are not always favourable for recruitment and there will be good and bad years for reproduction in many species (Plate 74). Favourable conditions may include a good food supply for adults to produce larvae, currents that take larvae or propagules from the donor area to the damaged site.
- **Dispersal potential.** Of key importance to conservation of existing communities and recovery of damaged ones is dispersal potential. If a species has a dispersal potential of a few centimetres (for instance, some corals) then a destroyed population is unlikely to recover and its place may be taken by opportunistic species that reproduce frequently, have long dispersal distances and grow rapidly. Although some species clearly have short larval dispersal distances and may have localised populations, the question has to be asked: how did they get there in the first place? Setting aside assisted dispersal (for instance, on the hulls of ships), it may be that some larvae remain viable for much longer than the short period which is the norm. In the case of the scarlet and gold star coral (Plate 75), Paul Tranter (pers. comm.), in aquarium conditions, observed that some larvae of *Balanophyllia regia* did not settle for up to two weeks after production – they had the capability to colonise new locations, but this rarely happened. Perhaps

these 'fit' larvae came from well-fed individuals and, every so often, conditions are just right for larger/fitter larvae to be produced.

- **Growth rate.** Whilst some species may settle soon after a habitat has been damaged, growth may be very slow. This seems likely to be the case for some sponges (see Plate 20).

Combinations of factors are also important. A combination of frequency of reproduction and dispersal potential (distance from the nearest intact population of a species) is relevant. In the case of ex *HMS Scylla* most species that were to be visually dominant settled in the first two years; but pink sea fans, *Eunicella verrucosa*, that had populations on bedrock as little as 40m away from the new reef, did not settle until year four: the new reef was close enough (to a species with probably limited dispersal capability) but perhaps year four was the first with successful reproduction in the donor population.

Biological traits are, however, often poorly known and extrapolations from species of the same genus are not necessarily relevant. Accumulating knowledge from monitoring, from experimental studies and from laboratory observations will provide essential information for management. Such work has been undertaken in Europe by MarLIN and is available from their website (www.marlin.ac.uk/biotic). Assessing recoverability potential is a component of sensitivity assessments (Hiscock and Tyler-Walters, 2006; www.marlin.ac.uk/sensitivityrationale.php). The definitions of recoverability used in the MarLIN programme are given in Chapter 7 (p112) and range from 'None: recovery is not possible' to 'Immediate: recovery immediate or within a few days'.

Where does recovery come from?

MPAs with adequate protection of sensitive habitats should provide a reservoir of species that will produce larvae and propagules that will be dispersed into the wider seas away from the MPA boundary and therefore assist recovery of damaged areas.

However, it is important for the those charged with management of MPAs to understand that recruitment will often, or usually, be local or from the wider (non-protected) marine environment and not solely or mainly from some nearby MPA. Work by Kinlan and Gaines (2003), Shanks *et al.* (2003) and Roberts *et al.* (2010) makes it clear that some species will have the ability to colonise new or damaged locations from afar. It is equally clear that some species are unlikely to colonise (including for recovery) habitats further than a few metres away from their parent colonies.

Taking off the pressure – is there a cost for wildlife?

Although the consequences of removing human pressures from marine ecosystems for biodiversity conservation are generally considered to result in 'benefits' (for naturalness, for survival and recovery of threatened species and habitats, etc.), there may be perceived 'costs'.

Some of those costs are predictable, especially from areas where conservation measures have been in place for some time or where experimental studies in natural systems have been carried out, but others may be surprises. Understanding how ecosystems function is important in predicting or accounting for changes after conservation measures have been put into place. Table 11.2 lists some of the benefits and costs for specific examples of conservation measures or outcomes of protection.

Table 11.2 Benefits and costs of conservation measures

Measures or outcomes	Benefit(s)	Cost(s)	References
Protection of seals (harbour seal, *Phoca vitulina*).	Increased populations of a charismatic species.	High density probably a contributory cause to outbreak of phocine distemper virus.	Lavigne and Schmitz (1990)
Protection of colourful anthozoan and sponge communities (species such as red coral and sea fans recover).	Attractive scenery for increased tourism and educational activities that provide 'value' to conservation.	Physical disturbance and damage to structural features through, for instance, clumsy finning, boulder turning, etc.	
Protection of lobster (*Homarus gammarus*) populations as part of no-take zone.	Increased population and larger individuals of lobsters. More and larger females produce more larvae to enter the fishery outside. Possible overcrowding leads to migration out of protected area and into fishery.	Minor increase in shell disease (low level) of large males within the NTZ.	Wootton et al. (2012)
Protection of fish stocks (yellowtail flounder) in no-fishing areas in Nantucket Lightship Closed Area.	In, for example, one of the protected areas, 17 positive, 2 negative and 6 equivocal effects noted.	Mass mortality of large scallops between 2004 and 2005 most likely due to effects of senescence, including parasitism by shell borers and prokaryotic infection.	Stokesbury et al. (2007)

The denser the population of a species is, the easier it is for disease and parasites to spread through the population. Facilitating the increased abundance of a species as a consequence of conservation measures may well increase likelihood of disease or parasitic infection. Whilst concern about disease is an animal welfare issue it is also important to realise that recovered populations may become self-limiting and even suffer occasional catastrophic outbreaks of disease or parasitism. A much-cited example is the sea otter population in California which recovered dramatically after exploitation ceased but then suffered from disease that reduced the population. Seal populations may also suffer increased incidence of disease as exploitation is reduced: for instance, canine distemper virus in Antarctic seals (Bengtson et al., 1991). The example of a high mortality event in scallops, *Placopecten magellanicus*, in 2004 and 2005 seemed to be the result of the scallops being 'allowed' to get old in the absence of fishing pressure. Such events often cause much hand-wringing by fishermen and calls for a cull of larger individuals to the financial benefit of the fishing community. If the measure had been put in place to prevent damage to fish stocks other than scallops (it was) or to seabed habitats and to understand natural change, the calls would be illegitimate.

Changes that are part of recovery following the removal of pressures are not necessarily predictable although some that are brought about through trophic cascades are well established. For instance, along the Pacific coast of North America, the virtual extirpation of sea otters led to increased abundance of their prey, sea urchins, which destroyed kelp forests and the associated community of species (Steneck et al., 2002; Estes et al., 2010).

Restoration – assisting recovery

Introduction

Recovery, or the rate of recovery, can be assisted by direct conservation action beyond 'taking off the pressure'. Determining what those actions might be is supported by the discipline of restoration ecology, which often uses experimental studies but also case studies to inform restoration projects. The direct actions that can be taken are catalogued in Lotze *et al*. (2011) and some examples are given below. The examples are intended to illustrate how effective (or not) interventions might be in restoring biodiversity, including returning locations to a situation that is as close as possible to natural or at least as a functioning ecosystem. In addition, there will be the practical need to prioritise action as not everything that is desired can be afforded.

Reintroduction or translocation

Reintroduction and translocation, methods commonly used for terrestrial and freshwater species, may only be appropriate for a very few marine species such as those that have become locally extinct and are unlikely to recolonise an area through their own dispersal mechanisms. Translocation as 'restocking' is commonly used in shellfisheries (see, for instance Norman *et al*., 2006 for scallops in Europe). Native European oysters, *Ostrea edulis*, are already subject to restoration programmes (Goulletquer, 2004) that involve spat collection and laying. In Chesapeake Bay (see Chapter 4, 'Oysters in Chesapeake Bay', p60) restoration work has included release of larvae from hatcheries and deposition of cultch. Despite some significant successes (Schulte *et al*., 2009), those restoration efforts have failed to return populations to anywhere near original amounts, and Wilberg *et al*. (2011) recommend a moratorium on fishing to minimise the risk of extirpation and provide an opportunity for recovery. Translocation of horse mussels, *Modiolus modiolus*, to areas of 'cultch' (broken scallop shells) in Strangford Lough, Northern Ireland as part of a programme of work to restore populations destroyed by scallop dredging, indicated that settlement of M. *modiolus* larvae was directly enhanced by the presence of adults on the seafloor. Translocation seemed essential and, as a part of the same study, Elsäßer *et al*. (2013) conclude that remnant populations of M. *modiolus* are largely self-recruiting with little connectivity between them or with populations outside the lough. They suggest that the best approach to accelerate the recovery and restoration of M. *modiolus* biogenic reefs in Strangford Lough is to provide total protection of all remaining larval sources and establish additional patches of mussels in areas where models predict certain larval densities to ensure that restoration sites are located where recovery has the highest likelihood of success.

Translocations of mobile species as a biodiversity conservation measure are unusual in the marine environment. One exception is the successful 'assisted migration' of rock lobsters, *Jasus edwardsii*, to locations in Tasmania where populations had been depleted by commercial fishing (Green *et al*., 2010). Although the assisted migration was greatly concerned with stock enhancement, coincidentally, range extension of the long-spined sea urchin (*Centrostephanus rodgersii*) due to seawater warming was having catastrophic consequences on the kelp forest communities through grazing (Ling *et al*., 2009). Lobsters eat sea urchins and restoring the lobster population should assist in the recovery of the kelp forest. In a later paper, Ling and Johnson (2012) explore the mechanisms underlying the utility of marine reserves to reinstate trophic dynamics and to increase resilience of kelp beds against climate-driven phase shift to sea urchin barrens on the rapidly warming Tasmanian east coast. They found that, in no-take zones, mortality of tethered urchins (unable to seek refuge in crevices) was approximately 7 times higher and for untethered urchins, about 3.3 times higher than in fished areas

Major efforts may be made to restore (including for recreation) habitats such as some coral reefs where coral nurseries are used to supply animals to rebuild damaged reef areas. Many of the most successful projects are described in Edwards (2010). The different ways in which nursery-grown corals are attached to existing reef or various frameworks of artificial material create coral gardens that may grow to look like natural reef. However, if a reef has been damaged by human activities, recovery will often occur anyway when the damaging activity is resolved and some rehabilitation activities seem more like creating gardens on land. Action may be needed where an unsuitable habitat for recovery has been created: for instance, coral rubble resulting from blast fishing. Raymondo et al. (2007) stabilised such rubble with plastic mesh and found that the fish community evolved to one similar to the adjacent healthy reef within three years, and coral recruitment and percent cover increased over time with 63.5 per cent recruit survivorship within consolidated plots compared with 6 per cent on rubble. Plate 76 shows a nursery of corals used to assist recovery of damaged coral reef habitat.

Edwards (2010, p10) provides a manual for the restoration of coral reefs and observes:

- Active reef restoration is *not* an alternative to proper coastal management.
- Rehabilitation of habitat is always more expensive than protecting it from degradation in the first place.
- There is no point in attempting active restoration unless the area to be restored is under effective management (e.g. within a marine protected area) or not under significant local anthropogenic pressure.
- Resilient reefs (generally those relatively unimpacted by mankind) are likely to recover from disturbances (e.g., storms, bleaching) without human intervention.
- Reefs significantly impacted by humans tend to recover poorly from disturbances (i.e. have lost resilience), but management can improve their resilience.
- Effective management at an adequate spatial scale needs to be in place before active restoration can succeed.
- Active restoration, where deemed appropriate, should be part of a broader integrated coastal management plan. It should not be an isolated act.

Fonseca et al. (2002) report that seagrasses can be readily transplanted and significant restoration successes have occurred. However, they warn that sites need to be appropriately selected and basic ecological principles applied to the restoration exercise. The appropriateness of locations may be judged by whether there is, or has been, seagrass there and that water quality is adequate. Campbell (2000) describes the factors to be taken into account in determining whether restoration is worth pursuing. Orth et al. (2006) describe how, in southern bays of the Delmarva coastal bays (USA) (Figure 11.8), extensive seeding of *Zostera marina* has been successful in re-instating the seagrass beds, but warn that continued recovery will depend on maintaining good water quality to avoid the macroalgal accumulations and phytoplankton blooms that have characterised other coastal lagoons. There has been much less success in Europe and Cunha et al. (2012) report that none of the seagrass restoration programmes developed in Europe by the participants during the ten years preceding a workshop in 2010 was successful.

Restoring a habitat to its previous state or something close to that state may include adding substratum to a damaged seabed. For instance, where larger sediment particles and particularly shell fragments have been removed, the deployment of waste shell 'cultch' may help to increase habitat diversity. Such an experimental restoration project was carried out in a dredged area to the east of the Isle of Wight (Collins and Mallinson, 2007) with limited success: scallop shells providing attachment and habitat for a range of epifaunal and crevice-dwelling animals.

Prioritising and taking action for recovery and restoration

Species

The establishment of species recovery plans can be traced back to the USA's Endangered Species Act of 1973, which requires the implementation of recovery plans to promote the conservation of endangered or threatened species. In 1992, the Convention on Biodiversity (Glowka et al., 1994) gave impetus to the creation of Biodiversity Action Plans (BAP) which would, for the few countries that developed them, create targets for conservation and restoration, establish actions to be taken and identify budgets, timelines and institutional partnerships for implementing each BAP. An example is the series of BAP for the UK, which includes 96 marine species. Hiscock et al. (2011) revisited species action plans for England, prepared action plans (as dossiers) and prioritised species according to criteria initially developed for terrestrial species.

For species that have declined, where there is a desire to reverse that decline, there will be questions of need, feasibility, likelihood of success and of costs to address. The objective for action may not be a return to some pristine state but for the species to become self-sustaining members of their ecosystem (see Hiscock et al., 2013). Some species may benefit from protection or restoration of their habitat and may not need a programme of their own. Some species may be highly mobile and localised protection will not assist the population as a whole. The following four groups (based on Hiscock et al., 2013) provide the basis for an initial sift of species to identify which might benefit from action:

- species with no evidence of significant decline and/or that are likely to be protected within well-managed MPAs and hence no further action is required;
- species that are likely to be protected within MPAs but will require additional targeted action;
- species that are unlikely to be protected within MPAs but where protection can be secured through wider measures;
- species that are too far ranging for protection to be secured within MPAs or through wider measures in national waters and hence require international action.

Inevitably, there will be lack of information about which are rare, scarce, in decline or threatened with decline species in a biogeographical or administrative area and about life history traits of species identified as in need of restoration including re-establishment.

The process of identifying recovery/conservation goals can be determined by a number of considerations but especially (from Hiscock et al., 2013, p92):

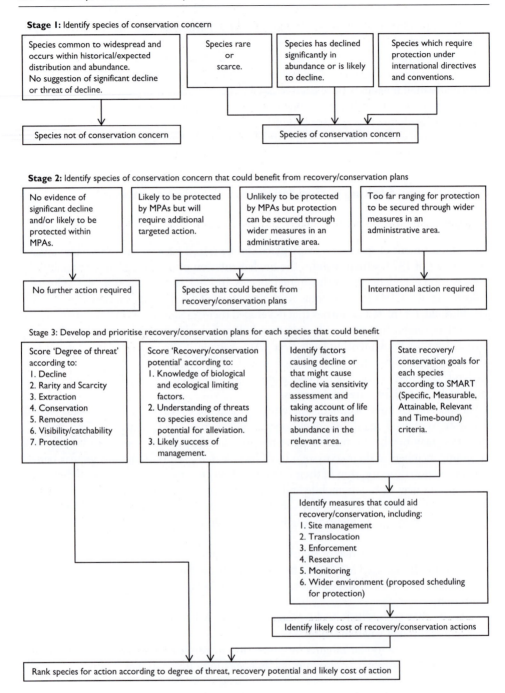

Figure 11.9 A decision tree for identifying species that are of conservation concern (Stage 1); of those, the species that would benefit from recovery/conservation plans (Stage 2); and development and prioritisation of recovery/conservation plans (Stage 3).

Source: Hiscock et al. (2013).

- Does the habitat for the species still exist and in a high quality state?
- Is the remaining species pool adequate to re-populate in the area under consideration?
- Do we know what caused a decline or threatens to cause decline (determines if any action to take can be identified)?
- Will management of human activities result in full or partial recovery/protection?
- If not full recovery/conservation of populations, how much and how extensive?
- Bearing in mind life-history traits, how long is recovery likely to take after action to remove pressures?

Conservation goals should be described according to SMART (Specific, Measurable, Attainable, Relevant/Realistic and Time-bound) criteria. Cost is an additional prioritising consideration.

Action plans will be needed. Likely actions for maintenance or recovery of a population of a species can be specified under the headings: 'Site Management', 'Translocation', 'Enforcement', 'Research', 'Monitoring' and 'Wider Environment'.

Examples of conservation/recovery objectives for some of the species of conservation importance researched for England are given in Table 11.3

The proposals for research associated with informing conservation and, in a few cases, recovery of populations of the species researched for England resulted in dossiers for each species and an estimate of costs which ranged from GBP6,000 to GBP160,000 for low-mobility benthic species but GBP3,500,000 for grouped elasmobranchs and GBP4,425,000 for grouped cetaceans. In a different study, hypothetical estimates of costs for restoration of deep-sea coral communities damaged by mobile fishing gear by transplanting nursery-grown corals to the Darwin Mounds came in at US$3,410,000 (Van Dover et al., 2014).

Many species are listed for protection in international directives and conventions and in national statutes. That protection may be a prohibition of any removal (for instance, most whales) or of trade in body parts (the Convention on Trade in Endangered Species). The success or otherwise of these measures can be assessed as most are large well-studied species such as whales, sharks and seabirds. Success is mixed and many threatened species are long-lived, slow growing and have a very low fecundity so that recovery is likely to be on a scale of tens of decades or even centuries. The example given is of recovery of the western Atlantic bowhead whale numbers from 1975 to 2002, with an estimated change in numbers from about 4,000 to 10,000 (Gerber et al., 2007). More examples are given in Lotze et al. (2011).

At the completion of their work on conservation and recovery of 'threatened' marine species in English waters, Hiscock et al. (2011, piv) concluded:

> Many of the results of this exercise are pessimistic – both with regard to the degree of threat and the recovery/conservation potential. For commercially exploited species or species impacted by commercial fishing activities, we may know that recovery is possible but obtaining necessary measures is problematic. For non-commercial species and species that are not obviously being impacted by human activities, the poor outlook is generally because, although there has clearly been decline, we do not know (for certain) why.

Habitats

In a paper on restoration, Hawkins et al. (1999) advocate removing, where possible, the pressures or activities adversely affecting systems and then different measures for 'open' and

Table 11.3 Degree of threat and recovery/conservation potential rankings for example species that are species of conservation importance around England. Full information on each species is given in the dossiers in Hiscock *et al.* (2011)

Species	Degree of threat	Conservation/ recovery potential	Conservation/recovery objective
Phymatolithon calcareum (maerl)	Mod.	High	Maintain the current distribution and extent of maerl beds and the associated plant and animal communities in the UK by protecting existing beds from damage and monitor status.
Armandia cirrhosa (lagoon sandworm)	Mod.	Mod.	Halt/reverse any decline/loss observed at the Eight Acre Pond and maintain/enhance populations at existing sites through site protection and management. Stable populations at known sites by 2015.
Hippocampus guttulatus (short-snouted seahorse	Low	High	Recovery or conservation will have been achieved when a constant level of abundance has been reached though removal of habitat degrading activities and negative pressures. If suggested measures are implemented, within five years the population at a site with a persistent population should be within a healthy state.
Eunicella verrucosa (pink sea fan)	Mod.	High	Recovery or conservation will have been achieved when the recent historical distribution and abundance has been maintained/restored by protection of existing populations and removal of (manageable) pressures causing decline. Research aimed at understanding reproductive characteristics and population genetics should be complete by end of 2014.
Leptopsammia pruvoti (sunset cup coral)	Mod.	Low	Maintain potential for survival and expansion by protection of existing and any newly discovered colonies and better understand reproduction and growth by laboratory studies in 2011–2015.
Palinurus elephas (crawfish; spiny lobster)	High	Low	Recovery will have been achieved when the general historical distribution and a constant level of abundance has been reached. If suggested measures are implemented, the goal should be reached within 50 years.
Atrina fragilis (fan mussel)	Mod.	Low	Ensure that *Atrina fragilis* individuals are protected wherever they are found to occur and that their habitat is protected wherever historically they have occurred.
Anguilla anguilla (European eel)	High	Low	Recovery will have been achieved when the general historical distribution and a constant level of abundance has been reached. If suggested measures are implemented, the goal should be reached within 60 years.
Raja clavata (thornback ray)	Mod.	Low	Conservation will have been achieved when there is a sustained and continuing increase in numbers in north-east Atlantic population by 2020 as well as restoring the species to its full North Sea range by 2030.

Table 11.3 (continued)

Species	Degree of threat	Conservation/ recovery potential	Conservation/recovery objective
Squatina squatina (angel shark; monk fish; angel fish)	Mod.	Low	Conservation goals should aim at continuing to ensure that the species is returned whenever taken as by-catch and establishing safe havens for the species. Recovery will have been achieved when the species abundance has been restored by maintenance of existing populations and recolonisation of at least some of its historical range and removal of pressures causing decline.
Phoca vitulina vitulina (harbour seal)	High	Low	Achieve and maintain sustained population increases towards the levels exhibited prior to the Phocine Distemper Virus outbreak in 1988 and by 2016–2021.
Tursiops truncatus (bottlenose dolphin)	Mod.	Low	Raise levels of knowledge of this species to a suitable level to allow the creation of meaningful management goals within 10–15 years, this includes sufficient time to assess trends in both population numbers and distribution.

'closed' systems (Figure 11.10). Those measures include reconstructing habitats including controlling physical processes and ensuring suitable water quality so that a suitable habitat is developed as well as (re)introducing species if considered necessary.

Recover to what?

Recovery in marine ecosystems is unlikely to be to some 'pristine' state – and anyway we do not know what that state was. Permanent damage to habitats and continued degradation in the wider marine environment from overfishing, from the spread of diffuse contaminants and from colonisation by non-native species is a reality that needs to be taken into account. However, marine conservationist need not be as disheartened as some terrestrial conservationists (see, for instance, Harris et al., 2006). Getting back to communities that are close to natural is probable – once damaging pressures have been taken off, providing that the habitat has not been destroyed and that colonists are available. Marine ecosystems change naturally and populations may have high and low points without having been affected by human activities.

Replacement

Habitats

Where habitats have been lost (for instance, because of extraction or deposition or because of damage by mobile fishing gear) or are about to be lost (for instance, because of coastal defence works or harbour construction), consideration may be given to replacing those habitats with something that will either mimic them or at least be attractive to high species diversity and a productive community. Although described here as 'Replacement',

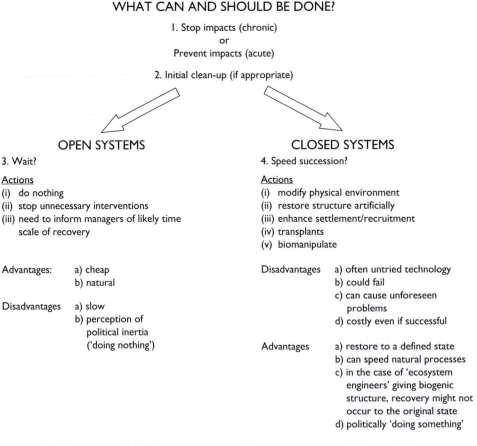

WHAT CAN AND SHOULD BE DONE?

1. Stop impacts (chronic)
or
Prevent impacts (acute)

2. Initial clean-up (if appropriate)

OPEN SYSTEMS

3. Wait?

<u>Actions</u>
(i)   do nothing
(ii) stop unnecessary interventions
(iii) need to inform managers of likely time
      scale of recovery

Advantages: a) cheap
               b) natural

Disadvantages a) slow
               b) perception of
                  political inertia
                  ('doing nothing')

CLOSED SYSTEMS

4. Speed succession?

<u>Actions</u>
(i)   modify physical environment
(ii) restore structure artificially
(iii) enhance settlement/recruitment
(iv) transplants
(v)   biomanipulate

Disadvantages   a) often untried technology
                b) could fail
                c) can cause unforeseen
                   problems
                d) costly even if successful

Advantages   a) restore to a defined state
                b) can speed natural processes
                c) in the case of 'ecosystem
                   engineers' giving biogenic
                   structure, recovery might not
                   occur to the original state
                d) politically 'doing something'

Figure 11.10 A summary of decision-making involved in recovery or restoration of marine
ecosystems.

Source: Based on Hawkins *et al.* (1999).

there is another descriptor that is becoming increasingly popular, that of 'ecological or biodiversity offsetting' where loss of a valued habitat at one location due to development is 'compensated for' by creating another similar habitat elsewhere, leading to no net loss of biodiversity. Biodiversity offsetting is defined as:

> measurable conservation outcomes resulting from actions designed to compensate for significant residual adverse biodiversity impacts arising from project development after appropriate prevention and mitigation measures have been taken. The goal of biodiversity offsets is to achieve no net loss and preferably a net gain of biodiversity on the ground with respect to species composition, habitat structure, ecosystem function and people's use and cultural values associated with biodiversity.
>
> (BBOP, 2009, p15)

That approach may work for intertidal habitats affected by coastal defence works (where defended coast is compensated for by removing defences and allowing flooding elsewhere) or transitory habitats such as saline lagoons (which may be lost in one location but can be excavated in a new location nearby) but trying to mimic many natural habitats, especially subtidal ones, is unlikely to work. Those habitats are too complex to mimic.

Although offset metrics should be based on considerations of area and quality of habitat and the type of damage caused, it is hard to intervene to enhance the quality of some benthic habitat types, leaving two broad options (from Dickie et al., 2013, p5):

- Offset through enhancements made to benthic biodiversity by trading up from one (lower ecological value) habitat type to another habitat type, such as biogenic reefs. Metrics for calculating damage and offsets are described based on species diversity and abundance.
- A more ecosystem-based approach, which considers several individual projects or for a development programme, for which pooled offsets larger areas of sea may provide more ecological benefits.

The same report used case studies to work through each stage of the process of developing biodiversity offsets requirements and concluded:

- Some damages cannot be offset … It appears that more biodiversity features are non-offsettable in the marine environment due to their dynamism, greater uncertainties, and difficulty of recreating marine environmental conditions for biodiversity.
- Marine offsets may require more lateral thinking on how to boost populations of species in order to offset impacts, making populations more resilient, rather than location specific actions.

(Dickie et al., 2013, p5)

Introduction of new structures to the sea to encourage growth of lost communities may be considered valuable if those communities were important for coastal productivity including of fish stocks. A large-scale and successful programme of introducing and then colonising artificial structures onto the shallow seabed off Korea resulted in the development of algal communities and trophic structures similar to those that were present in natural communities (Kang et al., 2008). Those structures were concrete pyramids and other hard substrata. Although replacing damaged seabed, the ethics of introducing artificial substrata to natural but damaged habitats needs careful consideration.

The prospect of replacement should not be an excuse (a 'licence to trash') for deliberately and unnecessarily destroying natural systems. But, in ecosystem-based management, humans are a part of the ecosystem and have requirements for transport, food and recreation and consideration of compensatory measures should be welcome.

Considerable effort has been put into designing coastal defence structures to encourage diversity. Such activity can be described as 'ecological engineering' (Bergen et al., 2001) and combines a knowledge of engineering and ecology to create habitats that are practical for their prime purpose (to protect coast or create infrastructure) but also to attract a community of species that will be close to natural. Chapman and Underwood (2011) provide a wide-ranging review of ecological engineering in intertidal marine habitats. They give examples of structures that create habitat diversity through incorporating water-retaining features or damp, shaded habitats and point to the need to understand the way that assemblages in coastal habitats develop and are maintained and, specifically, in a way that will support design, size and placement of coastal defence structures. Firth *et al.* (2013) further demonstrate the importance of water-retaining features on coastal defence structures and describe how such features support greater species richness than emergent substrata. Examples of building in water retaining or structurally complex features to coastal defences are shown in Plates 77 to 79.

Docks are a habitat that do not mimic situations that occur naturally but may provide a surrogate habitat to replace saline lagoons that have been lost due to development (sometimes of the very docks that might have replaced them). The water quality and the physical processes in such habitats may need manipulation to make them suitable for colonisation (see Figure 11.10). A significant study that 'created' a habitat suitable for diverse communities of species was in Liverpool, UK where the old docks were renovated and re-flooded (Allen *et al.*, 1995; Russell *et al.*, 1983).

Predicting likely colonisation on artificial structures will get better and better as more structures are designed, studied and monitored for their biology. Engineers, who work with straightforward knowledge of strength and size of the materials they need to use, may find it difficult to understand the uncertainties associated with ecology. Nevertheless, Moschella *et al.* (2005) provide evidence from existing structures and advice on design of structures to enhance species richness on them.

Artificial structures do not mimic natural features. This is particularly the case for reefs where sunken ships may be considered a replacement for damaged or destroyed reefs. The extent to which artificial structures can mimic natural habitats is questionable and comparisons are, as pointed out by Perkol-Finkel and Benayahu (2005), scarce. In a few cases, artificial structures have been specifically designed to mimic natural habitats but there has been no consistent evidence that these aims have been achieved (Svane and Petersen, 2001; Perkol-Finkel *et al.*, 2006; Burt *et al.*, 2009; Miller *et al.*, 2009). In the study of a sunken warship, ex HMS *Scylla*, in south-west England, Hiscock *et al.* (2010) found that, of the 122 conspicuous species noted for the warship and natural reefs in the vicinity, 39 species recorded on nearby bedrock reefs had not been recorded from *Scylla* by the end of the study and 9 species were recorded on *Scylla* but not the natural bedrock reefs. The conclusion by Perkol-Finkel *et al.* (2006) that, even after a century, an artificial reef will mimic its adjacent natural communities only if it possesses structural features similar to those of the natural surroundings seems likely to apply also to artificial reefs in temperate waters; but, furthermore, there may be species that are long-lived and slow growing or that have short larval dispersal times that should not be expected to colonise.

Whilst this section has addressed replacement of habitats, it is also relevant to the introduction of new habitats such as wind farm pylons, marinas, recreational reefs (usually sunken vessels) and bereavement balls.

Whilst many habitat replacements or modifications are on a fairly small scale, some affect several square kilometres of habitats. One such is the Oosterschelde in the Netherlands. Following disastrous floods in 1953, the Netherlands government decided to close off three of the four main estuaries of the Delta Region, a decision which would have created huge brackish or freshwater lakes. However, as a compromise between human safety and nature conservation, a four-kilometre section of defences across the Eastern Scheldt estuary included sluice-gate doors that are normally open. Changes to the Rhine, Meuse and Scheldt estuaries as a result of tidal barrier construction are described by Heip (1989) who suggests that only the Western Scheldt remained a true unchanged estuary. He points out that, from the original situation of four comparable estuaries entering the Delta region, many ecologically very different water bodies have been created. The now enclosed area became less subject to storms, tidal current velocity slowed, the water became clearer and the tidal range decreased from 3.40m to 3.25m. The area has, since 2002, been a national park with an area of 370km^2 and a shore length of 125km. The area was intensively studied before the barrier was completed and afterwards (Nienhuis and Smaal, 1994). The changes reported in the ecology of the area were in some cases significant with some faunal elements disappearing (de Kluijver and Leewis, 1994) but some communities remaining largely unchanged although with increased sedimentation causing a reduction in species diversity (Meijer and Waardenburg, 1994).

Species

Replacing a lost species with a different species that has the same structural or functional characteristics or fulfils the same role in cultural terms (for instance, for luxury food) is rarely undertaken in the sea. Native species, if the habitat was suitable, would most likely colonise naturally and so replacement is likely to involve non-native species and subsequent unintended consequences. An example is the replacement of declining native European oysters *Ostrea edulis* with Pacific oysters *Crassostrea gigas* (Padilla, 2010). Not only did the non-native oysters colonise and dominate natural habitats but they brought with them unwanted pest species (such as slipper limpets, *Crepidula fornicata*, and wire weed, *Sargassum muticum*). Replacement of native species with a non-native alternative in the sea is very dangerous for natural ecosystems and should not be undertaken.

Restoration and replacement – ecological, political and practical considerations

Whilst we can take action to restore or replace species and habitats, the questions need to be asked: 'should we?'; and, 'which ones?' There are considerations that go beyond feasibility and that are addressed by Elliott (2011, p652) as tenets of successful and sustainable environmental management:

• Environmentally/ ecologically sustainable	That the measures will ensure that the ecosystem features and functioning and the fundamental and final ecosystem services are safeguarded
• Technologically feasible	That the methods, techniques and equipment for ecosystem protection are available
• Economically viable	That a cost-benefit assessment of the environmental management indicates viability and sustainability
• Socially desirable/ tolerable	That the environmental management measures are as required or at least are understood and tolerated by society as being required; that societal benefits are delivered

- Legally permissible   That there are regional, national or international agreements and/or statutes which will enable and/or force the management measures to be performed
- Administratively achievable   That the statutory bodies such as governmental departments, environmental protection and conservation bodies are in place and functioning to enable successful and sustainable management
- Politically expedient   That the management approaches and philosophies are consistent with the prevailing political climate and have the support of political leaders

Often, restoration is a requirement, where practicable, of directives, conventions and statutes. Sometime the 'restore' imperative can be achieved by taking off whatever pressure was causing damage, but sometimes active restoration is possible and desirable or may be considered necessary because a directive says so. However, whether or not the intervention is economically viable is a very practical consideration that has to be taken into account. Attaching likely costs to the actions exemplified in Table 11.3 will reorder the priority that species are given for restoration action. For habitats affected by aggregate extraction, Cooper *et al.* (2010) review the benefits and costs of restoration measures. Restoration measures included dredging/placement, capping and bed levelling. They identify losses and gains from taking restorative action and the likely cost. Their conclusion, for the specific area studied, is that restoration would not be warranted when comparing costs and benefits. Their detailed analysis provides a case study for any policy advisor or manager considering the feasibility, desirability and cost of restoration.

Improving prospects or accepting impacts?

Understanding what was at one time (long ago) present at a location may help to provide targets for recovery and restoration but most often the 'damage is done' – the dredging has been done, the harbour walls have been built, the structurally complex habitats have been crushed and the invasive (non-native) species have arrived. The resulting impacts, especially in estuaries and coastal waters, may be severe (Lotze *et al.*, 2006). Understanding what a location used to be like long ago may not be helpful in informing conservation. Reise *et al.* (2008, p20) observe, in relation to changes in tidal flat communities in Königshafen Bay in the German Wadden Sea, 'Any historical reference is no more than a disconcerting ghost of the past, a delusive light, not likely to be approached again even if human impacts cease altogether'. That statement is pessimistic for a return to previous or close to previous communities even after pressures have been removed. It begs the question of what would we want the biota to be if return to a previous state is not going to happen. Some reversals may be possible (especially where contaminants and nutrients can be reduced) but the task now is to stop further degradation.

Prioritising action

If change is being caused by human activities (from eutrophication, through contamination to seawater warming), are there ways that management can increase resistance and resilience so that valued species and communities of species are not lost, including prevention of regime shifts? The science is largely hypothetical but has a strong basis in understanding the roles of different organisms in ecosystems and their biological traits. Brock *et al.* (2012) suggest guidelines for developing resilient MPAs especially in relation to climate change, summarised as:

1   Protect species and habitats with crucial ecosystem roles or those of special conservation concern.
2   Protect potential carbon sinks.
3   Protect ecological linkages and connectivity pathways for a wide range of species.
4   Protect the full range of biodiversity present in the target biogeographical area.

Bearing in mind that eutrophication is a major cause of change, maintenance or restoration of good water quality also seems a good idea. Not all species may be protected by management action but protecting those with crucial ecosystem roles (structural species, grazers, predators, etc.) is likely to be most important in maintaining the functioning of a community. The idea that areas where damaging human activities are kept to a minimum will resist undesirable change may seem aspirational but Micheli *et al.* (2012), in a paper entitled 'Evidence that marine reserves enhance resilience to climatic impacts', point to an example where numbers of the pink abalone, *Haliotis corrugata* (a key functional species), remained stable within reserves because of large body size and high egg production of the protected adults. Abalones are an exploited species and so the example may not be representative of unexploited populations except where, for instance, repeated physical disturbance prevents species reaching full size and reproductive capacity. However, Bates *et al.* (2014) demonstrate that protection from fishing has buffered fluctuations in biodiversity and provided resistance to the initial stages of tropicalisation in an MPA in Tasmania.

Actions taken to restore marine ecosystems that are successful will inform the measures that are likely to be successful in fighting against future impacts from human activities.

Conclusions

1   Many marine species and communities will recover within a few years (<5 is common) once a pressure is removed.
2   Full recovery will not occur if the habitat has been altered, if long-lived and slow-growing species or species with poor dispersal capability have been damaged, or if water quality has been compromised.
3   Maintaining or restoring good environmental quality including chemical and physical characteristics is essential for species and habitat conservation including recovery from damage.
4   Very often, knowledge of the life history traits of a species is needed to see what action is required for recovery or restoration and whether recolonisation by natural recruitment is likely, and that means research.
5   'Change' may be averted or diminished if resistance is encouraged through managing those environmental factors that can be managed. For instance, reducing nutrient inputs to enclosed areas or preventing the destruction of structural complexity in reef habitats.

6 A few species may benefit from reintroduction including translocation from healthy populations or from captive-bred individuals or colonies.

7 Conservation action that restores key structural or functional species is usually considered beneficial in (re)creating natural communities but there may be 'costs' in terms of reduced abundances of prey species, opportunist species or increased disease in the restored species.

8 It is usually impossible or extremely expensive to remove established non-native species but limitation may be possible.

9 Where reef habitats have been destroyed, introducing artificial hard substrata, including from 'bereavement balls' to sunken warships, is unlikely to reinstate the community that had existed on a natural reef but can have benefits for enhancing diversity in what might otherwise be a poor habitat for species.

10 Where destruction of natural habitats is inevitable, replacement with artificial constructs that encourage diverse communities may be possible.

11 Replacement may be pursued via the concept of 'biodiversity offsets' which are measures taken to compensate for damage to wildlife.

12 Whilst the 'recover' and 'restore' objectives are noble ones in conservation, the question has to be asked 'to what?' as recolonisation and reintroduction may not result in a return to what was present before, and, taking account of shifting baselines, we may not know what was the natural state of a habitat or species.

13 Rehabilitated habitats rarely look like their natural predecessors and the best management option is not to allow damage in the first place.

Chapter 12

Conclusions and the manager's 'toolbox'

Introduction

Before the mid 1980s, it seemed that human activities were having mainly localised and (apart from coastal developments) minor impacts on marine life. Then, from about that time, changes became much more significant or at least obvious. There were severe impacts in enclosed areas from TBT antifouling paints; regime shifts occurred most likely brought about by human activities especially eutrophication, overfishing and the arrival of several 'new' non-native pest species; fishing boats started to exploit previously inaccessible areas including seamounts, destroying communities that had built up over hundreds of years; we started to be aware of climate change in the form of warming; an explosion of mariculture destroyed habitats especially in mangroves but also in sheltered bays and fjords; coral bleaching and disease events became more common. And, as we moved into a new millennium, the impacts and threats continued with the development of offshore energy devices, the realisation that increased CO_2 in the atmosphere was causing ocean acidification, and so on. For many areas, the damage is done: what were intertidal areas are now car parks and container ports, the regime shifts have occurred and are unlikely to reverse, the non-native species are here to stay, the contaminants are in the sediments and politicians seem reluctant to take action to reduce damaging fishing methods let alone work towards sustainable fisheries. If we are serious about the conservation of biodiversity, we need to look after what we have left and, where possible, enable recovery, restoration or even replacement of what has been damaged.

Not all is doom and gloom. There are some promising signs of recovery in populations of large vertebrates. MPAs have been shown to have been successful in improving populations of fish and, where damaging pressures have been removed, recovery of seabed species. The management of threats, wherever they occur, to species and to biodiversity is beginning to show benefits and may be the most important way to minimise the adverse effects of human activities. Much more remains to be done to improve protection including vastly increasing our knowledge base.

The writing of this book has brought together much of the conservation-related research that I and many and varied colleagues have done since the 1970s. Many needs of marine biodiversity conservation, of what drives change in marine ecosystems and of what we can expect to happen when pressures are removed have become clearer to me as I have had the pleasure of reviewing the fast-expanding information base available to the conservation practitioner. My approach has been 'wide and shallow'. For the reader who wants to look at a topic 'narrow and deep', the literature cited and the descriptions given offer a starting point. Although I will, no doubt, have missed some key papers (and I apologise to the authors), this final chapter is a personal opportunity to outline some lessons learned, to express what I think 'really' matters and where progress needs to be made in marine biodiversity conservation. It concludes by addressing the fact that the world is changing and how we need to factor in those changes that relate especially to human use of the marine environment and to climate change effects.

Biodiversity conservation in the marine environment is different

All too often, it seems that marine conservation is using terrestrial concepts. Whilst we can 'adopt and adapt' some approaches to conservation from terrestrial experience, conservation practitioners need to understand that the character of marine ecosystems and the knowledge that we need to protect marine species and habitats are different to those for terrestrial ecosystems. In particular:

1   Our knowledge of what is where is, compared to terrestrial and freshwater habitats, is very poor. There are major areas of even inshore marine areas that we have not surveyed for habitats or biology.
2   Filling those gaps in knowledge is very expensive and difficult. There are no remote survey techniques the equivalent of aerial photography to even map broadscale habitats.
3   Although extensive parts of the sea have been impacted by human activities, some (mostly open coast rocky) inshore marine habitats are close to natural.
4   The physical and chemical processes (strength of wave action, tidal currents, light penetration, salinity, etc.) that shape and maintain marine biodiversity are very different to terrestrial environmental factors.
5   There is natural connectivity (for larvae, propagules, migratory species but also contaminants) via the water column between locations – and the water column is always there.
6   'Restoration' and 'Recovery' almost always rely on natural processes (not on gardening and reintroduction).
7   Information on changes in abundance of a species is rarely as quantitative as for terrestrial species. Criteria such as for Red List categories can rarely be applied to marine species which are therefore recorded as 'data deficient'.

Biodiversity conservation is different

Knowledge of impoverishment and of knock-on effects on marine ecosystems and of the science needed to address conservation overwhelmingly uses examples from depletion of fish stocks and incidental effects of fishing on other marine life. Whilst fish and their role in ecosystem structure and functioning is a part of the whole biodiversity 'picture', conclusions in scientific papers often lose sight of the source of their data – fish and fishing – and general statements forget wider biodiversity to the extent that published papers that appear to be about general principles have turned out to be just about fish and fisheries.

We know that recovery from damaging activities, even those activities which have been prevalent for many years, can be quite rapid (three to five years) – the seabed community returning to its previous state or something very close to it. However, it seems that for some species, even assisted recovery does not work and the character of the ecosystem has shifted to a new one. Some structural species such as oysters and horse mussels seem especially slow to show any signs of recovery and often do not recover at all, usually from damage by fisheries but also eutrophication. The message here must be not to break the ecosystem in the first place.

Some regime shifts may have occurred due to entirely natural reasons. Whether they are part of some long-term (decadal-scale) cycle and whether there will be a reversal at some time generally awaits much longer-term data than we have. Where regime shifts have occurred, it is often in relatively enclosed areas and due to eutrophication, damaging fishing practices and arrival of non-native pest species. At the very least, taking off those pressures that can be managed is likely to improve the diversity and functioning of the seabed communities and perhaps even return the site to its previous state.

The establishment of protected areas is a well-established approach, on land, to create islands of biodiversity, often in a devastated landscape. The concept of protected areas transfers well to the marine environment and the establishment of MPAs is a management option that can lead to identification and prevention of damaging activities and enable recovery locally. However, the enthusiasm for MPAs as a means of ensuring seabed biodiversity conservation needs to be tempered and some of the flawed concepts (such as required connectivity distances or minimum viable size) need much more careful scientific scrutiny. Furthermore, some MPAs have been established but with very weak, highly selective or no management of damaging activities. Whilst MPAs can be a focal point for particular conservation action, it seems much more important to stem damaging activities (particularly some fishing activities, nutrient enrichment and the spread of non-native species) that can be controlled and to ensure good water quality universally.

Whilst the practitioners' focus is on the best management option to protect and recover biodiversity using existing knowledge, it is very important to develop conservation science. Knowledge and experience needs to increase on relevant matters such as the distribution of habitats and species and on the assessment of sensitivity and 'importance' in terms of rarity and degree of threat. Understanding natural change and how quickly recovery occurs after a damaging event or activity are important to inform management and involve not only surveillance and monitoring but experimental studies.

Why a 'toolbox'?

The various criteria, decision trees and catalogues provided in this volume can be used as a manager's 'toolbox'. The tools are those that have already been developed and used: there will no doubt be improvements to those tools as well as new and helpful methods and reference points developed. However, by reading this book, I hope that conservation practitioners will not reinvent or leave behind the wheels already available. Now, those separate parts of the 'jigsaw' need to be brought together and their place in management made clear.

The various 'tools' that have been identified to inform conservation need to be used in a structured and selective way – they are relevant to particular objectives and often their use is sequential. The tools available to protect marine life are numerous and include fisheries regulation to close areas to certain sorts of (damaging) gear, regulation of contaminant input, reduction of nutrient inputs to enclosed areas, anchoring restrictions or placement of fixed moorings in delicate habitats, licensing activities within a spatial planning regime so that sensitive sites are avoided or protected, impact assessments that identify fragile features to be avoided by activities that will damage them, imaginative design of constructions to support biodiversity, assisting recovery after damage has occurred, etc.

This volume provides a summary of the 'evidence' available by early in 2014 to help promote and underpin marine biodiversity conservation. That evidence will be needed by advocates of environmental protection and management as a tool to persuade those who doubt the need for conservation. However, this text may also make uncomfortable reading for those who have been swept along by unsubstantiated myths and fairy tales about some of the techniques used to support such activities as habitat mapping, identifying 'important' species and habitats and designing sets of MPAs – some tools are not fit for purpose and should be at least used with caution. Using the information in this volume, policy advisors can give advice that, if implemented, will protect, recover and even enhance the very significant biodiversity that we still have. At the centre of that decision-making will be knowledge and experience. Knowledge comes in part from books such as this, whilst experience is something that is only obtained by getting out there and doing survey and conservation.

What is in the manager's toolbox?

Although the reader can scroll through this volume and itemise what should be the contents of the manager's toolbox, it is useful to list here what is likely to be in the toolbox. The list may not be complete or may need adjustment to suit the relevant geographical area and the human activities that are prevalent there, but that is an exercise for practitioners and students to undertake.

✗ Information on the environmental characteristics at a location, e.g.:

- bathymetry;
- currents (tidal and residual);
- tidal range;
- habitat types (substratum, depth);
- biotopes maps;
- species occurrences;
- existing impacts/degree of contamination.

✗ Manuals and guidance on methods to collect new information on marine life and environment.
✗ Formulated methodologies to take new survey data and:

- calculate indices that assess 'quality';
- apply criteria that assess 'importance' and 'sensitivity';
- identify structure and functional attributes that will inform management.

✗ Information on the expected dynamic or temporal features of the biology in the area: e.g. seasonal fluctuations, long-term natural fluctuations.
✗ Information on what is 'important' at a location (presence of protected habitats or designated species, etc.).
✗ Information on likely sensitivity of habitats and species to the pressure and/or activity being considered including knowledge of relevant case studies or experimental studies.
✗ Procedures to bring all of the above together to produce decisions.

✖ Licensing regimes that will prevent or minimise adverse effects of developments and activities on biodiversity.

✖ Regulatory measures, including the ability to create MPAs where focussed conservation is desirable, to ensure that protection is adequate.

The decision trees and lists of criteria that are included in this volume are the procedures that should aid the marine biodiversity conservation practitioner. Those procedures will be influenced by societal views and should be applied in collaboration with stakeholders. Whatever we do from a scientific point of view, our conclusions and advice have to inform and influence public support and political action. Our science has to be presented to the public, the media and to decision-makers in a way that is accurate and honest but understandable. 'State of nature' reports and indicators of improving or declining quality (probably within regional seas or the seas under the jurisdiction of a state) are a successful medium for identifying where there are problems (and successes) and for tracking progress. We may need to work towards meaningful indices and ways of presenting what could otherwise be impenetrable scientific gobbledegook.

The importance of regulation

If everyone in the world was sympathetic to the need to protect biodiversity, then voluntary agreements and codes of conduct would be all that was needed. But many will feel that they cannot afford such 'luxuries' and need to make a living, follow a 'growth' agenda, go where they want to go, take what they want to take, or pursue their engineering challenges, etc. Nevertheless, voluntary agreements, especially where backed up by peer pressure, can work. In areas subject to intense recreational pressure, diving facilities will not allow their customers to interfere with marine life, especially when that is part of what those customers come to see. Fishermen may agree not to trawl an area where fragile seabed marine life occurs or, perhaps, to allow only static gear to be used there. Those fishermen will police such agreements themselves. But more often than not, regulation and licensing is needed, backed up by monitoring and enforcement measures for the whole range of human activities that occur in the marine environment. Monitoring activities is very difficult but, for instance, it has suddenly become easy to know where a boat is with the advent of Vessel Monitoring Systems. Enforcement is for statutory authorities and needs to be robust.

Research needed

Introduction

Some aspects of the science that we have are reasonably straightforward to use in advising management. They include situations where the consequences of an activity are obvious or where there are case studies that inform us of likely consequences. They include locations where we know what the biodiversity resource is. We can then advise why some change has occurred or what will 'matter' (from the point of view of biodiversity conservation and/or ecosystem services) if some development is permitted. They are the 'known knowns'.

   Much less straightforward will be where we do not know what are the likely consequences of an activity or pressure and/or do not have reliable information on what biology is where. The possibility of synergistic effects of various stressors or of natural processes in causing change compounds or adds to those existing problems. These are the 'known unknowns'.

Most worrying are the problems that we are not yet aware of. Perhaps these problems will result from new chemicals being released into the sea with unexpected consequences or the arrival of a non-native species that becomes a pest. These are the 'unknown unknowns'.

Policymakers and regulators are increasing their expectations of what scientists can explain or predict and may ask scientists to identify how far an ecosystem can be 'pushed' before it collapses or switches to an alternative state. Whilst some of those expectations may be unreasonable, research needs to be focused on the key questions being asked or likely to be asked by those policymakers and regulators.

Knowledge gaps to be filled

Fundamental to biodiversity conservation is knowing where habitats and species occur. *In situ* observations and mapping of resources is mainly restricted to the coastal zone and even here it is very patchy. To fill those gaps, there seems a desperation to find technological fixes. Some of those, such as using multibeam sonar to map reef habitats, have proved highly effective. Others such as acoustic ground discrimination without adequate ground truthing have wasted enormous amounts of money to produce highly inaccurate coloured maps that look impressive to office-based policy advisors but are clearly incorrect when shown to field ecologists and fishermen. Worse still are the algorithms that have used physical measurements to predict seabed types: at the moment they are probably too simplistic to take account of all of the environmental factors that will determine the habitat present. Technology is bound to improve (see, for instance, Dunstan *et al.*, 2012) but, in the meanwhile, survey needs to use *in situ* imaging, sampling and observation.

There are many certainties about how human activities have affected and could affect marine biodiversity and about how most effectively to improve conservation. But there are major gaps in our understanding, some of which are being filled with untested hypotheses. Hypotheses need to be (further) tested by experiments and by sampling: for instance, the hypothesis that increased diversity (as species richness) increases resilience; that connectivity between MPAs by larvae or propagules of benthic species is any more than the general connectivity that exists through the water column; that only large protected areas will be effective, including for some attached or low-mobility species that may require only a small area protected; that seabed species will benefit from protected status when they have not previously been impacted by human activities; that artificial or newly created habitats can be designed to mimic and develop the same communities as lost or damaged habitats.

Few indicator species have been found that act as the 'canary in the coal mine', warning us when disaster is imminent or that recovery is on its way. It seems more practical to identify which are sensitive species that are likely to be adversely affected by particular factors. Assessing the sensitivity of species and, in turn, habitats relies on cataloguing species traits as well as on case studies or experimental studies where those species or habitats have been adversely affected. Researching traits is not something that attracts academic research funding and the opportunity to publish in high-impact peer-reviewed journals. It may attract funding related to the implementation of directives and conventions but the report will be 'grey literature'. Similarly, yet another survey of the biology of an area will add essential data and information to our knowledge of what is where but will not be attractive to funding by research councils or to publication in journals. High-quality scientists wishing to do such work and institutes wishing to host it may have to set aside their potential for 'high scores' in the various indices that now exist and on which the academic value of their work or the work of their institute is judged.

Undertaking surveys and interpreting the changes that are seen in ecosystems requires old-fashioned 'natural history' skills. But, experienced taxonomists and naturalists are mostly getting old and not being replaced to any great extent. Indeed, to be called a 'naturalist' brings forth an image of a slightly crazed individual in shabby clothes poring over their collection of dead organisms. Cataloguing the distribution of species, knowing how species behave and knowing about life cycles and fluctuations in abundance is essential in underpinning conservation. We need to record the knowledge that extant naturalists have before they become extinct but we also need to facilitate opportunities to train and employ a new generation of naturalists.

Do we have the means to record what we know about the biology of species and about changes and events in nature? To an extent, catalogues are being produced, particularly of species' distributions and of the biological traits that species exhibit. But not enough is being done to record observations of events (such that mass strandings of a particular species have always occurred, that disease events happen in a particular species, when breeding occurs, or what might be cyclical occurrences of a species including long-term fluctuations). Those observations of events and of fluctuations in abundance especially are essential in interpreting the results of monitoring or in separating unusual events (that need to be investigated) from events that should be expected. Recording phenological information may be particularly important in interpreting the effects of climate change and the possibility of trophic mismatches leading to declines in species abundance.

Long-term observations of change are essential. Those observations will help to reveal natural cycles of change and the length of time (if at all) some habitats take to recover. Some of the observations will be opportunistic (and need to be recorded) but systematic monitoring needs to be supported – and that means long-term commitment to research that is not going to be ready for publication for decades after it is started – not very attractive to an ambitious scientist!

Technological developments

Whilst some technologies have failed to deliver information that we can have confidence in, improvements are bound to occur and, for instance, seabed mapping using acoustic ground discrimination techniques may become much more reliable. Autonomous vehicles may offer a way of surveying large areas without expensive ships. Vessel Monitoring Systems will track where fishing vessels are and associated equipment will tell if their fishing gear is being deployed.

The future

The last 40 years have seen marine biodiversity conservation develop, follow some blind alleys and make some significant achievements. Our awareness of the marine environment and of the species and habitats in it has been greatly enhanced by what we see directly ourselves and through films, books and other media that have enriched our lives. Hopefully, we are inspired to do more to protect marine biodiversity but that protection has to be through the application of knowledge and experience. That knowledge and experience will grow but the science questions that we are asking need to be clear, relevant and feasible. Technology will help us more and more but seeing and doing will always be important.

Researching this volume has reminded or taught me an enormous amount about the diversity, beauty and importance of marine life. At the same time, it has been depressing to see how easily some parts of marine ecosystems can be damaged by human activities. It has never been more urgent or important to use the knowledge that we have to manage human activities for the benefit of biodiversity and to maintain the services that biodiversity provides.

Glossary

The glossary is of terms that the marine conservation professional might encounter in relevant scientific literature and in the conventions, directives and statutes that drive conservation action. Source references are given where a definition is not original.

Abyssal Pertaining to zones of great depths in the oceans into which light does not penetrate. In oceanography, usually restricted to depths below 2,000m (based on Lincoln *et al.*, 1998).

Acclimation/Acclimation capacity The gradual and reversible adjustment of physiology or morphology as a result of changing environmental conditions (Lincoln *et al.*, 1998). The change from one stable physiological state to another stable physiological state in experiments when conditions are altered (see, Peck *et al.*, 2014). Cf. 'acclimatisation'

Acclimatisation The gradual and reversible adjustment of physiology and morphology to changing environmental conditions; often used to refer to the changes observed in a species over a number of generations (Lincoln *et al.*, 1998). The modulation of physiological processes between long-term stable states in response to changes in environmental variables in the field (see, Peck *et al.*, 2014). Cf. 'acclimation'

Acidification See Ocean acidification.

Adaptive management A combination of scientific research and resource management, whereby management of a given system is continually adapted in light of ongoing research (Ruth and Lindholm, 2002). The integration of design, management and monitoring to systematically test assumptions in order to adapt and learn (Salafsky *et al.*, 2001). Cf. 'spatial planning'

Adequacy A criterion for MPA network design. Sometimes included with viability (see Ardron, 2008a) and sometimes separately (see Natural England and Joint Nature Conservation Committee, 2010), where it is described (p130) as 'the overall size of the MPA network and the amount of each feature protected within it, must be large enough to ensure the delivery of ecological objectives, and the features' long-term protection and recovery'.

Aggregates In the context of aggregate extraction, any granular material formed from a natural rock substance (www.bgs.ac.uk/planning4minerals/Resources_1.htm).

Alien species A non-established introduced species, which is incapable of establishing self-sustaining or self-propagating populations in the new area without human interference (www.marlin.ac.uk/glossary.php). Cf. 'introduced species', 'non-native', 'vagrant'

Anaerobic An environment in which the partial pressure of oxygen is significantly below normal atmospheric levels; deoxygenated (Lincoln *et al.*, 1998).

Anchialine   Coastal saltwater habitats having no surface connection to the sea (Lincoln *et al.*, 1998).

Anoxic   Devoid of oxygen.

Artificial reef   An artificial structure placed on the shore or seabed with the intention of increasing biodiversity but often as an addition to other purposes. For instance: coastal defence; oil rigs dropped to the seabed as a cheaper alternative to retrieval and providing recreational fishing; concrete structures that incorporate human ashes ('bereavement balls'); and vessels sunk to provide recreational opportunities for divers.

Assemblage   A generic term used chiefly by some British marine ecologists which does not assume interdependence within a community or association, but appears to have the same broad definition as 'community' (based on Hiscock and Connor, 1991). A subset of a community chosen for study. The term implies taxonomic incompleteness (Paine, 1994). Cf. 'community'

Bathyal   Pertaining to the seafloor between 400m and 4,000m (Lincoln *et al.*, 1998).

Benthos/Benthic species   Those organisms attached to, or living on, in or near, the seabed, including that part which is exposed by tides as the littoral zone (based on Lincoln *et al.*, 1998).

Biodiversity   'The variability among living organisms from all sources including, *inter alia*, terrestrial, marine and other aquatic ecosystems and the ecological complexes of which they are part; this includes diversity within species, between species and of ecosystems' (UN Convention on Biological Diversity, 1992: see www.cbd.int/convention/articles/?a=cbd-02).

Biodiversity hotspot   Areas of high species and habitat richness that include representative, rare and threatened features (Hiscock and Breckles, 2007).

Biodiversity offsetting   Measurable conservation outcomes resulting from actions designed to compensate for significant residual adverse biodiversity impacts arising from project development after appropriate prevention and mitigation measures have been taken (BBOP, 2009).

Biogenic   Produced by the action of living organisms (Lincoln *et al.*, 1998).

Biogeochemical cycles   Circulation of water, air and organic compounds through the Earth's organisms, atmosphere, oceans and land (Ruth and Lindholm, 2002).

Biogeography   The branch of biology concerned with the geographical distribution of plants and animals, and the factors affecting their distribution (Hiscock, 1996).

Biological traits   The particular features that a species has of a character or attribute. For instance, all species grow (an attribute) but the 'trait' describes the growth rate. Biological traits are described for such features as adult mobility, growth rate, adult dispersal potential, larval/propagule dispersal potential, sociability, feeding method, longevity and fragility. Cf. 'ecological traits', 'functional traits'

Biotic disturbance   Disruption of habitat or organisms caused by the nontropic activities of organisms. Usually leads directly or indirectly to mortality of the affected organisms (Paine, 1994).

Biomass   The total quantity of living organisms in a given area, expressed in terms of living or dry weight or energy value per unit area (www.marlin.ac.uk/glossary.php).

Biotope   1) The physical 'habitat' with its biological 'community'; a term which refers to the combination of physical environment (habitat) and its distinctive assemblage of conspicuous species. MNCR uses the biotope concept to enable description and comparison. 2) The smallest geographical unit of the biosphere or of a habitat that can be delimited by convenient boundaries and is characterised by its biota (Lincoln *et al.*, 1998).

Bioturbation   The mixing of a sediment by the burrowing, feeding or other activity of living organisms (Lincoln *et al.*, 1998).

Circalittoral   The subzone of the rocky sublittoral below that dominated by algae (the infralittoral), and that is dominated by animals (based on Hiscock, 1985).

Classification   1) Taxonomy – the placing of animals and plants in a series of increasingly specialised groups because of similarities in structure, origins, etc. that indicate a common relationship (Makins, 1991). 2) Biotopes – the process of identifying distinctive and recurrent groupings of species with their associated habitat and describing them within a structured framework.

Coastal zone   The space in which terrestrial environments influence marine (or lacustrine) environments and *vice versa*. The coastal zone is of variable width and may also change in time. Delimitation of zonal boundaries is not normally possible; more often, such limits are marked by an environmental gradient or transition. At any one locality the coastal zone may be characterised according to physical, biological or cultural criteria, which need not, and rarely do, coincide (based on Carter, 1988).

Coastal Zone Management (CZM)   See Integrated Coastal Zone Management.

Coherent   That which sticks or clings firmly together (Shorter Oxford English Dictionary). Cf. 'ecologically coherent network'

Community   A group of organisms occurring in a particular environment, presumably interacting with each other and with the environment, and identifiable from other groups by means of ecological survey (from Mills, 1969; see Hiscock and Connor, 1991 for a discussion).

Community structure   Collective expression referring to the 'appearance' of a community; determined by quantifying distribution, abundance, body size, tropic relationships and species diversity (Paine, 1994).

Community organisation   Collective expression referring to the mechanistic dynamics which can produce community structure; determined by evaluating the role of competition, predation, other biotic interactions, disturbance, colonisation and spatial and temporal heterogeneity (Paine, 1994).

Connectivity   The quality or condition of being connected or connective. Serving or tending to connect (www.dictionary.com). In the context of MPAs, a connection via larval or propagule dispersion or by active movement of adults between separate locations.

Conservation   'The regulation of human use of the global ecosystem to sustain its diversity of content indefinitely' (Nature Conservancy Council, 1984, p7).

Constancy   1) The frequency of occurrence of a species in samples from the same community (based on Makins, 1991). 2) The continued presence of a species or community at a particular location (www.marlin.ac.uk/glossary.php). Cf. 'persistence', 'resilience', 'stability'

Critically Endangered   A category of the IUCN Red List defined by a variety of measures (see IUCN, 2001). Cf. 'extinct', 'endangered', 'vulnerable'

Crypogentic   Of undetermined origin. (sensu Carlton, 1996 from Hewitt *et al.*, 2004). Cf. 'Introduced species'

Cultch   A mass of broken stones, shells and gravel which forms the basis of an oyster bed (Makins, 1991).

Demersal   Living at or near the bottom of a sea or lake, but having the capacity for active swimming (Lincoln *et al.*, 1998).

Deposit feeders   Any organisms which feed on fragmented particulate organic matter in or on the substratum; detritivores (Lincoln *et al.*, 1998).

Dispersant (oil)   A mixture of surfactants and solvents that break up an oil spill into droplets (http://en.wikipedia.org/wiki/Oil_dispersants).

Disturbance   'A chemical or physical process caused by humans that may or may not lead to a response in a biological system within an organism or at the level of whole organisms or assemblages. Disturbance includes stresses' (GESAMP, 1995, p4).

Diversity   The state or quality of being different or varied (Makins, 1991). In relation to species, the degree to which the total number of individual organisms in a given ecosystem, area, community or trophic level is divided evenly over different species; i.e. measure of heterogeneity. Species diversity can be expressed by diversity indices, most of which take account of both the number of species and number of individuals per species. (Based on Baretta-Bekker *et al.*, 1992.) Cf. Richness

Ecologically coherent network   The phrase comes from OSPAR Recommendation 2003/3 adopted by OSPAR 2003 (OSPAR 03/17/1, Annex 9), amended by OSPAR Recommendation 2010/2 (OSPAR 10/23/1, Annex 7). However, OSPAR (2013, p32) state 'no specific definition for the term "ecological coherence" has yet been formally agreed upon internationally and only a few theoretical concepts and practical approaches have been developed for an assessment of the ecological coherence of a network of MPAs'. OSPAR and HELCOM (OSPAR, 2013) have adopted the following working definition:

a.   An ecologically coherent network of MPAs:

i.   interacts with and supports the wider environment;

ii.   maintains the processes, functions, and structures of the intended protected features across their natural range; and

iii.   functions synergistically as a whole, such that the individual protected sites benefit from each other in order to achieve the above two objectives.

Additionally, an ecologically coherent network of MPAs may be designed to be resilient to changing conditions.

Cf. 'coherent'

Ecological engineering   Ecological engineering is the design of sustainable systems, consistent with ecological principles, which integrate human society with its natural environment for the benefit of both (from Bergen *et al.*, 2001).

Ecological traits   Traits that are related to habitat preferences such as in relation to salinity, depth (light regime), wave exposure, strength of tidal flow, environmental position (whether pelagic, infaunal, epifaunal, etc.), temperature, tolerance to organic pollution, biogeographic distribution, etc. Cf. 'biological traits', 'functional traits'

Ecologically extinct   Species whose populations are now so small that they can no longer play a significant ecological role in a particular community.

Ecosystem engineering   See 'ecological engineering'.

Ecosystem   A community of organisms and their physical environment interacting as an ecological unit (Lincoln *et al.*, 1998). Usage can include reference to large units such as the North Sea down to much smaller units such as kelp holdfasts.

Ecosystem-based management   An environmental management approach that recognises the full array of interactions within an ecosystem, including humans, rather than considering single issues, species, or ecosystem services in isolation (Christensen *et al.*, 1996; McLeod and Leslie, 2009).

Ecosystem engineer   Species that themselves create structure because of their physical presence or their activities, especially burrowing, are described as 'key structural species' or 'ecosystem engineers'.

Ecosystem services   The benefits people derive from nature (Liquete *et al.*, 2013).

Endangered   A category of the IUCN Red List defined by a variety of measures (see IUCN, 2001). Cf. 'Extinct', 'Critically Endangered', 'Vulnerable'

Endemic   Native to, and restricted to, a particular geographical region (Lincoln *et al.*, 1998).

Endogenous   Occurring within a system (Ruth and Lindholm, 2002).

Environment   The complex of biotic climatic, edaphic and other conditions which comprise the immediate habitat of an organism; the physical, chemical and biological surroundings of an organism at any given time (Lincoln *et al.*, 1998). Cf. 'habitat'

Epibenthic   Living on the surface of the seabed.

Epiphytic   Growing on the surface of a living plant (but not parasitic upon it).

Estuary   Any semi-enclosed coastal water, open to the sea, having a high freshwater drainage and with marked cyclical fluctuations in salinity, usually the mouth of a river (Lincoln *et al.*, 1998).

Euphotic zone   The upper area of the water column where photosynthetic activity occurs (Ruth and Lindholm, 2002).

Eutrophication   The overenrichment of an aquatic environment with inorganic nutrients, especially nitrates and phosphates, often anthropogenic (e.g. sewage, fertiliser run-off), which may result in stimulation of growth of algae and bacteria and can reduce the oxygen content of the water (www.marlin.ac.uk/glossary.php).

Exclusive Economic Zone   Ocean areas from the coast to usually 200 nautical miles offshore, where the adjacent nation has exclusive economic rights and the rights and freedoms of other states are governed by the relevant positions of the United Nations Convention on the Law of the Sea.

Exogenous   Occurring outside of a system (Ruth and Lindholm, 2002).

Extinct   A taxon is 'extinct' when there is no reasonable doubt that the last individual has died (IUCN, 2013). The term can be applied on a local or national basis as well as worldwide and is also used to refer to situations where a taxon no longer exists from a particular point of view (for instance: 'functionally extinct'; 'commercially extinct'). Cf. 'Critically Endangered', 'Endangered', 'Vulnerable'

Factor   Any causal agent. In statistics (but could be in ecology), any variable thought to influence the variable under investigation (based on Lincoln *et al.*, 1998). Cf. 'parameter'

Fecundity   The potential reproductive capacity of an organism or population, measured by the number of gametes (eggs) or asexual propagules.

Filter feeder   See Suspension feeder.

Flagship species   Species chosen strategically to raise public awareness or financial support for conservation action.

Focal species   Those species which, for ecological or social reasons, are believed to be valuable for the understanding, management and conservation of natural environments. (See Roff and Zacharias, 2011 for a detailed account.)

Functioning   The mode of action by which the system fulfils its purpose or role, as determined by its component elements. In terms of ecosystem functioning, the activities, processes or properties of ecosystems that are influences by its biota (Naeem *et al.*, 2004).

Functional diversity   Refers to the variety of biological processes, functions or characteristics of a particular ecosystem (www.marbef.org/wiki).

Functional traits   Those traits that define species in terms of their ecological roles – how they interact with the environment and with other species (see Díez and Cabildo, 2001). Cf. 'biological traits', 'ecological traits'

Habitat   The place in which a plant or animal lives. It is defined for the marine environment according to geographical location, physiographic features and the physical and chemical environment (including salinity, wave exposure, strength of tidal streams, geology, biological zone, substratum, 'features' (e.g. crevices, overhangs, rock pools) and 'modifiers' (e.g. sand scour, wave surge, substratum mobility)) (www.marlin.ac.uk/glossary.php). Cf. 'environment'

Heavy metal   A generic term for a range of metals with a moderate to high atomic weight, for example cadmium, mercury, lead. Although many are essential for life in trace quantities, in elevated concentrations most are toxic and bioaccumulate, and so are important pollutants (www.marlin.ac.uk/glossary.php).

Heuristics   Pertaining to a trial and error method of problem solving used when an algorithmic approach is impractical (http://dictionary.reference.com). Colloquially: 'rule of thumb'.

Holism, Holistic   The concept that all physical and biological entities form a single unified, interacting system, and that any complete system has a totality that is greater than the sum of the constituent parts (Lincoln *et al.*, 1998).

Hydrographic   Used with reference to the structure and movement of bodies of water, particularly currents and water masses (Lincoln *et al.*, 1998).

Hysteresis   The lag in response exhibited by a body in reacting to changes in the forces affecting it (www.dictionary.com).

Impact   In the case of human activities, man-induced modification to the physics, chemistry and biology of a system.

Imposex   An abnormality of the reproductive system in female gastropod molluscs, by which male characteristics are superimposed onto female individuals (Smith, 1980), resulting in sterility or, in extreme cases, death. This may be caused by hormonal change in response to pollution from organotin antifoulants, even at low concentrations.

Indicator   An indicator is considered to be a variable which supplies information on other variables that are difficult to access and can be used to take a decision. Indicators enable us to understand a complex system and distil it into its most important aspects (Healthy and Biologically Diverse Seas Evidence Group (HBDSEG) of the UK Marine Monitoring and Assessment Strategy (UKMMAS)).

Indicator species   An indicator species is an organism whose presence, absence or abundance reflects a specific environmental condition. Indicator species can signal a change in the biological condition of a particular ecosystem, and thus may be used as a proxy to diagnose the health of an ecosystem (Encyclopedia of Life: http://eol.org/info/465).

Infauna   Benthic animals which live within the seabed.

Infralittoral   A subzone of the sublittoral in which upward-facing rocks are dominated by erect algae, typically kelps; it can be further subdivided into the upper and lower infralittoral (based on Hiscock, 1985).

Integrated Coastal Zone management   A dynamic, multidisciplinary and iterative process to promote sustainable management of coastal zones (EC, cited in www.marbef. org/wiki/Integrated_Coastal_Zone_Management_(ICZM)).

Intolerance   The susceptibility of a habitat, community or species to damage, or death, from an external factor (based on www.marlin.ac.uk). Cf 'resistance'

Introduced species   Any species which has been introduced directly or indirectly by human agency (deliberate or otherwise), to an area where it has not occurred in historical times and which is separate from and lies outside the area where natural range extension could be expected (i.e. outside its natural geographical range). The term includes non-established introductions ('aliens') and established non-natives, but excludes hybrid taxa derived from introductions ('derivatives') (www.marlin.ac.uk/ glossary.php). Cf. 'alien species', 'non-native species', 'vagrants'

K-strategy   A life strategy optimally geared to living in a stable habitat with a high level of interspecific competition. Parental care is facilitated by low fecundity (small litters of large-size offspring), by longevity and size. K-strategists are unlikely to be well adapted to recover from population densities significantly below their equilibrium level and may become extinct if depressed to such low levels (Baretta-Bekker *et al.*, 1992). Cf. 'r-strategy'

Keystone species   A species which, through its predatory activities (for instance, grazing by sea urchins) or by mediating competition between prey species (for instance, by eating sea urchins), maintains community composition and structure. Removal of a keystone species leads to rapid, cascading changes in the structure they support (based on Raffaelli and Hawkins, 1996).

Lagoon (saline)   A shallow body of coastal saltwater (from brackish to hypersaline) partially separated from an adjacent sea by a barrier of sand or other sediment, or less frequently, by rocks (based on Ardizzone *et al.*, 1988).

Lecithotrophic   Pertaining to developmental stages that feed upon yolk, and to eggs rich in yolk (Lincoln *et al.*, 1998).

Littoral   The area of the shore that is occupied by marine organisms which are adapted to or need alternating exposure to air and wetting by submersion, splash or spray. On rocky shores (British Isles), the upper limit is marked by the top of the *Littorina/ Verrucaria* belt and the lower limit by the top of the laminarian zone (Lewis, 1964). It is divided into separate subzones, particularly marked on hard substrata.

Maerl   Twig-like unattached (free-living) calcareous red algae, often a mixture of species and including species which form a spiky cover on loose small stones – 'hedgehog stones' (www.marlin.ac.uk/glossary.php).

Macrobenthos   The larger organisms of the benthos, exceeding 1mm in length (from Lincoln *et al.*, 1998); often applied to organisms exceeding 0.5mm in length. Cf. 'meiobenthos'

Mangrove   A tidal salt marsh community found in tropical and subtropical regions dominated by trees and shrubs, particularly of the genus *Rhizophora*, many of which produce adventitious aerial roots (Lincoln *et al.*, 1998).

Mariculture   Cultivation, management and harvesting of marine organisms in their natural habitat or in specially constructed channels or tanks with a controlled environment (based on Lincoln *et al.*, 1998).

Marine Protected Area   A clearly defined geographical space, recognised, dedicated and managed, through legal or other effective means, to achieve the long-term conservation of nature with associated ecosystem services and cultural values (Dudley, 2008).

Marine reserve   Ocean areas that are fully protected from activities that remove animals or plants or alter habitats, except as needed for scientific monitoring (www.piscoweb. org). A marine reserve would correspond to IUCN Category Ia of protected areas in Day *et al.* (2012, p9): 'Strictly protected areas set aside to protect biodiversity and also possibly geological/geomorphological features, where human visitation use and impacts are strictly controlled and limited to ensure protection of the conservation values.'

Marine park   MPA that has a significant recreational element. A marine park would correspond to IUCN Category II of protected areas in Day *et al.* (2012, p9): 'Large natural or near natural areas set aside to protect large-scale ecological processes, along with the complement of species and ecosystems characteristic of the area, which also provide a foundation for environmentally and culturally compatible spiritual, scientific, educational, recreational and visitor opportunities.'

Marine spatial planning   A public process of analysing and allocating the spatial and temporal distribution of human activities in marine areas to achieve ecological, economic and social objectives that have been specified through a political process (www. unesco-ioc-marinesp.be).

Marxan   A software decision support tool for the 'optimal' design of marine reserve systems based on explicit trade-offs (Ball *et al.*, 2009).

Meiobenthos   Small benthic organisms which pass through a 1mm mesh sieve, but are retained by a 0.1mm mesh (Lincoln *et al.*, 1998). Typically, they inhabit interstitial space in sediments. May also be used to apply to organisms that pass through a 0.5mm mesh. Cf. 'macrobenthos'

Mesocosm   Tanks where environmental conditions can be manipulated.

Mesohaline   Pertaining to brackish water between 5 ‰ and 18 ‰ salinity (McLusky 1993). Cf. 'oligohaline' (The expression of salinity has changed since 1993. 'Parts Per Thousand' (PPT or ‰) and 'Practical Salinity Units' (PSU) are not generally used and the Thermodynamic Equation of Seawater 2010 (TEOS-10) is the latest iteration. All come out to about the same numerals. See: http://en.wikipedia.org/wiki/Salinity)

Meta-analysis   Procedures looking for overall effects or how variation in the strength of effects in individual studies can be accounted for by specific broadscale factors (Thrush and Dayton, 2010).

Mitigation   The reduction or control of the adverse environmental effects of a project, including restitution for any damage to the environment through replacement, restoration, or creation of habitat in one area to compensate for loss in another (Edwards, 2010).

Monitoring   Surveillance undertaken to ensure that formulated standards are being maintained (Davies *et al.*, 2001). Cf. 'Surveillance'

Natural history   The study of life at the level of the individual – what plants and animals do, how they react to each other and their environment, how they are organised into larger groupings like populations and communities (Bates, 1950).

Network of MPAs   A collection of individual MPAs that operates cooperatively and synergistically, at various spatial scales and with a range of protection levels in order to fulfil ecological aims more effectively and comprehensively than individual sites could alone (IUCN, 2007). In the context of separate protected areas, would be expected to mean an 'interconnected chain, group, or system' (Longman New Universal Dictionary).

Non-native (species)   A species which has been introduced directly or indirectly by human agency (deliberate or otherwise), to an area where it has not occurred in recent times (about 5,000 years BP) and which is separate from and lies outside the area where natural range extension could be expected (i.e. outside its natural geographical range). The species has become established in the wild and has self-maintaining populations; the term also includes hybrid taxa derived from such introductions ('derivatives') (www.marlin.ac.uk/glossary.php). Cf. 'alien species', 'introduced species'

Ocean acidification The increasing acidity of seawater as a result of rising atmospheric CO_2 levels from human activities such as fossil fuel burning (based on IGBP, IOC, SCOR, 2013).

Oligohaline Pertaining to brackish water between 0.5 ‰ and 5 ‰ salinity (McLusky 1993). Cf. 'mesohaline'

Parameter A variable or constant in a mathematical equation (Ruth and Lindholm, 2002). A quantity which is constant (as distinct from ordinary variables) in a particular case considered, but which varies in different cases (Shorter Oxford English Dictionary). Cf. 'factor'. ('Parameter' is often misused when referring to a 'factor'.)

Parasite An organism that lives in or on another living organism (the host), from which it obtains food and other requirements. The host does not benefit from the association and is usually harmed by it (www.marlin.ac.uk/glossary.php).

Pelagic zone The open sea and ocean, excluding the sea bottom. Pelagic organisms inhabit such open waters (www.marlin.ac.uk/glossary.php).

Persistence The continued presence of species or communities at a location (usually inferring in spite of disturbance or change in conditions) (www.marlin.ac.uk/glossary. php). Cf. 'constancy', 'stability', 'resilience'

Phase 1 survey Surveys aimed at identifying the range of habitats in an area, and may give an indication of their extent and distribution. This information can also be used to target the selection of sites for more detailed Phase 2 surveys (Hiscock, 1996).

Phase 2 survey Surveys aimed at describing the communities and their variation within habitats, thus providing information for assessing the marine natural heritage importance of sites (Hiscock, 1996).

Photosynthesis The biochemical process that utilises radiant energy from sunlight to synthesise carbohydrates from CO_2 and water in the presence of chlorophyll and other photopigments (based on Lincoln *et al.*, 1998).

Physical disturbance Disruption of habitat or organisms caused by the physical environment. Leads directly or indirectly to mortality, or temporary impairment, of the affected organisms (Paine, 1994).

Physiographic Related to physical geography and geomorphology (derived from: http:// dictionary.reference.com).

Phytoplankton Planktonic plant life: typically comprising suspended or motile microscopic algal cells such as diatoms, dinoflagellates and desmids (based on Lincoln *et al.*, 1998).

Planktotrophic Feeding on plankton (Lincoln *et al.*, 1998).

Pollution 'The introduction by man, directly or indirectly, of substances or energy into the marine environment (including estuaries) resulting in such deleterious effects as harm to living resources, hazards to human health, hindrance to marine activities including fishing, impairment of quality for use of seawater and reduction in amenities' (GESAMP, 1995, p4).

Predation Consumption of one species by another. It may be complete, resulting in victim mortality, or partial in which the victim survives (Paine, 1994).

Propagule   Any part of an organism, produced sexually or asexually, that is capable of giving rise to a new individual (Lincoln *et al.*, 1998).

r-strategy   A life strategy which allows a species to deal with changes of climate and food supply by responding to suitable conditions with a high rate of reproduction. r-strategists are continually colonising habitats of a temporary nature (Baretta-Bekker *et al.*, 1992). Cf. 'K-strategy'

Recent colonist   A species which, without any human intervention, has extended its natural geographical range (q.v.) in recent times and which has established new self-maintaining and self-regenerating populations in the wild (www.marlin.ac.uk/glossary.php). Cf. 'non-native', 'vagrant'

Recovery   A passive event that relies on recolonisation and regrowth of pre-existing species and an associated rebalancing of ecosystem structure and functioning. Cf. 'recoverability', 'rehabilitation', 'restoration', 'replacement'. Lotze *et al.* (2011) define five different types of 'recovery'.

Recoverability   The ability of a habitat, community or individual (or individual colony) of species to redress damage sustained as a result of an external factor (www.marlin.ac.uk/glossary.php). Cf. 'recovery'

Red List   The term used by IUCN to refer to their list of threatened species (see IUCN, 2013).

Regime shift   With regard to marine communities and habitats, where shifts have occurred in the community structure of a location, especially of regional seas, as a result of large-scale hydrographic and climatic factors (Scheffer and Carpenter, 2003; Collie *et al.*, 2004). Also applied to situations where it is most likely that it is human activities that have caused a shift.

Rehabilitation   The act of partially or, more rarely, fully replacing structural or functional characteristics of an ecosystem that have been diminished or lost, or the substitution of alternative qualities or characteristics than those originally present with the proviso that they have more social, economic or ecological value than existed in the disturbed or degraded state (Edwards, 2010). Cf. 'recovery', 'recoverability', 'restoration'

Reintroduction   A species which has been reintroduced by human agency, deliberate or otherwise, to an area within its natural geographical range (q.v.) but where it had became extinct in historical times. Cf. 'recovery', 'replacement'

Remediation   The act or process of remedying or repairing damage to an ecosystem.

Replacement   A habitat constructed in the place of one that has been lost or destroyed. A species introduced to recreate the structural of functional services of one that has been lost or destroyed. Cf. 'recovery', 'reintroduction', 'rehabilitation', 'restoration'

Representativity/Representivity/Representativeness   (conservation assessment). Typical of a feature, habitat or assemblage of species. Representative examples are identified from the range of natural or semi-natural habitats and associated communities (biotopes) within a biogeographically distinct area or the boundaries of a national territory (Hiscock, 1996).

Resident   A permanent inhabitant, non-migratory.

Resilience   The ability of an ecosystem to return to its original state after being disturbed (Makins, 1991). Cf. 'constancy', 'persistence', 'recoverablity', 'resistance', 'stability'

Resistance   capacity of a system to resist change in the face of a perturbation (Stachowicz *et al.*, 2007). Cf. 'constancy', 'persistence', 'resilience', 'stability'

Restoration   Restitution of something that has been taken away or lost (www.dictionary. com). 'Ecological restoration' is the process of assisting the recovery of an ecosystem that has been degraded, damaged or destroyed (SER, 2004). The act of bringing a degraded ecosystem back into, as nearly as possible, its original condition (Edwards, 2010). Cf. 'recovery', 'recoverability', 'rehabilitation'

Richness (species)   The number of species in a community, habitat or sample (www. marlin.ac.uk/glossary.php). Cf. 'diversity'

Salinity   A measure of the concentration of dissolved salts in seawater. Salinity is defined as the ratio of the mass of dissolved material in seawater to the mass of seawater (UNESCO, 1985).

Salt marsh   Areas of alluvial or peat deposits, colonised by herbaceous and small shrubby terrestrial vascular plants, almost permanently wet and frequently inundated with saline waters (Long and Mason 1983).

Scavenger   Any organism that feeds on dead organic material (www.marlin.ac.uk/glossary.php).

Sensitivity   (Conservation assessment) An assessment of the intolerance of a species or habitat to damage from an external factor and the time taken for its subsequent recovery (www.marlin.ac.uk/glossary.php).

Spatial planning   The allocation of human use (of the marine environment) in space and time. Explained as 'Adaptive maritime spatial planning' in Douvere and Ehler (2011, p305).

Stability   The ability of an ecosystem to resist change (Makins, 1991). Cf. 'constancy', 'persistence', 'resilience'

Stakeholder   Those people or organisations which are vital to the success or failure of an organisation or project to reach its goals. The primary stakeholders are (a) those needed for permission, approval and financial support and (b) those who are directly affected by the activities of the organisation or project. Secondary stakeholders are those who are indirectly affected. Tertiary stakeholders are those who are not affected or involved, but who can influence opinions either for or against (Dudley, 2008).

Stratification   The division of a water body into layers of different temperature and density, owing to the development of a thermocline (Eleftheriou, 1997). Stratification may also occur as a result of the development of a halocline (division of areas of high- and low-salinity water). The stratification prevents mixing between the different water layers.

Structure   The combination of mutually connected and dependant biological and non-biological elements of a system that determine its nature (Hiscock *et al.*, 2006).

Sublittoral   The zone exposed to air at its upper limit only by the lowest spring tides, although almost continuous wave action on extremely exposed coasts may extend the upper limit high into the intertidal region. The sublittoral extends, in temperate zones, from the upper limit of the large kelps and includes, for practical purposes in nearshore areas, all depths below the littoral. Various subzones are recognised (based on Hiscock, 1985).

Surveillance   A continued programme of biological surveys systematically undertaken to provide a series of observations in time (Davies *et al.*, 2001). Cf. 'monitoring'

Survey   A single event at a particular location with the objective of describing the character of that area, site or feature.

Suspension feeders   Suspensivores, filter-feeders, any organisms which feed on particulate organic matter, including plankton, suspended in the water column (Lincoln *et al.*, 1998).

Threatened   To be in danger. Refers especially to 'degree of threat' and the categories in the IUCN Red List (IUCN, 2001).

Tipping point   The point at which what may have been a slowly changing situation crosses a certain threshhold and gains significant momentum, triggered by some minor factor or change (based on www.dictionary.reference.com).

Traits   See Biological traits; Ecological traits; Functional traits.

Vagrant   Individuals of a species which, by natural means, move from one geographical region to another outside their usual range, or away from usual migratory routes, and which do not establish a self-maintaining, self-regenerating population in the new region (www.marlin.ac.uk/glossary.php). Cf. 'alien species'

Viability   A criterion for MPA network design. Sometimes included with adequacy (see Ardron, 2008) and sometimes separately (see Natural England and Joint Nature Conservation Committee, 2010) where it is described.

Vulnerable   Open or susceptible to damaging activities, contaminants, events or disease. A category of the IUCN Red List defined by a variety of measures (see IUCN, 2001). Cf. 'Critically Endangered', 'Endangered'

Water column   The water of the ocean, organised from the surface to the floor, rather than from coast to coast (Ruth and Lindholm, 2002).

Xenobiotics   A foreign (originating from outside) organic chemical: a non-biological compound that an organism must eliminate or neutralise by detoxification; used on environmental pollutants such as pesticides in river run-off (based on Lincoln *et al.*, 1998).

Acronyms and abbreviations

The following are acronyms and abbreviations used in this book together with some that may be found in conventions, directives and statutes.

AGDS	Acoustic Ground Discrimination Sonar
ANZEC TFMPA	Australia and New Zealand Environment and Conservation Council Task Force on Marine Protected Areas
BBOP	Business and Biodiversity Offsets Programme
CBD	Convention on Biological Diversity
Cefas	Centre for Environment, Fisheries and Aquaculture Science (UK)
CMECS	Coastal and Marine Ecological Classification Standard (USA)
COML	Census of Marine Life
CoP	Conference of Parties (to the Convention on Biological Diversity)
CPR	Continuous Plankton Recorder
DPSIR	Drivers - Pressures - State Change - Impact - Response
EAC	East Australian Current
EC	European Commission
EcIA	Ecological Impact Assessment
EEZ	Exclusive Economic Zone
EIA	Environmental Impact Assessment
EU	European Union
EUNIS	European Union Nature Information System
FAO	Food and Agriculture Organization of the United Nations
GBIF	Global Biodiversity Information Facility
GBRMP	Great Barrier Reef Marine Park
GES	Good Environmental Status (from the EU Marine Strategy Framework Directive)
GESAMP	IMO/FAO/UNESCO/WMO/WHO/IAEA/UN/UNEP Joint Group of Experts on the Scientific Aspects of Marine Environmental Protection
GIS	Geographical Information System
HELCOM	Baltic Marine Environment Protection Commission
IAEA	International Atomic Energy Agency
ICES	International Council for the Exploration of the Seas
ICZM	Integrated Coastal Zone Management
IEEM	Institute of Ecology and Environmental Management

IOC	Intergovernmental Oceanographic Commission
IODE	International Oceanographic Data and Information Exchange
IUCN	The World Conservation Union (formally the International Union for the Conservation of Nature)
IPIECA	International Petroleum Industry Environmental Conservation Association (IPIECA no longer use the full title)
JNCC	Joint Nature Conservation Committee (UK)
MarLIN	Marine Life Information Network for Britain and Ireland
MEECE	Marine Ecosystems Evolution in a Changing Environment
MLPA	Marine Life Protection Act (in California)
MNCR	Marine Nature Conservation Review (of Great Britain)
MPA	Marine Protected Area
NBN	National Biodiversity Network (UK)
NCCARF	National Climate Change Adaptation Research Facility (Australia)
OBIS	Ocean Biodiversity Information System
OSPAR	Convention for the Protection of the Marine Environment of the NE Atlantic (originally, the **Os**lo and **Par**is Commissions)
PISCO	Partnership for Interdisciplinary Studies of Coastal Oceans
ROV	Remote Operated Vehicle
SCOR	Scientific Committee on Oceanic Research
SCOS	Special Committee on Seals (UK)
SCUBA	Self-Contained Underwater Breathing Apparatus
SMART	Specific, Measurable, Achievable, Realistic, and Time-bounded (objectives)
SMRU	Seal Mammals Research Unit (UK)
TBT	Tributyltin
UKMMAS	UK Marine Monitoring and Assessment Strategy
UKMMASC	UK Marine Monitoring Assessment Strategy Community
UN	United Nations
UNEP	United Nations Environment Program
UNESCO	United Nations Educational, Scientific and Cultural Organization
WCED	World Commission on Environment and Development
WCMC	World Conservation Monitoring Centre
WCPA	World Commission on Protected Areas
WWF	World Wildlife Fund (WWF no longer uses the full title)

References

Abbreviations of organisations are spelt out in the list of acronyms.

Agardy, T., Notarbartolo di Sciara, G. and Christie, P. (2011) 'Mind the gap: addressing the short-comings of marine protected areas through large scale marine spatial planning', *Marine Policy*, vol. 35, no. 2, pp. 226–232.

Airoldi, L. and Beck, M. W. (2007) 'Loss, status and trends for coastal marine habitats of Europe', in R. N. Gibson, R. J. A. Atkinson and J. D. M. Gordon (eds) *Oceanography and Marine Biology Annual Review, Volume 45*, CRC Press, Boca Raton: FL, pp. 345–405.

Albins, M. A. and Hixon, M. A. (2008) 'Invasive Indo-Pacific lionfish *Pterois volitans* reduce recruit-ment of Atlantic coral-reef fishes', *Marine Ecology Progress Series*, vol. 367, pp. 233–238.

Allen, J. R., Wilkinson, S. B. and Hawkins, S. J. (1995) 'Redeveloped docks as artificial lagoons: the development of brackish-water communities and potential for conservation of lagoonal species', *Aquatic Conservation: Marine and Freshwater Ecosystems*, vol. 5, no. 4, pp. 299–309.

Alzieu, C. (1991) 'Environmental problems caused by TBT in France: assessment, regulations, pros-pects', *Marine Environmental Research*, vol. 32, no. 1, pp. 7–17.

André, M., Solé, M., Lenoir, M., Durfort, M., Quero, C., Mas, A., Lombarte, A., van der Schaar, M., López-Bejar, M., Morell, M., Zaugg, S. and Houégnigan, L. (2011) 'Low-frequency sounds induce acoustic trauma in cephalopods', *Frontiers in Ecology and the Environment*, vol. 9, no. 9, pp. 489–493.

ANZECC TFMPA (1998) *Guidelines for Establishing the National Representative System of Marine Protected Areas*, Environment Australia, Canberra.

Appeltans, W., Costello, M. J. and 108 others (2012) 'The magnitude of global marine species diver-sity', *Current Biology*, vol. 22, no. 23, pp. 2189–2202.

Ardizzone, G. D., Catandella, S. and Rossi, R. (1988) *Management of Coastal Lagoon Fisheries and Aquaculture in Italy*, Technical Paper No. 295, FAO Fisheries, Rome.

Ardron, J. A. (2008a) 'Three initial OSPAR tests of ecological coherence: heuristics in a data-limited situation', *ICES Journal of Marine Science*, vol. 65, no. 8, pp. 1527–1533.

Ardron, J. A. (2008b) 'The challenge of assessing whether the OSPAR network of marine protected areas is ecologically coherent', *Hydrobiologia*, vol. 606, pp. 45–53.

Atkins, J. P., Burden, D., Elliott, M. and Gregory, A. J. (2011) 'Management of the marine environ-ment: integrating ecosystem services and societal benefits with the DPSIR framework in a systems approach', *Marine Pollution Bulletin*, vol. 62, no. 2, pp. 215–226.

Augier, H. and Boudouresque, Ch.-F. (1967) 'Végétation marine de L'Ile de Port-Cros (Parc National). 1. La Baie de la Palu', *Bulletin du Muséum d'Histoire Naturelle de Marseille*, vol. 27, 93–124.

Babcock, R. C., Shears, N. T., Alcala, A. C., Barrett, N. S., Edgar, G. J., Lafferty, K. D., McClanahan, T. R. and Russ, G. R. (2010) 'Decadal trends in marine reserves reveal differential rates of change in direct and indirect effects', *Proceedings of the National Academy of Sciences*, vol. 107, no. 43, pp. 18256–18261.

Bak, R. P. M. (1987) 'Effects of chronic oil pollution on a Caribbean coral reef', *Marine Pollution Bulletin*, vol. 18, no. 10, pp. 534–539.

Baker, J. M. (ed.) (1976) *Marine Ecology and Oil Pollution*, Applied Science, Barking, UK.

Bakke, T., Klungsøyr, J. and Sanni, S. (2012) *Long-Term Effects of Discharges to Sea from Petroleum-Related Activitie:. The Results of Ten Years' Research*, Research Council of Norway, Oslo.

Ball, I. R., Possingham, H. P. and Watts, M. (2009) 'Marxan and relatives: software for spatial conservation prioritisation', in A. Moilanen, K. A. Wilson and H. P. Possingham (eds) *Spatial Conservation Prioritisation: Quantitative Methods and Computational Tools*, Oxford University Press, Oxford, pp. 185–195.

Ballantine, W. J. (1961) 'A biologically-defined exposure scale for the comparative description of rocky shores', *Field Studies*, vol. 1, no. 3, pp. 1–19.

Baltazar-Soares, M., Biastoch, A., Harrod, C., Hanel, R., Marohn, L., Prigge, E., Evans, D., Bodles, K., Behrens, E., Böning, C. W. and Eizaguirre, C. (2014) 'Recruitment collapse and population structure of the European eel shaped by local ocean current dynamics', *Current Biology*, vol. 24, no. 1, pp. 104–108.

Baretta-Bekker, J. G., Duursma, E. K. and Kuipers, B. R. (1992) *Encyclopedia of Marine Sciences*, Springer-Verlag, Berlin.

Barry, J. P., Baxter, C. H., Sagarin, R. D. and Gilman, S. E. (1995) 'Climate-related, long-term faunal changes in a California rocky intertidal community', *Science*, vol. 267, no. 5198, pp. 672–675.

Bates, A. E., Barrett, N. S., Stuart-Smith, R. D., Holbrook, N. J., Thompson, P. A. and Edgar, G. J. (2014) 'Resilience and signatures of tropicalization in protected reef fish communities', *Nature Climate Change*, vol. 4, no. 1, pp. 62–67.

Bates, M. (1950) *The Nature of Natural History*, Charles Scribner's Sons, New York.

Baum, J. K. and Blanchard, W. (2010) 'Inferring shark population trends from generalized linear mixed models of pelagic longline catch and effort data', *Fisheries Research*, vol. 102, no. 3, pp. 229–239.

BBOP (Business and Biodiversity Offsets Programme) (2009) *BBOP Biodiversity Offset Design Handbook*, BBOP, Washington DC.

Beare, D. J., Burns, F., Jones, E. G., Peach, K. and Reid, D. G. (2003) *Observations on long-term changes in prevalence of fish species with southern biogeographic affinities in the northern North Sea*, Paper CM 2003/Q:24, International Council for the Exploration of the Sea.

Beaugrand, G., Reid, P. C., Ibanez, F., Lindley, J. A. and Edwards, M. (2002) 'Reorganization of North Atlantic marine copepod biodiversity and climate', *Science*, vol. 296, no. 5573, pp. 1692–1694.

Bell, J. J. (2008) 'Connectivity between island Marine Protected Areas and the mainland', *Biological Conservation*, vol. 141, no. 11, pp. 2807–2820.

Bengston, J. L., Boveng, P., Franzén, U., Have, P., Heide-Jørgensen, M. P. and Härkönen T. J. (1991) 'Antibodies to canine distemper virus in Antarctic seals', *Marine Mammal Science*, vol. 7, no. 1, pp. 85–87.

Bergen, S. D., Bolton, S. M. and Fridley, J. L. (2001) 'Design principles for ecological engineering', *Ecological Engineering*, vol. 18, no. 2, pp. 201–210.

Beukema, J. J. (1974) 'Seasonal changes in the biomass of the macro-benthos of a tidal flat area in the Dutch Wadden Sea', *Netherlands Journal of Sea Research*, vol. 8, no. 1, pp. 94–107.

Beukema, J. J. (1995) 'Long-term effects of mechanical harvesting of lugworms *Arenicola marina* on the zoobenthic community of a tidal flat in the Wadden Sea', *Netherlands Journal of Sea Research*, vol. 33, no. 2, pp. 219–227.

Björklund, M. J. (1974) 'Achievements in marine conservation, I. marine parks', *Environmental Conservation*, vol. 1, no. 3, pp 205–223.

Blake, C. and Maggs, C. A. (2003) 'Comparative growth rates and internal banding periodicity of maerl species (Corallinales, Rhodophyta) from northern Europe', *Phycologia*, vol. 42, no. 6, pp. 606–612.

Bolam, S. G., Rees, H. L., Somerfield, P., Smith, R., Clarke, K. R., Warwick, R. M., Atkins, M. and Garnacho, E. (2006) 'Ecological consequences of dredged material disposal in the marine environment: a holistic assessment of activities around the England and Wales coastline', *Marine Pollution Bulletin*, vol. 52, no. 4, pp. 415–426.

Borja, Á., Dauer, D. M., Elliott, M. and Simenstad, C. A. (2010b) 'Medium- and long-term recovery of estuarine and coastal ecosystems: patterns, rates and restoration effectiveness', *Estuaries and Coasts*, vol 33, no. 6, pp. 1249–1260.

Borja, Á., Dauer, D. M. and Grémare, A. (2012) 'The importance of setting targets and reference conditions in assessing marine ecosystem quality', *Ecological Indicators*, vol. 12, no. 1, pp. 1–7.

Borja, Á., Elliott, M., Andersen, J. H., Cardoso, A. C., Carstensen, J., Ferreira, J. G., Heiskanen, A. –S., Marques, J. C., Neto, J. M., Teixeira, H., Uusitalo, L., Uyarra, M. C. and Zampoukas, N. (2013) 'Good Environmental Status of marine ecosystems: what is it and how do we know when we have attained it?', *Marine Pollution Bulletin*, vol. 76, no. 1–2, pp. 16–27.

Borja, Á., Elliott, M., Carstensen, J., Heiskanen, A.-S. and van de Bund, W. (2010a) 'Marine management – towards an integrated implementation of the European Marine Strategy Framework and the Water Framework Directives', *Marine Pollution Bulletin*, vol 60, no. 12, pp. 2175–2186.

Borja, Á., Franco, J. and Perez, V. (2000) 'A marine biotic index to establish the ecological quality of soft-bottom benthos within European estuarine and coastal environments', *Marine Pollution Bulletin*, vol. 40, no. 12, pp. 1100–1114.

Borja, Á., Muxika, I. and Franco, J. (2006) 'Long-term recovery of soft-bottom benthos following urban and industrial sewage treatment in the Nervión estuary (southern Bay of Biscay)', *Marine Ecology Progress Series*, vol. 313, pp. 43–55.

Bosence, D. and Wilson, J. (2003) 'Maerl growth, carbonate production rates and accumulation rates in the NE Atlantic', *Aquatic Conservation: Marine and Freshwater Ecosystems*, vol. 13, Supplement 1, pp. S21–S31.

Boulcott, P. and Howell, T. R. W. (2011) 'The impact of scallop dredging on rocky-reef substrata', *Fisheries Research*, vol. 110, no. 3, pp. 415–420.

Bradshaw, C., Collins, P. and Brand, A. R. (2003) 'To what extent does upright sessile epifauna affect benthic biodiversity and community composition?', *Marine Biology*, vol. 143, no. 4, pp. 783–791.

Bradshaw, C., Veale, L. O., Hill, A. S. and Brand, A. R. (2001) 'The effect of scallop dredging on Irish Sea benthos: experiments using a closed area', *Hydrobiologia*, vol. 465, pp. 129–138.

Bremner, J. (2008) 'Species' traits and ecological functioning in marine conservation and management', *Journal of Experimental Marine Biology and Ecology*, vol. 366, no. 1–2, pp. 37–47.

Brock, R. J., Kenchington, E. and Martínez-Arroyo, A. (eds) (2012) *Scientific Guidelines for Designing Resilient Marine Protected Area Networks in a Changing Climate*, Commission for Environmental Cooperation, Montreal, Canada.

Bryan, G. W., Gibbs, P. E., Hummerstone, L. G. and Burt, G. R. (1986) 'The decline of the gastropod *Nucella lapillus* around south-west England: evidence for the effect of Tributyltin from anti-fouling paints', *Journal of the Marine Biological Association of the United Kingdom*, vol. 66, no. 3, pp. 611–640.

Burt, J., Bartholomew, A., Usseglio, P., Bauman, A. and Sale, P. F. (2009) 'Are artificial reefs surrogates of natural habitats for corals and fish in Dubai, United Arab Emirates?' *Coral Reefs*, vol. 28, no. 3, pp. 663–675.

Burton, M., Lock, K., Newman, P. and Jones, J. (2014) *Skomer Marine Nature Reserve Project Status Report 2013*, Natural Resources Wales, Bangor, Wales.

Byrnes, J. E., Reynolds, P. L. and Stachowicz, J. J. (2007) 'Invasions and extinctions reshape coastal marine food webs', *PLoS ONE*, vol. 2, no. 3, e295.

Campbell, M. L. (2000) 'Getting the foundation right: a scientifically based management framework to aid in the planning and implementation of seagrass transplant efforts', *Bulletin of Marine Science*, vol. 71, no 3, pp. 1405–1414.

Cardoso, P. G., Leston, S., Grilo, T. F., Bordalo, M. D., Crespo, D., Raffaelli, D. and Pardal, M. A. (2010) 'Implications of nutrient decline in the seagrass ecosystem success', *Marine Pollution Bulletin*, vol. 60, no. 4, pp. 601–608.

Carlton, J. (2009) 'Deep invasion ecology and the assembly of communities in historical times', in G. Rilov and J. A. Crooks (eds) *Biological Invasions in Marine Ecosystems*, Springer, Berlin, pp. 13–56.

Carter, R. W. G. (1988) *Coastal Environments: An Introduction to the Physical, Ecological and Cultural Systems of Coastlines*, Academic Press, London.

Cattrijsse, A., Codling, I., Conides, A., Duhamel, S., Gibson, R. N., Hostens, K., Mathieson, S. and McLusky, D. S. (2002) 'Estuarine development/habitat restoration and re-creation and their role in estuarine management for the benefit of aquatic resources', in M. Elliott and K. L. Hemingway (eds) *Fishes in Estuaries*, Blackwell, Oxford, pp. 266–321.

Cebrian, E., Uriz, M. J., Garrabou, J. and Ballesteros, E. (2011) 'Sponge mass mortalities in a warming Mediterranean Sea: are cyanobacteria-harboring species worse off?', *PLoS ONE*, vol. 6, no. 6, e20211.

Centre for Conservation Geography (2011) *Critical Gaps in the Marine Sanctuary Network Proposed by the Federal Government for Australia's North and North-West Planning Regions*, Centre for Conservation Geography, Sydney, Australia.

Cerrano, C., Arillo, A., Azzini, F., Calcinai B., Castellano L., Muti C., Valisano, L, Zega. G. and Bavestrello, G. (2005) 'Gorgonian population recovery after a mass mortality event', *Aquatic Conservation: Marine and Freshwater Ecosystems*, vol. 15, no. 2, pp. 147–157.

Chapman, J. W., Carlton, J. T., Bellinger, M. R. and Blakeslee, A. M. H. (2007) 'Premature refutation of a human-mediated marine species introduction: the case history of the marine snail *Littorina littorea* in the northwestern Atlantic', *Biological Invasions*, vol. 9, no. 8, pp. 737–750.

Chapman, M. G. (2003) 'Paucity of mobile species on constructed seawalls: effects of urbanization on biodiversity', *Marine Ecology Progress Series*, vol. 264, pp. 21–29.

Chapman, M. G. and Underwood, A. J. (2011) 'Evaluation of ecological engineering of "armoured" shorelines to improve their value as habitat', *Journal of Experimental Marine Biology and Ecology*, vol. 400, no. 1–2, pp. 302–313.

Christensen, N. L., Bartuska, A., Brown, J. H., Carpenter, S., D'Antonio, C., Francis, R., Franklin, J. F., MacMahon, J. A., Noss, R. F., Parsons, D. J., Peterson, C. H., Turner, M. G. and Woodmansee, R. G. (1996) 'The report of the Ecological Society of America Committee on the scientific basis for ecosystem management', *Ecological Applications*, vol. 6, no. 3, pp. 665–691.

Christie, H., Leinaas, H. P. and Skadsheim, A. (1995) 'Local patterns in mortality of the green sea urchin, *Strongylocentrotus droebachiensis*, at the Norwegian coast', in H. R. Skjoldal, C. Hopkins, K. E. Erikstad and H. P. Leinaas (eds) *Ecology of Fjords and Coastal Waters*, Elsevier, Amsterdam, pp. 573–584.

Christie, H., Fredriksen, S. and Rinde, E. (1998) 'Regrowth of kelp and colonization of epiphyte and fauna community after kelp trawling at the coast of Norway', *Hydrobiologia*, vol. 375/376, pp. 49–58.

Christie, M. R., Tissot, B. N., Albins, M. A., Beets, J. P, Jia, Y., Ortiz, D. M., Thompson, S. E. and Hixon, M. A. (2010) 'Larval connectivity in an effective network of marine protected areas', *PLoS ONE*, vol. 5, no. 12, e15715.

Cicin-Sain, B. and Belfiore, S. (2005) 'Linking marine protected areas to integrated coastal and ocean management: a review of theory and practice', *Ocean & Coastal Management*, vol. 48, no. 11–12, pp. 847–868.

Clark, M. R., Schlacher, T. A., Rowden, A. A., Stocks, K. I. and Consalvey, M. (2012) 'Science priorities for seamounts: research links to conservation and management', *PLoS ONE*, vol. 7, no. 1, e29232.

Clark, M. R., Rowden, A. A., Schlacher, T., Williams, A. Consalvey, M., Stocks, K. I., Rogers, A. D., O'Hara, T. D., White, M., Shank, T. M. and Hall-Spencer, J. M. (2010) 'The ecology of seamounts: structure, function, and human impacts', *Annual Review of Marine Science*, vol. 2, pp. 253–278.

Clark, R. B. (2001) *Marine Pollution*, Oxford University Press, Oxford.

Clarke, A., Barnes, D. K. A. and Hodgson, D. A. (2005) 'How isolated is Antarctica?', *TRENDS in Ecology and Evolution*, vol. 20, no. 1, pp. 1–3.

Clarke, K. R. and Gorley, R. N. (2006) *PRIMER v6: User Manual/Tutorial*, PRIMER-E, Plymouth, UK.

Claudet, J., Osenberg, C. W., Benedetti-Cecci, L., Domenici, P., García-Charton, J.-A., Pérez-Ruzafa, A., Badalamenti, F., Bayle-Sempere, J., Brito, A., Bulleri, F., Culioli, J.-M., Dimech, M., Falcón, J. M., Guala, I., Milazzo, M., Sánchez-Meca, J., Somerfield, P. J., Stobart, B., Vandeperre, F., Valle, C. and Planes, S. (2008) 'Marine reserves: size and age do matter', *Ecology Letters*, vol. 11, no. 5, pp. 481–489.

Cloern, J. E. (1982) 'Does the benthos control phytoplankton biomass in the South San Francisco Bay?' *Marine Ecology Progress Series*, vol. 9, pp. 191–202.

Cloern, J. E. and Jassby, A. D. (2012) 'Drivers of change in estuarine-coastal ecosystems: discoveries from four decades of study in San Francisco Bay', *Review of Geophysics*, vol. 50, no. 4, *RG4001* (33pp).

Cohen, A. N. and Carlton, J. T. (1998) 'Accelerating invasion rate in a highly invaded estuary', *Science*, vol. 279, no. 5350, pp. 555–558.

Cole, M., Lindeque, P., Halsband, C. and Galloway, T. S. (2011) 'Microplastics as contaminants in the marine environment: a review', *Marine Pollution Bulletin*, vol. 62, no. 12, pp. 1596–1605.

Coleman, R. A., Hoskin, M. G., von Carlshausen, E. and Davis, C. M. (2013) 'Using a no-take zone to assess the impacts of fishing: sessile epifauna appear insensitive to environmental disturbances from commercial potting', *Journal of Experimental Marine Biology and Ecology*, vol. 440, pp. 100–107.

Collette, B. B., Carpenter, K. E., Polidoro, B. A., Juan-Jordá, M. J., Boustany, A., Die, D. J., Elfes, C., Fox, W., Graves, J., Harrison, L. R., McManus, R., Minte-Vera, C. V., Nelson, R., Restrepo, V., Schratwieser, J., Sun, C.-L., Amorim, A., Brick Peres, M., Canales, C., Cardenas, G., Chang, S.- K., Chiang, W.-C., de Oliveira Leite Jr., N., Harwell, H., Lessa, R., Fredou, F. L., Oxenford, H. A., Serra, R., Shao, K.-T., Sumaila, R., Wang, S.-P., Watson, R. and Yáñez, E. (2011) 'High value and long life – double jeopardy for tunas and billfishes', *Science*, vol. 333, no. 6040, pp. 291–292.

Collie, J. S., Richardson, K. and Steele, J. H. (2004) 'Regime shifts: can ecological theory illuminate the mechanisms?' *Progress in Oceanography*, vol. 60, no. 2–4, pp. 281–302.

Collins, K. J. and Mallinson, J. (2007) 'Use of shell to speed recovery of dredged aggregate seabed', in R. C. Newell and D. J. Garner (eds) *Marine Aggregate Extraction: Helping to Establish Good Practice*, Proceedings of the Marine Aggregate Levy Sustainability Fund (ALSF) Conference, Sept 2006, Cefas, Lowestoft, UK, pp. 152–155.

Connell, J. H. and Sousa, W. P. (1983) 'On the evidence needed to judge ecological stability or persistence', *The American Naturalist*, vol. 121, no. 6, pp. 789–824.

Connor, D. W., Allen, J. H., Golding, N., Howell, K. L., Lieberknecht, L. M., Northen, K. O. and Reker, J. B. (2004) 'The Marine Habitat Classification for Britain and Ireland, Version 04.05', http://jncc.defra.gov.uk/MarineHabitatClassification, accessed 24 December 2013.

Cook, R., Fariñas-Franco, J. M., Gell, F. R., Holt, R. H. F., Holt, T., Lindenbaum, C., Porter, J. S., Seed, R., Skates, L. R., Stringell, T. B. and Sanderson, W. G. (2013) 'The substantial first impact of bottom fishing on rare biodiversity hotspots: a dilemma for evidence-based conservation', *PLoS ONE*, vol. 8, no. 8, e69904.

Cooper, K. M., Frojan, C., Defew, E., Curtis, M., Fleddum, A., Brooks, L. and Patterson, D. M. (2008) 'Assessment of ecosystem function following marine aggregate dredging', *Journal of Experimental Marine Biology and Ecology*, vol. 366, no. 1–2, pp. 82–91.

Cooper, K., Burdon, D., Atkins, J. Weiss, L., Somerfield, P., Elliott, M., Turner, K., Ware, S. and Vivian, C. (2010) *Seabed Restoration following marine aggregate dredging: do the benefits justify the costs?*, Cefas, Lowestoft, UK.

Costanza, R., d'Arge, R., de Groot, R., Farber, S., Grasso, M., Hannon, B., Limburg, K., Naeem, S., O'Neill, R. V., Paruelo, J., Raskin, R. G., Sutton, P. and van den Belt, M. (1997) 'The value of the world's ecosystem services and natural capital', *Nature*, vol. 387, pp. 253–260.

Costello, M. J. (2009) 'Distinguishing marine habitat classification concepts for ecological data management', *Marine Ecology Progress Series*, vol. 397, pp. 253–268.

Costello, M. J., Coll, M., Danovaro, R., Halpin, P., Ojaveer, H. and Miloslavich, P. (2010) 'A census of marine biodiversity knowledge, resources, and future challenges', *PLoS ONE*, vol. 5, no. 8, e12110.

Cotton, A. D. (1912) 'Marine algae. Clare Island Survey: Part 15', *Proceedings of the Royal Irish Academy*, vol. 31, pp. 1–178.

Cowan, R. K. and Sponaugle, S. (2009) 'Larval dispersal and marine population connectivity', *Annual Review of Marine Science*, vol. 1, pp. 443–466.

Crain, C. M., Kroeker, K. and Halpern, B. S. (2008) 'Interactive and cumulative effects of multiple human stressors in marine systems', *Ecology Letters*, vol. 11, no. 12, pp. 1304–1315.

Crapp, G. B. (1973) 'The distribution and abundance of animals and plants on the rocky shores of Bantry Bay', *Irish Fisheries Investigations*, Series B, No. 9, Department of Agriculture and Fisheries (Fisheries Division), The Stationery Office, Dublin.

Crisp, D. J. (ed.) (1964) 'The effects of the severe winter of 1962–63 on marine life in Britain', *Journal of Animal Ecology*, vol. 33, no. 1, pp. 165–210.

Crisp, D. J. and Southward, A. J. (1958) 'The distribution of intertidal organisms along the coasts of the English Channel', *Journal of the Marine Biological Association of the United Kingdom*, vol. 37, no. 1, pp. 157–208.

Crowder, L. B., Lyman, S. I., Figueria, W. F. and Priddy, J. (2000) 'Source-sink population dynamics and the problem of siting marine reserves', *Bulletin of Marine Science*, vol. 66, no. 3, pp. 799–820.

Cunha, A. H., Marbá, N. N., van Katwijk, M. M., Pickerell, C., Henriques, M., Bernard, G., Ferreira, A., Garcia, S., Garmendia, J. M. and Manent, P. (2012) 'Changing paradigms in seagrass restoration', *Restoration Ecology*, vol. 20, no. 4, pp. 427–430.

Cushing, D. H. and Dickson, R. R. (1976) 'The biological response in the sea to climatic changes', *Advances in Marine Biology*, vol. 14, pp 1–122.

Davey, J. T. and Watson, P. G. (1995) 'The activity of *Nereis diversicolor* (Polychaeta) and its impact on nutrient fluxes in estuarine waters', *Ophelia*, vol. 41, no. 1, pp. 57–70.

Davies, C. E., Moss, D. and Hill, M. O. (2004) 'EUNIS Habitat Classification Revised 2004. Report to the European Topic Centre on Nature Protection and Biodiversity, European Environment Agency', http://eunis.eea.europa.eu/habitats.jsp, accessed 10 January 2014.

Davies, J., Baxter, J., Bradley, M., Connor, D., Khan, J., Murray, E., Sanderson, W., Turnbull, C. and Vincent, M. (2001) 'Marine Monitoring Handbook', http://jncc.defra.gov.uk/PDF/MMH-mmh_0601.pdf, accessed 10 January 2014.

Day, J., Dudley, N., Hockings, M., Holmes G., Laffoley, D., Stolton S. and Wells, S. (2012) *Guidelines for Applying the IUCN Protected Area Management Categories to Marine Protected Areas*, IUCN, Gland, Switzerland.

Dayton, P. K., Tegner, M. J., Edwards, P. B. and Riser, K. L. (1998) 'Sliding baselines, ghosts, and reduced expectations in kelp forest communities', *Ecological Applications*, vol. 8, no 2, pp. 309–322.

de Kluijver, M. J. and Leewis, R. J. (1994) 'Changes in the sublittoral hard substrate communities in the Oosterschelde estuary (SW Netherlands), caused by changes in the environmental parameters', *Hydrobiologia*, vol. 282/283, pp. 265–280.

de Wilde, P. A. W. J., Berghuis, E. M. and Kok, A. (1984) 'Structure and energy demand of the benthic community of the oyster ground, central North Sea', *Netherlands Journal of Sea Research*, vol. 18, no. 1–2, pp. 143–159.

del Monte-Luna, P., Lluch-Belda, D., Serviere-Zaragoza, E., Carmona, R., Reyes-Bonilla, H., Aurioles-Gamboa, D., Castro-Aguirre, J. L., del Próo, S. A. G., Trujillo-Millán, O. and Brook, B. W. (2007) 'Marine extinctions revisited', *Fish and Fisheries*, vol. 8, no. 2, pp. 107–122.

den Hartog, C. (1994) 'Suffocation of a littoral *Zostera* bed by *Enteromorpha radiata*', *Aquatic Botany*, vol. 47, no. 1, pp. 21–28.

Dernie, K. M., Kaiser, M. J., Richardson, E. A. and Warwick, R. M. (2003) 'Recovery of soft sediment communities and habitats following physical disturbance', *Journal of Experimental Marine Biology and Ecology*, vol. 285–286, pp. 415–434.

Derous, S., Agardy, T., Hillewaert, H., Hostens, K., Jamieson, G., Lieberknecht, L., Mees, J., Moulaert, I., Olenin, S., Paelinckx, D., Rabaut, M., Rachor, E., Roff, J., Stienen, E. W. M., van der Wal, J. T., Van Lancker, V., Verfaillie, E., Vincx, M., Weslawski, J. M. and Degraer, S. (2007) 'A concept for biological valuation in the marine environment', *Oceanologia*, vol. 49, no. 1, pp. 99–128.

Dethier, M. N. (1984) 'Disturbance and recovery in intertidal pools: maintenance of mosaic patterns', *Ecological Monographs*, vol. 54, no. 1, pp. 99–118.

Dickie, I., McAleese, L., Pearce, B. and Treweek, J. (2013) *Marine Biodiversity Offsetting – UK Scoping Study*, Report to The Crown Estate, London.

Dicks, B. (1976) 'The effects of refinery effluents: the case history of a saltmarsh', in J. M. Baker (ed.) *Marine Ecology and Oil Pollution*, Applied Science Publishers, Barking, UK, pp. 227–245.

Díez, I., Santolaria, A., Secilla, A. and Gorostiaga, J. M. (2009) 'Recovery stages over long-term monitoring of the intertidal vegetation in the "Abra de Bilbao" area and on the adjacent coast (N. Spain)', *European Journal of Phycology*, vol. 44, no. 1, pp. 1–14.

Díez, I., Muguerza, N., Santolaria, A., Ganzedo, U. and Gorostiaga, J. M. (2012) 'Seaweed assemblage changes in the eastern Cantabrian Sea and their potential relationship to climate change', *Estuarine, Coastal and Shelf Science*, vol. 99, no. 1, pp. 108–120.

Díez, S. and Cabildo, M. (2001) 'Vive la différence: plant functional diversity matters to ecosystem processes', *TRENDS in Ecology and Evolution*, vol. 16, no. 11, pp. 646–655.

Douvere, F. and Ehler, C. N. (2011) 'The importance of monitoring and evaluation in adaptive maritime spatial planning', *Journal of Coastal Conservation*, vol. 15, no. 2, pp. 305–311.

Douvere, F., Maes, F., Vanhulle, A. and Schrijvers, J. (2007) 'The role of marine spatial planning in sea use management: The Belgian case', *Marine Policy*, vol. 31, no 2, pp. 182–191.

Duarte, L., Viejo, R. M., Martínez, B., deCastro, M., Gómez-Gesteira, M. and Gallardo, T. (2013) 'Recent and historical range shifts of two canopy-forming seaweeds in North Spain and the link with trends in sea surface temperature', *Acta Oecologica*, vol. 51, pp. 1–10.

Dudley, N. (ed.) (2008) *Guidelines for Applying Protected Area Management Categories*, IUCN, Gland, Switzerland.

Dugan, J. E., Airoldi, L., Chapman, M. G., Walker, S. J. and Schlacher, T. (2011) 'Estuarine and coastal structures: environmental effects, a focus on shore and nearshore structures', in E. Wolanski and D. S. McLusky (eds) *Treatise on Estuarine and Coastal Science, Volume 8*, Academic Press, Waltham, pp. 17–41.

Dulvy, N. K. (2013) 'Super-sized MPAs and the marginalization of species conservation', *Aquatic Conservation: Marine and Freshwater Ecosystems*, vol. 23, no. 3, pp. 357–362.

Dunstan, P. K., Althaus, F., Williams, A. and Bax, N. J. (2012) 'Characterising and predicting benthic biodiversity for conservation planning in deepwater environments', *PLoS ONE*, vol. 7, no. 5, e36558.

Durán, L. R. and Castilla, J. C. (1989) 'Variation and persistence of the middle rocky intertidal community of central Chile, with and without human harvesting', *Marine Biology*, vol. 103, no. 4. pp. 555–562.

Earle, S. (2009) *The World is Blue: How Our Fate and the Ocean's are One*, National Geographic Books, Washington DC.

Edwards, A. J. (ed.) (2010) *Reef Rehabilitation Manual*, Coral Reef Targeted Research and Capacity Building for Management Program, St Lucia, Australia.

Edwards, A. and Garwood, P. (1992) 'The Gann Flat, Dale: thirty years on', *Field Studies*, vol. 8, no. 1, pp. 59–75.

Ehler, C. and Douvere, F. (2007) *Visions for a Sea Change. Report of the First International Workshop on Marine Spatial Planning*, Intergovernmental Oceanographic Commission and Man and the Biosphere Programme, IOC Manual and Guides no. 48, Paris, UNESCO.

Eklöf, J. S., de la Torre-Castro, M., Gullström, M., Uku, J., Muthiga, N., Lyimo, T. and Bandeira, S. O. (2008) 'Sea urchin overgrazing of seagrasses: a review of current knowledge on causes, consequences, and management', *Estuarine Coastal and Shelf Science*, vol. 79, no. 4, pp. 569–580.

Eleftheriou, A. (ed.) (2013) *Methods for the Study of Marine Benthos*, Wiley-Blackwell, Chichester, UK.

Eleftheriou, M. (ed.) (1997) *Aqualex: A Glossary of Aquaculture Terms*, John Wiley and Sons, Chichester, UK.

Elliott, M. (2011) 'Marine science and management means tackling exogenic unmanaged pressures and endogenic managed pressures – a numbered guide', *Marine Pollution Bulletin*, vol. 62, no. 4, pp. 651–655.

Elliott, M., Burdon, D., Hemingway, K. L. and Apitz, S. E. (2007) 'Estuarine, coastal and marine ecosystem restoration: confusing management and science – a revision of concepts', *Estuarine, Coastal and Shelf Science*, vol. 74, no. 3, pp. 349–366.

Elsäßer, B., Fariñas-Franco, J. B., Wilson, C. D., Kregting, L. and Roberts, D. (2013) 'Identifying optimal sites for natural recovery and restoration of impacted biogenic habitats in a Special Area of Conservation using hydrodynamic and habitat suitability modelling', *Journal of Sea Research*, vol. 77, pp. 11–21.

Engle, J. M. (2008) *Unified Monitoring Protocols for the Multi-Agency Rocky Intertidal Network*, U.S. Department of the Interior Minerals Management Service, Camarillo, California.

Engel, J. and Kvitek, R. (1998) 'Effects of otter trawling on benthic community in Monterey Bay National Marine Sanctuary', *Conservation Biology*, vol. 12, pp. 1204–1214.

Eno, N. C., Frid, C. L. J., Hall, K. Ramsay, K., Sharp, R. A. M., Brazier, D. P., Hearn, S., Dernie, K. M., Robinson, K. A., Paramor, O. A. L. and Robinson, L. A. (2013) 'Assessing the sensitivity of habitats to fishing: from seabed maps to sensitivity maps', *Journal of Fish Biology*, vol. 83, no. 4, pp. 826–846.

Essink, K., Beukema, J. J., Coosen, J., Craeymeersch, J. A., Ducrotoy, J.-P., Michaelis, H. and Robineau, B. (1991) 'Population dynamics of the bivalve mollusc *Scrobicularia plana* da Costa: comparisons in time and space', in M. Elliot and J.-P. Ducrotoy (eds) *Estuaries and Coasts: Spatial and Temporal Intercomparisons*, Olsen and Olsen, Fredensborg, Denmark, pp. 167–172.

Estes, J., Tinker, M. T. and Bodkin, J. L. (2010) 'Using ecological function to develop recovery criteria for depleted species: sea otters and kelp forests in the Aleutian archipelago', *Conservation Biology*, vol. 24, no. 3, pp. 852–860.

Fabricius, K. E., De'ath, G., Noonan, S. and Uthicke, S. (2014) 'Ecological effects of ocean acidification and habitat complexity on reef-associated macroinvertebrate communities', *Proceedings of the Royal Society B*, vol. 281, no. 1775, 20132479.

Federal Geographic Data Committee (Marine and Coastal Spatial Data Subcommittee) (2012) 'Coastal and Marine Ecological Classification Standard, FGDC-STD-018-2012', www.csc.noaa.gov/digitalcoast/_/pdf/CMECS_Version%20_4_Final_for_FGDC.pdf, accessed 11 August 2012.

Fernandes, L., Day, J., Lewis, A., Slegers, S., Kerrigan, B., Breen, D., Cameron, D. F., Jago, B., Hall, J., Lowe, D., Innes, J., Tanzer, J., Chadwick, V., Thompson, L., Gorman, K. and Possingham, H. (2005) 'Establishing representative no-take areas in the Great Barrier Reef: large-scale implementation of theory on marine protected areas', *Conservation Biology*, vol. 19, no. 6, pp. 1733–1744.

Firth, L. B., Thompson, R. C., White, F. J., Schofield, M., Skov, M. W., Hoggart, S. P. G., Jackson, J., Knights, A. M. and Hawkins, S. J. (2013) 'The importance of water-retaining features for biodiversity on artificial intertidal coastal defence structures', *Diversity and Distributions*, vol. 19, no. 10, pp. 1275–1283.

Foden, J., Rogers, S. I and Jones, A. P. (2009) 'Recovery rates of UK seabed habitats after cessation of aggregate extraction', *Marine Ecology Progress Series*, vol. 390, pp. 15–26.

Fonseca, M. S., Kenworthy, W. J., Julius, B. E., Shulter, S. and Fluke, S. (2002) 'Seagrasses', in M. R. Perrow and A. J. Davy (eds) *Handbook of Ecological Restoration, Volume 2*, Cambridge University Press, New York, pp. 149–170.

Ford, S. E. (1996) 'Range extension by the oyster parasite *Perkinsus marinus* into the Northeastern United States: response to climate change?', *Journal of Shellfish Research*, vol. 15, no. 1, pp. 45–56.

Fowler, S. and Laffoley, D. (1993) 'Stability in Mediterranean-Atlantic sessile epifaunal communities at the northern limits of their range', *Journal of Experimental Marine Biology and Ecology*, vol. 172, pp. 109–127.

Fox, H. E., Pet, J. S., Dahuri, R. and Caldwell, R. L. (2003) 'Recovery in rubble fields: long term impacts of blast fishing', *Marine Pollution Bulletin*, vol. 46, no. 8, pp. 1024–1031.

Frantz, B. R., Kashgarian, M., Coale, K. H. and Foster, M. S. (2000) 'Growth rate and potential climate record from a rhodolith using 14C accelerator mass spectrometry', *Limnology and Oceanography*, vol. 45, no. 8, pp. 1773–1777.

Fredette, T. J. and French, G. T. (2004) 'Understanding the physical and environmental conse-quences of dredged material disposal: history in New England and current perspectives', *Marine Pollution Bulletin*, vol. 49, no. 1–2, pp. 93–102.

Freiwald, A., Fosså, J. H., Grehan, A., Koslow, T. and Roberts, J. M (2004) *Cold-Water Coral Reefs: Out of Sight – No Longer Out of Mind*. UNEP-WCMC Biodiversity Series No 22, UNEP-WCMC, Cambridge, UK.

Gaines, S. D., White, C., Carr, M. H. and Palumbi, R. (2010) 'Designing marine reserve networks for both conservation and fisheries management', *PNAS*, vol. 107, no. 43, pp. 18251–18255.

Garrabou, J., Coma, R., Bensoussan, N., Bensoussan, N., Chevaldonné, P., Cigliano, M., Diaz, D., Harmelin, J. G., Gambi, M. C., Kersting, D. K., Lejeusne, C., Linares, C., Marschal, C., Pérez, T., Ribes, M., Romano, J. C., Serrano, E., Teixido, N., Torrents, O., Zabala, M., Zuberer, F. and Cerrano, C. (2009) 'Mass mortality in Northwestern Mediterranean rocky benthic communities: effects of the 2003 heat wave', *Global Change Biology*, vol. 15, no. 5, pp. 1090–1103.

Gerber, L. R., Keller. A. C. and DeMaster, D. P. (2007) 'Ten thousand and increasing: is the west-ern Arctic population of bowhead whale endangered?', *Biological Conservation*, vol. 137, no. 4, pp. 577–583.

GESAMP (1995) *Biological Indicators and Their Use in the Measurement of the Condition of the Marine Environment*, GESAMP Reports and Studies No. 55, UNEP.

Giani, M., Djakoyac, T., Degobbis, D., Cozzi, S., Solidoro, C. and Umani. S. F. (2012) 'Recent changes in the marine ecosystems of the northern Adriatic Sea', *Estuarine, Coastal and Shelf Science*, vol. 115, pp. 1–13.

Giller, P. S., Hillebrand, H., Berninger, U.-G., Gessner, M. O., Hawkins, S., Inchausti, P., Inglis, C., Leslie, H., Malmqvist, B., Monaghan, M. T., Morin, P. J. and O'Mullan, G. (2004) 'Biodiversity effects on ecosystem functioning: emerging issues and their experimental test in aquatic environ-ments', *Oikos*, vol. 104, no. 3, pp. 423–436.

Gleason, M., Kirlin, J. and Fox, E. (2013) 'California's marine protected area network planning pro-cess: introduction to the special issue', *Ocean & Coastal Management*, vol. 74, pp. 1–2.

Glowka, L., Burhenne-Guilmin, F. and Synge, H. (1994) *A Guide to the Convention on Biological Diversity*, IUCN, Gland, Switzerland and Cambridge, UK.

Golbuu, Y., Victor, S., Penland, L., Idip, D. Jr., Emaurois, C., Okaji, K., Yukihira, H., Iwase, A. and van Woesik, R. (2007) 'Palau's coral reefs show differential habitat recovery following the 1998-bleaching event', *Coral Reefs*, vol. 26, no. 2, pp. 319–332.

Goñi, R., Hilborn, R., Diaz, D., Mallol, S. and Adlerstein, S. (2010) 'Net contribution of spillover from a marine reserve to fishery catches', *Marine Ecology Progress Series*, vol. 400, pp. 233–243.

González-Correa, J. M., Bayle, J. T., Sánchez-Lizaso, J. L., Vallea, C., Sánchez-Jereza, P. and Ruizb, J. M. (2005) 'Recovery of deep *Posidonia oceanica* meadows degraded by trawling', *Journal of Experimental Marine Biology and Ecology*, vol. 320, no. 1, pp. 65–76.

Gorman, D. and Connell, S. D. (2009) 'Recovering subtidal forests in human-dominated landscapes', *Journal of Applied Ecology*, vol. 46, no. 6, pp. 1258–1265.

Gosse, E. (1906) *Father and Son*, Heinemann, London.

Gosse, P. H. (1865) *A Year at the Shore*, Alexander Strahan, London.

Goulletquer, P. (2004) *Cultured Aquatic Species Information Programme*. Ostrea edulis, FAO Fisheries and Aquaculture Department, Rome, www.fao.org/fishery/culturedspecies/Ostrea_edulis/en, accessed 23 December 2013.

Gray, J. S. (1977) 'Stability of benthic ecosystems', *Helgolander Wissenschaftliche Meeresuntersuchungen*, vol. 30, no. 1–4, pp. 427–444.

Gray, J. S. and McHardy, R. A. (1967) 'Swarming of hyperiid amphipods', *Nature*, vol. 215, no. 5096, p. 100.

Gray, J. S., Valderhaug, V. and Ugland, K. I. (1985) 'The stability of a benthic community of soft sediment', in P. E. Gibbs (ed.) *Proceedings of the 19th European Marine Biology Symposium*, Plymouth, Devon, UK, 16–21 September 1984, Cambridge University Press, Cambridge, UK.

Grebmeier, J. M., Overland, J. E., Moore, S. E., Farley, E. V., Carmack, E. C., Cooper, L. W., Frey, K. E., Helle, J. H., McLaughlin, F. A. and McNutt, S. L. (2006) 'A major ecosystem shift in the Northern Bering Sea', *Science*, vol. 311, no. 5766, pp. 1461–1464.

Green, B. S., Gardner, C., Linnane, A. and Hawthorne, P. J. (2010) 'The good, the bad and the recovery in an assisted migration', *PLoS ONE*, vol. 5, no. 11, e14160.

Greening, H. and Janicki, A. (2006) 'Toward reversal of eutrophic conditions in a subtropical estuary: water quality and seagrass response to nitrogen loading reductions in Tampa Bay, Florida USA', *Environmental Management*, vol. 38, no. 2, pp. 163–178.

Grorud-Colvert, K., Claudet, J., Carr, M. Caselle, J., Day, J., Friedlander, A., Lester, S. E., Lison de Loma, T., Tissot, B. and Malone, D. (2011) 'Networks – the assessment of marine reserve networks: guidelines for ecological evaluation', in J. Claudet (ed.) *Marine Protected Areas: A Multidisciplinary Approach*, Cambridge University Press, Cambridge, UK, pp. 293–321.

Guardiola, F. A., Cuesta, A., Meseguer, J. and Esteban, M. A. (2012) 'Risks of using antifouling biocides in aquaculture', *International Journal of Molecular Science*, vol. 13, no. 2, pp. 1541–1560.

Gubbay, S. and Knapman, P. A. (1999) *A Review of the Effects of Fishing within UK European Marine Sites*, English Nature, UK Marine SACs Project, Peterborough, UK.

Haapkylä, J., Ramade, F. and Salvat, B. (2007) 'Oil pollution on coral reefs: a review of the state of knowledge and management needs', *Vie et Milieu – Life and Environment*, vol. 57, no. 1–2, pp. 91–107.

Hagen, T. (1987) 'Sea urchin outbreaks and nematode epizootics in Vestfjorden, northern Norway', *Sarsia*, vol. 72, pp. 213–229.

Hale, S. S. (2010) 'Biogeographical patterns of marine benthic macroinvertebrates along the Atlantic coast of the northeastern USA', *Estuaries and Coasts*, vol. 33, no. 5, pp. 1039–1053.

Hall-Spencer, J. (1998) 'Conservation issues relating to maerl beds as habitats for molluscs', *Journal of Conchology*, Special Publication 2, pp. 271–286.

Hall-Spencer, J. M. and Moore, P. G. (2000) 'Scallop dredging has profound, long-term impacts on maerl habitats', *ICES Journal of Marine Science*, vol. 57, no. 5, pp. 1407–1415.

Hall-Spencer, J. M., Pike, J. and Munn, C. B. (2007) 'Diseases affect cold-water corals too: *Eunicella verrucosa* (Cnidaria: Gorgonacea) necrosis in SW England', *Diseases of Aquatic Organisms*, vol. 76, no. 2, pp. 87–97.

Hall-Spencer, J. M., Rodolfo-Metalpa, R., Martin, S., Ransome, E., Fine, M., Turner, S. M., Rowley, S. J., Tedesco, D. and Buia, M-C. (2008) 'Volcanic carbon dioxide vents show ecosystem effects of ocean acidification', *Nature*, vol. 454, no. 7200, pp. 96–99.

Halpern, B. S. (2003) 'The impact of marine reserves: do reserves work and does reserve size matter?', *Ecological Applications*, vol. 13, no. 1, pp. S117–S137.

Harris, J. A., Hobbs, R. J., Higgs, E. and Aronson, J. (2006) 'Ecological restoration and global climate change', *Restoration Ecology*, vol. 14, no 2, pp. 170–176.

Harrison, H. B., Williamson, D. H., Evans, R. D., Almany, G. R., Thorrold, S. R., Russ, G. R., Feldheim, K. A., van Herwerden, L., Planes, S., Srinivasan, M., Berumen, M. L. and Jones, G. P. (2012) 'Larval export from marine reserves and the recruitment benefit for fish and fisheries', *Current Biology*, vol. 22, no 11, pp. 1023–1028.

Harvell, C. D., Kim, K., Burkholder, J. M., Colwell, R. R., Epstein, P. R., Grimes, D. J., Hoffmann, E. E., Lipp, E. K., Osterhaus, A. D. M. E., Overstreet, R. M., Porter, J. W., Smith, G. W. and Vasta, G. R. (1999) 'Emerging marine diseases – climate links and anthropogenic factors', *Science*, vol. 285, no. 5433, pp. 1505–1510.

Harvell, D., Mitchell, C. E., Ward, J. R., Altizer, S., Dobson, A. P., Ostfeld, R. S. and Samuel, M. D. (2002) 'Climate warming and disease risks for terrestrial and marine biota', *Science*, vol. 296, no. 5576, pp. 2158–2162.

Harvey, W. H. (1857) *The Sea-Side Book: Being an Introduction to the Natural History of the British Coasts*, John Van Voorst, London.

Hawkins, S. J. and Southward, A. J. (1992) 'Lessons from the *Torrey Canyon* oil spill: recovery and stability of rocky shore communities', in G. W. Thayer (ed.) *Restoring the Nation's Marine Environment: Proceedings of the Symposium on Marine Habitat Restoration*, National Oceanic and Atmospheric Administration, Maryland Sea Grant College, Maryland, USA, pp. 584–631.

Hawkins, S. J., Allen, J. R. and Bray, S. (1999) 'Restoration of temperate marine and coastal ecosystems: nudging nature', *Aquatic Conservation: Marine & Freshwater Ecosystems*, vol. 9, no. 1, pp. 23–46.

Hawkins, S. J., Gibbs, P. E., Pope, N. D, Burt, G. R., Chesman, B. S., Bray, S., Proud, S. V., Spence, S. K., Southward, A. J. and Langston, W. J. (2002) 'Recovery of polluted ecosystems: the case for long-term studies', *Marine Environmental Research*, vol. 54, no. 3–5, pp. 215–222.

Hawkins, S. J., Sugden, H. E., Mieszkowska, N., Moore, P. J., Poloczanska, E., Leaper, R., Herbert, R. J. H., Genner, M. J., Moschella, P. S., Thompson, R. C., Jenkins, S. R., Southward, A. J. and Burrows, M. T. (2009) 'Consequences of climate-driven biodiversity changes for ecosystem functioning of North European rocky shores', *Marine Ecology Progress Series*, vol. 396, pp. 245–259.

Heinke, U. and Kowarik, I. (2010) 'What criteria should be used to select biodiversity indicators?', *Biodiversity Conservation*, vol. 19, no. 13, pp. 3769–3797.

Heip, C. (1989) 'The ecology of the estuaries of the Rhine, Meuse and Scheldt in the Netherlands', in J. D. Ros (ed.) *Topics in Marine Biology, 22nd European Marine Biology Symposium, Scientia Marina*, vol. 53, pp. 457–463.

Hewitt, C. L., Campbell, M. L., Thresher, R. E., Martin, R. B., Boyd, S., Cohen, B. F., Currie, D. R., Gomon, M. F., Keough, M. J., Lewis, J. A., Lockett, M. M., Mays, N., McArthur, M. A., O'Hara, T. D., Poore, G. C. B., Ross, D. J., Storey, M. J., Watson, J. E. and Wilson, R. S. (2004) 'Introduced and cryptogenic species in Port Phillip Bay, Victoria, Australia', *Marine Biology*, vol. 144, no. 1, pp. 183–202.

Hill, J. M., Marzialetti, S. and Pearce, B. (2011) *Recovery of Seabed Resources Following Marine Aggregate Extraction: Marine ALSF Science Monograph Series No. 2, MEPF 10/P148*, Cefas, Lowestoft, UK.

Hinz, H., Capasso, E., Lilley, M., Frost, M. and Jenkins, S. R. (2011) 'Temporal differences across a bio-geographical boundary reveal slow response of sub-littoral benthos to climate change', *Marine Ecology Progress Series*, vol. 423, pp. 69–82.

Hiscock, K. (1985) 'Aspects of the ecology of rocky sublittoral areas', in P. G. Moore and R. Seed (eds) *The Ecology of Rocky Coasts*, Hodder and Stoughton, London, pp. 290–328.

Hiscock, K. (1994) 'Marine communities at Lundy – origins, longevity and change', *Biological Journal of the Linnean Society*, vol. 51, no. 1–2, pp. 183–188.

Hiscock, K. (ed.) (1996) *Marine Nature Conservation Review: Rationale and Methods*, Joint Nature Conservation Committee, Peterborough, UK.

Hiscock, K. (1997) 'Use available data', *Marine Pollution Bulletin*, vol. 34, no. 2, pp. 74–77.

Hiscock, K. (1998a) *Marine Nature Conservation Review: Benthic Marine Ecosystems of Great Britain and the North-East Atlantic*, Joint Nature Conservation Committee, Peterborough, UK.

Hiscock, K. (1998b) *Biological Monitoring of Marine Special Areas of Conservation: A Review of Methods for Detecting Change*, Joint Nature Conservation Committee, Peterborough, UK.

Hiscock, K. (1999) 'Identifying marine "sensitive areas" – the importance of understanding life cycles', in M. Whitfield, J. Matthews and C. Reynolds (eds) *Aquatic Life Cycle Strategies: Survival in a Variable Environment*, Marine Biological Association of the UK, Plymouth, UK, pp. 139–149.

Hiscock, K. (2005) 'A re-assessment of rocky sublittoral biota at Hilsea Point Rock after fifty years', *Journal of the Marine Biological Association of the United Kingdom*, vol. 85, no. 4, pp. 1009–1010.

Hiscock, K. (2008a) 'Rocky shores of Lundy, 60 years on: the records of L.A. Harvey and initial comparisons', *Journal of the Lundy Field Society*, vol. 1, pp. 7–20.

Hiscock, K. (2008b) 'The role of marine protected areas for biodiversity conservation and for science', *Biologia Marina Mediterranea*, vol. 15, no. 1, pp. 457–462.

Hiscock, K. (2010) '"Mind the gap" – science that informs implementation of policy on marine protected areas', *Biologia Marina Mediterranea*, vol. 17, no. 1, pp. 16–22.

Hiscock, K. (2012) 'As if it was yesterday?', *Marine Scientist*, vol. 38, pp. 4–7.

Hiscock, K. and Mitchell, R. (1989) 'Practical methods of field assessment and conservation evaluation of nearshore/estuarine areas', in J. McManus and M. Elliott (eds) *Developments in Estuarine and Coastal Study Techniques*, Olsen and Olsen, Fredensborg, Denmark, pp. 53–56.

Hiscock, K. and Connor, D. W. (1991) *Benthic Marine Habitats and Communities in Great Britain: The Development of an MNCR Classification*, JNCC, Peterborough, UK.

Hiscock, K. and Tyler-Walters, H. (2006) 'Identifying sensitivity in marine ecosystems: the MarLIN programme', *Hydrobiologia*, vol. 555, pp. 309–320.

Hiscock, K. and Breckels, M. (2007) *Marine Biodiversity Hotspots in the UK: Their Identification and Protection*, WWF-UK, Godalming, UK.

Hiscock, K., Southward, A. J., Tittley, I. and Hawkins, S. (2004) 'Effect of changing temperature on benthic marine life in Britain and Ireland', *Aquatic Conservation*, vol. 14, no. 4, pp. 333–362.

Hiscock, K., Marshall, C., Sewell, J. and Hawkins, S. J. (2006) *The Structure and Functioning of Marine Ecosystems: An Environmental Protection and Management Perspective: Report to English Nature from the Marine Biological Association*, English Nature Research Report 699, Marine Biological Association, Plymouth, UK.

Hiscock, K., Sharrock, S., Highfield, J. and Snelling, D. (2010) 'Colonisation of an artificial reef in south-west England – ex-HMS *Scylla*', *Journal of the Marine Biological Association of the United Kingdom*, vol. 90, no. 1, pp. 69–94.

Hiscock, K., Bayley, D., Pade, N., Cox, E. and Lacey, C. (2011) 'A recovery/conservation programme for marine species of conservation importance', Report to Natural England from the Marine Biological Association and SMRU Ltd., Natural England Commissioned Research Report NECR065.

Hiscock, K., Bayley, D., Pade, N., Lacey, C., Cox, E. and Enever, R. (2013) 'Prioritizing action for recovery and conservation of marine species: a case study based on species of conservation importance around England', *Aquatic Conservation: Marine and Freshwater Ecosystems*, vol. 23, no. 1, pp. 88–110.

Hiscock, S. (1986) *Skomer Marine Reserve Subtidal Monitoring Project: Algal Results, August 1984 to February 1986*, Nature Conservancy Council, Peterborough, UK.

HM Government (2012) *Marine Strategy Part One: UK Initial Assessment and Good Environmental Status*, Defra, London.

Hoare, R. and Hiscock, K. (1974) 'An ecological survey of the rocky coast adjacent to the effluent of a bromine extraction plant', *Estuarine and Coastal Marine Science*, vol. 2, no. 4,, pp. 337–348.

Holme, N. A. (1961) 'The bottom fauna of the English Channel', *Journal of the Marine Biological Association of the United Kingdom*, vol. 41, no. 2, pp. 397–461.

Holme, N. A. (1966) 'The bottom fauna of the English Channel. Part II', *Journal of the Marine Biological Association of the United Kingdom*, vol. 46, no. 2, pp. 401–493.

Hore, J. P. and Jex, E. (1880) *The Deterioration of Oyster and Trawl Fisheries of England: Its Causes and Remedy*, Elliot Stock, London.

Hoskin, M. G., Coleman, R. A., von Carlshausen, E. and Davis, C. M. (2011) 'Variable population responses by large decapods crustaceans to the establishment of a temperate marine no-take zone', *Canadian Journal of Fisheries and Aquatic Sciences*, vol. 68, no. 2, pp. 185–200.

Houk, P. and Raubani, J. (2010) '*Acanthaster planci* outbreaks in Vanuatu coincide with ocean productivity, furthering trends throughout the Pacific Ocean', *Journal of Oceanography*, vol. 66, no 3, pp. 435–438.

Howarth, L. M., Roberts, C. M., Thurstan, R. H. and Stewart, B. D. (2013) 'The unintended consequences of simplifying the sea: making the case for complexity', *Fish and Fisheries*, doi: 10.1111/faf.12041.

Hughes, A. R., Bando, K. J., Rodriguez, L. F. and Williams, S. L. (2004) 'Relative effects of grazers and nutrients on seagrasses: a meta-analysis approach', *Marine Ecology Progress Series*, vol. 282, pp. 87–99.

Hughes, T. P., Bellwood, D. R., Folke, C., Steneck, R. S. and Wilson, J. (2005) 'New paradigms for supporting the resilience of marine ecosystems', *TRENDS in Ecology and Evolution*, vol. 20, no. 7, pp. 380–386.

Hughes, T. P., Rodrigues, M. J., Bellwood, D. R., Ceccarelli, D., Hoegh-Guldberg, O., McCook, L., Moltschaniwskyj, N., Pratchett, M. S., Steneck, R. S. and Willis, B. (2007) 'Phase shifts, herbivory, and the resilience of coral reefs to climate change', *Current Biology*, vol. 17, no. 4, pp. 360–365.

Hutching, G. and Walrond, C. (2009) 'Marine conservation – Māori and the sea', *Te Ara – the Encyclopedia of New Zealand*, www.TeAra.govt.nz/en/marine-conservation/1, accessed 2 August 2013.

IEEM (2010) *Guidelines of Ecological Impact Assessment in Britain and Ireland, Marine and Coastal*, Institute of Ecology and Environmental Management, London.

IGBP, IOC, SCOR (2013) *Ocean Acidification Summary for Policymakers – Third Symposium on the Ocean in a High-CO_2 World*, International Geosphere-Biosphere Programme, Stockholm, Sweden.

Iliffe, T. M. and Kornicker, L. S. (2009) 'Worldwide diving discoveries of living fossil animals from the depths of anchialine and marine caves', *Smithsonian Contributions to the Marine Sciences*, vol. 38, pp. 270–280.

IPIECA (1991) *Guidelines on Biological Impacts of Oil Pollution*, IPIECA, London.

IUCN (2001) *IUCN Red List Categories and Criteria: Version 3.1*, IUCN Species Survival Commission, IUCN, Gland, Switzerland and Cambridge, UK.

IUCN (2007) *Establishing Networks of Marine Protected Areas: A Guide for Developing National and Regional Capacity for Building MPA Networks. Non-technical summary report*, IUCN, Gland, Switzerland and Cambridge, UK.

IUCN (2013) 'The IUCN Red List of Threatened Species. Version 2013.2', www.iucnredlist.org, accessed 11 January 2014.

IUCN-WCPA (2008) *Establishing Resilient Marine Protected Area Networks: Making it Happen*, IUCN-WCPA, National Oceanic and Atmospheric Administration and The Nature Conservancy, Washington, DC.

Jackson, E. L., Langmead, O., Evans, J., Wilkes, P., Seeley, B., Lear, D. and Tyler-Walters, H. (2010) *Mapping Marine Benthic Biodiversity in Wales*, Countryside Council for Wales, Bangor.

Jackson, J. B. C., Kirby, M. X., Berger, W. H., Bjorndal, K. A., Botsford, L. W., Bourque, B. J., Bradbury, R. H., Cooke, R., Erlandson, J., Estes, J. A., Hughes, T. P., Kidwell, S., Lange, C. B., Lenihan, H. S., Pandolfi, J. M., Peterson, C. H., Steneck, R. S., Tegner, M. J. and Warner, R. R. (2001) 'Historical overfishing and the recent collapse of coastal ecosystems', *Science*, vol. 293, no. 5530, pp. 629–638.

Jensen, T., van de Bildt, M., Dietz, H. H., Andersen, T. H., Hammer, A. S., Kuiken, T. and Osterhaus, A. (2002) 'Another phocine distemper outbreak in Europe', *Science*, vol. 297, no. 5579, p. 209.

Jessopp, M. J. and McAllen, R. J. (2007) 'Water retention and limited larval dispersal: implications for short and long distance dispersers in marine reserves', *Marine Ecology Progress Series*, vol. 333, pp. 27–36.

Jones, H. P. and Schmitz, O. J. (2009) 'Rapid recovery of damaged ecosystems', *PLoS ONE*, vol. 4, no. 5, e5653.

Jones, P. J. S. (2014) *Governing Marine Protected Areas: Resilience Through Diversity*, Earthscan, London.

Jones, P. J. S. and Carpenter, A. (2009) 'Crossing the divide: the challenges of designing an ecologically coherent and representative network of MPAs for the UK', *Marine Policy*, vol. 33, no 5, pp. 737–743.

Kain, J. M. (1975) 'Algal recolonization of some cleared subtidal areas', *Journal of Ecology*, vol. 63, no. 3, pp. 739–765.

Kaiser, M. J., Attrill, M. J., Jennings, S., Thomas, D. N., Barnes, D. K. A., Brierley, A. S., Hiddink, J. G., Kaartokallio, H., Polunin, N. V. C. and Raffaelli, D. G. (2011) *Marine Ecology: Processes, Systems, and Impacts*, Oxford University Press, Oxford.

Kang, C.-K., Choy, E. J., Son, Y., Lee, J.-Y., Kim, J., Kim, Y. and Lee, K.-S. (2008) 'Food web structure of a restored macroalgal bed in the eastern Korean peninsula determined by C and N stable isotope analyses', *Marine Biology*, vol. 153, no. 6, pp. 1181–1198.

Kay, M. C., Lenihan, H. S., Kotchen, M. J. and Miller, C. J. (2012) 'Effects of marine reserves on California spiny lobster are robust and modified by fine-scale habitat features and distance from reserve borders', *Marine Ecology Progress Series*, vol. 451 pp. 137–150.

Keith, D. A., Rodríguez, J. P., Rodríguez-Clark, K. M., Nicholson, E., Aapala, K., Alonso, A., Asmussen, M., Bachman, S., Basset, A., Barrow, E. G.. Benson, J. S., Bishop, M. J., Bonifacio, R., Brooks, T. M., Burgman. M. A., Comer, P., Comín, F. A., Essl, F., Faber-Langendoen, D., Fairweather, P. G., Holdaway, R. J., Jennings, M., Kingsford, R. T., Lester, R. E., MacNally, R., McCarthy, M. A., Moat, J., Oliveira-Miranda, A. A., Pisanu, P., Poulin, B., Regan, T. J., Riecken, U., Spalding, M. D. and Zambrano-Martínez, S. (2013) 'Scientific foundations for an IUCN Red List of ecosystems', *PLoS ONE*, vol. 8, no. 5, e62111.

Kinlan, B. P. and Gaines, S. D. (2003) 'Propagule dispersal in marine and terrestrial environments: a community perspective', *Ecology*, vol. 84, no. 8, pp. 2007–2020.

Kirby, M. X. and Miller, H. M. (2005) 'Response of a benthic suspension feeder (*Crassostrea virginica* Gmelin) to three centuries of anthropogenic eutrophication in Chesapeake Bay', *Estuarine, Coastal and Shelf Science*, vol. 62, no. 4, pp. 679–689.

Kirlin, J., Caldwell, M., Gleason, M., Weber, M., Ugoretz, J., Fox E. and Miller-Henson, M. (2013) 'California's Marine Life Protection Act Initiative: supporting implementation of legislation establishing a statewide network of marine protected areas', *Ocean & Coastal Management*, vol. 74, pp. 3–13.

Knowlton, N. (2004) 'Multiple "stable" states and the conservation of marine ecosystems', *Progress in Oceanography*, vol. 60, no. 2–4, pp. 387–396.

Kortsch, S., Primicerio, R., Beuchel, F., Renaud, P. E., Rodrigues, J., Lønneb, O. J. and Gulliksen, B. (2012) 'Climate-driven regime shifts in Arctic marine benthos', *PNAS*, vol. 109, no. 35, pp. 14052–14057.

Koslow, J. A., Gowlette-Holmes, K., Lowret, J. K., O'Hara, T., Poore, G. C. B. and Williams, A. (2001) 'Seamount benthic macrofauna off southern Tasmania: community structure and impacts of trawling', *Marine Ecology Progress Series*, vol. 213, pp. 111–125.

Kraberg, A. C., Wasmund, N., Vanaverbeke, J., Schiedek, D., Wiltshire, K. H. and Mieszkowska, N. (2011) Regime shifts in the marine environment: the scientific basis and political context', *Marine Pollution Bulletin*, vol. 62, no. 1, pp. 7–20.

Kraufvelin, P., Moy, F. E., Christie, H. and Bokn, T. L. (2006) 'Nutrient addition to experimental rocky shores communities revisited: delayed responses, rapid recovery', *Ecosystems*, vol. 9, no. 7, pp. 1–19.

Krkošek, M., Crawford, W., Revie, P. G., Skilbrei, O. T., Finstad, B. and Todd, C. D. (2012) 'Impact of parasites on salmon recruitment in the Northeast Atlantic Ocean', *Proceedings of the Royal Society B*, vol. 280, no. 1750, 20122359.

Kroeker, J. J., Kordas, R. L., Crim, R., Hendriks, I. E., Ramajo, L., Singh, G. S., Duarte, C. M. and Gattuso, J.-P. (2013) 'Impacts of ocean acidification on marine organisms: quantifying sensitivities and interaction with warming', *Global Change Biology*, vol. 19, no. 6, pp. 1884–1896.

Lafferty, K. D. (1997) 'Environmental parasitology: what can parasites tell us about human impacts on the environment?', *Parasitology Today*, vol. 13, no. 7, pp. 251–255.

Lafferty, K. D. and Holt, R. D. (2003) 'How should environmental stress affect the population dynamics of disease?', *Ecology Letters*, vol. 6, no. 7, pp. 654–664.

Laffoley, D. d'A., Maltby, E., Vincent, M. A., Mee, L., Dunn, E., Gilliland, P., Hamer, J. P, Mortimer,

D. and Pound, D. (2004) *The Ecosystem Approach: Coherent Actions for Marine and Coastal Environments. A Report to the UK Government*, English Nature, Peterborough, UK.

Langlois, T. J. and Ballantine, W. J. (2005) 'Marine ecological research in New Zealand: developing predictive models through the study of no-take marine reserves', *Conservation Biology*, vol. 19, no. 6, pp. 1763–1770.

Langlois, T. J., Anderson, M. J. and Babcock, R. C. (2006a) 'Inconsistent effects of reefs on different size classes of macrofauna in adjacent sand habitats', *Journal of Experimental Marine Biology and Ecology*, vol. 334, pp. 269–282.

Langlois, T. J., Anderson, M. J., Babcock, R. C. and Kato, S. (2006b) 'Marine reserves demonstrate trophic interactions across habitats', *Oecologia*, vol. 147, no. 1, pp. 134–140.

Langmead, O. and Jackson, E. (2010) 'Large scale patterns of marine biodiversity: an evidence-based approach for prioritizing areas for protection', *Biologia Marina Mediterranea*, vol. 17, pp. 11–14.

Langmead, O., McQuatters-Gollop, A. and Mee, L. (eds) (2007) *European Lifestyles and Marine Ecosystems: Exploring Challenges for Managing Europe's Seas*, University of Plymouth Marine Institute, Plymouth, UK.

Lavigne, D. M. and Schmitz, O. J. (1990) 'Global warming and increasing population densities: a prescription for seal plagues', *Marine Pollution Bulletin*, vol. 21, no. 6, pp. 280–284.

Leinaas, H. P. and Christie, H. (1996) 'Effects of removing sea urchins (*Strongylocentrotus droebachiensis*): stability of the barren state and succession of kelp forest recovery in the east Atlantic', *Oecologia*, vol. 105, no. 4, pp. 524–536.

Leleu, K., Remy-Zephir, B., Grace, R. and Costello, M. J. (2012) 'Mapping habitats in a marine reserve showed how a 30-year trophic cascade altered ecosystem structure', *Biological Conservation*, vol. 155, pp. 193–201.

Lester, S. E., Halpern, B. S., Grorud-Colvert, K., Jane Lubchenco, J., Ruttenberg, B. I., Gaines, S. D., Airamé, S. and Warner, R. R. (2009) 'Biological effects within no-take marine reserves: a global synthesis', *Marine Ecology Progress Series*, vol. 384, pp. 33–46.

Levell, D., Rostron, D. and Dixon, I. (1989) 'Sediment macrobenthic communities from oil ports to offshore oilfields', in B. Dicks (ed.) *Ecological Impacts of the Oil Industry*, Institute of Petroleum, London, pp. 97–134.

Lewis, J. R. (1964) *The Ecology of Rocky Shores*, English Universities Press, London.

Lieberknecht, L. M., Vincent, M. A. and Connor, D. W. (2004) *The Irish Sea Pilot – Report on the Identification of Nationally Important Marine Features in the Irish Sea*, Joint Nature Conservation Committee, Peterborough, UK.

Lincoln, R., Boxshall, G. and Clark, P. (1998) *A Dictionary of Ecology, Evolution and Systematics*, Cambridge University Press, Cambridge, UK.

Lindeboom, H. J. and de Groot, S. J. (1998) *IMPACT-II: The Effects of Different Types of Fisheries on the North Sea and Irish Sea Benthic Ecosystems*, NIOZ Report 1998–1/RIVO-DLO Report C003/98, Netherlands Institute for Sea Research, Den Burg, Texel.

Lindeboom, H. J., Kouwenhoven, H. J., Bergman, M. J. N., Bouma, S., Brasseur, S., Daan, R., Fijn, R. C., de Haan, D., Dirksen, S., van Hal, R., Lambers, H. R., ter Hofstede, R., Krijgsveld, K. L., Leopold, M. and Scheidat, M. (2011) 'Short-term ecological effects of an offshore wind farm in the Dutch coastal zone; a compilation', *Environmental Research Letters*, vol. 6, no. 3, 035101.

Ling, S. D. and Johnson, C. R. (2012) 'Marine reserves reduce risk of climate-driven phase shift by reinstating size- and habitat-specific trophic interactions', *Ecological Applications*, vol. 22, no. 4, pp. 1232–1245.

Ling, S. D., Johnson, C. R., Frusher, S. D. and Ridgway, K. R. (2009) 'Overfishing reduces resilience of kelp beds to climate-driven catastrophic phase shift', *PNAS*, vol. 106, no. 52, pp. 22341–22345.

Lipp, E. K., Huq, A. and Colwell, R. R. (2002) 'Effects of global climate on infectious disease: the cholera model', *Clinical Microbiology Reviews*, vol. 15, no. 4, pp. 757–770.

Liquete, C., Piroddi, C., Drakou, E. G., Gurney, L., Katsanevakis, S., Charef, A. and Egoh, B. (2013)

'Current status and future prospects for the assessment of marine and coastal ecosystem services: a systematic review', *PLoS ONE*, vol. 8, no. 7, e67737.

Llope, M., Daskalov, G. M., Rouyer, T. A., Mihneva, V., Chan, K.-S., Grishin, A. N. and Stenseth, N. (2011) 'Overfishing of top predators eroded the resilience of the Black Sea system regardless of the climate and anthropogenic conditions', *Global Change Biology*, vol. 17, no. 3, pp. 1251–1265.

Long, S. P. and Mason, C. F. (1983) *Saltmarsh Ecology*, Blackie, Glasgow.

Lotze, H. K., Coll, M., Magera, A. M. Ward-Paige, C. and Airoldi, L. (2011) 'Recovery of marine animal populations and ecosystems', *TRENDS in Ecology and Evolution*, vol. 26, no. 11, pp. 595–605.

Lotze, H. K., Lenihan, H. S., Bourque, B. J., Bradbury, R. H., Cooke, R. G., Kay, M. C., Kidwell, S. M., Kirby, M. X., Peterson, C. H. and Jackson, J. B. C. (2006) 'Depletion, degradation, and recovery potential of estuaries and coastal seas', *Science*, vol. 312, no. 5780, pp. 1806–1809.

Lowe, S., Browne, M., Boudjelas, S. and De Poorter, M. (2000) *100 of the World's Worst Invasive Alien Species: A Selection from the Global Invasive Species Database*, Invasive Species Specialist Group of the Species Survival Commission of IUCN, Auckland, New Zealand.

Loya, Y. and Rinkevich, B. (1980) 'Effects of oil pollution on coral reef communities', *Marine Ecology Progress Series*, vol. 3, pp. 167–180.

Luckenbach, M., Shumway, S. and Sellner, K. (1993) '"Non-toxic" dinoflagellate bloom effects on oyster culture in Chesapeake Bay', *Journal of Shellfish Research*, vol. 12, p. 142.

Lundälv, T. (1971) 'Quantitative studies on rocky-bottom biocenoses by underwater photogrammetry: a methodological study', *Thallasia Jugoslavica*, vol. 7, pp. 201–208.

Lundälv, T. (1985) 'Detection of long-term trends in rocky sublittoral communities: representativeness of fixed sites', in P. G. Moore and R. Seed (eds) *The Ecology of Rocky Coasts*, Hodder and Stoughton, London, pp. 329–345.

Macdonald, D. S, Little, M., Eno, N. C. and Hiscock, K. (1996) 'Disturbance of benthic species by fishing activities: a sensitivity index', *Aquatic Conservation: Marine & Freshwater Ecosystems*, vol. 6, no. 4, pp. 257–268.

McLeod, K. L. and Leslie, H. M. (eds) (2009) *Ecosystem-Based Management for the Oceans*, Island Press, Washington DC.

McLusky, D. S. (1993) 'Marine and estuarine gradients – an overview', *Netherlands Journal of Aquatic Ecology*, vol. 27, no. 2–4, pp. 489–493.

McQuatters-Gollop, A. (2012) 'Challenges for implementing the Marine Strategy Framework Directive in a climate of macroecological change', *Philosophical Transactions of the Royal Society A*, vol. 370, no. 1980, pp. 5636–5655.

Makins, M. (1991) *Collins English Dictionary*, 3rd edition, HarperCollins, Glasgow.

Margules, C. R. and Pressey, R. L. (2000) 'Systematic conservation planning', *Nature*, vol. 405, no. 6783, 243–253.

Marine Biological Association (1957) *Plymouth Marine Fauna*, Marine Biological Association, Plymouth, UK.

Marine Ecological Surveys Limited, Ellwood, H., Askew, N., Cameron, A. and McBreen, F. (2011) *UKSeaMap 2010. Technical Report 7. External Review of Confidence Assessment Methods*, Joint Nature Conservation Committee, Peterborough, UK.

Meijer, A. J. M. and Waardenburg, H. W. (1994) 'Tidal reduction and its effects on intertidal hard-substrate communities in the Oosterschelde estuary', *Hydrobiologia*, vol 282/283, pp 281–298.

Micheli, F., Saenz-Arroyo, A., Greenley, A., Vasquez, L., Montes, J. A. E., Rossetto, M. and De Leo, G. A. (2012) 'Evidence that marine reserves enhance resilience to climatic impacts', *PLoS ONE*, vol. 7, no. 7, e40832.

Mieszkowska, N., Kendall, M. A., Hawkins, S. J., Leaper, R., Williamson, P., Hardman-Mountford, N. J. and Southward, A. J. (2006) 'Changes in the range of some common rocky shore species in Britain – a response to climate change?', *Hydrobiologia*, vol. 555, pp. 241–251.

Miller, M. W., Valdivia, A., Kramer, K. L. Mason, B., Williams, D. E. and Johnston, L. (2009)

'Alternate benthic assemblages on reef restoration structures and cascading effects on coral settlement', *Marine Ecology Progress Series*, vol. 387, pp. 147–156.

Mills, E. L. (1969) 'The community concept in marine zoology, with comments on continua and instability in some marine communities: a review', *Journal of the Fisheries Boards of Canada*, vol. 26, no. 6, pp. 1415–1428.

Mitchell, R. (1987) *Conservation of Marine Benthic Biocenoses in the North Sea and the Baltic: A Framework for the Establishment of a European Network of Marine Protected Areas in the North Sea and the Baltic*, Council of Europe, Strasbourg.

Montefalcone, M., Albertelli, G., Morri, C., Parravicini, V. and Bianchi, C. N. (2009) 'Legal protection is not enough: *Posidonia oceanica* meadows in marine protected areas are not healthier than those in unprotected areas of the northwest Mediterranean Sea', *Marine Pollution Bulletin*, vol. 58, no. 4, pp. 515–519.

Moore, C. G., Harries, D. B., Cook, R. L., Hirst, N. E., Saunders, G. R., Kent, F. E. A., Trigg, C. and Lyndon, A. R. (2013) *The Distribution and Condition of Selected MPA Search Features within Lochs Alsh, Duich, Creran and Fyne*, Scottish Natural Heritage, Edinburgh, Scotland.

Moore, J. (2006) 'Long term ecological impacts of marine oil spills', in *Proceedings of the Interspill 2006 Conference*, held at London ExCeL, 21–23 March 2006, www.interspill.com/previous-events/2006/pdf/marine_ecological_doc.pdf, accessed 2 August 2013.

Moran, M. J. and Stephenson, P. C. (2000) 'Effects of otter trawling on macrobenthos of demersal scalefish fisheries on the continental shelf of north-western Australia', *ICES Journal of Marine Science*, vol. 57, no. 3, pp. 510–516.

Moreno, C. A., Sutherland, J. P. and Jara, F. H. (1984) 'Man as a predator in the intertidal zone of southern Chile', *Oikos*, vol. 46, pp. 359–364.

Moschella, P. S., Abbiati, M., Åberg, P., Airoldi, L., Anderson, J. M., Bacchiocchi, F., Bulleri, F., Dinesen, G. E., Frost, M., Gacia, E., Granhag, L., Jonsson, P. R., Satta, M. P., Sundelöf, A., Thompson, R. C. and Hawkins, S. J. (2005) 'Low-crested coastal defence structures as artificial habitats for marine life: using ecological criteria in design', *Coastal Engineering*, vol. 52, no. 10–11, pp. 1053–1071.

Mumby, P. J. (2006) 'Connectivity of reef fish between mangroves and coral reefs: algorithms for the design of marine reserves at seascape scales', *Biological Conservation*, vol. 128, no. 2, pp. 215–222.

Naeem, S., Loreau, M. and Inchausti, P. (2004) 'Biodiversity and ecosystem functioning: the emergence of a synthetic ecological framework', in M. Loreau, S. Naeem and P. Inchausti (eds) *Biodiversity and Ecosystem Functioning*, Oxford University Press, Oxford, pp. 3–11.

Natural England and Joint Nature Conservation Committee (2010) *Marine Conservation Zone Project: Ecological Network Guidance*, Natural England and Joint Nature Conservation Committee, Peterborough, UK.

Nature Conservancy Council (1984) *Nature Conservation in Great Britain*, Nature Conservancy Council, Peterborough, UK.

Neira, C., Mendoza, G., Levin, L. A., Zirino, A., Delgadillo-Hinojosa, F., Porrachia, M. and Deheyn, D. D. (2011) 'Macrobenthic community response to copper in Shelter Island Yacht Basin, San Diego Bay, California', *Marine Pollution Bulletin*, vol. 62, no. 4, pp. 701–717.

Neubert, M. G. (2003) 'Marine reserves and optimal harvesting', *Ecological Letters*, vol. 6, no. 9, pp. 843–849.

Newell, R. C. and Woodcock, T. A. (eds) (2013) *Aggregate Dredging and the Marine Environment: An Overview of Recent Research and Current Industry Practice*, The Crown Estate, London.

Nichols, F. H. and Thompson, J. K. (1985) 'Time scales of change in the San Francisco Bay benthos', *Hydrobiologia*, vol. 129, pp. 121–138.

Nienhuis, P. H. and Smaal, A. C. (eds) (1994) 'The Oosterschelde Estuary (The Netherlands): a case-study of a changing ecosystem', *Hydrobiologia*, vol. 282/283, pp. 1–14.

Norman, M., Román, G. and Strand, Ø. (2006) 'European aquaculture', *Developments in Aquaculture and Fisheries Science*, vol. 35, no. 20, pp. 1059–1066.

Nozères, C., Vandepitte, L., Appeltans, W. and Kennedy, M. (2012) *Best Practice Guidelines in the Development and Maintenance of Regional Marine Species Checklists, Version 1.0, released August 2012*, Global Biodiversity Information Facility, Copenhagen.

Nybakken, J. W. (2001) *Marine Biology: An Ecological Approach*, 5th edition, Benjamin Cummings, San Francisco.

Nyström, M., Folke, C. and Moberg, F. (2000) 'Coral reef disturbance and resilience in a human-dominated environment', *TRENDS in Ecology and Evolution*, vol. 15, no. 10, pp. 413–417.

O'Gorman, E. J., Enright, R. A. and Emmerson, M. C. (2008) 'Predator diversity enhances secondary production and decreases the likelihood of trophic cascades', *Oecologia*, vol. 158, no. 3, pp. 557–567.

O'Gorman, E. J., Yearsley, J. M., Crowe, T. P., Emmerson, M. C., Jacob, U. and Petchey, O. L. (2010) 'Loss of functionally unique species may gradually undermine ecosystems', *Proceedings of the Royal Society B*, vol. 278, pp. 1886–1893.

Olesen, B. and Sand-Jensen, K. (1994) 'Demography of shallow eelgrass (*Zostera marina*) populations – shoot dynamics and biomass development', *Journal of Ecology*, vol. 82, pp. 379–390.

Olsen, E. M., Johnson, D., Weaver, P., Goñi, R., Ribeiro, M. C., Rabaut, M., Macpherson, E., Pelletier, D., Fonseca, L., Katsanevakis, S. and Zaharia, T. (2013) *Achieving Ecologically Coherent MPA Networks in Europe: Science Needs and Priorities: Marine Board Position Paper 18*, European Marine Board Working Group on Marine Protected Areas, European Marine Board, Ostend, Belgium.

Orth, R. J., Luckenbach, M. L., Marion, S. R., Moore, K. A. and Wilcox, D. J. (2006) 'Seagrass recovery in the Delmarva Coastal Bays, USA', *Aquatic Botany*, vol. 84, pp. 26–36.

Osinga, R., Lewis, W. E., Wopereis, J. L. M., Vriezen, C. and van Duyl, F. C. (1995) 'Effects of the sea urchin *Echinocardium cordatum* on oxygen uptake and sulphate reduction in experimental benthic systems under increasing organic loading', *Ophelia*, vol. 41, no. 1, pp. 221–236.

Osman, R. W. and Whitlatch, R. B. (1998) 'Local control of recruitment in an epifaunal community and the consequences to colonization processes', *Hydrobiologia*, vol. 375/376, pp. 113–123.

OSPAR (2007) *Background Document to Support the Assessment of whether the OSPAR Network of Marine Protected Areas is Ecologically Coherent*, OSPAR Commission, London.

OSPAR (2008) *OSPAR List of Threatened and/or Declining Species and Habitats*, Publication Number: 2008–6, OSPAR Commission, London.

OSPAR (2012) *2011 Status Report on the OSPAR Network of Marine Protected Areas*, Publication Number: 577/2012, OSPAR Commission, London.

OSPAR (2013) *2012 Status Report on the OSPAR Network of Marine Protected Areas*, Publication Number: 618/2013, OSPAR Commission, London.

Padilla, D. K. (2010) 'Context-dependant impacts of a non-native ecosystem engineer, the Pacific oyster *Crassostrea gigas*', *Integrative and Comparative Biology*, vol. 50, no. 2, pp. 213–225.

Paine, R. T. (1994) *Marine Rocky Shores and Community Ecology: An Experimentalists Perspective*, Excellence in Ecology Series, no. 4, Ecology Institute, Oldendorf, Germany.

Palumbi, S. R. (2003) 'Population genetics, demographic connectivity, and the design of marine reserves', *Ecological Applications*, vol. 13, no. 1, Supplement, pp. S146–S158.

Parnell, P. E., Dayton, P. K., Lennert-Cody, C. L., Rasmussen, L. L. and Leichter, J. J. (2006) 'Marine reserve design: optimal size, habitats, species affinities, diversity, and ocean microclimate', *Ecological Applications*, vol. 16, no. 3, pp. 945–962.

Parravicini, V., Micheli, F., Montefalcone, M., Morri, C., Villa, E., Castellano, M., Povero, P. and Bianchi, C. N. (2013) 'Conserving biodiversity in a human-dominated world: degradation of marine sessile communities within a protected area with conflicting human uses', *PLoS ONE*, vol. 8, no. 10, e75767.

Parsons, E. C. M., Dolman, S. J., Wright, A. J., Rose, N. A. and Burns, W. C. (2008) 'Navy sonar and cetaceans: how much does the gun need to smoke before we act?', *Marine Pollution Bulletin*, vol. 56, no. 7, pp. 1248–1257.

Pauly, D. (1995) 'Anecdotes and the shifting baseline syndrome of fisheries', *TRENDS in Ecology and Evolution*, vol. 10, no. 10, p. 430.

Pauly, D. (2005) 'The ecology of fishing down marine food webs', *Society for Conservation Biology Newsletter*, vol. 12, no. 4, 2pp.

Pauly, D., Christensen, V., Dalsgaard, J., Froese, R. and Torres, F., Jr. (1998) 'Fishing down marine food webs', *Science*, vol. 279, no. 5352, pp. 860–863.

Pawson, M. G. (1995) *Biogeographical Identification of English Channel Fish and Shellfish Stocks, Fisheries Research Technical Report No. 99*, Ministry of Agriculture Fisheries and Food Directorate of Fisheries Research, Lowestoft, UK.

Pearsall, J. (ed.) (1999) *Concise Oxford Dictionary*, 10th edition, Oxford University Press, Oxford.

Pearson, R. G. (1981) 'Recovery and recolonization of coral reefs', *Marine Ecology Progress Series*, vol. 4, pp. 103–122.

Pearson, T. H. and Rosenberg, R. (1978) 'Macrobenthic succession in relation to organic enrichment and pollution of the marine environment', *Oceanography and Marine Biology: An Annual Review*, vol. 16, pp. 229–311.

Pearson, T. H., Josefson, A. B. and Rosenberg, R. (1985) 'Petersen's benthic stations revisited. I. Is the Kattegat becoming eutrophic?' *Journal of Experimental Marine Biology and Ecology*, vol. 92, pp. 157–206.

Peck, L. S., Morley, S. A., Richards, J. and Clark, M. S. (2014) 'Acclimation and thermal tolerance in Antarctic marine ectotherms', *Journal of Experimental Biology*, vol. 217, no. 1, pp. 16–22.

Pelc, R., Gaines, S. D., Warner, R. R. and Paris, C. B. (2010) 'Detecting larval export from marine reserves', *PNAS*, vol. 107, no. 43, pp. 18266–18271.

Perkol-Finkel, S. and Benayahu, Y. (2005) 'Recruitment of benthic organisms onto a planned artificial reef: shifts in community structure one decade post-deployment', *Marine Environmental Research*, vol. 59, no. 2, pp. 79–99.

Perkol-Finkel, S., Shaskar, N. and Benayahu, Y. (2006) 'Can artificial reefs mimic natural reef communities? The roles of structural features and age', *Marine Environmental Research*, vol. 61, no. 2, pp. 121–135.

Petchey, O. and Gaston, K. (2009) 'Effects on ecosystem resilience of biodiversity, extinctions, and the structure of regional species pools', *Theoretical Ecology*, vol. 2, no. 3, pp. 177–187.

Petersen, C. G. J. (1914[1913]) *Valuation of the sea. II. The animal communities of the sea-bottom and their importance for marine zoogeography: Report of the Danish Biological Station, 21*, pp. 1–44 and appendices 1–67.

Pitcher, C. R., Lawton, P., Ellis, N., Smith, S. J., Incze, L. S., Wei, C.-L., Greenlaw, M. E., Wolff, N. H., Sameoto, J. A and Snelgrove, P. V. R. (2012) 'Exploring the role of environmental variables in shaping patterns of seabed biodiversity composition in regional-scale ecosystems', *Journal of Applied Ecology*, vol. 49, no. 3, pp. 670–679.

Planes, S., Jones, G. P. and Thorrold, S. R. (2009) 'Larval dispersal connects fish populations in a network of marine protected areas', *Proceedings of the National Academy of Sciences of the United States of America*, vol. 106, pp. 5693–5697.

Poloczanska, E. S., Brown, C. J., Sydeman, W. J., Kiessling, W., Schoeman, D. S., Moore, P. J., Brander, K., Bruno, J. F., Buckley, L. B., Burrows, M. T., Duarte, C. M., Halpern, B. S., Holding, J., Kappel, C. V., O'Connor, M. I., Pandolfi, J. M., Parmesan, C., Schwing, F., Thompson, S. A. and Richardson, A. J. (2013) 'Global imprint of climate change on marine life', *Nature Climate Change*, vol. 3, no. 10, pp. 919–925

Pranovi, F., Raicevich, S., Franceschini, G., Farrace, M. G. and Giovanardi, O. (2000) 'Rapido trawling in the northern Adriatic Sea: effects on benthic communities in an experimental area', *ICES Journal of Marine Science*, vol. 57, no. 3, pp. 517–524.

Qui, W. and Jones, P. J. S. (2013) 'The emerging policy landscape for marine spatial planning in Europe', *Marine Policy*, vol. 39, pp. 182–190.

Quintino, V., Freitas, R., Mamede, R., Ricardo, F., Rodrigues, A. M., Mota, J., Pérez-Ruzafa, Á. and

Marcos, C. (2010) 'Remote sensing of underwater vegetation using single-beam acoustics', *ICES Journal of Marine Science*, vol. 67, no. 3, pp. 594–605.

Raffaelli, D. and Hawkins, S. (1996) *Intertidal Ecology*, Chapman and Hall, London.

Rahel, F. J. (1990) 'The hierarchical nature of community persistence: a problem of scale', *American Naturalist*, vol. 136, no. 3, pp. 328–344.

Raymundo, L. J., Maypa, A. P., Gomex, E. D and Cadiz, P. (2007) 'Can dynamite-blasted reefs recover? A novel low-tech approach to stimulating natural recovery in fish and coral populations', *Marine Pollution Bulletin*, vol. 54, no. 7, pp. 1009–1019.

Rees, H. L., Waldock, R., Matthiessen, P. and Pendle, M. A. (2001) 'Improvements in the epifauna of the Crouch estuary (United Kingdom) following a decline in TBT concentrations', *Marine Pollution Bulletin*, vol. 42, no. 2, pp. 137–144.

Reid, P. C., Fischer, A. C., Lewis-Brown, E., Meredith, M. P., Sparrow, M., Andersson, A. J., Antia, A., Bates, N. R., Bathmann, U., Beaugrand, G., Brix, H., Dye, S., Edwards, M., Furevik, T., Gangstø, R., Hátún, H., Hopcroft, R. R., Kendall, M., Kasten, S., Keeling, R., Le Quéré, C., Mackenzie, F. T., Malin, G., Mauritzen, C., Ólafsson, J., Paull, C., Rignot, E., Shimada, K., Vogt, M., Wallace, C., Wang, Z. and Washington, R. (2009) 'Impacts of the oceans on climate change', in David W. Sims (ed.) *Advances in Marine Biology, Volume 56*, pp. 1–150.

Reise, K. and Schubert, A. (1987) 'Macrobenthic turnover in the subtidal Wadden Sea: the Norderaue revisited after 60 years', *Helgoländer Meeresuntersuchungen*, vol. 41, no. 1, pp. 69–82.

Reise, K. and Kohlus, J. (2008) 'Seagrass recovery in the northern Wadden Sea?', *Helgoland Marine Research*, vol. 62, no. 1, pp. 77–84.

Reise, K., Herre, E. and Sturm, M. (2008) 'Mudflat biota since the 1930s: change beyond return?', *Helgoland Marine Research*, vol. 62, no. 1, pp. 13–22.

Ridgway, K. and Hill, K. (2009) 'The East Australian Current', in E. S. Poloczanska, A. J. Hobday and A. J. Richardson (eds) *A Marine Climate Change Impacts and Adaptation Report Card for Australia 2009*, NCCARF Publication 05/09.

Riegl, B. and Luke, K. E. (1998) 'Ecological parameters of dynamited reefs in the Northern Red Sea and their relevance to reef rehabilitation', *Marine Pollution Bulletin*, vol. 37, no. 8–12, pp. 488–498.

Rilov, G. and Galil, B. (2009) 'Marine bioinvasions in the Mediterranean Sea – history, distribution and ecology', in G. Rilov and J. A. Crooks (eds) *Biological Invasions in Marine Ecosystems*, Springer, Berlin, pp. 549–576.

Rindi, F. and Guirey, M. D. (2004) 'A long-term comparison of the benthic algal flora of Clare Island, County Mayo, western Ireland', *Biodiversity and Conservation*, vol. 13, no. 3, pp. 471–492.

Roberts, C. (2007) *The Unnatural History of the Sea*, Island Press, Washington DC.

Roberts, C. (2012) *Ocean of Life: How our Seas are Changing*, Penguin, London.

Roberts, C. and Hawkins, J. P. (2012) 'Establishment of fish stock recovery areas: report to the European Parliament Committee on Fisheries', www.europarl.europa.eu/studies, accessed 20 July 2013.

Roberts, C. M., Hawkins, J. P., Fletcher, J., Hands, S., Raab, K. and Ward, S. (2010) *Guidance on the size and spacing of Marine Protected Areas in England*, Natural England, Sheffield, UK.

Roberts, C., Branch, G., Bustamante, R., Castilla, J. C., Dugan, J., Halpern, B. S., Lafferty, K. D, Leslie, H., Lubchenco, J., Mcardle, D., Ruckelshaus, M. and Warner, R. R. (2003) 'Application of ecological criteria in selecting marine reserves and developing reserve networks', *Ecological Applications*, vol. 13, no. 1, S215–228.

Robinson, L. A. and Frid, C. L. J. (2008) 'Historical marine ecology: examining the role of fisheries in changes to North Sea benthos', *Ambio*, vol. 37, no. 5, pp. 362–371.

Robinson, L. M., Elith, J., Hobday, A. J., Pearson, R. G., Kendall, B. E., Possingham, H. P. and Richardson, A. J. (2011) 'Pushing the limits in marine species distribution modelling: lessons from the land present challenges and opportunities', *Global Ecology and Biogeography*, vol. 20, no. 6, pp. 789–802.

Roff, J. C. (2014) 'Networks of marine protected areas – the demonstrability dilemma', *Aquatic Conservation: Marine and Freshwater Ecosystems*, vol. 24, no. 1, pp. 1–4.

Roff, J. C. and Evans, S. (2002) 'Frameworks for marine conservation – non-hierarchical approaches and distinctive areas', *Aquatic Conservation: Marine and Freshwater Ecosystems*, vol. 12, no. 6, pp. 635–648.

Roff, J. C. and Zacharias, M. (2011) *Marine Conservation Ecology*, Earthscan, London and Washington DC.

Rondinini, C. (2010) *Meeting the MPA Network Design Principles of Representation and Adequacy: Developing Species-Area Curves for Habitats*, JNCC, Peterborough, UK.

Rosenberg, R. (1976) 'Benthic faunal dynamics during succession following pollution abatement in a Swedish estuary', *Oikos*, vol. 27, no. 3, pp. 414–427.

Rosenberg, A. A., Swasey, J. H. and Bowman, M. (2006) 'Rebuilding US fisheries: progress and problems', *Frontiers in Ecology and the Environment*, vol. 4, no. 6, pp. 303–308.

Rothschild, B. J., Ault, J. S., Goulletquer, P. and Héral, M. (1994) 'Decline of the Chesapeake Bay oyster population: a century of habitat destruction and overfishing', *Marine Ecology Progress Series*, vol. 11, pp. 29–39.

Russell, B. D., Thompson, J.-A. I., Falkenberg, L. J. and Connell, S. D. (2009) 'Synergistic effects of climate change and local stressors: CO2 and nutrient-driven change in subtidal rocky habitats', *Global Change Biology*, vol. 15, pp. 2153–2162.

Russell, F. S., Southward, A.J., Boalch, G. T. and Butler, E. I. (1971) 'Changes in biological conditions in the English Channel off Plymouth during the last half century', *Nature*, vol. 234, no. 5330, pp. 468–470.

Russell, G., Hawkins S. J., Evans, L. C., Jones, H. D. and Holmes, G. D. (1983) 'Restoration of a disused dock as a habitat for marine benthos and fish', *Journal of Applied Ecology*, vol. 20, pp. 43–58.

Ruth, M. and Lindholm, J. (eds) (2002) *Dynamic Modelling for Marine Conservation*, Springer-Verlag, Berlin.

Saarman, E., Gleason, M., Ugoretz, J., Airamé, S., Carr, M., Fox, E., Frimodig, A., Mason, T. and Vasques, J. (2013) 'The role of science in supporting marine protected area network planning and design in California', *Ocean & Coastal Management*, vol. 74, pp. 45–56.

Sala, E., Aburto-Oropeza, O., Paredes, G., Parra, I., Barrera, J. C. and Dayton, P. K. (2002) 'A general model for designing networks of marine reserves', *Science*, vol. 298, no. 5600, pp. 1991–1993.

Sala, E., Ballesteros, E., Dendrinos, P., Franco, A., Ferretti, F., Foley, D., Fraschetti, S., Friedlander, A., Garrabou, J., Güçlüsoy, H., Guidetti, P., Halpern, B. S., Hereu, B., Karamanlidis, A. A., Kizilkaya, Z., Macpherson, E., Mangialajo, L., Mariani, S., Micheli, F., Pais, P., Riser, K., Rosenberg, A. A., Sales, M., Selkoe, K. A., Starr, R., Tomas, F. and Zabal, M. (2012) 'The structure of Mediterranean rocky reef ecosystems across environmental and human gradients, and conservation implications', *PLoS ONE*, vol. 7, no. 2, e32742.

Salafsky, S., Margoluis, R. and Redford, K. (2001) *Adaptive Management: A Tool for Conservation Practitioners*, Biodiversity Support Program, World Wildlife Fund, Washington DC.

Salm, R. V., Clarke, J. R. and Siirila, E. (2000) *Marine and Coastal Protected Areas: A Guide for Planners and Managers*, 3rd edition, IUCN, Washington DC.

Salomon, A. K., Gaichas, S. K., Shears, N. T., Smith, J. E., Madin, E. M. and Gaines, S. D. (2010) 'Key features and context-dependence of fishery-induced trophic cascades', *Conservation Biology*, vol. 24, no. 2, pp. 382–394.

Sammarco, P. W., Atchison, A. D. and Boland, G. S. (2004) 'Expansion of coral communities within the Northern Gulf of Mexico via offshore oil and gas platforms', *Marine Ecology Progress Series*, vol. 280, pp. 129–143.

Sanderson, W. G. (1996) 'Rarity of marine benthic species in Great Britain: development and application of assessment criteria', *Aquatic Conservation: Marine and Freshwater Ecosystems*, vol. 6, no. 4, pp. 245–256.

Scheffer, M. and Carpenter, S. R. (2003) 'Catastrophic regime shifts in ecosystems: linking theory to observation', *TRENDS in Ecology and Evolution*, vol. 18, no. 2, pp. 648–656.

Schmalenbach, I., Mehrtens, F., Janke, M. and Buchholz, F. (2011) 'A mark-recapture study of hatchery-reared juvenile European lobsters, *Homarus gammarus*, released at the rocky island of Helgoland (German Bight, North Sea) from 2000 to 2009', *Fisheries Research*, vol. 108, pp. 22–30.

Schulte, D. M., Burke, R. P. and Lipcius, R. N. (2009) 'Unprecedented restoration of a native oyster metapopulation', *Science*, vol. 325, no. 5944, pp. 1124–1128.

Sciberras, M., Jenkins, S. R., Kaiser, M. J., Hawkins, S. J. and Pullin, A. S. (2013) 'Evaluating the biological effectiveness of fully and partially protected marine areas', *Environmental Evidence*, vol. 2, no. 4, pp. 1–31.

SCOS (2009) *Scientific Advice on Matters Related to the Management of Seal Populations*, SMRU, St Andrews, Scotland.

Sebens, K. P. (1985) 'Community ecology of vertical rock walls in the Gulf of Maine, U.S.A.: small-scale processes and alternative community states', in P. G. Moore and R. Seed (eds) *The Ecology of Rocky Coasts*, Hodder and Stoughton, London, pp. 346–371.

Sewell, J. and Hiscock, K. (2005) *Effects of Fishing Within UK European Marine Sites: Guidance for Nature Conservation Agencies. Report to the Countryside Council for Wales, English Nature and Scottish Natural Heritage from the Marine Biological Association*, Marine Biological Association, Plymouth, UK.

Shanks, A. L., Grantham, B. A. and Carr, M. H. (2003) 'Propagule dispersal distance and the size and spacing of marine reserves', *Ecological Applications*, vol. 13, no. 1, pp. S159–S169.

Sheehan, E. V., Cousens, S. L., Nancollas, S. J., Strauss, C, Royle, J. and Atrill, M. J. (2013a) 'Drawing lines at the sand: evidence for functional vs. visual reef boundaries in temperate marine protected areas', *Marine Pollution Bulletin*, vol. 76, pp. 194–201

Sheehan, E. V., Stevens, T. F., Gall, S. C., Cousens, S. L. and Attrill, M. J. (2013b) 'Recovery of a temperate reef assemblage in a marine protected area following the exclusion of towed demersal fishing', *PLoS ONE*, vol. 8, no. 12, e83883.

Sheppard, C. R. C., Harris, A. and Sheppard, A. L. S. (2008) 'Archipelago-wide coral recovery patterns since 1998 in the Chagos Archipelago, Central Indian Ocean', *Marine Ecology Progress Series*, vol. 362, pp. 109–117.

Short, F. T., Ibelings, B. W. and den Hartog, C. (1988) 'Comparison of a current eelgrass disease to the wasting disease in the 1930s', *Aquatic Botany*, vol. 30, no. 4, pp. 295–304.

Sims, D. W. and Reid, P. C. (2002) 'Congruent trends in long-term zooplankton decline in the northeast Atlantic and basking shark (*Cetorhinus maximus*) fishery catches off west Ireland', *Fisheries Oceanography*, vol. 11, no. 1, pp. 59–63.

Sloan, N. and Aldridge, T. (1981) 'Observations on an aggregation of the starfish *Asterias rubens* L. in Morecambe Bay, Lancashire, England', *Journal of Natural History*, vol. 15, no. 3, pp. 407–418.

Smale, D. A. and Wernberg, T. (2013) 'Extreme climatic event drives range contraction of a habitat-forming species', *Proceedings of the Royal Society B*, vol. 280, 20122829.

Smale, D. A., Burrows, M. T., Moore, P., O'Connor, N. and Hawkins, S. J. (2013) 'Threats and knowledge gaps for ecosystem services provided by kelp forests: a northeast Atlantic perspective', *Ecology & Evolution*, vol. 3, no. 11, pp. 4016–4038.

Smith, B. S. (1980) 'The estuarine mud snail, *Nassarius obsoletus*: abnormalities in the reproductive system', *Journal of Molluscan Studies*, vol. 46, no. 3, pp. 247–256.

Smith, J. E. (ed.) (1968) '*Torrey Canyon' Pollution and Marine Life*, Cambridge University Press, Cambridge, UK.

Smith, J. R., Fong, P. and Ambrose, R. F. (2006) 'Dramatic declines in mussel bed community diversity: response to climate change?' *Ecology*, vol. 87, no. 5, pp. 1153–1161.

Smith, S. D. A and Rule, M. J. (2001) 'The effects of dredge-spoil dumping on a shallow water soft-sediment community in the Solitary Islands Marine Park, NSW, Australia', *Marine Pollution Bulletin*, vol. 42, no. 11, pp. 1040–1048.

Southern, R. (1915) 'Clare Island survey. Part 67: Marine ecology', *Proceedings of the Royal Irish Academy*, vol. 31, pp. 1–110.

Southward, A. J. (1979) 'Cyclic fluctuations in population density during eleven years recolonisation of rocky shores in west Cornwall following the "Torrey Canyon" oil-spill in 1967', in E. Naylor and R. G. Hartnoll (eds) *Cyclic Phenomena in Marine Plants and Animals*, Pergamon Press, Oxford, pp. 85–477.

Southward, A. J. (1980) 'The western English Channel – an inconstant ecosystem?', *Nature*, vol. 285, no. 5764, pp. 361–366.

Southward, A. J. and Southward, E. C. (1988) 'Disappearance of the warm water hermit crab *Clibanarius erythropus* from south west Britain', *Journal of the Marine Biological Association of the United Kingdom*, vol. 68, no. 3, pp. 409–412.

Southward, A. J., Hiscock, K., Moyse, J. and Elfimov, A. S. (2004) 'Habitat and distribution of the warm-water barnacle *Solidobalanus fallax* (Crustacea: Cirripedia)', *Journal of the Marine Biological Association of the United Kingdom*, vol. 84, no. 6, pp. 1169–1177.

Southward, A. J., Langmead, O., Hardman-Mountford, N. J., Aiken, J., Boalch, G. T., Dando, P. R., Genner, M. J., Joint, I., Kendall, M. A., Halliday, N. C., Harris, R. P., Leaper, R., Mieszkowska, N., Pingree, R. D., Richardson, A., J., Sims, D. W., Smith, T., Walne, A. W. and Hawkins, S. J. (2005) 'Long-term oceanographic and ecological research in the western English Channel', *Advances in Marine Biology*, vol. 47, pp. 1–105.

Spalding, M. D., Fox, H. E., Allen, G. R., Davidson, N., Ferdaña, Z. A., Finlayson, M., Halpern, B. S., Jorge, M. A., Lombana, A., Lourie, S. A., Martin, K. D., McManus, E., Molnar, J., Recchia, C. A. and Robertson, J. (2007) 'Marine ecoregions of the world: a bioregionalization of coastal and shelf areas', *Bioscience*, vol. 57, no. 7, pp. 573–583.

Stachowicz, J. J., Bruno, J. F. and Duffy, J. E. (2007) 'Understanding the effects of marine biodiversity on communities and ecosystems', *Annual Review of Ecology, Evolution and Systematics*, vol. 38, pp. 739–766.

Stebbing, P., Johnson, P., Delahunty, A., Clark, P. F., McCollin, T., Hale, H. and Clark, S. (2012) 'Reports of American lobsters, *Homarus americanus* (H. Milne Edwards, 1837) (Crustacea: Decapoda: Astacidea: Nephropoidea) in Great British waters', *BioInvasions Records*, vol. 1, no. 1, pp. 17–23.

Stebbing, P. D., Pond, M. J., Peeler, E., Small, H. J., Greenwood, S. J. and Verner-Jeffreys, D. (2012) 'Limited prevalence of gaffkaemia (*Aerococcus viridans* var. *homari*) isolated from wild-caught European lobsters *Homarus gammarus* in England and Wales', *Diseases of Aquatic Organisms*, vol. 100, no. 2, pp. 159–167.

Steneck, R. S., Vavrinec, J. and Leland, A. V. (2004) 'Accelerating trophic level dysfunction in kelp forest ecosystems of the western North Atlantic', *Ecosystems*, vol. 7, no. 4, pp. 323–331.

Steneck, R. S., Leland, A., McNaught, D. C. and Vavrinec, J. (2013) 'Ecosystem flips, locks, and feedbacks: the lasting effects of fisheries on Maine's kelp forest ecosystem', *Bulletin of Marine Science*, vol. 89, no. 1, pp. 31–55.

Steneck, R. S., Graham, M. H., Bourget, B. J., Corbett, D., Erlandson, J. M., Estes, J. A. and Tegner, M. J. (2002) 'Kelp forest ecosystems: biodiversity, stability, resilience and future', *Environmental Conservation*, vol. 29, no. 4, pp. 436–459.

Steyl, I., Sakellariadou, F. and Bray, S. (2013) *Quantification of Pollution Levels in Harbour Sediments: A Geospatial Perspective*, Tahoka Press, Clearwater, USA.

Stokesbury, K. D. E., Harris, B. P, Marino II, M. C. and Nogueira, J. I. (2007) 'Sea scallop mass mortality in a Marine Protected Area', *Marine Ecology Progress Series*, vol. 349, pp. 151–158.

Svane, I. and Petersen, J. K. (2001) 'On the problems of epibioses, fouling and artificial reefs, a review', *Marine Ecology*, vol. 22, no. 3, pp. 169–188.

Tett, P., Gowen, R., Mills, D., Fernandes, T., Gilpin, L., Huxham, M., Kennington, K., Read, P., Service, M., Wilkinson, M. and Malcolm, S. (2007) 'Defining and detecting undesirable disturbance in the context of eutrophication', *Marine Pollution Bulletin*, vol. 53, no. 1–6, pp. 282–297.

Thrush, S. F. and Dayton, P. K. (2010) 'What can ecology contribute to ecosystem-based management?', *Annual Review of Marine Science*, vol. 2, pp. 419–441.

Thurstan, R. H. and Roberts, C. M. (2010) 'Ecological meltdown in the Firth of Clyde, Scotland: two centuries of change in a coastal marine ecosystem', *PLoS ONE*, vol. 5, no. 7, e11767.

Tillin, H. M., Hiddink, J. G., Jennings, S. and Kaiser, M. J. (2006) 'Chronic bottom trawling alters the functional composition of benthic invertebrate communities on a sea-basin scale', *Marine Ecology Progress Series*, vol. 318, pp. 31–45.

Timmers, M. A., Bird, C. E., Skillings, D. J., Smouse, P. E. and Toonen, R. J. (2012) 'There's no place like home: crown-of-thorns outbreaks in the central Pacific are regionally derived and independent events', *PLoS ONE*, vol. 7, no. 2, e31159.

Todd, C. D. (1998) 'Larval supply and recruitment of benthic invertebrates: do larvae always disperse as much as we believe?', *Hydrobiologia*, vol. 365/376, pp. 1–21.

Tomascik, T., van Woesik, R. and Mah, A. J. (1997) 'Rapid coral colonization of a recent lava flow following a volcanic eruption, Banda Islands, Indonesia', *Coral Reefs*, vol. 15, no. 3, pp. 169–175.

Törnroos, A. and Bonsdorf, E. (2012) 'Developing the multitrait concept for functional diversity: lessons from a system rich in functions but poor in species', *Ecological Applications*, vol. 22, no. 8, pp. 2221–2236.

Toropova, C., Meliane, I., Laffoley, D., Matthews, E. and Spalding, M. (eds) (2010) *Global Ocean Protection: Present Status and Future Possibilities*, IUCN, Gland, Switzerland.

Trathan, P. N., Sala, E., Merkl, A., Beumer, J. and Spalding, M. (2012) 'The MPA math: how to reach the 10% target for global MPA coverage', *MPA News*, vol. 13, no. 5, pp. 1–4.

Turner, S. J., Thrush, S. F., Pridmore, R. D., Hewitt, J. E, Cummings, V. J. and Maskery, M. (1995) 'Are soft-sediment communities stable? An example from a windy harbor', *Marine Ecology Progress Series*, vol. 120, pp. 219–230.

Tyler, E. H. M., Somerfield, P. J., Vanden Berghe, E., Bremner, J., Jackson, E., Langmead, O., Palomares, M. L. D. and Webb, T. J. (2012) 'Extensive gaps and biases in our knowledge of a well-known fauna: implications for integrating biological traits into macroecology', *Global Ecology and Biogeography*, vol. 21, no. 9, pp. 922–934.

UKMMASC (2010) *Charting Progress 2: An Assessment of the State of UK Seas*, Department for Environment, Food and Rural Affairs, London, http://chartingprogress.defra.gov.uk/resources, accessed 2 January 2014.

Underwood, A. J. (1999) 'Physical disturbances and their direct effect on an indirect effect: responses of an intertidal assemblage to a severe storm', *Journal of Experimental Marine Biology and Ecology*, vol. 232, no. 1, pp. 125–140.

UNEP (1984) *Thermal Discharges in the Marine Environment*, United Nations Environment Programme, UNEP Regional Seas Reports and Studies, No. 45, UNEP.

UNEP-WCMC (2008) *National and Regional Networks of Marine Protected Areas: A Review of Progress*, UNEP-WCMC, Cambridge, UK.

UNESCO (1985) *The International System of Units (SI) in Oceanography*, UNESCO Technical Papers in Marine Science, No. 45, UNESCO, Paris.

UNESCO (2009) *Global Open Oceans and Deep Seabed (GOODS) – Biogeographic Classification*, UNESCO-IOC, Paris.

UNESCO (2013) 'Convention concerning the protection of the world cultural and natural heritage', World Heritage Committee. Thirty-seventh session. Phnom Penh, Cambodia, 16–27 June 2013. State of conservation of World Heritage properties inscribed on the World Heritage List, http://whc.unesco.org/archive/2013/whc13–37com-7B-en.pdf, accessed 13 January 2014.

United Nations (2002) *Report of the World Summit on Sustainable Development, Johannesburg, South Africa, 26 August–4 September 2002*, United Nations, New York.

Utne-Palm, A. C., Salvanes, A. G. V., Currie, B., Kaartvedt, S., Nilsson, G. E., Braithwaite, V. A., Stecyk, J. A. W., Hundt, M., van der Bank, M., Flynn, B., Sandvik, G. K., Klevjer, T. A., Sweetman, A. K., Brüchert, V., Pittman, K., Peard, K. R., Lunde, I. G., Strandabø, R. A. W.

and Gibbons, M. J. (2010) 'Trophic structure and community stability in an overfished ecosystem', *Science*, vol. 329, no. 5989, pp. 333–336.

Vadas, R. L. and Steneck, R. S. (1995) 'Overfishing and inferences in kelp–sea urchin interactions', in H. R. Skjoldal, C. Hopkins, K. E. Erikstad and H. P. Leinaas (eds) *Ecology of Fjords and Coastal Waters*, Elsevier, Amsterdam, pp. 509–524.

van Denderen, P. D., van Kooten, T. and Rijnsdorp, A. D. (2013) 'When does fishing lead to more fish? Community consequences of bottom trawl fisheries in demersal food webs', *Proceedings of the Royal Society B*, vol. 280, no. 1769, 20131883.

van der Kooij, J., Kupschus, S. and Scott, B. E. (2011) 'Delineating the habitat of demersal fish assemblages with acoustic seabed technologies', *ICES Journal of Marine Science*, vol. 68, no. 9, pp. 1973–1985.

VanDover, C. L., Aronson, J., Pendleton, L., Smith, S., Arnaud-Haond, S., Moreno-Mateos, D., Barbier, E., Billett, D., Bowers, K., Danovaro, R., Edwards, A., Kellert, S., Morato, T., Pollard, E., Rogers, A. and Warner, R. (2014) 'Ecological restoration in the deep sea: Desiderata', *Marine Policy*, vol. 44, pp. 98–106.

van Woesik, R., Sakai, K., Ganase, A. and Loya, Y. (2011) 'Revisiting the winners and loser a decade after coral bleaching', *Marine Ecology Progress Series*, vol. 434, pp. 67–76.

van Woesik, R., Hoek, P., Isechal, A. L., Idechong, J. W. Victor, S. and Golbuu, Y. (2012) 'Climate-change refugia in the sheltered bays of Palau: analogs of future reefs', *Ecology and Evolution*, vol. 2, no. 10, pp. 2474–2484.

Vaudrey, J. M. P., Kremer, J. N., Branco, B. F. and Short, F. T. (2010) 'Eelgrass recovery after nutrient enrichment reversal', *Aquatic Botany*, vol. 93, no. 4, pp. 237–243.

Vezzulli, L., Previati, M., Pruzzo, C., Marchese, A., Bourne, D. G., Cerrano, C. and VibrioSea Consortium (2010) 'Vibrio infections triggering mass mortality events in a warming Mediterranean Sea', *Environmental Microbiology* vol. 12, no 7, pp. 2007–2019.

Voerman, S. E., Llera, E. and Rico, J. M. (2013) 'Climate driven changes in subtidal kelp forest communities in NW Spain', *Marine Environmental Research*, vol. 90, pp. 119–127.

Von Nordheim, H., Boedeker, D. and Krause, J. C. (eds) (2006) *Progress in Marine Conservation in Europe*, Springer, Berlin.

Ward, J. R. and Lafferty, K. D. (2004) 'The elusive baseline of marine disease: are diseases in ocean ecosystems increasing?' *PLoS Biol*, vol. 2, no. 4, e120.

Warwick, R. M. and Clarke, K. R. (2001) 'Practical measures of marine biodiversity based on relatedness of species', *Oceanography and Marine Biology: An Annual Review*, vol. 39, pp. 207–231.

Watts, M. E., Ball, I. R., Stewart, R. R., Klein, C. J., Wilson, K., Steinback, C., Lourival, R., Kircher, L. and Possingham, H. P. (2009) 'Marxan with Zones: software for optimal conservation based land- and sea-use zoning', *Environmental Modelling and Software*, vol. 24, pp. 1513–1521.

Waycott, M., Duarte, C. M., Carruthers, T. Orth, R., Dennison, W., Olyarnik, S., Calladine, A., Fourqurean, J., Heck, K., Hughes, A. and Kendrick, G. (2009) 'Accelerating loss of seagrasses across the globe threatens coastal ecosystems', *PNAS*, vol. 106, no. 30, pp. 12377–12381.

WCED (World Commission on Environment and Development) (1987) *Our Common Future*, Oxford University Press, Oxford.

Weslawski, J. M., Snelgrove, P. V. R., Levin, L. A., Austen, M. C., Kneib, R. T., Iliffe, T. M., Garey, J. R., Hawkins, S. J. and Whitlatch, R. B. (2004) 'Marine sedimentary biota as providers of ecosystem goods and services', in D. H. Wall (ed.) *Sustaining Biodiversity and Ecosystem Services in Soils and Sediments*, Scientific Committee on Problems of the Environment, Island Press, Washington, pp. 73–98.

Widdicombe, S., Austen, M. C., Kendall, M. A., Olsgard, F., Schaanning, M. T., Dashfield, S. L. and Needham, H. R. (2004) 'Importance of bioturbators for biodiversity maintenance: indirect effects of fishing disturbance', *Marine Ecology Progress Series*, vol. 275, pp. 1–10.

Wilberg, M. J., Livings, M. E., Barkman, J. S., Morris, T. and Robinson, J. M. (2011) 'Overfishing, disease, habitat loss, and potential extirpation of oysters in upper Chesapeake Bay', *Marine Ecology Progress Series*, vol. 436, pp. 131–144.

Wilding, T. A., Sayer, M. D. J. and Provost, P. G. (2003) 'Factors affecting the performance of the acoustic ground discrimination system RoxAnn™', *ICES Journal of Marine Science*, vol. 60, no. 6, pp. 1373–1380.

Wilkinson, T., Wiken, E., Bezaury-Creel, J. Hourigan, T., Agardy, T., Herrmann, H., Janishevski, L., Madden, C., Morgan, L. and Padilla, M. (2009) *Marine Ecoregions of North America*, Commission for Environmental Cooperation, Montreal, Canada.

Wollermann, U., Koenemann, S. and Iliffe, T. M. (2007) 'A new remipede, *Cryptocorynetes longulus*, n. sp., from Cat Island, Bahamas', *Journal of Crustacean Biology*, vol. 27, no. 1, pp. 10–17.

Wootton, E. C., Woolmer, A. P., Vogan, C. L., Pope, E. C., Hamilton, K. M. and Rowley, A. F. (2012) 'Increased disease calls for a cost-benefits review of marine reserves', *PLoS ONE*, vol. 7, no. 12, e51615.

Worm, B., Barbier, E. B., Beaumont, N., Duffy, J. E., Folke, C., Halpern, B. S., Jackson, J. B., Lotze, H. K., Micheli, F., Palumbi, S. R., Sala, E., Selkoe, K. A, Stachowicz, J. J. and Watson, R. (2006) 'Impacts of biodiversity loss on ocean ecosystem services', *Science*, vol. 314, no. 5800, pp. 787–790.

Worm, B., Hilborn, R., Baum, J. K., Branch, T. A., Collie, J. S., Costello, C., Fogarty, M. J., Fulton, E. A., Hutchings, J. A., Jennings, S., Jensen, O. P., Lotze, H.K., Mace, P. M., McClanahan, T. R., Palumbi, S. R., Parma, A. M., Rikard, D., Rosenberg, A. A., Zeller, D. and Minto, C. (2009) 'Rebuilding global fisheries', *Science*, vol. 325, no. 5940, pp. 578–585.

Wyn, G., Brazier, P., Birch, K., Bunker, A., Cooke, A., Jones, M., Lough, N., McMath, A. and Roberts, S. (2006) *Handbook for Marine Intertidal Phase 1 Biotope Mapping Survey*, Countryside Council for Wales, Bangor, Wales.

Yager, J. (1981) 'A new class of Crustacea from a marine cave in the Bahamas', *Journal of Crustacean Biology*, vol. 1, no. 3, pp. 328–333.

Yonge, C. M. (1949) *The Sea Shore*, Collins, London.

Zacharias, M. A., Howes, D. E., Harper, J. R. and Wainwright, P. (1998) 'The British Columbia marine ecosystem classification: rationale, development, and verification', *Coastal Management*, vol. 26, no. 2, pp. 105–124.

Zettler, M. L., Proffitt, C. E., Darr, A., Degraer, S., Devriese, L., Greathead, C., Kotta, J., Magni, P., Martin, G., Reiss, H., Speybroeck, J., Tagliapietra, D., Van Hoey, G. and Ysebaert, T. (2013) 'On the myths of indicator species: issues and further consideration in the use of static concepts for ecological applications', *PLoS ONE*, vol. 8, no. 10, e78219.

Index